How I Discovered World War II's Greatest Spy

and Other Stories of Intelligence and Code

How I Discovered World War II's Greatest Spy

and Other Stories of Intelligence and Code

David Kahn

Author of
The Codebreakers: The Comprehensive History of Secret Communication from Ancient Times to the Internet

Foreword by Bruce Schneier

CRC Press
Taylor & Francis Group
Boca Raton London New York

CRC Press is an imprint of the
Taylor & Francis Group, an **informa** business
AN AUERBACH BOOK

CRC Press
Taylor & Francis Group
6000 Broken Sound Parkway NW, Suite 300
Boca Raton, FL 33487-2742

© 2014 by Taylor & Francis Group, LLC
CRC Press is an imprint of Taylor & Francis Group, an Informa business

No claim to original U.S. Government works

Printed on acid-free paper
Version Date: 20140811

International Standard Book Number-13: 978-1-4665-6199-1 (Hardback)

Library of Congress Cataloging-in-Publication Data

Kahn, David, 1930-
    How I discovered World War II's greatest spy and other stories of intelligence and code / David Kahn.
        pages cm
    Includes bibliographical references and index.
    ISBN 978-1-4665-6199-1 (hardback)
    1. World War, 1939-1945--Military intelligence. 2. World War, 1939-1945--Electronic intelligence. 3. World War, 1939-1945--Cryptography. I. Title.

    D810.S7.K253 2013
    940.54'85--dc23
                                                                        2013037016

Visit the Taylor & Francis Web site at
http://www.taylorandfrancis.com

and the CRC Press Web site at
http://www.crcpress.com

To Donald and Susan Newhouse
Friends of a Lifetime

Contents

Foreword

In the beginning, the only useful works about cryptography were written by David Kahn.

That is not entirely true. There are many historical cryptography texts, and in the early twentieth century there were some books about pencil-and-paper ciphers. Certainly, the NSA and similar agencies had all sorts of information buried in their classified libraries, but when *The Codebreakers* was published in 1967, there was nothing else like it anywhere.

It was a history of cryptography from the beginning of time until the 1960s. I devoured it.

Things started to change in the early 1980s. An academic research community sprang up, and Springer-Verlag started publishing proceedings from the Crypto and Eurocrypt academic conferences. A few books that examined computer cryptography were published: Denning, Konheim, and Meyer and Matyas. The journal *Cryptologia* appeared in 1988—with Kahn as one of the founding editors—publishing both academic and historical papers. More mathematicians wrote books, and cryptography papers began to be regularly presented at both mathematics and engineering conferences.

Still, as a student of cryptography, I found myself returning to Kahn again and again. Cryptographer Whitfield Diffie once compared *The Codebreakers* to the Veda. "In India, if a man loses his cow, he looks for it in the Veda." Because, of course, everything is in the Veda. For people like Whit and me, *The Codebreakers* was like that.

David Kahn's second book was *Kahn on Codes*. Published in 1983, it is a collection of essays on cryptography from a variety of publications. It, too, was a cornucopia of ideas and stories. Kahn's historical understanding of the role of cryptography is unmatched, and his ability to tell a good historical story is remarkable. *Kahn on Codes* was an invaluable tool as I began to understand cryptography and its role in society.

Now, 30 years later, cryptography research has blossomed, and the use of cryptography on the Internet has exploded. I have nine shelves of books, journals, conference proceedings, and papers on cryptography. But Kahn's writings are no less important today. What you have in your hand is another collection of essays, all previously published but never before collected in a single volume. They appeared in such journals as *Military History Quarterly*, *Cryptologia*, *Foreign Affairs*, and *Intelligence and National Security* over the past two decades. And while it sometimes seems that stories of World War II spying and military codebreaking are worlds apart from the problems of Facebook security, computer viruses, and Internet surveillance, history still has lessons for us today. These essays are timeless. They are worth reading, and they are worth rereading. No matter what cow we have lost or where we have lost it, Kahn's writings contain clues to where it might be found.

Bruce Schneier

Preface

These articles are collected here because they seem to have some lasting value to historians of intelligence and its subaltern, cryptology, yet are hard to find because they were published in a variety of journals.

They have appeared in *Intelligence and National Security*, in *Foreign Affairs*, in *The Journal of Military History*, in *Military History Quarterly*, and in *Cryptologia*, and elsewhere. Their unity, such as it may be, comes from their dealing with a single topic, broadly conceived, and from their being the product of a single brain.

Yet they range over a pretty broad field. Some are more personal than others, like the lead piece, basically a detective story. Others seek a broader and more permanent effect, like "An Historical Theory of Intelligence." Some deal with curiosities, as "Garbles."

These articles complement my other publications, such as *The Codebreakers* published in 1967 and updated since then where needed, my other books, and an earlier collection of articles, *Kahn on Codes*, which tells about some of my experiences in interviewing cryptologists.

If these pieces, as well as my books, have any literary merit, the credit belongs to my first editor, the late Al Marlens. We worked at *Newsday*, the Long Island daily, a tabloid. Tabloid articles cannot run long, and Marlens would give me a story length too short for what I thought the event merited. But he was inflexible. I learned to write tight. I learned to ask whether an activity had been done elsewhere or before. If not, I could say it was a first. And often Al would ask for "art," meaning a photograph or an illustration. I learned to look for "art," and so some of these entries, like my books, include pictures, often fresh, that enhance the text and sometimes turn skimmers into readers—even buyers. All this I owe to Al Marlens.

With him looking over my shoulder, I offer them here to the world of cryptologists and intelligence historians.

PART I

INTRODUCTION

Jewels may be found in out-of-the-way places. Not only diamonds; not only gold. Nuggets of scholarship lie in obscure articles. Maybe they were forgotten in the advancing crush of scholarship. Maybe they appeared before people understood their significance.

Perhaps that has happened with some of these articles. Can they change our views of military intelligence? Maybe in some cases they have. Mostly they just add a few bits to our knowledge or correct what I believe to be wrong or incomplete views. The fact that various editors have published them means that at least some people thought that they had value. And they deal with an always fascinating part of human activity—the part that deals with knowing what others are hiding, with knowing without others knowing that you know. It is like the fly on the wall, watching and hearing all without being noticed, Harun al Rashid at night walking unrecognized through the bazaar and learning what his subjects are thinking and planning. This is spying with its adjunct, codebreaking. They imply hidden power with the added charm of lack of responsibility. Though they attract many people, writers and readers alike, no one has yet, to my knowledge, investigated the psychology or sociology or philosophy of political and military intelligence, though the German sociologist Georg Simmel has touched upon an aspect of it. These papers do not claim to provide a comprehensive theory of intelligence, though they are offered in the hope that they may advance some of it.

They have appeared in a variety of publications. Many deal with only a corner, secret writing, of that vast storehouse, but that corner has interested, and even fascinated, many people, and has sometimes played a significant role in world affairs. These papers may help us understand the evolution and significance of the whole field of military intelligence, and so benefit humankind as any advance in knowledge does.

I am thinking particularly of (1) the observation that military intelligence agencies owe their institution (in nineteenth-century armies) to a defeat, (2) the recognition that interception of radio communications first enabled armies repeatedly to win battles, and (3) the extension of Clausewitz's view that intelligence matters more to the defense than to the offense to show why generals—who want not just to not lose but to win—tend to neglect it. I believe that these are the most important conclusions in this collection and that they deserve to be "rescued" from their relative obscurity in scholarly publications to this more accessible book. Those points may seem obvious when stated, but nobody seems ever to have expressed them before. And that the United States is defending against terrorism helps show why intelligence interests so much of the nation today.

Other articles deal with some perennially fascinating questions: Did President Roosevelt know that Japan was going to attack at Pearl Harbor and cold-bloodedly let it happen to bring America into the war on the side of the Allies? Why did the intelligence of Nazi Germany, which seemed to be so efficient a society and have so effective a military, fail in comparison with the Allies? Why did the Allies keep their solution of the German Enigma cipher machine secret for decades after they had won the war? How good was at least some Soviet communications intelligence during the Cold War? And the book includes some nuggets that, while less significant, tell good stories or offer useful theories: How General Erwin Rommel used his intercepts of American messages in his victories—until British solutions of Enigma messages disclosed the leak. The role of a young American diplomat in the most important intelligence success in history. A couple of concepts that might help to quantify intelligence and to explain intelligence failures. How garbles in encrypted messages have affected the course of history. And more.

I offer them in the hope that they may interest and enlighten readers.

HOW I DISCOVERED WORLD WAR II'S GREATEST SPY*

Who Was the Greatest Spy of World War II? By that I don't mean the most colorful, the most James Bondlike, the most romantic, or the most skilled tradecraftsman. I mean the most effective. I mean the spy who most affected the course of the war.

Some will say it was Richard Sorge—the motorcycle-riding, womanizing, blue-eyed German secret Communist in Japan who concealed his spying by freelancing as a newspaper and magazine correspondent. After Adolf Hitler attacked Russia, Sorge had to learn what Japan would do. Would the empire move north to strike its traditional enemy from behind while in a life-and-death struggle, or would Japan move south, toward oil and the white man's empire in Asia? And indeed, at the end of September 1941, Sorge reported, "The Soviet Far East can be considered safe from Japanese attack."

But his achievement was not unalloyed. Russian codebreaking had revealed that Japanese troops were not moving north. Moreover, necessity drove Joseph Stalin to pull troops out of the Far East to fight the Germans approaching Moscow. Sorge's influence is thus at best clouded, so he therefore cannot stand clearly as the greatest spy of World War II.

How about Juan Pujol, code-named "Garbo"? This thirty-two-year-old anti-Fascist Spaniard had promised the Germans that he could provide them information from England, where he would be going for business reasons. Once there, he convinced the British that he could serve them as a double agent. And indeed, under their tutelage he fed the Germans information that was accurate but insignificant, or assumed to be already known to them.

Then, when their trust had solidified, he radioed them the big lie: that the Anglo-American assault on Normandy served merely as a

---

* From *MHQ: The Quarterly Journal of Military History*, 20 (Autumn 2007), 28–33.

feint for the main invasion, which would come farther north, opposite Dover, in France's Pas de Calais. The Germans believed him. His report sped to Berlin and back down to the Western Front—where four divisions were held in northern France to await what the Germans thought would be the real assault.

This certainly contributed to the success of the invasion, and may even be said to have driven the final nail into the deception plan. However, it was indeed only one nail in a huge operation. Valuable as Garbo was, he cannot be regarded as the greatest spy of the war. At best, he confirmed a German misconception; he did not create it.

A couple of Germans defied the Gestapo and delivered information to Allen Dulles, the Office of Strategic Services spymaster in Switzerland. Hans Bernd Gisevius, a counterintelligence agent operating under cover as a vice consul in Zurich, reported, for example, that the Germans were preparing two types of missiles—later called V-1 and V-2—that enabled the Allies to understand seemingly contradictory intelligence reports.

However, this information was provided after British aerial photographs had found the installations in Peenemünde. Fritz Kolbe, code-named "George Wood," a staffer under a high Foreign Office official, passed photographs of diplomatic messages to Dulles. They described the V-weapons, the Reich's transportation problems, the *Volkssturm*, and the so-called Alpine redoubt. His biographer has called Kolbe "the most important spy of World War II." A more sober assessment by historian Christoph Mauch says that "When it was realized how valuable the material presented by Wood really was, a good portion of its significance had already been lost."

On the Axis side, "Cicero" holds pride of place. He was an Albanian swindler, Elyesa Bazna, who had wormed himself into a job as butler for the British ambassador to Turkey. In the fall of 1943, he copied the diplomat's key to his safe, took secret documents from it, photographed them, and sold the films to the Germans. Turkey, a World War I ally of Germany and an old enemy of Russia, could threaten Allied control of the Mediterranean, but Allied advances precluded any significant action based on this inside information. Cicero's information, though interesting, did not matter.

No, I believe the greatest spy was one who worked before the war but whose information affected that conflict more than any other secret agent. His name is… but that is getting ahead of my story.

In 1973, I was at Oxford University writing my dissertation on German military intelligence in World War II. My supervisor was Hugh Trevor-Roper, whose job in British intelligence during the war had been to study that very subject.

One day in the spring, I received a note from an acquaintance, J. Rives Childs. A retired U.S. career ambassador who in World War I had broken codes for the American Expeditionary Forces, Childs had lent me his papers from that work when I was writing *The Codebreakers*. Later we met in New York and in Paris.

Childs was now inviting me to lunch with some English friends near Oxford. During the meal, the conversation turned to a new French book by General Gustave Bertrand, a retired French intelligence officer. He had run a spy early in the 1930s who provided information about the main German cipher machine that led to its solution. This machine, called Enigma (See Figure 1.1), was put into service in the German navy in 1926 and the German army in 1928. It concealed many of the Wehrmacht's transmitted secrets throughout World War II. Bertrand told the story of the spy in his book *Enigma, ou la Plus Grande Énigme de la Guerre 1939-1945*.

Figure 1.1   A three-rotor Mark 4 Enigma machine that Germany introduced on February 1942 for use in its U-boats.

If this man had indeed provided the information that enabled the Allies to crack Enigma messages and so gain access to key German military information, such as U-boat orders, he would indeed be the greatest spy of World War II. But who was he?

I bought Bertrand's book. It detailed how in October 1932 an employee of the German Defense Ministry's *Chiffrierstelle*, or Cipher Center, "offered his services" to the French. It provided much color about Bertrand's eighteen meetings with the spy in cities and resorts throughout Europe, and some details about the information he supplied, at first about Enigma, later about other German cryptosystems and the work of the *Forschungsamt*, Hermann Göring's wiretapping agency, to which the spy transferred in 1934.

Even with this help, however, the French cryptanalysts could not solve the Enigma cryptograms. Bertrand related how, with his supervisors' permission, he gave the spy's information to other countries concerned about German revanchism: Britain, Czechoslovakia, and Poland. Alone among all these countries—and "thanks to the information" from the agent, as the head of the Polish cryptanalysts acknowledged to Bertrand—Poland reconstructed the machine in December 1932 and read messages enciphered in it.

At a meeting in Warsaw in July 1939, the Poles told the British and French how three young Polish cryptanalysts had solved Enigma. Poland gave its friends two copies each of the Enigma. Both used them after the war broke out—France less successfully than Britain. But throughout his story, Bertrand used only the spy's cover name—the initials H.E., pronounced in French *asché*. He never provided the real name.

There the matter rested until the summer of 1974, when retired Royal Air Force Group Captain Frederick William Winterbotham obtained permission to disclose that the Allies had been intercepting, solving, and exploiting German Enigma-enciphered messages, thus helping them win World War II. His book *The Ultra Secret* exploded in headlines in the British press. The story was utterly surprising and extremely significant. No previous writings in English, French, or German had even hinted at it. Churchill had purged his memoirs of any references to intercepts and solutions. The official historians had not been told about Ultra—the interception, solution, and exploitation of coded German messages during World War II.

Winterbotham's revelations showed how much Allied commanders knew about German plans, supplies, order of battle, and much more—and thus how the Allies had won the war more quickly and more cheaply in men and materiel than they otherwise might have done. Some journalists and historians said that the Ultra revelations would require a total rewriting of the war.

This was hyperbole. At best, knowledge of Ultra helped explain why some things happened; it did not change the events. Still, as literary critic George Steiner has said, the breaking and exploitation of the German cryptograms was Britain's greatest achievement of the twentieth century.

I do not know why Winterbotham, who had merely run the system of extremely limited distribution of solved intercepts to military commanders, was allowed to reveal this tightly held secret before any of the other tens of thousands of World War II codebreakers. Many of them had been more central to the production and employment of this vital intelligence than he was, and had kept the secret for decades.

I did learn later why Her Majesty's government had decided to release the story after three decades of silence. At the end of European hostilities in 1945, the Allies gathered up thousands of Enigma machines from the Luftwaffe, the Kriegsmarine, the SS, the land forces of the former Wehrmacht, even the railroad administration. Soon decolonization began, and the newly independent members of the British Commonwealth—India, Pakistan, Nigeria, Ghana, and the others—clamored for cryptosystems for their diplomats and their soldiers. Only one firm in the world, the Swede Boris Hagelin's Cryptoteknik, then sold cipher machines in any quantity. Some of the new countries bought these machines. Others turned to the former mother country for help. Britain offered them the surplus Enigmas, systems more secure than Hagelin's.

Now, officials in these countries were not so naïve as to think that, if Britain was giving them cipher machines, it could not read them. But they were less concerned about Britain than about their neighbors—Pakistan was worried about India, for example. Those countries, many of them in the Third World, did not have and could not buy the cryptanalytic expertise to break Enigma. Many countries purchased the code machines.

However, the Enigma was electromechanical. It had rotors and pawls and contacts. By the early 1970s, the machines had worn out. Countries replaced them with more advanced cryptosystems, often electronic. At this point, Britain no longer had to keep secret the fact that it could read Enigma-encrypted messages.

Sir Joe Hooper, a former head of Britain's codebreaking agency, explained all this to me. We were standing in an ornate hall in Britain's Foreign and Commonwealth Office, the same building in which Foreign Secretary Sir Edward Grey, watching the lamplighters in Whitehall on the eve of World War I, said: "The lamps are going out all over Europe. We shall not see them lit again in our lifetime." For me, as a historian of cryptology, the moment was almost as historic.

Winterbotham's book amazed, fascinated—and chagrined—me perhaps more than anybody else. My book *The Codebreakers*, published in 1967, had nothing about the biggest cryptologic story of all time. I knew that ten thousand people worked at Bletchley Park (Figure 1.2), the British codebreaking center, but I could not find out what they did, or what effect they had had. I knew no one who might talk, and although while researching that book I had written Winston

Figure 1.2   Some of the ten thousand British military and civilian personnel at Bletchley Park's Hut 3 in 1943 work to penetrate Enigma's mysteries.

Churchill and Dwight Eisenhower, asking what effect codebreaking had had on the war, neither had responded.

Later in the summer of 1974, my wife and son were vacationing with her parents in Jesolo, near Venice, and I was to join them. I wanted to learn more about the Enigma solution. France was on the way to Italy, and General Bertrand agreed to let me interview him. I met him on July 12 in the Hôtel la Tour de l'Esquillon, atop a cliff on the edge of the Mediterranean in Théoule-sur-Mer, near Nice. Among other details, such as what French cryptanalysis had achieved in the first months of the war, I wanted to learn the identity of the spy.

But although Bertrand was helpful on other matters, saying that the man had been caught and shot shortly before the war and that his brother was a famous panzer general, he declined to name him. I excused myself and placed a telephone call to Walther Seifert in Osnabrück, West Germany. I had interviewed him twice for my book *Hitler's Spies*. Seifert, short, pug-nosed, cigar-smoking, had been chief of evaluation of the *Forschungsamt*, the agency in which Bertrand's spy had later worked. The *Forschungsamt* had left few documentary traces in Nazi Germany, and I needed to learn about it. Seifert had been extremely interested in his work and good at it. He and I got along very well; they were among my most productive interviews.

When he answered my telephone call from Théoule, I asked him whether any employees of the Defense Ministry's *Chiffrierstelle* and then the *Forschungsamt* had ever been arrested for betraying secret information. He first gave the name of one Plaas, shot in 1944, but then reconsidered and observed that Plaas had never served in the *Chiffrierstelle*.

Then he said that Hans-Thilo Schmidt (Figure 1.3), a *Forschungsamt* employee under him, had worked in the *Chiffrierstelle*. He said that around 1942 he was caught and shot for giving information to the enemy. He had done it for money and women. Seifert characterized him as a *Waschlappen*—a dishrag, a weakling. And he said that his brother was a panzer general! (This was Colonel-General Rudolf Schmidt, who commanded the XXXIX Panzer Corps in Russia and then replaced General Heinz Guderian, Germany's famed apostle of tank warfare, as commander of the Second Panzer Army. He was a favorite of Hitler's.)

I thanked Seifert, hung up, returned to Bertrand, and presented this information to him. I hoped that it would shock him into a

Figure 1.3   Hans-Thile Schmidt was shot in 1943 for giving secrets to the enemy "for money and women." This is his photograph on his Nazi Party application.

confirmation. It didn't. He declined to confirm or deny the identification, saying that the man's wife and children were still alive and should not be exposed to this further mortification.

A few weeks later, on August 7, Seifert typed out Schmidt's name in a letter and added that he was a member of the Nazi Party. I checked the party records in the Berlin Document Center, an archive under American control, and found Hans-Thilo Schmidt's membership card. Born May 13, 1888, he had joined the party on December 1, 1931, as member number 738,736.

Then, obtaining the service record of his brother, I learned the names of his parents—his father was a "Professor Doktor," a prestigious title in Germany, and his mother was a baroness. That record also showed that Rudolf (Figure 1.4), a signals officer in World War I, had as a captain served from 1926 to 1928 as head of the *Chiffrierstelle*, the unit that both broke foreign codes and devised and authorized cryptosystems for the German army. In depression- and inflation-ridden Germany, he had given his younger brother a job in that unit.

I now knew the identity of the greatest spy of World War II. But I had no occasion to use it. Then, when Winterbotham's book was published in America later in 1974, I reviewed it for *The New York Times*. I praised it, saying that the British—and later American—codebreaking was "the greatest secret of World War II after the atom bomb." I told

Figure 1.4   Panzer General Rudolf Schmidt was the brother of the spy Hans-Thilo Schmidt.

the story of the spy and gave his name. It was the first time he had been publicly identified, and I believe all subsequent references may be traced to this statement.

I sent a copy of the review to Bertrand, thinking it would interest him. Back came a furious note saying, "I will not hide from you that I am very angry at the indiscretion that you have committed in unveiling the name of the employee of the Cipher Center, which I had always carefully concealed, since his brother and his wife (as well as his children) are still living." Bertrand thus inadvertently confirmed that the identification was correct.

Actually, the brother had died in 1957; I don't know about the widow, but a daughter still lived. Further confirmation came, I discovered later, from two German sources. A 1967 article by the German intelligence historian Gert Buchheit stated that "Thilo Schmidt" had delivered some details about Enigma to the French; he expanded this in his 1975 book *Spionage in Zwei Weltkriegen*. And the diaries of Nazi propaganda minister Joseph Goebbels, published in partial English translation in 1948, mention in the entry for May 10, 1943, the arrest for treason of the brother of Colonel-General Schmidt. (Bertrand had been wrong when he said that Schmidt had been caught before the war.) The traitor was not named, and no one seems to have paid attention to the item.

Finally, for his book on Allied codebreaking, *Enigma* (2001), British author Hugh Sebag-Montefiore amazingly tracked down the daughter of a man whose family name was Schmidt. She told of a father who seduced his housemaids, somewhat substantiating the statement that he had betrayed his country for money and women. He thus filled out the human picture of the man who is, in my view, not only the greatest spy of World War II but also possibly the most important spy of all time.

Schmidt's contribution, however, tells only half the story of the Enigma solution. How did the Poles achieve it when the British and French, who also had that information, had failed? The story again revolves around Oxford.

Around the turn of 1973-1974, the head of Oxford's faculty of modern history asked me to help another doctoral student with his dissertation on intelligence during the Napoleonic wars. The student, Alfred Piechowiak, met me in February at my house. I offered what little help I could, and in conversation then or later he said that his father, a retired lieutenant colonel in the Polish army, had been in intelligence in World War II and had some papers dealing with codebreaking. Naturally, I asked if I could see them. He readily assented, and on July 26 we went to their house in South Hinksey, a suburb of Oxford.

They gave me a thirty-two-page purple carbon copy of an anonymous typescript titled "Enigma, 1930–1940." It was in Polish and heavily mathematical. I could understand none of it, but Piechowiak orally translated part of it for me. With his permission, I photocopied it.

By then Tadeusz Lisicki, a retired colonel living in England, had contacted me, probably because the Enigma story was breaking and he knew I had written about cryptology. He told me that Henryk Zygalski, one of the three original solvers of Enigma, was living in England. On July 29, Lisicki and I interviewed Zygalski at his home in Liss, some 30 miles southwest of London. I was thrilled to meet a man who had contributed to a cryptanalysis that had had such far-reaching effects. He provided me not with technical details, which in any event would be foggy sixty years after the event, but with color: where the cryptanalysts worked, in particular.

He also wrote out for me the name and address in Warsaw of his former colleague, Marian Rejewski, who turned out to be the chief solver of the

Enigma and the author of the anonymous typescript. Besides Zygalski, Rejewski was the only survivor of the three original cryptanalysts.

Lisicki identified the corrections on the typescript as in Rejewski's handwriting. Eventually, I believe through Lisicki, it reached a wider audience. This contributed to explaining why Poland had been the only nation to solve the Enigma though two other countries had the information from Schmidt.

One reason was that Poland had greater need: Germany thundered out threats against it more than against the others, hating that much of Poland's land had once been held by Germany, furious that the Polish corridor divided East from West Prussia, resenting the independence of what had once been the German port of Danzig, demanding the "rectification" of its borders.

The other reason was that Poland had greater cryptanalytic ability. With more foresight than the other countries, it was the only one to employ mathematicians as cryptanalysts—and only mathematics could make it possible to reconstruct the Enigma rotor's internal wirings. Subsequently, I corresponded in German—our best mutual language—with Rejewski, filling in some details of the work.

His memorandum was later translated and published. It described how the cryptanalysis had advanced pretty well—but then had stalled. Then Rejewski received Schmidt's information. It converted some of the unknown terms in the cryptanalytic equations to known terms, enabling Rejewski to resolve them. In a commentary, he generously acknowledged, "the intelligence material furnished to us should be regarded as having been decisive to the solution of the machine." Thus he independently implied what I had already concluded: that Hans-Thilo Schmidt was the most important spy of World War II.

This story cannot be completed without mentioning two remarkable coincidences. One is that author Sebag-Montefiore's great-great-grandfather, Sir Herbert Leon, had once owned Bletchley Park, the home of British World War II codebreaking.

The other is the most exquisite irony in intelligence history. As head of the *Chiffrierstelle*, Rudolf Schmidt approved for use the Enigma cipher machine that his brother later betrayed!

How Hans-Thilo Schmidt Got the Information He Sold to the French

He didn't steal it. He didn't copy it or photograph it. He didn't buy it. He didn't blackmail anybody or seduce anybody for it. He just asked for it—and the officials gave it to him!

A German document tells the story. A few years after I wrote the preceding article, I was in Berlin, examining German documents dealing with cryptology that the British had restituted to the German Foreign Office archive. These are designated as Bestand Rückgabe TICOM. Among the office files of Heimsoeth & Rinke, the firm that manufactured Enigmas, I found under number T-1717 a 20 May 1943 certified copy of a 1930 memorandum revealing Schmidt's method. The matter apparently came up in 1943 because Schmidt had just been arrested for spying. Propaganda Minister Joseph Goebbels mentions it in his copious diary on 10 May.

The memorandum shows that Schmidt, an employee of the Army Cipher Branch, simply requested a drawing and blueprint of the rotors–the heart of the Enigma. Nobody seemed to have asked why he wanted them. The firm's engineer, Willi Korn, gave them to Schmidt on the orders of Lieutenant Seifert, almost certainly the Walther Seifert who identified Schmidt in our telephone call. During that call, he said nothing to me about this event, whether because he didn't remember or because he didn't want to reveal it, I don't know. I believe that in 1930 Seifert just wanted to help a colleague. I don't know what Schmidt's job was or how it related to Enigma or what he said to his colleagues about why he wanted the information. The memorandum:

Re: Hans-Thilo Schmidt

The above-mentioned was often present with our Mr. Korn in the factory of our production firm Konski & Krieger in the years 1930-33 in the matter of Wehrmacht cipher machines.

In addition Sch. participated in the following discussion in the Defense Ministry of which the following memo of our Mr. Korn gives details.

Memorandum: Secret

On 28 August 1930 I was asked to come to First Lieutenant Seifert. He asked me in the presence of Mr. Sch. for the preparation of a drawing and blueprint that deals with our rotor principle at Ch 11 [not clear what that is] and is given on the first rotor positions. The rotor wiring may not agree with that of Ch 11 E but must be entirely random. The documents are said to be for a special assignment of the Reich Defense Ministry, which was not specified to me.

First Lieutenant S. emphasized expressly to me personally that no disadvantages would accrue either to the cryptography or to me personally. On the other hand, he asked me whether giving the information of the wiring would be harmful to us by enabling conclusions about the Enigma cipher system. I denied this on account of the great theoretical possibilities that such wiring makes possible.

I spoke personally about this with Mr. Ritter [an engineer and colleague of Arthur Scherbius, the inventor of the Enigma] on 1 October 1930. Mr. R. had nothing against it.

I gave an original of Ch 8 Tx 35 [not known what these are] and a blueprint of it in the presence of Frau Rinke [who ran the firm] and Mr. Sch. on 6 October 1930.

With this a similar matter was again assured from both sides as above.

Mr. Ritter and Frau Rinke of the cipher side have been informed of the matter.

Signed Korn

For the correctness of the copy [signature illegible]

Berlin, 20.5.43

*Original of this given to Branch Chief [Wilhelm] Fenner, Cipher Branch,
High Command of the Armed Forces, 20.5.43*

PART II
AMERICAN
STORIES

Many people know that the United States was solving Japanese codes and reading secret Japanese messages before the attack on Pearl Harbor. How then, they ask, could the attack have surprised the nation? Could Roosevelt have deliberately allowed or even invited it to bring a united and infuriated nation into war against the Axis? This revisionist position was most strongly put in a popular book critically reviewed in "Did Roosevelt Know?" (although the idea that a leader would start a war by sacrificing much of his strength should show the stupidity of the theory). "Pearl Harbor and the Inadequacy of Intelligence" outlines the intelligence that the United States was missing before Pearl Harbor. "U.S. Intelligence Views Germany and Japan in 1941" describes the information that the United States had on Germany and Japan in 1941 and what effect it had on American policy. "Roosevelt, MAGIC and ULTRA" tells how codebreaking intelligence—the best the nation had—was refined and presented to the president. "Edward Bell…" spotlights the role of an American diplomat in the most significant case in history of secret intelligence affecting events. Secret telephony completely protected the transatlantic calls of Roosevelt and Churchill; the technique—spread spectrum—owed much to an invention by the movie star, Hedy Lamarr.

2

DID ROOSEVELT KNOW?*

Every dozen years or so a new book comes out about Pearl Harbor. Some of these books merely tell how the attack succeeded. The more interesting ones seek to explain why. Why was it possible for a far-off country to surprise the mighty United States and sink some of its most powerful warships? The puzzle has been deepened by the knowledge that the United States had been breaking some of Japan's codes and reading some of its secret messages.

Orthodox historians argue that Japan had cloaked its attack in such complete secrecy that no form of intelligence then used by the United States could have penetrated it. Revisionists offer a different answer. The attack succeeded, they say, through treachery—at the highest level. President Franklin D. Roosevelt is the traitor. They argue that Roosevelt, eager to get America into World War II to save Britain and defeat Hitler, needed an enemy attack on American forces to unite the nation. To ensure that such an attack would succeed, he and his subordinates withheld intelligence from Admiral Husband E. Kimmel, commander-in-chief of the Pacific Fleet, and Lieutenant General Walter C. Short, commanding general of the Hawaiian Department. Roosevelt thus was responsible for the deaths of 2,400 Americans and the sinking of eleven warships to get his war.

Among the revisionists are some distinguished historians: Charles A. Beard, a former president of the American Historical Association, for example, and John Toland, a Pulitzer Prize–winning author. The newest, most ambitious revisionist author, Robert B. Stinnett, a former photographer on the staff of the *Oakland Tribune,* is not in their class. He has spent a decade and a half on *Day of Deceit* but has come up with the most irrational of the revisionist books.

Stinnett posits a conspiracy so immense as to dwarf anything the earlier revisionists had proposed. One theory, for example, required

---

* From *The New York Review of Books* (November 2, 2000), 59–60.

only that the chief of naval operations sneak into the office of a subordinate, find in his files an intercept revealing the coming attack, and destroy it. Stinnett contends, however, that many naval officers passed documents to Roosevelt and his advisers while keeping them from Kimmel; they then concealed their acts from congressional investigators and historians—until Stinnett unearthed the conspiracy. He maintains that newly released documents, new interviews with aging survivors, and government suppression of papers support his view. But he misreads the record, misunderstands intelligence, mishandles facts, and misdirects readers.

One expert on communications intelligence found 23 pages containing technical errors in the first third of Stinnett's book before publication, but the author refused to correct any.[1] Another concluded a detailed review of Stinnett's book in the journal *Cryptologia* by saying.

> To those of us who are familiar with Japanese naval codes and communications procedures at the time, available documentation in the Pearl Harbor arena as well as the pertinent personnel and history of OP-20-G [the Navy's communication intelligence center], it is abundantly clear that the book fails to prove any part of its massive revisionist conspiracy theory.[2]

Central to the surprise was the radio silence of the strike force. The Japanese, commanders and radio operators alike, say unanimously that they never transmitted any messages whatever, not even on low-power ship-to-ship messages. Except for Homer "Charlie" Kisner, an American intercept operator now near ninety, everyone else who was listening for Japanese messages says the same thing.[3] And the naval communications intelligence summaries produced in Hawaii have only one statement to make about the Japanese aircraft carriers after November 26, when the strike force sailed: "Carriers are still located in home waters." On December 3, in the last mention before the attack, the summaries say, "No information on submarines or Carriers."

But Stinnett says the strike force did transmit at least one message and that US naval intelligence heard and located it. The US Navy did this by the well-known procedure of radio direction-finding. In this method, radio receivers determine the direction in which a transmitter lies by rotating and listening, just as people turn a portable radio to get the best reception. If two receivers report their bearings to a central listening post, it can draw lines on a map to locate the transmitter at the point where the lines intersect. Stinnett claims that bearings were taken from the Philippines and Alaska and that the fix or fixes were transmitted to Hawaii. He does not give a precise enough citation for researchers to find such reports in the million or so documents in the relevant section of the National Archives' Record Group 38, containing materials from the Navy. But the Hawaii summaries contain no such fixes. Stinnett contends that they do, but he misleads the reader.

For example, he says that the intelligence summary of November 25 told Kimmel that "a large Japanese force of fleet subs and long-range patrol aircraft was heading eastward toward Hawaii from Japan." He cites Box 41 in the records of the Pearl Harbor Liaison Office, Record Group 80, and claims it is a newly discovered document, although it, or a carbon copy of it, is photoduplicated on page 2629 of Part 17 of the Joint Congressional Committee hearings on Pearl Harbor. But the summary says not what he claims it does, only that "Fourth Fleet is still holding extensive communications with the Commander Submarine Fleet." It refers in no way and in no place to any messages from any forces heading toward Hawaii. Moreover, the previous day's summary placed the Fourth Fleet in Truk, far south of Japan and Hawaii. Stinnett also says that, according to a summary of December 5, the Japanese commander-in-chief, Admiral Isoroku Yamamoto, "originated several [radio] messages to the Carriers" (Stinnett's brackets). The summary he cites mentions no such messages. His book contains many other such misstatements.

Moreover, Stinnett seems unaware that a single bearing does not fix a vessel's location. The line of bearing from the Philippines runs not only through the Kurile Islands north of Japan, from which the strike force sailed, but also through the home waters of the Japanese fleet. So it cannot be said to have located the strike force.

Stinnett states that before Pearl Harbor, the United States had broken the main Japanese naval code, the five-numeral system later called JN 25 B. This codebook replaced Japanese words and phrases with groups of five digits, so that, say, "Tokyo" would become 43181; to these were added key digits, such as 52001, and the sum, 95182, was transmitted as the cryptogram. Deciphering the code, he says, enabled the United States to read messages from the Japanese naval command ordering the strike force to attack. As one example, he cites an intercept of December 6 beginning, "A special message on the occasion of the Declaration of War." Stinnett thinks that it was broken before the Pearl Harbor attack the next day and should have been interpreted by the US as revealing the impending attack. The intercept is one of tens of thousands of recently declassified Japanese naval intercepts. They were read in 1945 and 1946 by American crypt-analysts awaiting demobilization. All bear such annotations similar to the one made on the December 6 intercept: "Navy Trans. 10/14/45."

Stinnett refuses to accept this plain statement. He contends that the dates have been falsified as part of the conspiracy to cover up Roosevelt's culpability. But the month-by-month reports of the Navy's cryptanalytic center, declassified in December 1998, discovered by Stephen Budiansky and used by him in his new book, *Battle of Wits*,[4] tally the number of code groups deriving from the five-numeral system that the Navy recovered each month. They show that by December 7 only 3,800 of the code's estimated 30,000 groups had been recovered—and many of the 3,800 stood for numerals. This was not enough to read more than fragments of each message and could not produce any significant intelligible messages. A wartime report gives the number of messages read in this code in 1941 as "none." All this fits perfectly with the unanimous statements by navy codebreakers that no five-numeral messages were read before Pearl Harbor.

According to *Day of Deceit*, the Japanese order for war, "Climb Mount Niitaka December 8," was transmitted in uncoded Japanese, even though the photocopy of the intercept shown in the book plainly shows the designation "JN 25 B" and even though the Japanese preceded the directive with "This despatch is Top Secret." Stinnett then charges that "deceit took over" after the message was intercepted: Lieutenant Commander Edwin T. Layton, Kimmel's intelligence officer, denied ever receiving it, and it "remained in locked vaults." The intercept operator, he writes, was never called to testify by anyone investigating the Pearl Harbor debacle.

Layton was only one of the many involved in Stinnett's Pearl Harbor conspiracy. Among the others who illegally withheld information from Kimmel were not only Roosevelt and Admiral Harold Stark, chief of naval operations, but also Admiral Walter Anderson, the battleships commander at Pearl Harbor; Captain Irving Mayfield, the intelligence officer for the 14th Naval District, in Hawaii; Lieutenant

Commander Thomas Dyer, chief cryptanalyst in the Navy's Hawaiian communications intelligence unit; and Lieutenant Commander Arthur McCollum, the Far Eastern specialist in the Office of Naval Intelligence in Washington.

The list of suspects also includes, among other specialists in communications intelligence, Lieutenant Commander Joseph J. Rochefort, head of the Hawaii communications intelligence unit, even though he often met with Kimmel, who initialed many of Rochefort's summaries. Of Mayfield, Stinnett writes, "For the six days prior to the attack, Captain Mayfield supervised the handling of the coded radiograms. He had one paramount responsibility, to get the intercepts to Admiral Kimmel. His failure to do so has escaped scrutiny." According to Stinnett, this huge conspiracy has remained secret until he uncovered it.

Stinnett rests his argument that Roosevelt wanted to provoke the Japanese into firing the first shot on a memorandum that he says he found in McCollum's personnel file. Dated October 7, 1940, and addressed to Anderson, at the time director of naval intelligence, and Dudley W. Knox, chief of the ONI library, it "suggested" giving all possible aid to China and embargoing "all trade with Japan," among other proposals. "If by these means Japan could be led to commit an overt act of war, so much the better," McCollum wrote. Stinnett does not mention or seem to realize that McCollum's points about aid to China and the embargo of Japan reflected longstanding American policies in support of China and opposition to Japan's aggression and fascism. Stinnett admits that he has no record of Roosevelt's having seen McCollum's document, but says that the fact that its eight points were put into effect—as most of them were—proves that Roosevelt did see it and follow it. But it is much more likely that McCollum was following national policy and adding his own view on the risk of war than that Roosevelt was taking guidance on American policy from a mid-level Navy officer.

Aside from its basic errors of fact and its tendentious interpretations, *Day of Deceit* is an extraordinarily sloppy book. Topics that should stand together are separated and information is occasionally repeated in the space of a few pages. Citations are often inadequate, and Stinnett sometimes contradicts himself. For example, after saying repeatedly that Kimmel was denied codebreaking intelligence, he says that such information was sent to him on "apparently the slowest boat in the Navy." Moreover, in mentioning Roosevelt's last-minute appeal to Hirohito, he writes that the American ambassador was not granted an audience—implying that the message never got to the emperor. He doesn't say that it was in fact delivered in an audience granted by the foreign minister at 3 AM. He calls "F-2" McCollum's "code name," when it merely designated his office: OP-20-F-2. He says letters were engraved on the rims of the code wheels of a Japanese cipher machine: no code wheels ever existed. He claims that Rochefort's description of the Japanese naval code called "AD" by the Americans "appears to be a cover story." It's not. He misreads the date of 15-5-41 on an illustrated document as December 5, 1941. These and many other blunders discredit his work.

It is further undermined by three of its assumptions. One is that the plot would work. Any of the naval officers who were more loyal to Kimmel than to Roosevelt could have slipped information to him. If the army lieutenant supervising a radar on the morning of December 7 had not told the two operators who spotted the approach of the Japanese airplanes to "forget it," surprise would have been lost. And if Kimmel and Short had done their jobs despite less than perfect knowledge and driven off the attackers, the conspiracy would have failed.

Another erroneous assumption is that Roosevelt needed the destruction of major American forces to get into war. A Japanese attack on a few antiquated battlewagons left as bait would have achieved Roosevelt's alleged goal. And although the deaths of men and the sinking of ships appalled Americans, it was the sneakiness of the attack while negotiations were still underway that enraged them.

Finally, Stinnett is simply wrong when he writes, "If Japan could be provoked into committing an overt act of war against the United States, then... mutual assistance provisions [of the Axis Tripartite Pact] would kick in." They wouldn't. The pact—it is in English in the original—reads in part:

> Germany, Italy and Japan agree to co-operate their efforts on the aforesaid lines [the distribution of spheres of influence]. They further undertake to assist one another with all political and economic military means when one of the three Contracting Parties is attacked by a power at present not involved in the European War or in the Sino-Japanese Conflict.

The treaty did not require assistance if one of the parties mounted an attack on another nation. And in fact Japan had not attacked its old foe Russia when Hitler invaded the Soviet Union. So Japan could not be sure that Germany would fight on Japan's side after Pearl Harbor. When Hitler, who was surprised by the event, declared war on December 11, he did not do so because he was complying with the treaty. His reasons have never been made clear and remain a subject of controversy among historians. Roosevelt could not be certain of his reaction any more than the Japanese were.

Stinnett does not see what nearly all other students of the attack agree on: Pearl Harbor succeeded because of Japan's total secrecy about the attack. Even the Japanese ambassadors, whose messages the United States was reading, were never told of it.

The ultimate problem with his book, as with most conspiracy theories, is that it refuses to admit that it can be in error. Conspiracies certainly exist, but those who propound a theory must be open to evidence that can prove them wrong. Otherwise rational argument cannot take place. Unfortunately Stinnett is such a passionate believer in conspiracy that he is unwilling to consider the countervailing evidence. He is offering not a theory but a definition, which cannot be contradicted. It may be expected to have the same fate as all of the other Pearl Harbor conspiracy arguments made during the last fifty-five years.

Notes

1. Captain Duane Whitlock, USN Ret., letters and telephone conversation.
2. Lieutenant Commander Philip H. Jacobsen, USN Ret., "A Cryptologic Veteran's Analysis of 'Day of Deceit,'" *Cryptologia*, Vol. 24 (April 2000), pp. 110–17.
3. According to Stinnett, Kisner said he "verified that several Japanese intercepts heard by his operators were transmitted in plain language to December 7" (p. 57). Philip Jacobsen, Kisner's one-time subordinate, believes Kisner is misremembering, perhaps under Stinnett's suggestions.
4. Stephen Budiansky, *Battle of Wits: The Complete Story of Codebreaking in World War II* (New York: Free Press, 2000).

3

PEARL HARBOR AND THE INADEQUACY OF CRYPTANALYSIS*

Fifty years later, Pearl Harbor still haunts Americans. The nation remains mystified about how Japan's surprise attack on the proud Pacific Fleet could have succeeded. The Joint Congressional Committee that in 1945 and 1946 investigated the attack put the question sharply:

> Why, with some of the finest intelligence available in our history, with the almost certain knowledge that war was at hand, with plans that contemplated the precise type of attack that was executed by the Japanese on the morning of December 7—Why was it possible for a Pearl Harbor to occur?[1]

The "finest intelligence" came from codebreaking. This is nearly always the best form of intelligence. It is faster and more trustworthy than spies, who have to write up and transmit their reports and who are always suspected of setting up a deception. It sees further into the future than aerial reconnaissance, which detects only what is present. It is broader in scope than the interrogations of prisoners, who know little more than what they have experienced. And it is usually cheaper and less obtrusive, hence more secret, than all of these. But it has a serious double-barreled failing. It cannot provide information that a nation has not put onto the airwaves, while its apparent omniscience and its immediacy seduce its recipients into thinking they are getting all the other nation's secrets.

This is one of the lessons of Pearl Harbor. American codebreakers performed prodigies, giving remarkable insight into Japanese thinking. But that insight was not total, and so even the extraordinary U.S. cryptanalysis could not warn policymakers of Japan's secret intentions.

---

* From *Cryptologia,* 15 (October 1991), 273–294.

This article attempts, therefore, two things: to provide information about the codebreaking leading up to Pearl Harbor that has become available since the 1967 publication of *The Codebreakers*, and to explain why even the voluminous information that cryptanalysis did provide did not prevent surprise.

After World War I, which taught or retaught the great powers the value of cryptanalysis, they extended or refounded their codebreaking agencies to provide in peace the benefactions gained in war.[2] The United States was one of these. In 1919, the head of the wartime Section 8 of the Military Intelligence Division of the Army General Staff, or MI-8, persuaded officials to establish a joint State Department–War Department codebreaking agency, formally called the Cipher Bureau but later widely known as the American Black Chamber. He was Herbert O. Yardley, 30, short, balding, and charismatic; he set up shop in New York. The Navy, which after a short-lived effort by naval intelligence had let MI-8 do its codebreaking during the war,[3] talked about organizing its own agency[4] but in fact did nothing in cryptanalysis until 1923. In that year, naval intelligence rifled the steamer trunk of a Japanese naval officer in New York, yielding a 1918 Japanese naval codebook.[5] This trove inspired the Navy to establish a codebreaking agency[6] under the director of naval communications, calling it the Research Desk for security.

Its first head was Lieutenant Laurance F. Safford, who thus became the father of U.S. naval cryptography. Fifteenth in the Annapolis class of 1916, "Saffo" – rumpled, with wavy blond hair that seemed permanently on end ("as if he had been scratching his head in perplexity," a staff member said), whose speech emerged in disconnected bursts – had a flair for mechanics and mathematics and a love for cryptology,[7] though his abilities lay more in making ciphers and cipher machines than in breaking them. He began work in January 1924[8] with four civilians in Room 1621[9] of Main Navy, a temporary building on what is now Constitution Avenue, near the Lincoln Memorial. One of the first things he did was to start setting up radio intercept stations in the Pacific to furnish more material for codebreaking than was provided by the haphazard monitoring by ships and the naval radio station in Shanghai.[10]

Safford concentrated on Japan because it was generally felt that she constituted the greatest danger to the United States. She had, not many years before, defeated China and then Russia to become mistress of the western Pacific. Now she was building a fleet to match America's and had occupied, under a League of Nations mandate, islands that menaced the ocean routes to the Philippines. Japan was a main concern of America's foreign policy, a main focus of America's naval war planning,[11] a main target of America's codebreaking. Yardley, for example, sent Japanese cables that he had cryptanalyzed to U.S. diplomats at the Washington disarmament conference of 1921-22. This gave them knowledge of Japan's negotiating position, which they used to drive her to a lower capital-ship ratio with the United States than she wanted, costing her the equivalent of three battleships.

Soon thereafter, Safford took one of his most important strides in building up his agency when, in August 1924, he hired Mrs. Agnes Meyer Driscoll, 32, as a cryptanalyst. Tall, slender, secretive, a graduate of Ohio State University, she had taught mathematics and music in Texas, had worked in cryptography for the Navy, had studied crypt-analysis at the Riverbank Laboratories, had worked for Yardley's Cipher Bureau for five months and then for cipher-machine inventor Edward H. Hebern in California before accepting Safford's offer and rejoining the Navy, this time as a cryptanalyst.[12] She soon proved out-standing and became the Navy's principal civilian cryptanalyst (most of the Navy's cryptanalysts were officers). Among her first assignments was to work on the photographed code. The Research Desk had found that it was not used plain; rather, its codegroups were themselves enci-phered by a columnar transposition. The first job of Miss Aggie, as she was called, was to solve the transposition. At first, she found, the key remained the same for several weeks; later it changed more fre-quently. Incessantly turning the pages of the photographed book with the rubber tip of her eraser to check codegroups, she took a couple of years to complete the job,[13] enabling the Research Desk to turn the coded messages into Japanese. A husband-and-wife pair translated the Japanese into English.[14]

By then, in 1926, Safford had gone to sea and had been succeeded by one of the first American naval officers to have studied Japanese in Japan: Lieutenant Joseph J. Rochefort. He was a "mustang" – a for-mer enlisted man who had won a commission. This had made him tough and independent in a world dominated by Annapolis graduates; he neutralized his caustic speech with a conciliatory smile. Rochefort became one of the very few Americans capable both in Japanese and in codebreaking.[15]

One of his subordinates described work at the unit:

> Hours went by without any of us saying a word, just sitting in front of piles of indexed sheets on which a mumbo jumbo of figures or letters was displayed in chaotic disorder, trying to solve the puzzle bit by bit like fitting together the pieces of a jigsaw puzzle. We were just a few then…, young people who gave ourselves to cryptography with the same ascetic devotion with which young men enter a monastery.[16]

The hardest part of breaking a code is the beginning. Rochefort explained it in colorful terms:

> It first off involved what I call the staring process. You look at all of these messages that you have, you line them up in various ways, you write them one below the other, and you'd write them in various forms and you'd stare at them. Pretty soon you'd notice a definite pattern between these messages. This was the first clue…. You notice a pattern that when you follow through, you say this means so-and-so; you'd run that through, and it doesn't work out. Then you'd proceed on some other effort and eventually, if you're lucky and the other fellow makes mistakes, which he invariably will, then you come up with a solution that will stand up under test, and this gives your first lead-in.[17]

Rochefort said he felt good while doing this work "because you have defied these people who have attempted to use a system they thought was secure, that is, it was unreadable. It was always somewhat of a pleasure to defeat them or challenge them." But the work took its toll. While engaged in the actual cryptanalysis, he said, he generally felt frustrated. The tension was so great that after work he had to lie down for two or three hours before he could eat anything; he developed ulcers anyway, and this, together with the fact that duty in communications intelligence hurt a man's career, drove him to get out of the work when his tour in the Research Desk ended in 1927.[18] At least for a while.

Safford returned in June 1929. He had the photographed code, called Code No. 1, whose translation had originally been put together in 10 "volumes" with metal-strip Acco office binders, retyped in four copies on huge 12-by-18-inch forms and bound in two volumes in red buckram McBee binders, far more convenient to use. This gave the code its more common name, the Red Code.[19] On 1 December 1930, however, the Japanese replaced it with a new code. But Miss Aggie, who had by then learned the ships' names, the communications patterns, and the frequently used phrases of the Japanese fleet, solved its transposition encipherment and then reconstructed the 85,000-group, two-part code, later called, from its binding, the Blue Code. It was a remarkable feat of cryptanalysis, and it gave the U.S. Navy insight into Japanese forces and tactics for years.[20]

Two events in 1929 led the Army to expand its codebreaking. In May, after giving the new secretary of state a little time to understand the realities of the job, Yardley passed him some solved messages. Henry L. Stimson was shocked at what he regarded as a dishonorable and counterproductive activity – "Gentlemen do not read each other's mail," he said later, maintaining that "the way to make men trustworthy is to trust them." He withdrew State Department support from the Cipher Bureau.[21] In the meantime, the Army had decided that Yardley was not doing what it needed most: training cryptanalysts for immediate use in case of war.[22] These events doomed the unit, which was dissolved as of October 31, 1929[23] – two days after the great stock market crash.

Its people were released; its papers went to the Army Signal Corps, which had charge of Army codes and ciphers.[24] The Signal Corps had in 1921 hired a 29-year-old who was on his way to becoming the world's greatest cryptologist. William F. Friedman, natty, uptight, brilliant, had written some theoretical treatises of landmark importance and had solved German codes in France during World War I. His new job was nominally to improve the Army's own cryptosystems. But doing this properly required him to test cryptosystems offered to it. This gave him experience in cryptanalysis and expanded the Army's knowledge of it.[25] With the closing of Yardley's agency, the Signal Corps added codebreaking to its responsibilities, and Friedman became the head of a new Signal Intelligence Service. He hired as junior cryptanalysts at $2,000 a year three young men who knew languages and mathematics. The first to report was Frank B. Rowlett, 21, a Virginian, a former teacher, fair-haired, with an all-American look to him, who at 8 a.m. April 1, 1930, found himself entering Room 3406 of the Munitions Building on B Street (now Constitution Avenue) near the Lincoln Memorial in Washington (Figure 3.1).[26]

Figure 3.1   Frank B. Rowlett on May 2, 1930, his 22nd birthday, a month after joining the Signal Intelligence Service.

Two months later, he and his colleagues were excitedly combing through the secret files of Yardley's organization. This most clandestine and most valuable form of intelligence thrilled them. They went on to study basic cryptography and the solution of machine ciphers, clearly the wave of the future. In 1932, their training completed, they attacked Japanese diplomatic cryptosystems, working on messages provided by the Army's new intercept service. They first cracked a simple code, the LA, so called from the indicator group that preceded its messages. It did little more than put kata kana, a Japanese syllabary, into Latin letters for telegraphic transmission and to secure some abbreviations for cable economy. It was rather regular in construction. For example, all kata kana syllables that ended in *e* had as code equivalents groups beginning with A, so that *ke* = AC and *se* = AD. This arrangement facilitated solution. When the young cryptanalysts discovered that LA encrypted only insignificant messages, such as those dealing with expenses or vacations, and when they had gained experience and knowledge of Japanese diplomatic language and communications practices, they turned their attention to the more important messages, apparently protected by a machine system. It served on two main Japanese diplomatic communication networks—one covering the Far East, one linking Tokyo with major world capitals.[27]

The cryptanalysts recognized messages in it because they consisted of 5-letter groups like RWOBA preceded by a 5-digit group like 77181. Study showed that vowels had a relatively higher frequency than consonants. It appeared that the machine divided the 26 letters of the Latin alphabet into two subsets, the 6 vowels and the 20 consonants. They perhaps got some help from Navy Lieutenant Jack S. Holtwick's solution of a Japanese cipher machine that enciphered kana. Eventually, the Army cryptanalysts discovered that the machine they were working on used the same cryptographic principles as the Holtwick machine but enciphered not 50 syllables but the 26 letters of the Latin-alphabet form of Japanese, called Romaji, with a mechanism appropriately adapted.[28] Rowlett and one of the other original junior cryptanalysts, Solomon Kullback, one day struck gold. Among their tentative recoveries of partial plaintext were three letters, an unknown, and another letter: *oyo?i*. They knew then they had broken the system, because *oyobi* was Japanese for *and*. They named it RED, the first of the primary colors.[29] By 1937, for the first time in American history, solutions began going to the White House,[30] probably to President Franklin D. Roosevelt. The intercepts revealed, for instance, advance information about Italy's possible adherence to the German-Japanese Anti-Comintern Pact—providing this in March 1937, six months before American diplomats began reporting on it. Later they provided part of the text of the treaty.[31]

The next year, messages began to appear suggesting that a new machine would supplement and probably eventually replace the older one, which was physically wearing out. On March 20, 1939, three messages in the new system were intercepted, and over the next three months messages in RED gradually disappeared. Japan's major diplomatic messages had become unreadable. Faced with the loss of the nation's paramount intelligence, the Signal Intelligence Service mounted a concentrated attack to solve the new machine. Friedman put Rowlett in charge, with he himself exercising overall supervision. The Americans called the new machine PURPLE (Figure 3.2).[32]

Figure 3.2 Women work with U.S. Army analogue of the Japanese PURPLE cipher machine. (Photo by US Government.)

In the absence of any American spies almost anywhere in the world,[33] these half-dozen cryptanalysts would be able to provide the United States with its best secret intelligence on Japan as relations with that nation, which persisted in its aggression against China, deteriorated. They plunged into their work in Rooms 3416 and 3418 in the Munitions Building. Room 3418, about 25 feet square with a steel door and barred windows, was known as the vault. As additional cryptanalysts were assigned to the PURPLE problem, the group moved into larger quarters, finally occupying about eight rooms. Rowlett worked in 3416. He arrived at 7, an hour early, and left at 5, an hour late. His desk was usually neat, for he spread out his work-sheets on a nearby table. Rowlett was extremely focused on the work. He never hummed or chewed his pencil or muttered to himself; he looked out the window only when something attracted his attention; he never drank coffee at work, but did puff on a pipe. His mind didn't dwell on the cryptanalytic problems during the 15-minute drive to work from Arlington County, but he would awaken each night after a few hours of sleep and, lying there in the dark, would review the day's work and think of ways of improving it.[34] In the morning, at work he would exchange ideas with the other cryptanalysts—Assistant Cryptanalyst Robert O. Ferner, Rowlett's principal helper, and Junior

Cryptanalysts Albert W. Small, Genevieve Grotjan, and Samuel S. Snyder, occasionally assisted by Cryptographic Specialists Cyrus C. Sturgis, Jr., Kenneth D. Miller, and Glenn S. Landig[35] (their names deserve to be remembered!). After the conference, all would return to their desks. Quiet reigned as they pored over the intercepts, most of which had been teletyped in from the monitoring stations; sometimes they puzzled over statistical and alphabetical tables compiled by hand from intercepts. To Rowlett, the atmosphere was like that of a library. Only the rustling of papers and the scratching of pencils and an occasional discussion broke the brooding silence.

PURPLE had carried over from RED the 6-and-20 division of letters. But this time the "sixes" were not exclusively vowels. Nevertheless, within a few weeks, the cryptanalysts ascertained how the sixes were enciphered. This enabled them to recover the plaintext for those letters. The process was slow and painstaking. A new recruit, Leo Rosen, was assigned to devise a way to mechanize this pencil-and-paper process. He hit upon the idea of using standard 6-level, 25-point telephone selector switches, used in dialing. They worked like a dream, and the solution process was considerably speeded.[36]

Despite Rosen's remarkable advance, the totality of PURPLE still resisted the Americans. Friedman, who had been supervising the work rather loosely, was asked by his bosses—all extremely supportive, financially as well as psychologically[37]—to participate personally.[38] But he was busy with administrative and communication security and, aside from the fundamental and important job of assembling the team, did not contribute directly to solving PURPLE.[39] The Navy, though its main effort continued to be against Japan's naval codes, lent a hand. It and the Army organized their files the same way to facilitate cooperation. After about four months, the Navy dropped its effort[40] and returned to Japanese naval cryptosystems. The S. I. S. pushed ahead. Within Rowlett's group, teamwork was extremely close. No one complained that a task was too menial. Determination pervaded the team. Rowlett was confident from the start that they would break PURPLE the way he and others had broken RED. He never grew depressed, even as one month after another went by without a solution.[41]

As the breakthrough was being sought, the cryptanalysts spent much of their time matching proposed plaintext—a guess as to the text of the original message—against the text of the cryptograms, the ciphertext. The proposed plaintext came from various sources. During the gradual replacement of RED with PURPLE, circular messages were sent to embassies and legations around the world in both systems. RED's solution gave the plaintext to the circulars in PURPLE. In a few cases, the State Department gave them the texts of notes to or from the Japanese ambassadors, which the codebreakers used as cribs. And the cryptanalysts' guessed at plaintexts. They knew, for example, that many diplomatic dispatches began "I have the honor to inform Your Excellency that…" and they often tried that as the plaintext start.

Among the things they were looking for, apparently, were letter intervals that would reveal the advancement of PURPLE's mechanism. Exactly what these intervals were has never been revealed, but one possibility is that two occurrences of a probable plaintext letter, such as *a*, stood at a certain distance from one another, say two places, as in *Japan*, and that the ciphertext letters that represented them were separated in the alphabet by the same interval, as X and Z. This would show that the machine had moved forward one space each time a letter was enciphered. C. A. Deavours thinks that the search was for identical ciphertext letters, so that in a situation like

```
1  2  3  4  5  6  7
a  d  v  a  n  c  e
X  G  A  R  X  G  V
```

the cryptanalysts looked for an alphabet where the *a* in alphabet 1 was represented by the same letter as plaintext *n* in alphabet 5, and *d* in alphabet 2 was represented by the same ciphertext letter as *c* in alphabet 6. A plugboard, which monoalphabetically enciphered the cipher alphabet table, complicated things. Either way, two or more intervals were needed for the hypothesis to be confirmed.

More than a year of tedious work passed.[42] Then, about 2 p.m. on Friday, 20 September 1940, a sunny day on which the temperature reached 88 degrees, in the middle of Roosevelt's running for an unprecedented third term, as Britain anxiously awaited a German invasion from occupied France, Albert Small noticed that Grotjan, a dignified, 26-year-old statistician, seemed to be concentrating extremely intently. He spoke to her about it, and learned that she had just discovered a couple of the needed intervals and was looking hard for others. He took her in to see Rowlett. He was conferring with Ferner.

She said she had something to show him.[43] All moved to her desk. She pointed to her instances, then a third leaped out at the codebreakers. At once, they grasped the significance of what she was showing them. The ebullient Small dashed around the room, hands clasped above his head. Ferner, normally phlegmatic, shouted "Hooray!" Rowlett jumped up and down, crying "That's it!" Everybody crowded around. Friedman came in. "What's all the noise about?" he asked. Rowlett showed him Grotjan's findings. He understood immediately. Grotjan's discovery verified the team's theory of how the PURPLE machine worked. It marked the climax of one of the greatest cryptanalyses of all time. And how did the egghead codebreakers celebrate this great moment in the history of American codebreaking? They sent out for Cokes![44]

When the euphoria and the effects of the Coca-Colas had worn off, the cryptanalysts drifted back to work. Grotjan, who seems to have gotten excited about the breakthrough mainly because everybody else was, regarded it soberly as just one step in a series of steps. A week later, the day after Japan started to occupy French Indo-China and the very day the Tripartite Pact establishing the Rome-Berlin-Tokyo axis was signed, the Signal Intelligence Service handed in its first two solutions of PURPLE messages.[45] This did not mean its work was done. The settings for the machine changed each day, and the cryptanalysts had to recover these. But this work was facilitated by Rosen's construction of two American analogues of the Japanese PURPLE machine. The cost: $684.65.[46] Later, other copies of the machine were built—several at the Washington Navy Yard; some were given to the Navy, which had rejoined the PURPLE work to help with the heavy volume of solutions, and some to the British, so they could read the messages without having to wait for American solutions to be forwarded to them. Soon Navy Lieutenant Francis A. Raven discovered a pattern to the daily machine setting changes. With this knowledge, the United States was able to read reports from and instructions to Japan's ambassadors on average within a day or so, sometimes within hours. It had gained access to the most secret diplomatic dispatches of Japan as U.S. relations with that empire continued to worsen.

In cryptology, the beginning of wisdom is to know that there is no such thing as "the" Japanese code. PURPLE was not the only cryptosystem of the Foreign Ministry, much less of the empire. The Foreign Ministry employed a hierarchy of systems, of which PURPLE was the apex.

Under it lay several codes that—unlike PURPLE, which served embassies exclusively—were used at both embassies and consulates. LA, the simplest, lay at the bottom.[47] Above it rested a two-part system, PA-K2. The PA was a code, like LA, though more extensive and with its codegroups disarranged in relation to their kata kana plaintexts. The K2 part shuffled the letters of the PA codegroups. American cryptanalysts could restore them to their original positions and then solve the PA code message in three days on the average.[48] More complex still was the J series of codes. These codes were more extensive and more thoroughly disarranged than PA, and their codegroups were transposed in a far more complicated manner than the K2: an irregular columnar transposition with a pattern of blanks that broke up the columns. (See Appendix 1.) Moreover, the code was changed every several months, and the transposition blank pattern—called K plus a number by the Americans—was, by November 1941, changed every 10 days; the transposition's columnar transcription key changed daily, so the codebreakers had to make a fresh analysis for each day's messages.[49] Thus J17-K6 was replaced on 1 March 1941 by J18-K8, and that in turn by J19-K9, whose K9 transposition was itself replaced by K10, which served from 11 to 20 November.[50] Some 10 to 15 percent of J-code messages were not solved at all, and those that were took an average of a week from interception through translation to distribution. This situation contrasts with that of PURPLE, in which most messages were solved within hours and all but 2 to 3 percent of keys were recovered. Did the Japanese err in assessing the security of their cryptosystems? Yes and no. PURPLE was a much more difficult system to solve in the first place, but once solved it was easier to keep up with.

While the Army was concentrating on Japan's diplomatic systems (though the Navy later joined in recovering daily keys and solving and translating messages), the Navy's codebreaking agency—except for some help to the Army—focused on Japan's naval systems. This agency, again under Safford, now a commander, was now called OP-20-G: the OP for the Office of the Chief of Naval Operations, the 20 for Office of Naval Communications, the G for its Communication Security Section, which included codebreaking. During the 1930s it read messages in the Blue code, gaining considerable knowledge about Japan's naval maneuvers.[51] The Japanese replaced this with a new code on 1 November 1938. But the paucity of intercepts in it meant that almost no progress was made in reading it.[52]

On 1 June 1939, the Japanese introduced yet another code. Called JN25 by the Americans, for the 25th Japanese naval code attacked, it soon became the main fleet code, enshrouding messages dealing with naval operations. It was a two-part code of 33,333 five-digit groups, each of which had the peculiarity of being divisible by 3: for example, 52884; this checked against garbles. It was superenciphered with an additive—a string of numbers, printed in a book, that the cipher clerk added to the codegroups, disguising them. Miss Aggie attacked it, greatly helped by reserve Lieutenant Prescott Currier. She stripped off the additive, exposing the original codegroups, then recovered their meanings. A year and a half later, in almost the very week that the Army was producing its first PURPLE solutions, the first JN25 solutions emerged.[53] The Navy's satisfaction did not last long. On 1 December 1940, the Imperial Navy replaced it with a new edition, called by the Americans JN25b. But Japan's cryptographers foolishly kept the first edition's last additive book in force for the first two months of the second edition's service. Since this additive book had been reconstructed, OP-20-G gained easy access to the basic codegroups of JN25b and quickly determined the meaning of 2,000 of them. When new additive tables went into effect, the I. B. M. tabulators generated the difference tables necessary for stripping off the additives.[54] As Safford remarked, "We could always trust the Japanese themselves to do something that would assist us in the solution of their systems: they have never yet failed us."[55] Nevertheless, progress continued slow.

So in March 1941, OP-20-G in Washington ordered the radio intelligence unit on Corregidor Island in the Philippines to help with the solution of JN25b. A British codebreaking unit in Singapore exchanged recoveries of JN25b codegroups with Corregidor.[56] But despite all these efforts, the code remained readable to but a very small degree. By December 1941, only 10 to 15 percent of each message could be understood.[57]

This, then, was the cryptanalytic situation early in December 1941: the main Japanese diplomatic system could be read rapidly and completely; Japanese consular systems could be read with a few days' delay; the main naval system could be read only spottily. The diplomatic solutions provided Washington with the instructions to and reports from Japan's ambassadors to the United States and so with considerable insight into Japan's foreign plans, and it did so with great speed, accuracy, and volume. By November 1941, 50 to 75 messages a day poured out of the U.S. codebreaking agencies.

Why did all this information not enable the United States to foresee the Pearl Harbor attack? The most basic answer is this: Japan never sent any message to anybody saying anything like "We shall attack Pearl Harbor." The ambassadors in Washington were never told of the plan. Nor were any other Japanese diplomats or consular officials. The ships of the strike force were never radioed any message mentioning Pearl Harbor. It was therefore impossible for the cryptanalysts to solve one.

Some historians have contended that, if only the intelligence officers of the Army and the Navy, and perhaps State Department officials as well, had found the time to analyze all the intercepts as a group, they would have discerned a pattern that pointed to Pearl Harbor. This argument resembles that made by Roberta Wohlstetter in her book *Pearl Harbor: Warning and Decision*,[58] in which she holds that the noise of the false evidence drowned out the indications of the true signals. "We failed to anticipate Pearl Harbor not for want of the relevant materials, but because of a plethora of irrelevant ones."[59] This is wrong. There were no true signals, no clear indications of the attack.

What then is the answer to the Joint Congressional Committee's question? What about that "finest intelligence"? The simple answer is that fine though it was, it was not good enough. A nation can't cryptanalyze what is not there. In that elementary fact lies the inadequacy of cryptanalysis at Pearl Harbor.

Appendix 1: A Japanese Cryptosystem

The most complicated of Japan's pencil-and-paper cryptosystems was the J19-K10 enciphered code. J19 was a two-part code. A Japanese plaintext was first encoded using the J19 code, then this codetext was transposed using the K10 transposition.

An example of this system is one of the messages from Tokyo to Washington setting up the so-called "winds" code. If it had been drafted in English, Circular 2352 would have read:

Regarding the broadcast of a special message in an emergency:
In case of emergency (danger of cutting off our diplomatic relations),
and the cutting off of international communications, the following

warning will be added in the middle of the daily Japanese language short wave news broadcast.

(1) In case of Japan-U.S. relations in danger: *HIGASHI NO KAZE AME.*

(2) Japan-U.S.S.R. relations: *KITA NO KAZE KUMORI.*

(3) Japan-British relations (including Thailand, Malaya, and Netherlands East Indies): *NISHI NO KAZE HARE.*

This signal will be given in the middle and at the end as a weather forecast and each sentence will be repeated twice. When this is heard please destroy all code papers, etc. This is as yet to be a completely secret arrangement.

Forward as urgent intelligence.

The phrases relate to the position of the various countries from Japan and mean, respectively, "East wind rain," "North wind cloudy," and "West wind clear."

The text in Romaji (Japanese syllabary in Latin letters) version began: *Kancho fugo atsukai. Kokusai jigyo no hippaku no kekka itsu saiaku no jitai ni tachi itaru kamo....* This was first encoded in J19 (see Figure 3.3).

Most of the codewords are two-letter groups that replace syllables in kata kana, punctuation, numbers, and whole words. But some are four-letter groups that replace words. An M was added at the end, perhaps as a dummy to fill out the last five-letter group. The dash before the B in the third to last group indicates that that letter is missing from the intercepted texts.

The code clerk next took out a sheet of paper with that day's transposition block printed on it (see Figure 3.4). This consisted of a grid of lines and columns in which several of the cells were blacked out (■) topped by a row of numbers from 1 to 19 in scrambled order. He wrote the coded message— XEICNCSTWYNYKYES... — horizontally into the grid, skipping the blacked out squares.

Then he transcribed the letters vertically by columns beginning with the column numbered 1. The result

NEWZUCNFXALEKFKOHTZVGONHEWKWWK...

was the cryptogram that would be sent. He divided it into five-letter groups for ease of transmission and to detect any dropped letters, placed the system and key indicators in two five-letter groups at the top,

```
Kancho fugo atsukai     Kokusai jigyo no hip pa ku no kekka
      XEIC              NC   ST   WYNY  KY  ES  NI  CU  KY  MTAN

itsu saiaku no jitai ni tachi itaru kamo hakararezaru tokoro
WEUF DB  TH  ZW JXHZ  US GKIY IO    WV           MTGS       WU

kakaru baai waga ho to aitekoku to no tsushin wa tadachi ni
  YK   UQEQ  XF  UX KZRS LJ   SC   FW  AO AD    CE     CY

teishi serarubeki wo waga ho no gaiko kankei kiken ni hinsuru
SI LW   BS  BN    FK    XF  ZW LUGS XEYM  LZFF  US  TR GD

baai ni wa waga kaigai hoso no kakuchi muke nihoho news no
UQEQ XG    FH   EK  FG XJKC KY  PE IY  ZTVE FJ FX  VAIX ZW

chukan oyobi saigo ni oite tenki yoho to shite   1  .  Nichibei
MS  ZP  KR  DB    NX  AE  NE LZ LJXJ   CT      NC LA BO   TMWD

kankei no baai ni wa "  higashi no kaze  ame "    2  .  Nichiso
XEYM  KY  UQEQ XG    HL  CUOM LW KY FEXD DWLD VB NC JG BO  EF  PB

kankei no baai ni wa "  kita no kaze kumori "    3  .  Nichiei
XEYM  ZW UQEQ XG    HL  VM  KY FEXD CUCNJM  VB NC TK BO  OCXP

kankei no baai (  "  tai "  shinchu mare  "
XEYM  KY  UQEQ WM HL HZ  VB  AO MS  MD QC VB

Netherlands East Indies koryoku oboe fukumu "  "  nishi no kaze
            MTOV           ER CX   NV  FAXPZT VB HL ZA LW KY FEXD

hare "   o  2  do   zutsu kurikaeshi hoso seshimeru koto to
KPQV VB NC NV JG UP QOAF UF   XEEQ    XJKC  GG       BV  UX

seru wo motte migi ni yori ango  . Shorui to tekito shobun
NJ   FX     DM    MG    RA VD BO AD BE  RV TMKD  AD  JB

aritashi    Nao migi wa gen ni gokuhi atsukai to seraretashi
  GQ      NC NU DM  AG VP  US BDZK   -B    UX     ZH
```

Figure 3.3   The "East Wind Rain" message encoded in J19.

some other indicators at the end, typed it up, and handed it to a communications officer for transmission (probably by a commercial radio company) to the embassy in the United States.

When a cryptogram like this was intercepted by U.S. Army or Navy radio monitors and teleprinted to Washington, cryptanalysts there faced two steps. They had, first, to determine the pattern of blanks in the grid and the order of the keynumbers at the top. They did this by trying various arrangements until repetitions of pairs of quadruplets or letters indicated that that arrangement had produced codewords. Then the codebreakers had to ascertain the original Japanese words or syllables for which the codewords stood. These two steps could not be completed on the basis of a single message; dozens were needed (Figure 3.5). When a message was finally solved, translators would render it into English. Then it would be distributed to the very limited circle of those high officials entitled to see the intercepts.

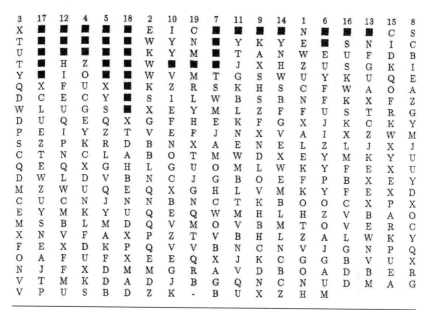

3	17	12	4	5	18	2	10	19	7	11	9	14	1	6	16	13	15	8
X	■	■	■	■	■	E	I	C	■	■	■	■	N	■	■	■	C	S
T	■	■	■	■	■	W	Y	N	■	Y	K	Y	E	■	S	N	I	C
U	■	■	■	■	■	K	Y	M	■	T	A	N	W	E	U	F	D	B
T	■	H	Z	■	■	W	■	■	■	J	X	H	Z	U	S	G	K	I
Y	■	I	O	■	■	W	V	M	T	G	S	W	U	Y	K	U	Q	E
Q	X	F	U	X	■	K	Z	R	S	K	H	S	C	F	W	A	O	A
D	C	E	C	Y	■	S	I	L	W	B	S	B	N	F	K	X	F	Z
W	L	U	G	S	■	X	E	Y	M	L	Z	F	F	U	S	T	R	G
D	U	Q	E	Q	X	G	F	H	E	K	F	G	X	J	K	C	K	Y
P	E	I	Y	Z	T	V	E	F	J	N	X	V	A	I	X	Z	W	M
S	Z	P	K	R	D	B	N	X	A	E	N	E	L	Z	L	J	X	J
C	T	N	C	L	A	B	O	T	M	W	D	X	E	Y	M	K	Y	U
Q	E	Q	X	G	H	L	G	U	O	M	L	W	K	Y	F	E	X	U
D	W	L	D	V	B	N	C	J	G	B	O	E	F	P	B	X	E	Y
M	Z	W	U	Q	E	Q	X	G	H	L	V	M	K	Y	F	E	X	D
C	U	C	N	J	N	Q	N	B	N	C	T	K	B	O	O	C	X	P
E	Y	M	K	Y	U	Q	E	Q	W	M	H	L	H	Z	V	B	A	O
M	S	B	L	M	D	Q	V	M	O	V	B	M	T	O	V	E	R	C
X	N	V	F	A	X	P	Z	T	V	B	H	L	Z	A	L	W	K	Y
F	E	X	D	K	P	Q	V	V	B	N	C	N	V	J	G	N	P	Q
O	A	F	U	F	X	E	E	Q	X	J	K	C	G	G	B	V	U	X
N	J	F	X	D	M	M	G	R	A	V	D	B	O	A	D	B	E	R
V	T	M	K	D	A	D	J	B	G	Q	N	C	N	U	D	M	A	R
V	P	U	S	B	D	Z	K	-	B	U	X	Z	H	M				

Figure 3.4 Code clerk's sheet of one day's transposition block.

```
SF DE JAB                                    8 NOV 41
361 SDCE TOKIO 90 19 9 40S JP P1/50                        3805
RIYOJI SANFRANCISCO
MWZHU BUWTJ NEWZU CNFXA LEKFK OHTZV GONHE WKWWK SXGVB BLNQV
QQPQE MDZXT UTYQD WDPSC QDMCE MXFON VVZOU CGEYK CXDUN KLFDU
XKSXY SQZRL GVQJY MAKFD DBEUY FFUJI ZYYPY OZOAJ GAUMT SWMEJ
AMPGH CWOVB XAGBS CBIEA ZGYMJ UDYDX OCYQX RGKAX SHSZF XNDLO
VKHBH CKDNX IYYVZ IEFEN OGCXB EVZVE GJKYT JGKBL
                                   1320   S RJ
                                   9160


SF DE JAB                                    8 NOV 41
P2/360 41W KOS WASHN                                       3804
KNEWM BLTMV BNJVQ UHIFE UQIPN QLWCM BVXFF MUNFG UAXTA ZJKEX
EXBEW UVBMY NHWSB FGVEX WEMBL MLNCB CZCID KQOFR KWXYX EXPAR
KPUEA SUSKW KSKXL MFBFC VVLGB DDXCL UEZTE WZUYS NEAJT PXTDA
HBENU DXPXM ADCNM MRLYH FXTUJ GNQMT VQRB 84444 BDSHD TAKAO
TOGO
      ( VQRB ) AS SENT                         1317  S RJ
                                               9160
```

Figure 3.5 The Japanese cryptogram of Circular 2353, as intercepted in two parts by American monitors.

Appendix 2: The Woman Who Made the Key Discovery

In a small brick ranch house exactly like the others lined along the wooded suburban street near Washington, D.C., lives an important piece of America's secret history—and of its feminist.

The young neighbors on either side have no inkling that the structure between them houses a woman who detected data that led to perhaps the nation's most important cryptanalytic breakthrough. To them, she and her husband are just an old couple with a less than manicured lawn.

But the woman, the former Genevieve Grotjan, discovered, on 20 September 1940, significant characteristics in intercepted Japanese code messages. A week later, the team of U.S. Army civilian codebreakers, of which she was a part, had solved Japan's main diplomatic cipher machine, which the Americans called the PURPLE machine. Solutions of the messages enciphered in it gave President Franklin D. Roosevelt and other high-ranking members of the U.S. Government extraordinary insight into the thoughts and plans of the Foreign Ministry and its envoys in Washington through all of 1941.

Grotjan was born in Buffalo on April 30, 1913. She attended the University of Buffalo, hoping to become a mathematics teacher. But no such work was available at the time, so she accepted a position in Washington as a statistical clerk with the Railroad Retirement Board. Later she took an examination for a professional grade of mathematician and was offered a job by the Signal Intelligence Service, which naturally never told her that she would be breaking codes but asked only whether she would be interested in working with codes. She was; she was hired; she proved good enough to be assigned to the premier task of the unit—and she became the one who made the critical find.

Why her? "Maybe I was just lucky in getting the right series of papers," she said. "I perhaps had a little more patience than [Al] Small. [Bob] Ferner might have done it but he was working on something else." When she spotted the intervals, she aside, "I was elated up to a point but I didn't think 'This is it!' because there was so much more to do. I was looking forward to working on the mechanism. I regarded it more as just one step in a series of steps."

So she makes no great claims for herself. Interviewed in her cluttered living room, she thought long before offering a carefully worded answer to each question. She was evidently trying both to reconstruct transient events of more than half a century ago and to be as accurate

Figure 3.6   Genevieve Grotjan in 1935.

as she could. She did not exaggerate her importance, did not suggest that without her discovery PURPLE would not have been cracked or the war lost. She recognized that only chance gave her the breakthrough. It was a commendable display of modesty.

Though the solution of PURPLE did not prevent Pearl Harbor, it had enormous effects on the war. Not the war in the Pacific, but that in Europe. "Our main basis of information regarding Hitler's intentions in Europe is obtained from [Japanese ambassador] Baron Oshima's messages from Berlin," wrote Army Chief of Staff General George C. Marshall. These and other solutions, he noted, "contribute greatly to the victory and tremendously to the saving in American lives." It was a remarkable tribute to America's cryptanalysts: including Grotjan, who lives obscure, forgotten, unsung in a low house with a scruffy lawn, but who helped, more than most, to shorten America's biggest war (Figure 3.6).

Notes

1. U.S., Congress, Joint Committee on the Investigation of the Pearl Harbor Attack, *Investigation of the Pearl Harbor Attack*, Report, 79th Congress, 2d Session (Document No. 244) (Washington, DC: Government Printing Office, 1946), p. 253.

2. "Codebreaking in World Wars I and II: The Major Successes and Failures, Their Causes and Their Effects," in David Kahn, *Kahn on Codes: Secrets of the New Cryptology* (New York: Macmillan, 1983), pp. 99–119; David Kahn, *Seizing the Enigma: The Race to Break the German U-Boat Codes, 1939–1943* (New York: Houghton Mifflin, 1991), pp. 82–85.

3. J. S. Holtwick, "Naval Security Group History to World War II," Appendix I, p. 003, SRH-355, Record Group 457, National Archives (since all SRH documents are from this record group, that designation is omitted in other references); William F. Friedman, "A Brief History of the Signal Intelligence Service," SRH-029, p. 01.

4. SRH-355, p. 026.

5. Jeffery M. Dorwart, *Conflict of Duty: The U. S. Navy's Intelligence Dilemma, 1919–1945* (Annapolis: Naval Institute Press, 1983), pp. 39–40, giving March 1923 as the terminus ad quem; I have been unable to find the report in the source given by Dorwart, apparently through some error; Laurance F. Safford, "A Brief History of Communications Intelligence in the United States," pp. 3–12 in Ronald H. Spector, ed., *Listening to the Enemy: Key Documents on the Role of Communications Intelligence in the War with Japan* (Wilmington, DE: Scholarly Resources, 1988), 6, giving date as "about 1922"; Ladislas Farago, *The Broken Seal: The Story of "Operation Magic" and the Pearl Harbor Disaster* (New York: Random House, 1967), pp. 36–37, giving 1920 as the date. Farago's source is the memoir of Rear Admiral Ellis M. Zacharias, *Secret Missions* (New York: Putnam, 1946), which Farago co-authored.

6. L. F. Safford, "The Undeclared War: 'History of R[adio]. I[ntelligence].' 15 November 1943," SRH-305, p. 03.

7. Edwin T. Layton with Roger Pineau and John Costello, *"And I Was There": Pearl Harbor and Midway – Breaking the Secrets* (New York: Morrow, 1985), p. 32.

8. Russell Willson, "The Birthday of the Naval Security Group," in *A History of Communications Intelligence in the United States*, ed. Graydon A. Lewis (Denver, CO: Naval Cryptologic Veterans Association, 1982), p. 41.

9. Layton, 33.

10. Safford, "A Brief History," 5; Willson, 41.

11. Edward S. Miller, *War Plan Orange: The U. S. Strategy to Defeat Japan, 1897–1945* (Annapolis, MD: Naval Institute Press, 1991).

12. Susan M. Lujan, "Agnes Meyer Driscoll," *Cryptolog* (Naval Cryptologic Veterans Association), Vol. 9 (August Special 1988), pp. 4–6.

13. "Reminiscences of Captain Joseph J. Rochefort, U. S. N., Ret." Transcript of oral history interview (U. S. Naval Institute, 1969), p. 30; Layton, 31.

14. SRH-305, p. 01; Layton, 31–32.

15. David Kahn, *The Codebreakers: The Story of Secret Writing* (New York: Macmillan, 1967), p. 7 (henceforth as Kahn); Layton, 33, 34; Jasper Holmes, *Double-Edged Secrets: U.S. Naval Intelligence Operations in the Pacific During World War II* (Annapolis, MD: Naval Institute Press, 1979), p. 3.

16. Zacharias 89.

17. Rochefort, 17.

18. Rochefort, 16, 17, 45–46.

19. SRH-305, p. 03.

20. Safford, 8–9; Layton, 46; SRH-305, pp. 11–12.

21. Louis Kruh, "Stimson, The Black Chamber, and the 'Gentlemen's Mail' Quote," *Cryptologia*, 12 (April 1988), pp. 65–89.

22. SRH-029, Paragraph 6; Frank B. Rowlett, "Comments on [an early draft of this] David Kahn Article," 22 May 1991.

23. Kahn, 360.

24. SRH-029, Paragraph 8.

25. Kahn, 384–385.

26. Theodore M. Hannah, "Frank B. Rowlett: A Personal Profile," *Cryptologic Spectrum*, 11 (Spring 1981), pp. 4–21 at 5.

27. *Ibid.*, passim.

28. Rowlett, "Answers to David Kahn's Questions," 22 March and 31 May 1991. The U. S. Navy solved the following Japanese cipher machines: (1) The IKA machine, perhaps so called because messages encrypted in it used the Japanese character *ika*, written as a double slash, as a separator. (2) Its successor, called the M1, a kana machine used by the Japanese navy for about four years starting in 1933 whose analogue was designed by Holtwick, who presumably had solved the machine. (3) M2, contemporaneous with M1 but used by naval attachés and producing text in Latin letters rather than kana. It passed through several models, each more complicated than its predecessor. (4) M3, used by the Japanese Foreign Office. The Navy gave this an additional, alphabetical designation and called it the A machine. The Army called it RED. (5) M4. No other information available. (6) M5, which the Navy called the B machine and the Army PURPLE. (SRH-355, Appendix VIII.) M2 would appear to be the Romaji machine utilizing the same cryptographic principles as the kana machine on which it was based, namely the machine solved by the Army, but M3 is stated to be RED, or that machine. I cannot clear up the discrepancy.

29. Hannah, 14–15. I have written (Kahn, 20) that the machine solved by the Army was probably codenamed RED as a successor to the likely codename ORANGE — the Navy's codeword for Japan — for the machine Holtwick solved, and that RED's successor, PURPLE, was so named because the colors deepened as did the strength of the machine. Alas for this elegant theory, both Rowlett, in his Answers, and Holtwick, in SRH-355, Appendix VIII, pp. 090E-090F, deny that this was the basis for the naming. Holtwick even specifies that "These colors had no connection with color covernames for foreign nations in war plans, such as ORANGE for Japan."

30. Frank Rowlett, telephone interview, 22 April 1986.

31. Solved Japanese messages declassified by the National Security Agency; United States, State Department, *Foreign Relations of the United States: Diplomatic Papers, 1937*, 1 (Washington, DC: Government Printing Office, 1954), 608.

32. Hannah, 15–16.

33. United States, Congress, Joint Committee on the Investigation of the Pearl Harbor Attack, *Pearl Harbor Attack*, Hearings (79th Congress, 1st and 2nd Sessions) (Washington, DC: Government Printing Office, 1946), 2:785 (henceforth *PHA*, following by volume and page number); Anthony Cave Brown, *Wild Bill Donovan: The Last Hero* (New York: Times Books, 1982), pp. 176–177; Thomas F. Troy, *Donovan and the CIA: A History of the Establishment of the Central Intelligence Agency* (Frederick, MD: University Publications of America, 1981), pp. 105–107.

34. Rowlett, Answers.

35. William F. Friedman, "Preliminary Historical Report on the Solution of the 'B' Machine," October 14, 1940, SRH-159, p. 8.

36. Rowlett, Answers.

37. *Ibid.*

38. *PHA*, 34:84–85.

39. Rowlett, telephone interview.

40. *Ibid.*

41. *Ibid.*

42. Rowlett, Answers, says that nothing in the romantic and hypothetical paragraph on pages 21–22 of Kahn is accurate.

43. Grotjan, interview, 12 May 1991.

44. Hannah, 5.

45. *Ibid.*, 18.

46. *Ibid.*

47. Kahn, 14–15.

48. *Ibid.*, 15–16. This does seem long for this system, but this was in fact the time given.

49. *Ibid.*, 15–18.

50. Some J19-K10 solved intercepts and transposition worksheets are in Box 13, Records of the Pearl Harbor Liaison Office, Record Group 80, National Archives.

51. Safford in *Listening to the Enemy*, 8–9, 12; SRH-305, 12–19; Layton, 46.

52. Safford in *Listening to the Enemy*, 8; Layton, 77.

53. Safford in *Listening to the Enemy*, 9; Layton, 77–78.

54. Layton, 78.

55. SRH-305, 12.

56. Kahn, 10. James Rusbridger and Eric Nave, in *Betrayal at Pearl Harbor: How Churchill Lured Roosevelt into World War II* (New York: Summit Books, 1991), claim that the British unit was reading JN25 pretty fully and was passing its knowledge of Japanese fleet movements, and hence its foreknowledge of the Pearl Harbor attack, to Britain, where Prime Minister Winston Churchill suppressed it to make sure the attack would bring the United States into the war on the side of Britain. Aside from the fact that Churchill wanted the United States to fight Germany, not Japan, the claim is not only not substantiated by any documents (it is based chiefly on hypotheses and "must have beens"), but is vitiated by technical errors. The chief one is the belief that JN25b was merely a new additive book to the unchanged basic code. In fact JN25b was a new, improved,

and enlarged codebook, which is why the Americans had made such little progress into it. It is improbable that the British would have made much more, and also unlikely that they would have limited exchanging code-group recoveries with the Americans, when they would have benefited as much if not more than the Americans from learning as much as they could about the Japanese.

57. Layton, 231–232, 547. Captain Thomas H. Dyer, U. S. N., states, in his U.S. Naval Institute oral history, p. 231, that JN25 produced no intelligence about the Pearl Harbor attack.

58. (Stanford, CA: Stanford University Press, 1962).

59. *Ibid.*, 387.

4

How the United States Viewed Germany and Japan in 1941*

Intelligence had little to do with American assessments of Germany and Japan before December 1941. The actions of the Nazi government convinced Americans, high and low, that the United States might someday be the target, if not the victim, of its aggression. On the other hand, American racism and rationalism kept the United States from thinking that Japan would attack it.

Geography made danger from Germany appear imminent. As President Franklin D. Roosevelt explained in a fireside chat early in 1941, German occupation of the Azores or Cape Verdes would put hostile bombers in range of South America and thereby jeopardize North America.[1]

Japan was not only more distant; since she had no more than half of America's population and only one-ninth of America's industrial output, rationality seemed to preclude her attacking the United States. And disbelief in a Japanese attack was reinforced by belief in the superiority of the white race. Americans looked upon the Japanese as bucktoothed, bespectacled little yellow men, forever photographing things with their omnipresent cameras so that they could copy them. Such opinions were held not only by common bigots but by opinion-makers as well. Witness comments on Japanese aviation by the widely known writer on naval subjects, Fletcher Pratt:

> Every observer concurs in the opinion that the Japanese are daring but incompetent aviators; hardly any two agree on the reason. Four main

* From E.R. May (ed.), *Knowing One's Enemies: Intelligence Assessment before the Two World Wars*. Princeton, NJ: Princeton University Press, 1984, pp. 475–501. Used with permission.

theories have been advanced, explaining it on a) medical, b) religious, c) psychological and d) educational grounds.

According to the first postulate the Japanese as a race have defects of the tubes of the inner ear, just as they are generally myopic. This gives them a defective sense of balance, the one physical sense in which an aviator is not permitted to be deficient.

The second explanation places the blame on Bushido and the Japanese code that the individual life is valueless. Therefore, when the plane gets into a spin or some other trouble, they are apt to fold their hands across their stomachs and die cheerfully for the glory of the Empire, where Westerners, with a keener sense of personal existence, make every effort to get the plane out of trouble, or bail out at the last minute. This explanation has been advanced by several aviation instructors who have been in Japan.

The psychological theory points out that the Japanese, even more than the Germans, are a people of combination. "Nothing is much stupider than one Japanese, and nothing much brighter than two." But the aviator is peculiarly alone, and the Japanese, poor individualists, are thus poor aviators.

Finally the educational explanation points out that Japanese children receive fewer mechanical toys and less mechanical training than those of any other race.[2]

Captain W. D. Puleston, a former director of the Office of Naval Intelligence, wrote that "Japan has been energetic in her efforts to create naval aviation, but she is usually a phase behind. She cannot match in numbers the planes carried on American carriers, and what is equally important, her personnel cannot send planes aloft or take them aboard as rapidly as American personnel." These remarks were in no way exceptional. They paralleled others in official documents and in the military and general press.[3]

If there had been no American intelligence agencies, Americans would probably still have seen Germany and Japan as potential foes. It took little more than reports of their aggression, gross statistics, a glance at the globe, and attitudes like those of Pratt and Puleston to provide a rationale for the policy in Joint Army and Navy Basic War Plan Rainbow No. 5 of May 26, 1941: "Since Germany is the predominant member of the Axis Powers, the Atlantic and European area is considered to be the decisive theater.... If Japan does enter the war, the military strategy in the Far East will be defensive."[4]

Even in designing and procuring military forces, planning deployments, and preparing for possible military surprises, American leaders made comparatively little use of military intelligence. Such matters as whether Germany had 100 divisions or 300 and whether Japan had 10 carriers or 20 were not even raised when policy-makers examined the basic issues of strategy. When, on June 13, 1940, Roosevelt put several questions to his army and navy intelligence chiefs, not one dealt with Axis plans, and only one with Axis strength.[5] When, in December 1940, the head of army war plans asked the head of military intelligence "to prepare an Estimate of the Situation for use in formulation of Joint Army and Navy Basic War Plan Rainbow 5," the only question specifically on enemy countries concerned "the effect on Germany and Italy of steadily augmented air operations, combined with economic starvation through blockade."[6] When, at the same time, General George C. Marshall, the Army Chief of Staff, discussed, in a memo to Admiral Harold R. Stark, the Chief of Naval Operations, keeping the fleet in the Pacific until a major offensive began against the Axis in the Atlantic instead of moving it at once to the Atlantic, he did not mention German or Japanese forces or plans and, indeed, did not seem to be thinking of them at all.[7] He was concentrating on American capabilities. And when, in October 1941, the army's War Plans Division prepared a strategic estimate, it likewise based it largely on geography and the political situation.[8]

The omission of intelligence data from all these discussions of high policy shows how subsidiary intelligence was. Intelligence did nevertheless reach American leaders. The six most important sources were diplomatic reports; information from friendly nations; military attaché reports (technically a subspecies of the diplomatic reports, but distinct enough in practice to merit a separate category); radio intelligence; the press in all forms (newspapers, magazines, books, radio, and newsreels); and information from private individuals. The list omits spies, for, owing to congressional stinginess, a belief that spy rings would not produce information justifying the effort or potential damage, and a lingering rectitude, the United States did not have, in the years before the Second World War, any secret agents in foreign countries.[9]

The diplomatic reports were based on personal observation, newspapers (or translations made by embassy staffs), talks with officials and private citizens of the host countries, and exchanges with other diplomats.

Most top American representatives in the Axis countries were experienced diplomats, not political hacks. Several had personal ties to the President. Joseph C. Grew, the ambassador to Japan, for example, though a professional diplomat, had gone to Groton and Harvard with Roosevelt and once worked on the Harvard Crimson with him. Information on Germany, Japan, and Italy also came from American diplomats in countries that feared becoming objects of Axis aggression. Especially after war broke out, officials of these countries passed on information. Chief recipients were the ambassadors in Paris and in London. In France, William C. Bullitt, a brilliant, charming, financially independent sophisticate who had served as the first American ambassador to the Soviet Union, attained extremely intimate relations with the statesmen of his host nation. In Britain, Joseph P. Kennedy, a longtime supporter of Roosevelt whom the British correctly regarded as defeatist, received less information than Bullitt.[10]

Sometimes information about the Axis was passed to American officials by foreign diplomats in Washington. Much of it was, of course, calculated to win American support. Some attempts were less subtle than others. The chief of U.S. army intelligence noted in February 1941, for example, that the British, who had been pressing for the dispatch of four American cruisers to defend Singapore, had reported almost simultaneously in Washington and from Tokyo, Vichy, and London the imminence of a Japanese attack. "It is difficult to believe that all of this pressure… is coincidental," he minuted. "It all looks very like concerted British pressure on us to commit ourselves in the Far East."[11]

Some information came directly to American leaders from the leaders of the nations fighting the Axis. Winston Churchill and Roosevelt began corresponding when Churchill was still First Lord of the Admiralty and continued when he became Prime Minister.[12] At the Atlantic Conference of August 1941, where the two met, the British Chiefs of Staff passed assessments of Germany to the American chiefs and discussed strategy with them.[13]

Information about Axis military capabilities came chiefly from the military and naval attachés, their assistants, and their air specialists. They constituted part of the staff of, and had their offices in, the

United States embassies in Berlin, Tokyo, and Rome. Like the other diplomats, they gathered information from newspapers and official publications. They read training manuals, talked with officers of the host armed forces, observed equipment and troops at parades and maneuvers, toured army camps and naval vessels, and exchanged tidbits with other attachés. Sometimes, attachés were attached to host country army units for extended periods. In August 1937, for example, Captain Merritt B. Booth was assigned for ten days to the 38th Infantry Regiment of the Imperial Japanese Army at Nara. Discussing a 6.5-mm. automatic rifle, Model 11 (1932), he wrote, "I fired 12 rounds and hit all targets many times. I noted also that excellent results were being obtained by all engaged in this exercise."[14] Later in the year, he was attached for three and a half months to the 27th Infantry Regiment at Asahigawa on Hokkaido. During the first part of that period he "observed and participated in infantry battalion and regimental field exercises and maneuvers, machine gun training, range firing of the rifle, light machine gun and heavy machine gun, combat firing of the above weapons, and a maneuver of the medical bridge." He also took part in the annual fall maneuver of the 7th Division. In his long and detailed report, Booth also submitted drawings from Japanese manuals of the light machine gun and the Japanese infantry rapid-fire gun.[15] Another observer, attached to a different unit, took many photographs of Japanese weapons, both standing alone and being served, and submitted them in his report.[16] Reports like these often ran to 90 pages.

Observation sometimes provided not just this static intelligence but also current operational information. Booth wrote that he "not only counted troops of war organization marching to the station to depart for China, but also witnessed final inspection of organizations by the divisional commander preparatory to the departure."[17] Indeed, observation was, another officer wrote, "the principal means of garnering information on organization and to a large extent on tactics and material." The reason, he said, was "the mania for secrecy which prevails in the Japanese army."[18] Of course, even without this mania, Japan, like other countries, did not give foreign observers their real secrets. An American Signal Corps lieutenant, attached to Japan's communications school, wrote that he was told candidly by its commanding general that, because of the secrecy surrounding research being done there, the American "would be asked to remain away from a portion—this later proved to be a major slice indeed—of the school's activities." He noted about codes and ciphers that "I was able neither to attend classes nor to get any of the students or other officers to discuss, in general terms, the type of codes and ciphers used nor their methods of using them."[19] In general, the attachés got only the data that their hosts wanted them to have: none seemed to have any secret sources inside the governments.

Despite this limitation, the attachés in Japan and Germany gathered a great deal of information, which they analyzed very carefully, sometimes generating accurate conclusions. All this they poured into Washington in many voluminous reports. In 1940, for example, a package arrived in Washington from Tokyo about every two weeks. The one that came in on June 18 included, in addition to administrative papers such as requests for home leave, a report on the national defense budget, population statistics for 1940, an estimate of men reaching military age, and a report on field operations in China. The next package, which arrived on July 8, included biographical sketches of seven lieutenant generals, discussions of air transport of troops and supplies, of parachute training, of field operations in China, of military and industrial installations in Tokyo, and still more.[20] The material from Germany comprised similar topics and was even more voluminous.[21] In both cases, however, volume and importance declined as war approached and arrived. In 1939, for example, the one-line listing of items from Japan required eight pages; in 1940, five. The cause was probably tightening restrictions on movement. In the spring of 1941, for instance, Germany limited foreign attachés to 50 gallons of gasoline a month and refused to let them travel outside of greater Berlin.[22] This forced the attachés to obtain a greater proportion of their information from controlled publications and propaganda handouts—a far skimpier source than observation. Still, the attachés provided more military information about America's probable enemies than any other source.

Second to them was radio intelligence. This consisted of radio direction-finding, radio fingerprinting, traffic analysis, and cryptanalysis.[23] In the United States, as in other countries, radio intelligence came into permanent existence in the First World War. By the 1930s, the navy's unit was headquartered in the wooden temporary World War I Navy Building that disfigured the Mall in Washington. It was called OP-20-G, the OP for the Office of the Chief of Naval Operations, the 20 for the 20th division, the Office of Naval Communications, and the G for the Communications Security Section; this latter protected the navy's own communications as well as analyzed those of other navies. It consisted of some 700 officers and men, many of them in its nine intercept posts, others in its Mid-Pacific Strategic Direction-Finder Net, whose monitor posts curved in a gigantic arc from the Philippines through Guam, Samoa, Midway, and Hawaii to Dutch Harbor, Alaska. In addition, small communications-intelligence units were located in Hawaii and the Philippines.

The army concentrated its work in a branch of the Signal Corps called the Signal Intelligence Service. Headquartered in the Munitions Building, the next-door counterpart to the Navy Building, it consisted of about 330 officers and men there and in eight intercept posts scattered around the continental United States and overseas. Its technical head was one of the greatest cryptanalysts of all time, William F. Friedman, a rather uptight man given to bow ties, then in his late 40s.

The navy utilized direction-finding, radio fingerprinting, and traffic analysis more than the army because it had more occasion to do so; compared with, say, the French army, the U.S. army had little opportunity to overhear the maneuvers of nearby foreign forces. The U.S. navy listened mainly to Japanese naval communications, and even without cryptanalysis its other techniques of radio intelligence told it a great deal about the Japanese navy. Washington's weekly communications intelligence reports named the battleships and aircraft carriers, listed the numbers of cruisers, destroyers, and auxiliaries, and specified their locations and command organizations. On November 25, for example, the report noted with loupe-like precision the presence of a single destroyer of the Third Fleet near Maizuru, a port on the Sea of Japan. But radio intelligence was not omniscient. The same report conceded that "The composition of the Fifth Fleet is still unknown."[24] Hawaii issued daily communication-intelligence reports that concentrated more on activity than organization. "The entire fleet traffic level is still high which leads to the conclusion that organizational arrangements or other preparations are still not complete," it noted on the same day, November 25.[25]

OP-20-G was attacking the cryptosystems of the Japanese, Italian, and German navies, but had made hardly any progress with Italian and German and little more with Japanese, on which it concentrated. It was reading about 10 percent of Imperial Navy traffic, but most of this was in minor cryptosystems such as those used for weather reports; it read the main fleet code only spottily and the flag officers' code not at all.[26] In part this stemmed from a lack of intercepts, in part from a lack of cryptanalysts.

In the same way, the Signal Intelligence Service was trying to solve, in the late 1930s, the cryptosystems of the armies of Germany, Italy, and Japan. Even by the time of Pearl Harbor, no Japanese army codes could be read, chiefly because of a paucity of material.[27] Little effort had been expended against Italy; consequently, results were almost nil. Likewise, the service did not work much on German military messages, many of them enciphered in the Enigma, because the British had these "under control" and the Americans believed that the British would supply any vital information obtained from their solutions that might help the Americans.[28] It began working on the big German diplomatic code in 1938. The Federal Bureau of Investigation photographed a new code that a German businessman, acting as a courier, was bringing to South America. This alone did not permit the service to read messages in it, for a numerical sequence was added to the codenumbers to disguise them. Only when a lazy code clerk in Buenos Aires repeated portions of the sequence—in violation of regulations— could the service break it.[29] In 1938, with the threat from Japan growing and that from Germany still contained by England and France, the service concentrated its limited manpower on Japanese diplomatic messages, and kept it there as negotiations intensified.

These were in several quite different cryptosystems. The most secret was a machine cipher which the Americans called PURPLE.[30] A team headed by Friedman, with considerable help from OP-20-G, reconstructed the PURPLE machine in August 1940, after 18 months of arduous work. Thereafter, the Americans read top Japanese diplomatic messages almost as fast as (and sometimes even faster than) the Japanese diplomats themselves. Messages in lower systems, in particular one called J-19, sometimes took longer to read than PURPLE. In part this was a characteristic of the cryptosystems—PURPLE was harder to break in the first place, but once solved was easier to keep up with—and in part it was because the cryptanalysts put messages in secondary systems aside until those in higher-level systems were read.

The cryptanalytic results were copious: 50 to 75 messages a day in the fall of 1941. Some of these, such as the diplomatic notes, were in English; others were in Japanese and required translation. The top officers of the army and navy Far Eastern intelligence sections selected the important intercepts and brought them in locked briefcases to Roosevelt, the secretaries of state, war, and navy, the Chief of Staff, the Chief of Naval Operations, and the heads of the army and navy War Plans and Intelligence divisions. They stood by while these leaders read them, and then took them back and burned them.

These intercepts were known collectively as MAGIC. Those who received MAGIC were, in Secretary of State Cordell Hull's words, "intensely interested" in it. When the army suspended deliveries to the White House, partly because of a security breach, partly because it felt these diplomatic matters should go to the President through the State Department, Roosevelt requested MAGIC. The navy war plans chief thought that MAGIC, which was then largely diplomatic, affected his estimates by about 15 percent. The army intelligence chief regarded it as the most reliable and authentic information that the War Department was receiving on Japanese intentions and activities.[31]

Like all sources, however, MAGIC had limitations. It could not provide more information than the Japanese transmitted to their diplomats—and they did not tell their envoys everything. It could not provide information from areas to which it had no access—and it had not penetrated Japanese and German military and naval communications. MAGIC's amazing capabilities tended to lull its recipients into thinking they were learning everything that the Japanese were plotting. But MAGIC was not omniscient.

Nor was a source that lay at the opposite end of the secrecy spectrum from MAGIC. This was the press.

The American correspondents in Germany during the prewar years of Hitler's power were among the best the American press had. Their names are famous: William L. Shirer of the Columbia Broadcasting System, Louis Lochner and Richard C. Hottelet of the Associated Press, Joseph C. Harsch of the *Christian Science Monitor*, Edgar Ansel Mowrer of the *Chicago Daily News*, Otto Tolischus of *The New York Times*, Karl von Wiegand of the Hearst papers. They were experienced reporters; virtually all spoke German, had spent several years in Germany (Lochner, for instance, had been there since 1924), and knew German history and culture.[32] Three won Pulitzer Prizes for their dispatches from Berlin: Mowrer in 1933, Lochner in 1939,

Tolischus in 1940. Martha Dodd, the pretty young daughter of the American ambassador, felt that the newspapermen were "on a pretty high level." "On the whole," she wrote, "the stories that came from Germany… presented a pretty accurate picture of what was happening there…. The newspapermen I knew were amazingly conscientious, had excellent sources, both German, foreign, and diplomatic, and knew Germany and the developments better than most people."[33]

This contrasted sharply with the situation in Japan. The correspondents in Tokyo were mostly young and relatively inexperienced newcomers—a great many had been there only since around 1937. None knew Japanese; few had much previous knowledge of Japan. Even the experienced men, such as Tolischus, transferred there from Berlin, and Wilfred Fleisher of the *New York Herald Tribune*, had little background in Japan and few contacts there. These handicaps reduced the quantity and quality of copy coming out of Japan as compared with that out of Berlin.[34] This difference, together with Germany's closer social and cultural ties to the United States, meant that Germany got more and better coverage in the American press. *The New York Times Index* for 1938 gives twenty columns to Germany and six to Japan. And the stories out of Germany show an insight that those from Japan do not. The correspondents in Germany often filed, for example, on the bitter rivalry between the army, once the most powerful institution in the country, and the paramilitary SS, rapidly coming to run the German police state.[35] The correspondents in Japan showed much less feel for Japanese politics.

Among private individuals who provided information on Axis countries, the most famous was Charles A. Lindbergh, who visited Germany three times in the 1930s. More obscure, and deservedly so, was one Dr. F. M. Sebree of Los Angeles. Billing himself as a lecturer and teacher of mental science, he wrote the War Department in 1935 that later that year Japan would attack Hawaii and California. This information he "obtained metaphysically," he said. The war Department expressed its appreciation of his "patriotic interest in our National Defense."[36] Such, then, were the main sources of information. To whom did it go? And what did the recipients do with it?

It did not all go to all the same places. Some material, such as that in newspapers, went to everybody. Some filtered through evaluating agencies on its way to policy-makers. Some, such as MAGIC, went only to a few top individuals. They received this material raw, and it was they who analyzed and judged it.

Among the evaluating agencies was the bureaucracy of the State Department. Probably all the innumerable reports from diplomatic posts were read by somebody or other, but few got to the desk of Secretary of State Hull, fewer to Roosevelt's, and almost certainly fewer still to their memories. What little effect the dispatches had is shown by the attitude of William Phillips, at the time Undersecretary of State, when he visited Ambassador William E. Dodd in Germany in 1935. After a morning conference with embassy specialists, including the military attaché, who told him that "Germany is one vast military camp," and the commercial attaché, who said that "In two years Germany will be manufacturing oil and gas enough out of soft coal for a long war," Phillips was "amazed and distressed." Dodd noted that "all this information has been going to the Department for two whole years. But no high official can master all the reports as they pile up there."[37] Though the reports were filed by subject in the State Department's useful decimal file, no mechanism existed to assemble the various files—economic, political, military—into a current whole for analysis. Nor do the reports seem to have been reviewed periodically in an attempt to determine any trends.

This operation, in which the general bureaucracy served as the organ for evaluating information, differed from that in the armed services, both of which had specialized agencies to analyze information. The army's Military Intelligence Division (MID), a headquarters unit that dated in various forms to 1885, was headed by the Assistant Chief of Staff (G-2), Brigadier General Sherman Miles. The son of a former commanding general of the army, Nelson Miles, he had had extensive experience abroad, having served as an attaché in Russia, Turkey, and Britain, and with commissions or embassies in Austria, Yugoslavia, and Czechoslovakia; he had served in the Military Intelligence Division from 1919 to 1921 and, in addition to holding various field posts, had served four years with the War Plans Division. He had headed the Military Intelligence Division since May 1, 1940. In 1941, that body had 856 people in Washington.[38]

Its opposite number, the Office of Naval Intelligence (ONI), founded in 1882, was designated OP-16, the 16th division of the Office of the Chief of Naval Operations. It had 600 people in Washington and had been headed since October 15, 1941, by Rear Admiral Theodore S. Wilkinson. He was bright—he had graduated first in the class of 1909 from the U.S. Naval Academy—and he had served abroad at the limitation of arms conferences in Geneva in 1933 and London in 1934. But his previous assignments—office work on shore and the command of ships at sea—had never included an intelligence post.[39] The work of both MID and ONI included counterintelligence, and the evaluating sections for Germany and for Japan in each were rather small. The Far Eastern section of MID, for example, consisted of 11 officers, only three of them assigned to Japan.[40]

The sources that they used most seemed to be the attaché reports, news stories, and, for the highest officials only, MAGIC. The officers in each section read this incoming material, rejected what they considered were false reports, determined the possible core of truth in the sometimes contradictory or exaggerated data, judged how much weight to give to the remaining facts and opinions on such bases as the motives of the sources and their congruence with other data, and from all this inferred the probable strength and intentions of other countries. They issued these conclusions in both periodic and special reports. Since the officers who drafted these were usually low-ranking officers who did not have access to MAGIC and since the ultimate sources of their information did not differ much from those exploited by the American correspondents, the reports often resembled a weekly summary in *The New York Times*. As with the news stories, the intelligence reports sometimes included predictions of foreign moves. But mostly they just summarized the situation.

Two other intelligence agencies were getting their work under way at the time of Pearl Harbor. Cooperation between MID and ONI existed but was spotty, so the Joint Army–Navy Board, the father of the Joint Chiefs of Staff, brought them together formally by establishing a Joint Intelligence Committee as "an agency responsible to the Joint Board."[41] This happened in October 1941, but the committee first met formally on December 3.[42] It had issued no reports by the time the United States entered the war. The second agency was created when William J. Donovan, a Columbia Law School fellow student of Roosevelt's, a World War I hero, and a prominent Republican politician, proposed a unified intelligence agency to Roosevelt after making two trips to Europe to gather information for him. Roosevelt accepted the idea, and, on July 11, 1941, named Donovan Coordinator of Information. He was "to collect and analyze all information and data which may bear upon national security; ... and to make such information and data available to the President and to such departments and officials of the Government as the President may determine."[43] After the United States entered the war, his organization evolved into the Office of Strategic Services.

Throughout the years and months preceding the German declaration of war on the United States, information poured into Washington about Germany. It ranged from the details that serve to make up a picture of the whole to judgments about Germany's next moves.

The details covered an amazing range. The military attaché for many years was Major Truman Smith, an observant, lively, intelligent Germanophile.[44] He reported, in a powerful but undisciplined prose, that Hitler wanted peace.[45] In technical matters, he was rather more accurate. Often he succeeded in providing remarkably precise figures on the strength of the German army. In July 1939, just before the outbreak of the war, he counted the number of German army formations almost exactly. He was one under on the number of infantry divisions one under on the number of panzer divisions, one over on the number of motorized infantry divisions and right on target on the number of mountain and light divisions and on the single cavalry brigade. On the other hand, he greatly overestimated the number of available reserve formations. He figured on 123; in fact only 103 were available.[46] He hated the press, which painted what he thought was a false picture: "Hitler looking around for new nations to conquer" and "marching gray-clad armies and a succession of German conquests in Eastern Europe."[47] But the press was more prescient than he was. On the level of particulars, it reported during the prewar years a great variety of useful details: the creation of the XIV Corps, with headquarters probably at Würzburg, a new steel helmet, new weapons, and the 1938 shake-up in the high commands (this even before the official announcement).[48] Moreover, it provided a flood of information about Germany's politics, economics, labor conditions, racial measures, and foreign relations—the context of the military activities. The diplomats, too, poured out information on the same subjects.

Everybody paid a great deal of attention to the age's new wonder weapon, the airplane. The American attachés had been following its growth as a military weapon in Germany since before the Luftwaffe's existence was formally disclosed in 1935. In November 1934, an attaché calculated, on the basis of figures for civilian airplanes and for pilots' tests, that Germany had 1,200 training airplanes and about 1,000 combat planes. This was close to the actual 1,300 trainers but considerably overestimated the actual 670 combat planes.[49] As Germany's rearmament progressed, security tightened. To breach the secrecy, Smith and his air assistant cleverly called for help upon the man who was possibly the most famous in the world: Charles A. Lindbergh.[50]

Lindbergh acceded, and paid the first of three annual inspection visits to Germany in July 1936. He visited aircraft factories and Luftwaffe airfields, examined planes and flew them, talked with pilots and high air officials, including German Air Force Chief Hermann Göring. In 1936, the leader of an elite fighter unit gave him what proved to be accurate information about the speed, armament, and ceiling of the Messerschmidt Me-109, which later became Germany's basic single-seater fighter; in 1937, he examined one and watched it fly at the Rechlin testing field. Before he left that year, he and Smith prepared a "General Estimate" of Germany's air power. It was an apocalyptic document. "Germany is once more a world power in the air," it began. It spoke of the "astounding growth of German air power," which it called "one of the most important world events of our time;" of the "remarkable" German advance in aeronautics; and of how the United States could be "doomed to... inferiority." It asserted that "Technically Germany has outdistanced France in practically all fields" and, at the end, warned that "Germany should obtain technical parity with the U.S.A. by 1941 or 1942."[51] A few months later, Lindbergh wrote a memorandum for Ambassador Kennedy in London about his trip. "Germany is probably the strongest air power in Europe," he declared. At a factory near Berlin, where Dornier Do-17 bombers were in production, he noted, "There were twenty wings and twenty fuselages in the final assembly hangar. These were moving through on tracks and made one complete round of the hangar during the process of assembly so that as the plane left its assembly jig the jig was back at the beginning of the line, ready for a new fuselage." This memorandum went to Roosevelt, who sent it on February 10, 1938, to Marshall and Stark.[52] Lindbergh also reported on his impressions orally to General Henry H. "Hap" Arnold, chief of staff of the Army Air Corps, to naval officers to the secretary of war, and to Roosevelt himself.[53]

In France in October 1938, Lindbergh was told by French authorities that Germany could build 24,000 planes a year (compared with the French production of 540) and already had 6,000 modern planes. In Germany a few weeks later, he again visited factories and this time did not merely view the Me-109 but actually flew it. It "handled beautifully," he said.[54] Perhaps it was from Lindbergh that Arnold got the frightening information that he gave Congress early in 1939: that Germany had approximately 1,700 planes capable of flying from the west coast of Africa to the east coast of South America.[55]

Roosevelt's concern about German aviation was heightened by other sources. In January 1938, a French visitor told him that German planes could fly over France with impunity; in October, Bullitt, his trusted ambassador in France, said that the Germans would be able to bomb Paris at will. When war broke out in Europe, he cabled that "There is an enormous danger that the German air force will be able to win this war for Germany before the planes can begin to come out of our plants in quantity."[56]

And at the same time everybody was warning against underestimating Germany. Truman Smith wrote that American leadership in the air "must... not lead to an underestimate of what Germany will achieve in the future."[57] Undersecretary of State Sumner Welles said during his 1940 trip to Europe that the two most experienced members of the diplomatic corps in Berlin believe "that the Allied governments grossly underestimate Germany's military strength."[58] A few months later, the American naval attaché declared that "Germany as a fighting nation is tremendously powerful. Under no circumstances should she be underestimated."[59] Yet the problem was not underestimating Germany. On the contrary, everybody was overestimating her.

The naval attaché estimated airplane production in February 1940 at 1,800 to 2,000 planes a month.[60] The actual figure for all of 1940 averaged under 900 a month.[61] The French premier said Germany had ten times as many planes as France; the actual figures around then were France, 3,289, Germany, 4,665.[62] The Military Intelligence Division issued on July 11, 1941, after the German attack on the Soviet Union, a strategic estimate of the situation that set the number of planes for the Luftwaffe at 11,000, a figure which in September it specified referred to "front-line combat airplanes."[63] In fact, on July 5, 1941, the Luftwaffe had only 3,094 fighters and bombers.[64] The Coordinator of Information attained almost Wagnerian proportions in his over-estimations. On December 12, 1941, using figures no doubt worked up previously, he credited the Germans with 29,000 planes. Yet on the eastern front, outside of Africa the only combat area, the German Army chief of staff counted on that very day 950 fighters and bombers. The Coordinator estimated, also on December 12, that Germany had 30,000 tanks at the start of the invasion of Russia. There were 3,332. He guessed that the Reich was producing 1,000 to 17,000 tanks a month, or 12,000 to 204,000 a year. In fact, in all of 1941 Germany built only 3,256.[65] All this was the other side of racism. America underrated the little yellow men of Japan, but overrated the blue-eyed blonds of Germany.[66]

American estimates of the ground troops were closer to the mark. Though the Coordinator's estimates of casualties in Russia doubled the actual number, his figure of 9,000,000 men in the German armed forces in June 1941 stood only a quarter higher than the actual 7,234,000.[67] Comparisons of the estimated with the actual numbers of German army divisions are difficult to make for two reasons. First, the published German documents list only divisions at the fronts whereas the American estimates include divisions at home. And second, with a gross disregard for the needs of historians, MID failed to issue its estimates on the same day the German Army General Staff's organization section tabulated units. But a rough index of accuracy may be attained by comparing American estimates and German listings close in time and by choosing easily matched portions of the force total. On July 11, 1941, MID estimated 60 German army divisions in the west; on June 27, there were 49.[68] On December 1, 1941, ONI, no doubt getting its information from MID, counted 27 divisions in Holland, Belgium, and France; on January 2, 1942 there were 29.[69] The over-estimation followed by an underestimation depicts no pattern. But MID did have solid information on German strength in an area of importance. When MID stated in August 1941 that Germany had 20 armored divisions in Europe and 1 in Libya its figures were exact.[70]

When it came to Hitler's intentions toward the United States, few people ventured to prophesy. The military and the naval attaché reports in the latter part of 1941 do not mention the possibility of war. Nor do the diplomatic reports. When Churchill and his advisers met Roosevelt and his at the Atlantic Conference, no one even mentioned that Hitler might declare war on America. And all were then correct in not doing so. Hitler had just invaded Russia. For the next several months, he would be "thoroughly occupied in beating Russia," as Secretary of War Stimson put it, "immersed in the conflict with the U.S.S.R.," as MID put it.[71] While engaged in that struggle, he would not want to clash with the United States, their thinking seemed to run.

And indeed, he apparently did avoid problems. He restrained his admirals, who wanted to let their U-boats sink American ships bringing supplies to Britain.[72] Even Churchill sensed, in August, that Hitler's current naval policy gave little prospect of an incident that might bring America into the war. Three did occur—those of the American destroyers *Greer, Reuben James*, and *Kearny*—but Roosevelt, blocked by isolationists, could not use them as an excuse for war.[73] Fears persisted about German subversion in Latin America, but these were groundless: Hitler had talked about "a new Germany" in Brazil but had taken no concrete action to realize this either there or in other Latin American countries. On the other hand, German spying in the United States—exposed in the summer of 1941 by 29 headline-making arrests—implied at least preparation for some hostile action or other.[74]

A "Brief Periodic Estimate of the World Situation" issued by MID on September 5, 1941, made, in an almost offhand manner, the only reference to Germany's possibly warring on the United States that the intelligence documents seem to contain: "It is estimated that Germany has large submarine forces in hand, which she will use with the utmost caution in the North Atlantic until she is ready to run the risk of provoking the United States or until hostilities with America begin." In its conclusions, however, the report did not mention war with the United States.[75] This suggests that the remark about hostilities was unimportant and was perhaps only a case of MID's protecting itself with a throwaway prediction in case war did come.

In October, the army's War Plans Division issued a War Department Strategic Estimate. Examining Germany's possible lines of action, it declared that Germany "will not be in a position to attempt major offensive operations in the Western Hemisphere for at least a year, and then only if she acquires large numbers of British ships, both commercial and war vessels. The effect of U.S. active participation in the war would probably cause Germany to accelerate her operations in the Russian theater in order to bring about the defeat of the

Russians before our fighting capacity reaches decisive proportions. Further, the early defeat of Russia would release much-needed manpower for employment in German industry to match U.S. expanding war industries."[76]

All these views are speculation. None of them cite any hard evidence about Hitler's intentions toward America. None of them imply that they obtained their information from codebreaking or an attaché's honorable spying or the secret agents of a friendly power. And this for a very good reason: astonishing though it may be, Hitler had no plans on how he would conduct a war against the United States. The Japanese attack on Pearl Harbor was as much a surprise to him as it was to the Americans, and his notification to his armed forces high command that he was about to declare war on the United States exposed the embarrassing lack of even a contingency plan for hostilities with that country.[77]

His decision was unpremeditated, precipitated by the Pearl Harbor attack.[78] There was therefore no way in which any intelligence agency could have obtained foreknowledge of it. The United States' first solid information of Hitler's intention came from a MAGIC intercept of a Japanese message from Berlin to Tokyo on December 8.[79] A warning was flashed to American defense commands, but the United States did nothing else until, on December 11, Hitler had the Reichstag declare war. The Congress replied with a similar declaration that same day, and the potential enemies became real ones.

If with Germany capabilities attracted more interest than intentions, with Japan it was just the reverse. Diplomats, correspondents, intelligence evaluators, and policymakers focused, not upon the forces available to Japan as they had concentrated, for example, on the Luftwaffe, but upon where the Japanese might strike next. Perhaps the reasons for this were in part that it was easier to gain information on Germany than Japan, in part that Germany seemed to have no real options until after she had beaten Russia, while Japan had many, all in a region in which the United States had possessions and interests.

Throughout 1941, American intelligence officers and the policymakers they served tried with growing urgency to determine what Japan would do. But racism and the presumption of rationality prevented current details from being assembled into a pattern that might indicate what was happening in Japan. "The Japanese, brave, self-confident and ingenious, are the most willing of all nations to stake their chances of success on some tactical or technical trick," wrote Pratt. "But even they would hardly engage the United States Fleet in anything but a battle of desperation; the material superiority is too great.... Japan dares provoke or enter no war in which the United States Fleet will be engaged on the opposite side."[80] Puleston concurred: "... a sober estimate of the situation could convince leaders in Japan that they could not reasonably hope to defeat the United States, whose population, resources and military position are superior to their own. There are no economic reasons that could justify the Japanese Government in accepting the hazards of war with the United States." Then he became more specific. "The greatest danger from Japan, a surprise attack on the unguarded Pacific Fleet, lying at anchor in San Pedro harbor [California], under peacetime conditions, has already been averted. The Pacific Fleet is at one of the strongest bases in the world—Pearl Harbor—practically on a war footing and under a war regime. There will be no American Port Arthur." Other writers expressed the same opinion: "there is no danger of Japan attacking Hawaii in any force so long as it harbors the battle fleet" and a "Japanese attack upon Hawaii is a strategical impossibility."[81]

American intelligence officers shared this view. Though they acknowledged that an attack on Pearl Harbor was not impossible, they dismissed it as improbable. And it was from within this framework that they scrutinized the latest details of the intelligence picture.

These included information on the land forces of Japan. Throughout the fall of 1941, the Military Intelligence Division was refining its figures on the Japanese army. By December 5, army intelligence chief Sherman Miles was reporting to Marshall that Japan had 62 active divisions, 22 independent and 5 cavalry brigades, 13 tank regiments, 15 depot divisions in Japan and Manchuria as well as garrison and railway guard units. He listed their locations: 30 divisions in Manchuria, 8 in north China, 10 in central China, and so on. His figures were over the true numbers. At the time of Pearl Harbor, Japan had only 48 active infantry divisions, 13 depot divisions, and 24 independent mixed brigades.[82] In combat aircraft production, military intelligence underestimated the Japanese. It figured 200 planes a month; the actual rate was 426.[83]

Of far greater interest than the army was the Japanese navy, for the island empire would need her naval forces for any move, and American radio intelligence might be able to track them.

And indeed, the United States had, for much of 1941, good radio intelligence on the composition and movements of Japan's naval units. It was admittedly not complete: the coded orders of the major commands remained sealed to Americans. But its basic excellence, combined with a fluke in history, paradoxically led OP-20-G and the outpost units into a fatal misapprehension.

In July, the Japanese, taking advantage of Vichy France's weakness, occupied French Indochina. The naval preparations for this grab were clearly indicated in the radio traffic. During it, however, not only were no messages heard from the aircraft carriers, none were sent to them either. Naval communications intelligence reasoned that the carriers were standing by in home waters as a covering force in case of counterattack and that communications to and from them were not heard because they were transmitted on short-range, low-powered transmissions that died away before reaching American receivers. A similar blank of carrier communications had obtained in a similar tactical situation in February. American intelligence had drawn the same conclusion then and had been proven right. Events soon confirmed the July assessment as well. When, early in December, the carriers again vanished from the radio picture while observers and other intelligence told of ships moving south, the February and July situations seemed to be recurring. OP-20-G and the Hawaiian radio intelligence unit thought the carriers were again in home waters. But the carriers were not in home waters—they were in the central Pacific, heading east, under silence.[84] Moreover, not only did they send no messages, they received only one, to confirm that the attack was to be carried out. This consisted of an open-language code phrase ("Climb Mount Niitaka") used just that once: its meaning was impossible to determine.

As the U.S. navy gathered radio intelligence and made false deductions from it, the diplomats sought clues to Japanese intentions. They found nothing concrete. On November 17, Grew cabled Hull that "recent reports from our consuls at Taihoku and at Harbin point to Japanese troop concentrations in both Taiwan and Manchuria, and all other available indications are that since the general mobilization of July last, troop dispositions have been made to enable new operations to be carried out on the shortest possible notice in either Siberia or the southwest Pacific or both."[85] This was a fancy way of saying that he didn't know whether Japan would move north or south.

Nor did specific information come from MAGIC. To a degree, in fact, MAGIC may have obscured the likelihood of an attack on Pearl Harbor. Its numerous intercepts of Japanese diplomatic messages told of espionage interest in Latin America, of observations of Soviet submarines and minesweepers at Vladivostok, of attention to Thailand and Burma.[86] What American policy-makers read of this must have fragmented their attention, rendering it more difficult to conceive of a Pearl Harbor attack. In the same way, military intercepts revealing that Japanese agents were reporting on the arrival, presence, and departure of warships in major American ports presented a misleading picture. For they pointed away from Pearl Harbor. The number of ship-movement messages translated between August 1 and December 6 dealing with Pearl Harbor totaled 20; those dealing with the Panama Canal totaled 23; and those with the Philippines, 59.[87]

The intercepts of dispatches to the Japanese ambassadors in Washington likewise yielded no specific clues to a Pearl Harbor attack. For they were never told about it and remained ignorant of their government's intentions. So MAGIC could not foretell where Japan would move. What it could and did do was provide a constantly increasing sense of urgency, an indication of the constantly rising tension. Intercepts made clearer and clearer that Japan was going to rupture relations with, and perhaps even go to war with, the United States. On November 22, Tokyo told its ambassadors in Washington that after the 29th, "things are automatically going to happen." On November 30, a dispatch to Berlin ordered the ambassador to "Say very secretly to them [Hitler and Foreign Minister Joachim von Ribbentrop] that there is extreme danger that war may suddenly break out between the Anglo-Saxon nations and Japan through some clash of arms and add that the time of breaking out of this war might come quicker than anyone dreams." There followed a rash of messages about destroying codes, and on the evening of December 6 the first 13 parts of a 14 part note rupturing negotiations. Roosevelt read it in his lamplit office in the presence of his aide, Harry Hopkins, and a MAGIC courier and said, in effect, "This means war."[88] But knowing that war is coming does not mean that one knows where or when it is coming.

The lack of information about where the Japanese would strike was reflected in MID's estimates. On November 2, Miles submitted a report that listed the alternatives that Japan could take, without stating which he thought was the most likely. On December 5 he repeated the list, merely adding that "The most probable line of action for Japan is the occupation of Thailand."[89]

Two days later, airplanes from the Japanese carrier force attacked Pearl Harbor, to the utter consternation and astonishment of everybody in the United States and the Territory of Hawaii. Surprise was complete.

Why was it so surprising? Roberta Wohlstetter has argued that "We failed to anticipate Pearl Harbor not for want of the relevant materials, but because of a plethora of irrelevant ones...."[90] But there *was* a want of relevant materials. Sufficient indications of an attack simply did not exist within the mass of American intelligence data. Not one intercept, not one datum of intelligence ever said anything about an attack on Pearl Harbor or on any other possession. That there were many distractions is true but irrelevant; the most refined analysis cannot bring out what is not present. More information was needed for intelligence officers to have overcome their preconceptions and to have foreseen the attack, and that information could only have been generated if the United States, years before, had insinuated spies into Japanese government offices, or flown regular aerial reconnaissance of the Imperial Japanese Navy, or put intercept units aboard ships sailing close to Japan to pick up naval messages that a greatly expanded code-breaking unit might have cracked, or recruited a network of marine observers to report on ship movements. The intelligence failure at Pearl Harbor was one not of analysis, but of collection.

That failure was due to deep-seated factors that, in the 1920s and 1930s, kept legislators from expending a great deal of money on the U.S. armed forces, much less on intelligence, which was regarded as less important than arms, unnecessary for a country with the only undefeated army and navy in the world, and sneaky and un-American anyway.

This widespread disregard for intelligence permitted the generals and admirals to downgrade that function, which they viewed as a threat to their power. The army general staff, Dwight D. Eisenhower has written, treated intelligence as a "stepchild."[91] The reason lay in the antagonism of line officers to intelligence, as to every new specialty that technology created.[92] For if a specialty became important, its officers would be able to compete for higher posts, giving the officers in the older branches difficulties they otherwise would not have had.

For these reasons, intelligence remained marginal to American decision making before Japan's surprise attack. But that trauma taught Americans the need for intelligence. They have never forgotten that lesson, and that is why they still remember Pearl Harbor.

Notes

1. *The Public Papers and Addresses of Franklin D. Roosevelt*, ed. By Samuel I. Rosenman, 8 vols. (New York: Russell and Russell, 1969) [hereafter, *PPA*], VIII, p. 185. See also Stetson Conn and Byron Fairchild, *The Framework of Hemisphere Defense* (Washington, DC: Government Printing Office, 1960), pp. 68–129.
2. Fletcher Pratt, *Sea Power and Today's War* (New York: Harrison-Hilton, 1939), pp. 178–79.
3. W. D. Puleston, *The Armed Forces of the Pacific: A Comparison of the Military Power of the United States and Japan* (New Haven, CT: Yale University Press, 1941), p. 226; Howard V. Young, Jr., "Racial Attitudes of United States Navy Officers as a Factor in American Unpreparedness for War with Japan," Paper delivered at the Fifth Naval History Symposium, U.S. Naval Academy, Annapolis, Oct. 2, 1981—a remarkable and eye-opening study.
4. *PHA*, XXXIII, p. 958.
5. WPD 4250-3, OP-12B-McC, June 26, 1940, RG 165, NARS.
6. Gerow to Assistant Chief of Staff G-2, Dec. 14, 1940, WPD 4175-18, *ibid.*
7. Marshall to Stark, Dec. 2, 1940, WPD 4175-15, *ibid.*
8. War Department Strategic Estimate, Oct. 1941, WPD 4494, *ibid.*
9. *PHA*, II, p. 785; Anthony Cave Brown, *Wild Bill Donovan: The Last Hero* (New York: Times Books, 1982), pp. 176–77; Thomas F. Troy, *Donovan and the CIA: A History of the Establishment of the Central Intelligence Agency* (Frederick, MD: University Publications of America, 1981), pp. 105–7.
10. Examples of the American diplomats' reports on Axis matters are in *FRUS*, 1939, I, pp. 49, 170, 178–79, 192, 195, 422; *1940*, I, pp. 39, 50, 228, 230. See also Purport Book for Department of State Decimal File 862.00, RG 59, NARS. On Bullitt, see introduction by George F. Kennan to Orville H. Bullitt, ed., *For the President: Personal and Secret: Correspondence between Franklin D. Roosevelt and William C. Bullitt* (Boston, MA: Houghton Mifflin, 1972), pp. v–viii. Michael Beschloss, *Roosevelt and Kennedy: The Uneasy Alliance* (New York: Norton, 1980), cites no instances of Kennedy's mentioning German strength, but he does give numerous examples of Kennedy's expressing belief that Britain would not survive (e.g., pp. 195, 197, 203, 206, 208, and 212), which may be regarded as a reference in negative terms to German power.

11. Miles to Chief of Staff, Feb. 11, 1941, WPD 4175-18, RG 165, NARS.

12. See *Roosevelt and Churchill: Their Secret Wartime Correspondence,* ed. by Francis L. Loewenheim, Harold D. Langley, and Manfred Jonas (New York: Saturday Review Press, 1975), pp. 105, 126, 129, 130. Joseph P. Lash, *Roosevelt and Churchill, 1939–1941: The Partnership That Saved the West* (New York: Norton, 1976), gives excellent background on the Roosevelt-Churchill relationship.

13. WPD 4402-62, RG 165, NARS.

14. Report No. 8958, p. 4, MID 2023–948, *ibid.*

15. Report No. 9210, *ibid.*

16. Report No. 8267, *ibid.*

17. Report No. 9210, *ibid.*

18. Report No. 10,099, MID 2023–1011, *ibid.*

19. Report No. 7765 MID 2023–962, *ibid.*

20. Japan: Dispatch Books and Cross-References, MID, *ibid.*

21. Germany: Dispatch Books and Cross-References, *ibid.*

22. Secret Naval Attachés Reports, Vol. I, Document 24, RG 38, NARS.

23. For the techniques of radio intelligence and the organization of the American agencies engaged in it, see David Kahn, *The Codebreakers: The Story of Secret Writing* (New York: Macmillan, 1967), esp. ch. 1.

24. *PHA,* XV, pp. 1882–83.

25. *Ibid.,* XVII, p. 2629.

26. *Ibid.,* XVIII, p3335; X, p. 4673; Kahn, *Codebreakers,* p. 47.

27. *PHA,* XXXV, p. 106.

28. Telephone interview with Abraham Sinkov, May 12, 1980; personal interview, Oct. 27, 1979, and telephone interview, July 4, 1980, with Solomon Kullback.

29. Kullback interviews.

30. Contrary to speculations in Kahn, *Codebreakers,* pp. 18–19, the PURPLE machine was not a descendant of the German Enigma machine, even though the Japanese had purchased an Enigma. The two utilized entirely different cryptographic principles. As a consequence, the statement in several books that the American solution of PURPLE was merely an offshoot of the Polish-British solution of Enigma is erroneous. The two solutions were independent.

31. Kahn, *Codebreakers,* pp. 30–31.

32. Telephone interview with William L. Shirer via Mrs. Mary Thomas, July 7, 1980; J. Schaleben, "Louis P. Lochner: Getting the Story Out of Nazi Germany, 1933–1941" (M.A. Thesis, University of Wisconsin-Madison, Madison, WI, 1942).

33. Martha Dodd, *Through Embassy Eyes* (New York: Harcourt, Brace, 1939), pp. 96, 98, 99.

34. Ernest R. May, "U.S. Press Coverage of Japan, 1931–1941," in *Pearl Harbor as History: Japanese-American Relations 1931–1941,* eds. Dorothy Borg and Shumpei Okamato (New York: Columbia University Press, 1973), pp. 511–32.

35. See, for example, the stories headlined "Schacht's Diatribe Bares Basic Clash," *New York Times*, Aug. 25, 1935, and "Reich Split Widens in Army-Nazi Row; Blomberg Has Quit," *ibid.*, Feb. 3, 1938.

36. Folder 2023–949, Jan. 4 and 29, 1935, MID, RG 165, NARS.

37. [William E. Dodd], *Ambassador Dodd's Diary, 1933–1938*, ed. by William E. Dodd, Jr. and Martha Dodd (New York: Harcourt, Brace, 1941), p. 292.

38. Marc B. Powe, "The Emergence of the War Department Intelligence Agency, 1885–1918" (M.A. Thesis, Kansas State University, Manhattan, KS, 1974), p. 15; *PHA*, II, p. 777; Harold C. Relyea, "The Evolution and Organization of the Federal Intelligence Function: A Brief Overview," in 94th Congress, 2d Session, Select Committee to Study Governmental Operations with Respect to Intelligence Activities, Final Report: *Supplementary Reports on Intelligence Activities*, Book VI, Report No. 94–755 (Washington, DC: Government Printing Office, 1976), p. 185; "General Miles, Intelligence Aide," *New York Times*, Oct. 8, 1966.

39. Jeffrey M. Dorwart, *The Office of Naval Intelligence: The Birth of* America's *First Intelligence Agency, 1865–1918* (Annapolis, MD: Naval Institute Press, 1979), p. 16; *PHA*, IV, pp. 1727,1724; United States Navy, Public Information Office, official biography of Theodore Stark Wilkinson.

40. *PHA*, XIV, p. 1419; II, p. 829; XV, p. 1864; IV, p. 1726; Roberta Wohlstetter, *Pearl Harbor: Warning and Decision* (Stanford, CA: Stanford University Press, 1962), p. 314.

41. *PHA*, II, p. 785; Patrick Beesly, *Very Special Admiral* (London, U.K.: Hamish Hamilton, 1980), p. 180.

42. Memorandum from Marshall, Oct. 20, 1941, WPD 4584-3, RG 165, NARS; Minutes of the First Formal Meeting, Dec. 3, 1941, WPD 4584-6, *ibid.*

43. Troy, *Donovan and the CIA.*

44. Anne Morrow Lindbergh, *The Flower and the Nettle: Diaries and Letters of Anne Morrow Lindbergh, 1936–1939* (New York: Harcourt, Brace, Jovanovich, 1976), p. 84.

45. *FRUS, 1938*, I, pp. 716–20; Folder 2016-1297, Report No. 17, 128, Mar. 1, 1940 MID, RG 165, NARS.

46. Wilhelm Deist, "Die Deutsche Aufrüstung in amerikanischer Sicht: Berichte des US-Militärattachés in Berlin aus den Jahren 1933–1939," in *Russland-Deutschland-Amerika: Festschrift für Fritz T. Epstein zum 80. Geburtstag*, ed. Alexander Fischer et al. (Wiesbaden, Germany: Steiner, 1978), pp. 279–95.

47. *FRUS*, 1938, I, p. 716.

48. *The New York Times Index* for 1935, 1936, 1937, 1938, 1939.

49. Deist, "Die Deutsch Aufrüstung," p. 282.

50. Walter S. Ross, *The Last Hero: Charles A. Lindbergh* (New York: Harper & Row, 1968), pp. 264–65.

51. *Ibid.*, pp. 268–70, 273–76. See also Wayne S. Cole, *Charles A. Lindbergh and the Battle against American Intervention in World War II* (New York: Harcourt, Brace, Jovanovich, 1974), pp. 31–34

52. Folder "Navy 1938-Jan.-Feb." PSF 87, Franklin D. Roosevelt Library, Hyde Park, New York [hereafter, FDRL].
53. [Charles A. Lindbergh], *The Wartime Journals of Charles A. Lindbergh* (New York: Harcourt, Brace, Jovanovich, 1970), pp. 183–84, 185. 186.
54. *Ibid.*, pp. 82–84.
55. *The New York Times*, Feb. 22, 1939.
56. Robert Dallek, *Franklin D. Roosevelt* and *American Foreign Policy, 1932–1945* (New York: Oxford University Press, 1979), pp. 172, 213.
57. Ross, *The Last Hero*, p. 275.
58. *FRUS*, 1940, I, p. 50.
59. Secret Naval Attaché Reports, No. 69, Dec. 18, 1940, RG 38, NARS.
60. Estimate of Potential Military Strength Summaries, Feb. 17, 1940, *ibid.*
61. Cajus Bekker, *The Luftwaffe War Diaries,* trans, and ed. by Frank Ziegler (Garden City, NY: Doubleday, 1968), p. 377.
62. Bullitt, *For the President*, p. 419 and note at p. 421.
63. *PHA*, XIV, p. 1336; "Brief Periodic Estimate of the Situation," Sept. 5, 1941, Tab A, WPD 4494, LB. 122, RG 165, NARS.
64. "Die Stärke der deutschen Luftwaffe am 5.7.1941, 3.1.1942, und 31.5.1943," *Wehrwissenschaftliche Rundschau*, Vol. XI (Nov. 1961), pp. 641–44.
65. Coordinator of Information, "The German Military and Economic Position: Summary and Conclusions," Monograph No. 3, Dec. 12, 1941, p. 1, Folder Germany, PSF, Box 4, FDRL. (The figure of 29,000 airplanes is derived by beginning with the figure given of 24,000 at the start of the Russian war, subtracting the estimated losses of 4,500, and adding the estimated monthly production of 1,960 for five months). Franz Halder, *Kriegstagebuch*, 3 vols. (Stuttgart, Germany: W, Kohlhammer, 1962–64), III, p. 341; Burkhart Müller-Hillebrand, *Das* Heer 1933–1945, 3 vols. (Frankfurt, Germany: 1954–56), II, pp. 106–7. The Coordinator was not the only one to err. When the Wehrmacht armaments office set a monthly production goal of 800 to 1,200 tanks and assault guns for the panzer army of 1944, an official in a rival office calculated that it would take the whole machine-tool industry two years to produce the necessary tools— provided that, in the first place, 100,000 specialists had been recalled from the army to do the work. Alan S. Milward, *The German Economy at War* (London, U.K.: Athlone, 1965), p. 26.
66. The question arises why, if Americans overestimated German air production at least in part because of racism, the French and British also overestimated it. See, for example, F. H. Hinsley et al., *British Intelligence in the Second World War*, 2 vols. (Cambridge: Cambridge University Press, 1979–), I, pp. 75, 228–29, 299–300, 308–9; Robert J. Young, "French Military Intelligence and Nazi Germany," above; R. J. Overy, "The German Pre-War Aircraft Production Plans; November 1936– April 1939," English *Historical Review*, XC (Oct. 1975), pp. 778–97; and Central Intelligence Agency, Office of Research and Development, and Mathtech, Inc., Covert Rearmament in Germany, 1919–1939: "Deception and Misperception" (1979). Did a sense of German superiority play a role

in their overestimations as well? I think it not improbable that a belief in German efficiency may well have colored their views. I concede I know of no evidence for or against this possibility but on the other hand none of the other reasons adduced for the British and French overestimations provides satisfactory explanations.

67. Coordinator of Information, "The German Military and Economic Position," p. 1; Müller-Hillebrand, *Das Heer*, I, p. 102.

68. *PHA*, XIV, p. 1336. Germany, Oberkommando der Wehrmacht [OKW], Wehrmachtführungsstab, *Kriegstagebuch* ... 1940–1945, eds. Helmuth Greiner and Percy Ernst Schramm, I: 1. *August* 1940–31. *Dezember* 1941, ed. Hans Adolf Jacobsen (Frankfurt, Germany: Bernard und Graefe, 1965), pp. 1125–38.

69. *PHA*, XV, p. 1785; OKW, *Kriegstagebuch*, II, pp. 1356–57.

70. Undated memorandum signed ACW [Albert Coady Wedemeyer], WPD 4494–21, *RG* 165, NARS; Müller-Hillebrand, *Das Heer*, II, p. 182.

71. Robert Sherwood, *Roosevelt and Hopkins: An Intimate History* (New York: Harper, 1948), p. 304; "Brief Periodic Estimate of the Situation," Sept. 5, 1941, I.B. 122, WPD 4494–17, RG 165, NARS.

72. Holger H. Herwig, *Politics of Frustration: The United States in German Naval Planning* (Boston, MA: Little, Brown, 1976), pp. 216–34.

73. Dallek, *Franklin D. Roosevelt*, p. 287.

74. See *ibid.*, pp. 287, 291–92, 233–35; Herwig, *Politics of Frustration*, p. 187; *The New York Times*, June 30, 1941.

75. LB. 122, Tab. A, WPD, 4494, RG 165, NARS.

76. "Strategic Estimate," Oct. 1941, WPD, 4494, *ibid.*

77. Walter Warlimont, *Inside Hitler's Headquarters 1939–45*, trans, by R. H. Barry (London, U.K.: Weidenfeld and Nicolson, 1964), p. 208.

78. The best summary of Hitler's decision to declare war on the United States is Gerhard L. Weinberg, *A World at Arms: A Global History of World War II* (Cambridge: Cambridge University Press, 2005), pp. 249–253 and 262–633.

79. *PHA*, XII, p. 253.

80. Pratt, *Sea Power and Today's War*, pp. 236, 182.

81. Puleston, Armed *Forces of the Pacific*, pp. 259, 116–17; Young, "Racial Attitudes," citing Charles B. Gary, *War in the Pacific: A Study of Navies, Peoples and Battle Problems* (New York, 1936), p. 277, and George Fielding Eliot, "The Impossible War with Japan," *American Mercury*, Vol. XLV (Sept. 1938), p. 19.

82. *PHA*, XIV, p. 1380; Japan, Defense Agency, Office of Military History, *Riku-kaigun Nenpyu* (Tokyo, Japan: Showa 55 [1980]), CII. I am grateful to Dr. Alvin Coox for this reference and for translating the relevant data.

83. Wohlstetter, *Pearl Harbor*, p. 337.

84. Kahn, *Codebreakers*, pp. 8–9, 39.

85. *PHA*, XIV, p. 1059.

86. United States, Department of Defense, The *"MAGIC" Background to Pearl Harbor* 8 vols. (Washington, DC: Government Printing Office, 1978), I, p. A-81; II, p. 132; IV, p. 165.

87. *PHA*, XII, pp. 254–316.

88. *Ibid.*, XII, pp. 165, 204, 137, 208–9, 215–16, 231, 236, 237, 249; XXXV, pp. 472, 679; X, pp. 4659–65, 4662–63.
89. *Ibid.*, XIV, pp. 1363, 1372. Tab. A to the December 5 report contains the astonishing statement that Japan's leaders "want to avoid a general war in the Pacific" (*ibid.*, p. 1381). But this was probably written by a junior office who did not have access to MAGIC and its warnings, and it seems to have been overlooked or ignored by everybody. The G-2 Regional File has nothing of value about Japanese war plans at this time (G-2 Regional File, Box 2362, RG 165, NARS).
90. Wohlstetter, Pearl Harbor, p. 387. Wohlstetter's use of the terms of information theory, "signals" and "noise," which can illuminate, mislead in this case. She suggests that the "noise," or nonsignificant data, drowned out the "signals," or indications of the attack. But the implication that the signal could have been detected— perhaps through more careful correlation and evaluation— is false. There was simply not enough signal to do so. As information theory would say, the signal-to-noise ratio was too great. The only way the signal could have been recovered would have been to strengthen it, which meant adding indications of and attack.
91. Dwight D. Eisenhower, *Crusade in Europe* (New York: Doubleday, 1948), p. 37.
92. For an analysis of the same situation in the German army, where it was even more pronounced, see David Kahn, *Hitler's Spies: German Military Intelligence* in *World War II* (New York: Macmillan, 1978), pp. 531–34.

5

ROOSEVELT, MAGIC, AND ULTRA*

Part I

What MAGIC and ULTRA information went to President Franklin D. Roosevelt during World War II, and how did he use it?

It may as well be said at once that exhaustive research provides only a sketchy answer to the first question and merely unproved hypotheses for the second.

Extant records specify only a few of the solved German and Japanese messages that went to the president. Moreover, no documents or recollections have come to light suggesting any action that he took based on, or even influenced by, these intercepts.

Despite these disappointing results, it may be worthwhile to set out what has been learned about the production of MAGIC (Japanese solutions) and ULTRA (German) and their selection for and presentation to Roosevelt. Doing so will at least outline how one intelligence organization operated in preparing information for the highest authority in the land. And it will provide a framework in case any papers are discovered that answer, or at least shed more light on, the fundamental questions about Roosevelt, MAGIC, and ULTRA.

Foreign intercepts began going to the White House for the first time in 1937.[1] They came from the Army's Signal Intelligence Service, the Signal Corps' codemaking and codebreaking agency. Founded in 1929[2] under the great cryptanalyst William F. Friedman, SIS directed its first nontraining codebreaking at Japan, starting in 1932.[3] At first it solved Japanese diplomatic codes.[4] But these turned out to encrypt only insignificant messages. High-level, important traffic was

---

* From *Cryptologia*, XVI(4), October 1992, 289–313. Used by permission.

apparently protected by a machine cipher.[5] In 1935, when SIS realized this and had obtained more experience and greater knowledge of Japanese communication habits from its code solutions, it attacked the machine.[6] By 1936, cryptanalysts Frank B. Rowlett and Solomon Kullback,[7] perhaps helped by information about a simpler Japanese Navy machine cipher that the U. S. Navy had solved,[8] cracked what the Japanese Foreign Office called its "A" machine and what the Americans called RED. With this, the United States gained access to more and better intelligence than ever before.[9]

This included advance information starting in March 1937 about Italy's possible adherence to the German-Japanese anti-Comintern pact of the previous November. The intercepts revealed the early indications that Italy might join, the start of negotiations, the discussion over whether Italy should accede to the existing treaty or sign a separate agreement with Japan, a statement that Hitler wanted Italy to participate in the existing agreement, Italy's apparent acceptance, the emperor's approval, and part of the text of the treaty, which was signed 6 November 1937.[10]

U. S. diplomats did not start reporting until October on this rapprochement between three aggressive nations, to the east and to the west of the United States—and even then their information was far less specific than the intercepts.[11] So these seized the attention of officials in Army and Navy intelligence, in the State Department, and in the White House. Information from solved foreign cryptosystems, which had never before been of sufficient value to reach the topmost level of government, began going to the White House,[12] probably to the president.

On 20 February 1939, the Japanese introduced a new and more complicated cipher machine to supersede RED, whose mechanisms were wearing out. The Japanese called it their "B" machine; the Americans, PURPLE.[13] There followed nineteen months of concentrated cryptanalytic attack by a team under the general supervision of Friedman and the immediate direction of Rowlett, with some help from the Navy (which resumed diplomatic cryptanalysis to assist with PURPLE after having abandoned that field around 1938 or 1939 to concentrate on Japanese naval solutions). Their efforts were crowned with success in September 1940.[14] Thus, even after Japan discontinued use of the RED machine on 21 August 1941,[15] the PURPLE solution assured American officials of being able to read Japan's most secret diplomatic messages.

Part II

Growing cryptanalytic production—from an average of about one diplomatic solution a day in the first half of 1937[16] to fifty a day in the last half of 1941[17]—compelled the Army and the Navy to share the burden. In August 1940, SIS and the Navy's OP-20-G arranged that diplomatic messages originating in Tokyo on odd-numbered days would be handled by the Navy, those on even-numbered days, by the Army.[18] The two agencies exchanged the solutions.

Then, on 23 January 1941, the Army and the Navy agreed that their codebreaking results, which had been given the covername MAGIC, would be delivered to the White House by the Army in odd months, by the Navy in even.[19] But after a few months the Army stopped taking MAGIC to the White House.[20] In part this was because it felt that diplomatic intelligence should go to the president through the State Department, in part because the president's military aide, Brigadier General Edwin M. (Pa) Watson, had breached security by forgetfully throwing a MAGIC summary into his wastebasket some time after the Army's turn either in May or in July.[21] The final delivery in one or the other of those months seems to have been the last time an Army officer brought intercepts to Roosevelt. Henceforth, the naval aide was the person by whose hand MAGIC went to him.[22] This apparently came about because of the following events.

Near the end of September, an Army month, during which no intercepts were delivered to the White House, the president said he wanted to see them. In October, the Navy continued to send him memoranda based on MAGIC. Early in November, an Army month, during which again nothing was delivered to him, Roosevelt again told his naval aide, Captain John R. Beardall, that he wanted to see MAGIC. The aide told him it was an Army month. The president replied that he knew that and that he was either seeing MAGIC or being told what it said by Secretary of State Cordell Hull but that he still wanted to see the original intercepts. Beardall thought the reason was that the president grasped things more quickly by eye than by ear. On Monday, 10 November 1941, a conference changed the distribution setup. Henceforth, the Army would bring MAGIC to the State Department and the Navy to the White House. At 4:15 p. m. Wednesday, 12 November the first intercepts were delivered to the White House under this system.[23]

Neither war nor changes in the production of MAGIC affected this arrangement. On 25 January 1942, a month and a half after hostilities began, the cryptological officers of the Army and the Navy agreed orally that the Army would intercept and cryptanalyze all diplomatic traffic as well as enemy army and air force messages. This was formalized in a written agreement of 30 June 1942, which specified that the Navy would solve enemy naval messages and that the Army would continue to give the Navy the diplomatic solutions. The Joint Chiefs of Staff approved this on 6 July.[24] Another agreement on distribution matters, made 25 May 1942, between representatives of the Army, the Navy, and the Federal Bureau of Investigation, likewise did not alter Navy responsibility for White House delivery. It merely stated that, while the president should see diplomatic intelligence, he should not be given enemy naval, enemy military, western hemisphere clandestine (spy messages), or international clandestine intercepts.[25] (The reason was certainly not to conceal information from him but rather not to burden him with that which he could barely use.) Thus, although the Navy no longer generated the cryptanalytic intelligence that went to the White House, the naval aide continued to take it in to Roosevelt, who had been an assistant secretary of the Navy in World War I. By then, it was coming from a new Army agency.

Part III

After recovering from the shock of Pearl Harbor, the secretary of war, Henry L. Stimson, decided that a centralized analysis of the intercepted Japanese messages might have prevented the surprise.[26] He felt that an organization should be set up to study the intelligence from cryptanalysis more fully and carefully than before. Stimson, a lawyer, consulted with his assistant secretary, John McCloy, a lawyer, and they decided that the job should be handled by a lawyer, particularly one having experience in large cases involving many and complicated facts. They settled upon a former partner of McCloy in one of New York's most prestigious Wall Street firms who had represented Edwin Armstrong in his suits to protect his invention of the regenerative circuit. This was Alfred McCormack, a big, brilliant, demanding Brooklyn-born graduate of Princeton University and Columbia Law

School.[27] He was appointed special assistant to Stimson on 19 January 1942, six days after his 41st birthday.[28]

Because the Signal Corps had for years produced the raw material—the intercepted and solved messages—that went to Army intelligence, one of the two slots allotted to the Signal Corps in the General Staff was in G-2, or intelligence. It was filled, at that time, by Colonel Carter W. Clarke (Figure 5.1), a tall, slim, energetic career officer with strong likes and dislikes, salty modes of expression, and very good common sense.[29] Clarke had no signal intelligence background—he had replaced an officer who had signal intelligence experience but had been shifted to prepare for censorship as war approached[30]—but was extremely capable. On 15 May 1942, he was placed in charge of the new organization; McCormack, who was commissioned in June, became his deputy.[31] They worked very well together, each recognizing that the other had strengths that he lacked. McCormack was ideally qualified to run an intelligence unit while Clarke was just right to fit it into the Army.

Figure 5.1 Brigadier General Carter Clarke, head of the Special Branch, which processed German and Japanese intercepts for delivery to President Franklin D. Roosevelt and other high officials, congratulates his deputy, Alfred McCormack, a lawyer in civilian life, whom he has just awarded the Distinguished Service Medal for his work during World War II. (National Cryptologic Museum.)

The new unit, named Special Branch, was a highly secret element of the Military Intelligence Division;[32] the coordinate branches were administration, intelligence, counterintelligence, operations, and plans. All depended directly from the Army's assistant chief of staff for intelligence, the G-2.[33] A reorganization of the Military Intelligence Division in June 1944 changed some titles—McCormack became director of intelligence within the Military Intelligence Service, of which Clarke was deputy director[34]—but had little effect on the work and output of Special Branch.

The intercepts being distributed early in 1942 still consisted merely of the translations of Japanese messages with some footnotes. These gave the dates and intercept numbers of earlier messages referred to in those texts or said that those earlier messages were "not available."[35] This was raw intelligence. McCormack felt that the persons who got this exceptionally valuable information were entitled to have each detail in it illuminated by other information and the intercept itself placed into a larger context.[36] This would provide the recipients with finished—and therefore much more useful—intelligence. It would be presented to them in the form of a daily report. Moreover, surveying the intercepts over days or weeks would develop data that could be processed into long-range and specialized intelligence.[37]

For these jobs, McCormack sought men whose training "teaches them to deal with evidence, to be inquisitive and skeptical, to pursue an investigation through to a conclusion, to meet unfamiliar situations of fact and, most important, to do very detailed work without losing their sense of values."[38] He found these abilities not among historians, not among journalists, not among scientists or detectives or even parents of quarreling siblings, but exclusively among lawyers, and he began recruiting among members and former members of his law firm, Cravath, de Gersdorff, Swaine and Wood.

Clarke, meanwhile, handled administrative, security, and external matters. He prevailed upon the Signal Corps to expand its intercept facilities—the radio posts that monitored the foreign transmissions and so supplied the codebreakers with cryptograms to solve. He instructed the Signal Corps on assignment priorities—which cryptosystems intelligence wanted broken, which enemy circuits should be monitored. Perhaps most important of all, he alleviated the residual friction between SIS, a Signal Corps unit, and Special Branch, the glamorous organ of intelligence.[39]

Part IV

When Special Branch started, its offices were on the second floor of the front wing of Washington's Munitions Building, an ugly World War I temporary structure on Constitution Avenue between the Washington Monument and the Lincoln Memorial. In the rear wing of the same floor was SIS. Both moved in the fall of 1942: Special Branch to the newly built Pentagon, SIS to Arlington Hall, a former girls' school in Arlington, Virginia, half a dozen miles from the Pentagon.[40] As Special Branch grew, it expanded from its original single room into neighboring offices. The walls were temporary partitions that were constantly being shifted for new people. From time to time the branch moved;[41] for a while, at least, it was located in Rooms 2D715, 719, and 732.[42]

Though Clarke, McCormack, and some of the specialists had individual offices or offices shared with one or two people, the men preparing the daily intelligence reports—the heart of the operation—worked in a largish open area with desks facing each other in two rows. This enabled them to talk easily back and forth, to pass papers to one another, to go quickly and informally to another's desk to look at something to discuss it.[43]

The branch grew rapidly. From the dozen officers and civilians at the start, it swelled to 400 officers, enlisted men, and civilians in Washington and 80 abroad.[44]

Officers of Special Branch could not at first enter the supersensitive codebreaking agency,[45] even though the two organizations adjoined one another. But many questions arose in their work:[46] Was a message translated correctly? Did the codebreakers have other messages on the same subject? Could the intercept facilities pick up wanted traffic? In the first months, these matters were resolved by Clarke's consulting personally with the head of the Signal Intelligence Service, a fellow Signal Corps officer, at first Lieutenant Colonel Rex Minckler, and after April 1942, Lieutenant Colonel Frank W. Bullock.[47] Clarke carried written questions from his staff members to the codebreakers. Later a single officer of each agency handled liaison. But it was still a bottleneck.

Figure 5.2　Brigadier General W. Preston Corderman, head of the Signal Security Agency.

Then, in February of 1943, Lieutenant Colonel W. Preston (Red) Corderman (Figure 5.2), who had studied in the SIS School in the 1930s, took charge of the codebreaking agency, now called the Signal Security Agency (SSA). It was Corderman who had been moved to handle censorship and whom Clarke had replaced in intelligence in the General Staff; they had known each other since 1927, when Corderman reported at Fort Monmouth, New Jersey, to the 51st Signal Battalion's B Company, whose commander was Lieutenant Clarke.[48]

At once the liaison situation eased. Special Branch added several officers to handle the work. Secret teletype and secure telephone communications were established between Arlington Hall and the Pentagon.[49] The chief liaison officer with the codebreakers, Captain Thomas Ervin, a lawyer who had a flair for telling stories, would spend half his day with Special Branch and half with the codebreakers. He brought them questions Special Branch's analysts wanted answered and got from them both questions and requests for information that would help in their solving, such as which one of five possible solutions of a name was the right one.[50] Finally, toward the end of the war, the ultimate step was taken and many Special Branch evaluators began working in the same room as the codebreakers,[51] greatly facilitating the work of both sides.

Once a day, and perhaps later in the war several times a day, a courier driven in a staff car brought the hundreds of daily translated intercepts to Special Branch from Arlington Hall.[52] Urgent ones were tele-typed.[53] Most were Japanese army or diplomatic—the Japanese army material comprised 150 intercepts a day in the middle of the war, 700 at the end—a few were low-level German diplomatic, the higher-level German diplomatic codes not having been solved.[54] Italian messages did not figure prominently. It seems likely that every message solved and translated was sent to Special Branch: if Arlington Hall thought it worth translating, it was sent over.[55] In addition, an American unit under Colonel Telford Taylor at the British codebreaking agency at Bletchley Park, the Government Code and Cypher School, selected and then cabled to Special Branch, as it did to high military com-mands in the European theater, German military, air, and naval solu-tions, called ULTRA.[56] This began 27 August 1943.[57]

All messages, when they arrived at Special Branch, went to McCormack. He skimmed them to keep track of what was going on,[58] then, from 1943, divided them into diplomatic and military and dis-tributed them respectively to Henry Rigby and Benjamin Shute. These two lawyers, both in their early thirties (Rigby formerly of Cravath, and Shute on leave from it),[59] read the intercepts more closely. They kept those that dealt with immediate matters and gave those that dealt with longer-range or background matters to the specialists.[60]

Many of the specialists were academics with backgrounds in par-ticular areas. They related the intercepts to other sources of informa-tion that flowed to Special Branch,[61] such as newscast transcripts and prisoner-of-war interrogations, to produce a full-fledged report on a particular aspect of an enemy nation's economy, military organiza-tion, internal unrest, new technology, and the like.[62] These were pub-lished as completed or as needed.

The messages that were kept by Rigby, Shute, and later another lawyer, William R. Perdue, were edited by them and by the two other lawyers under each to produce the daily intercept reports.[63] These were the MAGIC Summary (later called the MAGIC Diplomatic Summary), edited by Rigby; the Military and Diplomatic Supplement to the MAGIC Summary (which began in the summer of 1943 and which from 1 July 1944 was called the MAGIC European Summary), edited by Shute; and the Far Eastern Summary (which began 10 February 1944 and dealt with Japanese military matters), edited by Perdue.[64] For these, the teams studied the day's file of translated decodes from the Signal Security Agency. They passed some to the specialists for information or comment.[65] They scanned other material for background. The editors working on the Far Eastern Summary, for example, looked at the 300 daily Japanese Navy intercepts; at cables from the field; outgoing cables on MAGIC intelligence; diplomatic and commercial intercepts; other MAGIC intelligence such as Japanese order of battle; the codebreaking agency's Weekly Report, giving the status of cryptanalysis of Japanese army systems; at the Boston Series of plaintext German diplomatic messages obtained by the Office of Strategic Services; and at noncodebreaking intelligence material, such as field command intelligence reports, photo interpretations, and Allied operational cables.[66]

From the translated decodes the editors selected the most important messages. That was their basic job. Most of their effort went into deciding what to leave out.[67] In addition, they spoke with the cryptanalysts and translators, often over the secure telephone, to rectify errors or fill in lacunae caused by garbles in the ciphertext and to clarify ambiguities in the Japanese and in the English. Even after this, many messages were, by themselves, scarcely intelligible.[68] To squeeze the maximum out of them, the editors called for files on items mentioned in the intercepts and sought elucidation.[69] They asked research personnel at the Military Intelligence Service to provide information about lesser known people, places, or things, about obscure events or allusions to forthcoming operations. They visited the who's who section, in which each mention of a name or operation was card-indexed, and determined who the person or what the event was.[70] This would be inserted as a footnote to the intercept. The editors conferred with one another on the meaning of a word. Some important intercepts were run verbatim in the summaries, but most were summarized. Rarely, if ever, were comments made beyond identifications; the editors did not evaluate the significance of the information.[71] The editors assembled the several summaries or texts and the identifications into a single writing, which went to Rigby and then to McCormack for final editing. McCormack was an extremely meticulous editor, who often spent a great deal of time making sure that the reports would be quickly and fully intelligible to their readers.[72]

The manuscript then went for typing to one of the two chief secretaries, both male legal stenographers who had worked at Cravath. One of them, at least, Vincent Fontana, followed the Cravath form book in typing the summaries: indent text 15 spaces from the left, indent 25 spaces for a paragraph start, indent 20 fewer for a quotation set apart in the text.[73] Reports averaged ten to twelve pages. The typescripts then were reproduced in bluish-purple ink by the Ditto process in about ten copies—later apparently more. Each was bound in a spiral binder, using a device that Special Branch had for this.[74] Then each was put in a locked leather briefcase,[75] called a pouch, and distributed by officer couriers in regularly scheduled staff cars. The diplomatic summary went out early in the afternoon; the military ones were reproduced and bound in the evening and distributed the next morning.[76]

The Army delivered its copies of the MAGIC Summary to the secretary of war (Stimson), the chief of staff (General George C. Marshall), the assistant chief of staff for war plans, the assistant chief of staff for intelligence, the Navy for further distribution, the secretary of state (Cordell Hull) and the assistant secretary of state who followed signal intelligence (probably Adolf A. Berle).[77] The Navy passed the 10 copies it got to the White House, the secretary of the navy (Frank Knox), the commander-in-chief of the U.S. Fleet and chief of naval operations (Admiral Ernest J. King), the chief of war plans, the director of naval intelligence, the vice chief of naval operations, the director of naval communications, the radio intelligence center, the domestic intelligence section and a file.[78] The Far Eastern Summary also went to the president. It was at first distributed in 23 copies; by the end of the war the number of copies had risen to 75.[79]

Part V

Delivery to the president was made by the naval aide. This had been the practice since before Pearl Harbor. For a few months in 1941, Roosevelt's physician, Admiral Ross T. McIntire, acted as naval aide and so brought the intercepts to the chief executive.[80] Once, in the summer, when McIntire was not available, a naval intelligence specialist, who did not want to entrust the pouch to the president's private secretary and who felt that the intercept he had could not wait, brought a message to the president. He was Lieutenant Commander Alwin D. Kramer, a Japanese language expert who headed the translation section of OP-20-G and who, because of his expertise on Japan and MAGIC, carried the intercepts to the high-level naval recipients so that he could answer their questions on MAGIC.[81] The intercept perhaps concerned Japanese-American negotiations the next day.[82]

When, a little later, Rear Admiral John Beardall became naval aide, Kramer—a methodical and dedicated man whom some called "The Shadow"[83]—took the intercepts to him for delivery to the president.[84] Kramer explained to Beardall points in the summaries about which the president was asking. Beardall, whose office, like Kramer's, was in the Navy Building, would ask Kramer late in the afternoon whether any MAGIC would be coming over for the president. Kramer would say, "There is no MAGIC ready for the president now" or "There might be something later" or "Nothing until tomorrow morning."[85] When there was something, Beardall would receive the intercepts in his office from Kramer and would carry them to the White House, a few blocks away, arriving around 5:30 or 6:00.[86]

About the first week in December 1941, a junior naval officer was assigned to bring MAGIC to the president when Beardall was off duty or at dinner or otherwise unavailable. This was a communications intelligence specialist, Lieutenant Lester R. Schulz.[87] He was assisted, beginning 6 December, by an Ensign Carson.[88] This was the system in effect at the time of Pearl Harbor.

Beardall had a key to the MAGIC pouch and sometimes opened it for the president, sometimes not. Normally, the president returned the sheaf of papers to Beardall when he had finished with it, though on 2 or 3 December 1941 he said he wanted to keep a copy of a Tokyo-Berlin intercept warning that "War may suddenly break out between the Anglo-Saxon nations and Japan… quicker than anyone dreams." Kramer prepared the copy and gave it to Beardall; he never got it back.[89] Though Beardall never discussed the intercepts with the president, he sometimes called attention to what he considered were important ones. On 4 or 5 December, for example, he said to Roosevelt of an intercept revealing that the Japanese were burning their codes: "Mr. President, this is a very significant dispatch." Roosevelt read it carefully, and then said to Beardall, "When do you think it will happen?" Beardall, thinking that Roosevelt meant the start of war, said, "Most any time."[90]

The most dramatic case of Roosevelt's receiving intercepts took place on the evening of Saturday, 6 December 1941. Schulz had been ordered by Beardall to stand by and bring some MAGIC expected that evening to the president. It was the first time that MAGIC was delivered after the close of the ordinary working day.[91] Schulz was waiting in Beardall's small office in the corner of the White House's basement mail room when Kramer arrived about 9:15. He was bringing the first thirteen parts of a fourteen-part PURPLE message; the Japanese had deliberately delayed transmitting the fourteenth part, which would break off negotiations with the United States. Schulz obtained permission to bring the MAGIC to the president and an usher accompanied him to the oval study on the second floor and announced him.

Roosevelt, who had excused himself from a dinner party, was seated at his desk. Only his confidante, Harry Hopkins, was with him in the quiet lamplit room. Schulz unlocked the briefcase in which the MAGIC was distributed with the key Beardall had given him, removed the sheaf of intercepts, and handed it to the president. Roosevelt read the thirteen parts in about ten minutes, while Hopkins paced slowly up and down. Then Hopkins read them. The thirteenth part rejected the final American offer and, when Hopkins passed the papers back to the president, Roosevelt said, in effect, "This means war." Hopkins agreed, and for about five minutes they discussed the situation, the deployment of Japanese forces, the movement towards Indochina, and similar matters. The president mentioned a message for peace he had sent the emperor of Japan. Hopkins replied that it was too bad that the United States could not strike the first blow and prevent any kind of surprise in the inevitable war.

"No," the president said in effect, "we can't do that. We are a democracy and a peaceful people." He raised his voice. "But we have a good record." He tried unsuccessfully to get the chief of naval operations on the telephone, deciding against having him paged at the National Theater for fear of causing undue alarm.

The president then returned the papers to Schulz, and, about half an hour after he had entered the study, Schulz left. He returned the papers to Kramer, who was waiting on a bench in the mail room, and soon thereafter went home.[92]

The next morning, Beardall brought the president the fourteenth part, which had been intercepted and solved during the night. It expressed the Japanese government's regret that "it is impossible to reach an agreement through further negotiations." It was about 10 a.m., and the president was in his bedroom. He said "Good morning" to Beardall, read the contents of the pouch, and then commented, in substance, "It looks like the Japanese are going to break off negotiations." There was no further discussion; Beardall took the pouch back to the Navy Department, and was as surprised as everybody else when news came of the attack on Pearl Harbor.[93]

Beardall was replaced as naval aide in January 1942 by Captain John McCrea. He saw or telephoned the president almost every day. To him went the MAGIC intercepts, brought over by an army courier. He also received copies of important naval dispatches that high naval officers thought should be shown to the president. Much of this arrived at his office in the Navy Building. Twice a day, McCrea picked out the naval dispatches he thought would be of interest to the president, added to these all the MAGIC intercepts, stuck them in his pocket or his briefcase, and headed for the White House, where he was expected.

When McCrea arrived in the morning, Roosevelt would usually be either in bed, in which case McCrea would hand him the papers, or in the bathroom, shaving. If the latter, the naval officer would go in, close the toilet cover, sit down on it, and in that inglorious setting would read the leader of the most powerful nation in the world some of the most secret documents of the greatest war in history. In the afternoon, the president, if he were not in the Map Room, a chart-lined office in the basement of the White House, would be seated in a neighboring room in a chair like a dentist's, having his sinuses packed by McIntire or his polio-deformed legs rubbed down by a masseur. Here again, McCrea would read the documents aloud to him.[94]

When the president was at his home in Hyde Park or at his Maryland mountain retreat, Shangri-La, McCrea would tell him about the documents by telephone.[95]

In 1942, the MAGIC documents were reaching McCrea's office in the Navy Department about 2:30 p.m.[96] OP-20-G had, since before Pearl Harbor, flagged the important items by sliding paper clips on them.[97] McCrea commented that although the selection was in general "accurate as to the possibility of their interest to the president," he often spotted other items that only he knew would also interest Roosevelt. After showing the documents to the president, he returned them to the courier for destruction by OP-20-G. In the summer of

Figure 5.3   Roosevelt smiles as he pins a Distinguished Service Medal on his departing naval aide, Vice Admiral Wilson Brown, April 28, 1942.

1942, when Admiral William D. Leahy became Roosevelt's chief of staff, MAGIC documents may have been addressed to him,[98] though he himself rarely took them in to Roosevelt.[99] That function was still mainly exercised by McCrea, his 1943 successor Rear Admiral Wilson Brown (Figure 5.3), Brown's assistant, Commander John A. Tyree and a young naval officer working in the Map Room under Leahy, Lieutenant Commander William C. Mott (Figure 5.4). All briefed the president orally in the morning and in the afternoon, often when he was getting his sinuses packed and was, Mott said, "a captive audience." They reported the intercept intelligence with the other information that they taught he would want to know and that they had boiled down for his consumption. If Roosevelt wanted to read some papers, they would give them to him; the intercept material was on separate sheets. Mott often underlined on these pages what he thought the president ought to know. The president struck the aides as extremely well informed.[100]

During Roosevelt's trip to the Casablanca conference with British Prime Minister Winston Churchill in January 1943, he was sent

Figure 5.4 Lieutenant Commander William C. Mott, assistant naval aide.

messages from Washington that were based on MAGIC Diplomatic Summaries. They were "from Colonel Boone"—almost certainly Marine Corps Colonel Ronald Aubry Boone (Figure 5.5), an Annapolis graduate who had been in naval intelligence in Washington since February 1939 and had spent eight years in Peking and Shanghai on language, intelligence, diplomatic, and public-relations missions.[101] One such "Colonel Boone" message, of 17 January 1943, identical with MAGIC Diplomatic Summary 296 of the day before, states that "Yamaguchi in Berlin reports to Tokyo that Nazis are upset about American military supplies reaching Vladivostok in Russian bottoms X. They reach Moscow quickly by rail X Germans say until this supply route is cut off, any advance in Russia quite impossible X…"[102] On 27 January, "Colonel Boone has indicated for last three days that a Jap movement in strength toward southern Solomons is shaping up X…"[103] There are about half a dozen such messages to Roosevelt during the conference.

Churchill sometimes sent Roosevelt ULTRA—which the prime minister referred to by his own codename for it, BONIFACE. While they were at the Quebec conference in September, 1944, for example, Churchill passed some to him, which he later said "appeared to me to be of profound significance." More often Churchill gave him documents based on intercepts or referred to information based on them. In a note to the president of 13 August 1943, while both were at the

Figure 5.5 Marine Corps Colonel Ronald A. Boone (right), deliverer of MAGIC and ULTRA to the president, arrives on assignment in Alaska. (National Cryptologic Museum.)

president's home in Hyde Park, New York. Churchill provided an analysis of the situation in Yugoslavia of which he said, "Much of it is taken from BONIFACE sources." In October, he wrote about movements in Italy that "We know from BONIFACE that the enemy is withdrawing to the north."[104]

Likewise, during Roosevelt's visit to Canada for the QUADRANT conference of July and August 1943 and his subsequent fishing trip, he was sent two Colonel Boone messages. One was on 21 August: "Colonel Boone indications that Jap barge traffic from Shortland to Kolombangara and Vella area (in the Solomon Islands) may be proceeding along south Choiseul coast to vicinity Sami Head (7 22 S 156 08 E) then across the channel to destination."[105] The other, four days later, dealt with a report of the Japanese ambassador in Hanoi.[106]

In November of 1943, a Marshall aide and Churchill sent Roosevelt intercepts that they wanted him to see. But he was away at the conferences at Cairo and Teheran when they arrived. He first saw them when he returned on 16 December 1943. After transferring from the battleship *Iowa* to the presidential yacht *Potomac* for the trip up to Washington, he was handed a brown manila envelope in a briefcase that a Map Room watch officer, naval reserve Lieutenant (j. g.) R. H. Myers, had brought with him on the yacht. The intercepts dealt with German forces and forts that would be defending against the Allied invasion of Europe. The Japanese ambassador, General Hiroshi Oshime, and his aides had inspected the Atlantic Wall and reported to Tokyo in great detail on the German measures: "... All the German fortifications on the French coast are very close to the shore and it is quite clear that the Germans plan to smash any enemy attempt to land as close to the water edge as possible.... The coastal defence divisions are distributed as follows: Netherlands Defence Army (covering the Netherlands down to the mouth of the Rhine), 4 divisions; Fifteenth Army (covering the area extending from the mouth of the Rhine to west of Le Havre), 9 divisions; Seventh Army (extending thence to the southern bank of the Loire), 8 divisions...." These messages, all probably decrypted from PURPLE radiograms intercepted at Asmara, Ethiopia, where SSA monitored Berlin-Tokyo traffic in the dun-colored block building of a former Italian radio station, have been called the greatest military intelligence coup of all time—and it certainly gave an insight into enemy plans unprecedented in history in both detail and scope. In July of 1944, Churchill asked that Roosevelt be shown another message. But, Clarke noted in a memo, that one had already been reported in Special Branch's Far Eastern Summary of 20 July 1944 and had been delivered to the White House that day. It was a Japanese message saying that the enemy must not be given any pretext to use chemical warfare.[107]

Part VI

Roosevelt's confidence in the MAGIC decrypts had been settled well before Pearl Harbor. When he was given the solution of the Japanese ambassador's report of a private audience with himself, he appeared much impressed and commented, as he read the translation, "Yes, I said that" and "That is correct; he said that."[108]

But did ULTRA and MAGIC, which had to compete with so many other messages and problems, capture his interest? The evidence is contradictory.[109]

In February 1944, Marshall wrote the president, "I have learned that you seldom see the Army summaries of 'Magic' material."

Marshall's remedies—improving the presentation, separating the wheat from the chaff and correlating the items with other information, binding the summaries in a Black Book for convenience of reading—suggest that the president was not particularly interested in the information.[110]

On the other hand, McCormack said of his MAGIC summaries that the president and his advisers "read them avidly."[111] He commented that "the fight for personnel was made easier by high praise which the [Special] Branch received from time to time by General Marshall and other high officials, and occasionally from the President."[112] General Corderman said that although none of the Signal Service Agency's many commendations were ever known to have come from the president, he had the impression that Roosevelt was a great user of the intercepts and a great supporter of those who produced them.[113] Frank Rowlett, the cryptanalyst whose solution of the RED machine had started it all, said that the usefulness of the intercepts to the top leadership was made clear to the cryptanalysts in the most valuable way possible: the cryptanalysts were asked, "Do you have anything more on this? Give it priority!" That request for more of their results was, said Rowlett, "better than any pat on the back."[114]

No doubt the president was glad for the information he got—hence the appreciation sensed by the codebreakers and the evaluators. Nevertheless, the impression remains that the intercepts had only a secondary interest for Roosevelt. The reason may be that—unlike the military and naval men—he could not much use the information they gave him.

During hostilities, intercepts on diplomatic affairs—either of the Axis or of neutral nations—dealt at best with nonbelligerents. But geography and the war situation influenced them far more than Allied pressure. Roosevelt understood this, and so perhaps interested himself but little in the intercepts dealing with these matters. For instance, the Allied invasion of North Africa had given rise to fears that Spain might admit German troops who could close the Strait of Gibraltar and trap Allied forces in the Mediterranean.[115] McCormack later claimed that Special Branch had provided the best intelligence about Spain's postinvasion intentions.[116] But however valuable the information Roosevelt may have gleaned from MAGIC, he seems

not to have acted upon it: he sent no instructions to his ambassador in Madrid and did not mention guarding against the German
threat in any of his postinvasion messages to Churchill.[117] In August
of 1942, however, a MAGIC solution seemed of unusual importance.
Marshall pointed out to Roosevelt intercepts showing that Japan had
decided not to attack the Soviet Union and urged that Roosevelt tell
Soviet leader Joseph Stalin about this. Roosevelt did—without, however, specifying the source of his information, which he affirmed was
"definitely authentic."[118]

The MAGIC and ULTRA dealing with military matters was,
of course, of extraordinary value to the generals and admirals, and
Roosevelt urged it upon them. "Be sure Ernie King sees that!" he
would sometimes tell McCrea when shown an intercept. But neither
McCrea nor Mott nor Tyree remembered cases in which an intercept
impelled the president to take a particular action.[119] In part this was
because he delegated the detailed running of the war to his military
chiefs and seldom interfered.

In this Roosevelt contrasted sharply with Churchill. Soon after
messages were solved at the codebreaking center at Bletchley Park,
they were sent, together with their interpretations, to MI6 headquarters at Broadway Buildings in London, where a selection was
made, put in a special buff-colored box, and taken by messenger to
10 Downing Street, five minutes away. The prime minister, who carried the key to the box on his key ring, sometimes read up to 200
ULTRA intercepts a day, discussed them at his daily meetings with
his chiefs of staff, drew the attention of his field commanders to individual items, was told of such technical successes as the solution of
a U-boat key, and in general utilized the intercepts in directing the
war. But Churchill was much closer to the fighting and bombing
than Roosevelt and, as minister of defense, much more intimately
involved in the details. The intercepts were therefore of far greater
value to him. Not to know what he saw would distort the picture of
how he worked during World War II.[120]

Can the same be said of Roosevelt? Not with our present knowledge. Perhaps he used MAGIC and ULTRA extensively in his
running of the war, and perhaps he did not. All known sources
do not provide enough facts to permit a conclusion one way or
the other. He and his advisors cannot be asked, and the chances

seem slight that papers yielding direct evidence on the matter will come to light. Possibly comparisons of MAGIC and ULTRA with actions taken in the war will develop a pattern convincing enough to let historians say that the one affected the other. But here, too, the uncertainty even about what intercepts Roosevelt saw and the tenuosness of such influence even with solid data reduce the likelihood of success. Of the two efforts made so far, one fails to convince—even its proposer offers it diffidently—and the other, more plausible, awaits a documentary basis.[121] The almost complete lack of traces of Roosevelt's use of MAGIC and ULTRA despite the great volume of material may indeed suggest that Roosevelt did not much use them. But this is at best a negative argument, and in no way conclusive. In the end, we historians can only say that we do not now know how Roosevelt used MAGIC and ULTRA. And probably we never will.

Notes

A name alone refers to an interview. Numbers for SRH items beginning with 0 or 00 when under 10 or 100 are the page numbers stamped on the document by archivists; they differ from the document's original typewritten page numbers.

Though this article concludes that cryptologic information was little used by Roosevelt, such material was of enormous value in military operations, including at the highest level. Special Branch prepared the material for use by these high officials. But because this article focuses on Roosevelt, it excludes many details of the workings of the Special Branch. Almost every sentence dealing with that operation could—and some day should—be expanded into an article. The sources offer clues to this.

My claim of exhaustive research requires that I list the sources that I checked for information about Roosevelt and MAGIC and ULTRA. They are:

- Franklin D. Roosevelt Library, Hyde Park, New York. The only records of MAGIC for the president are those for some of his trips away from Washington. These are cited below. The Map Room files have no logs of ULTRA or MAGIC documents or the summaries based on them that went to the president, nor any mention of the couriers who brought him ULTRA or MAGIC documents, nor any record of what the naval aides (as Captain McCrea) brought him in its noting of their visits to him.

- William Emerson, at the time of my inquiry director of the Roosevelt Library. He knew of no unpublished documentary material concerning Roosevelt's receipt of or use of ULTRA or MAGIC.

- Robert Dallek, *Franklin D. Roosevelt and American Foreign Policy, 1932–1945* (New York: Oxford University Press, 1979). The work does not mention ULTRA, and Dallek, who went through all or nearly all the papers dealing with Roosevelt and foreign policy, said on the telephone 14 April 1986 he does not remember seeing anything about it in the documents. He believes that such material would have jumped out at him and that he would have used it in his book as a good story.

- Robert Myers of the White House Map Room staff said that both he and George Elsey of that staff picked up intercepts from the commander in chief, U. S. Fleet (Admiral Ernest King), and Admiral John Tyree, assistant to the naval aide, said that Myers picked up intercepts from the Navy. On the other hand, Elsey said that, although he dealt with messages of Winston Churchill and Joseph Stalin to Roosevelt, he knew nothing about MAGIC or ULTRA documents or summaries going to the president. I have not been able to clear up the contradiction. Asked for any intercepts sent by the Navy to the White House during World War II, the Navy Security Group Command headquarters replied in a letter of 18 April 1988 (Ser GH/4057) that it had only duplicates of Army-originated diplomatic intercepts.

- All of the interviewees were asked about how the Special Branch summaries went to Roosevelt and what use he made of that information; they knew little about the distribution and none knew anything about the president's use of the material.

- Archive of Contemporary History, University of Wyoming. I was told 16 April 1986 by Professor Emmet Chisum that he has never seen anything about distribution of MAGIC to Roosevelt in the papers of Laurance Safford, Dundas Tucker, and C. C. Hiles, all naval officers who worked in or knew about communications intelligence.

- Dundas P. Tucker, "Rhapsody in Purple: A New History of Pearl Harbor," ed. Greg Mellen, *Cryptologia*, 6 (July 1982), 193–228, (October 1982), 346–367, has nothing on MAGIC or ULTRA to Roosevelt.
- Library of Congress, Manuscript Division, Papers of William D. Leahy, Diary. A skim showed nothing dealing with ULTRA or MAGIC. Moreover, these papers became available to the public before ULTRA material was declassified.
- National Archives, Record Group 218, Joint Chiefs of Staff, Leahy Papers. None of the following folders have anything about MAGIC or ULTRA to Roosevelt:
  - Folder 54, Value of OSS
  - Folder 82, Miscellaneous Messages 1945–1946
  - Folder 83, Dispatches 1944 Miscellaneous
  - Folder 84, Miscellaneous 1944
  - Folder 89, Conference Teheran 1943
  - Folder 100, Prime-President 1944
  - Folder 101, Prime-President 1943
  - Folder 102, Hurley— "Special"— and Harriman
  - Folder 104, High-Level (not Prime), 1945
  - Folder 105, High-Level Message 1943 1944 not Prime
  - Folder 125, Memoranda to and from President 1945
  - Folder 127, Memos to and from President July 1, 1943 to Nov. 1943
  - Folder 128, Correspondence signed by the President
  - Folder 138, Messages between President and Admiral Leahy
- U. S. Naval Institute, Annapolis, Maryland, "Reminiscences of Vice Admiral William R. Smedberg III, U. S. Navy, Retired," an oral history, July 1979, has nothing on Roosevelt on pages 281–313, which deal with Smedberg's service from September 1944 to March 1946 as combat intelligence officer on the staff of the commander in chief, U. S. Fleet.

I have not credited or used the statements in William Stevenson's *A Man Called Intrepid: The Secret War* (New York: Harcourt Brace Jovanovich, 1976) ascribed to Sir William Stephenson, head of British Security Coordination during World War II, that he brought ULTRA information to Roosevelt. These statements are unsupported by other evidence and my confidence in the book's unsubstantiated statements has been undermined by its basic and numerous errors.

Sources

Published Documents

United States. Congress. Joint Committee on the Investigation of the Pearl Harbor Attack. *Pearl Harbor Attack*. Hearings. 79th Congress: 1st and 2nd Sessions. Washington: Government Printing Office, 1946. 39 vols. Cited as *PHA* followed by volume and page number.

——. Department of State. *Foreign Relations of the United States: Diplomatic Papers*. Washington: Government Printing Office. Cited as *FRUS* with year followed by volume and page.

   1937, 1: *General*; 2: *British Commonwealth, Europe, Near East, Africa*; 3 and 4: *The Far East* (all 1954).

   Japan, 1931–1941, 2 (1943).

   1942, 2: *Europe* (1961); 3: *Europe* (1961).

   1943, 2: *Europe* (1964).

Unpublished Documents

National Archives. Record Group 457. Records of the National Security Agency.

   SRH-061. "Allocation of Special Security Offices to Special Branch, Military Intelligence Service, War Department, 1943–45." 33pp.

   SRH-111. "MAGIC Reports for the Attention of the President 1943–1944." 32pp.

   SRH-116. "Origin, Functions and Problems of the Special Branch, M. I. S." [A memorandum by McCormack to Clarke, 15 April 1943.] 55pp.

   SRH-118. "Incidental Exhibits re Pearl Harbor Investigation" [Collection of Japanese Diplomatic Messages 12 July 1938–21 January 1942. Department of the Army Intelligence Files.] 481pp.

   SRH-141. "Papers from the Personal Files of Alfred McCormack." Parts 1 and 2. 570pp.

   SRH-145. "Collection of Memoranda on Operations of S. I. S. [Signal Intelligence Service] Intercept Activities and Dissemination 1942–45." 293pp.

   SRH-153. "M. I. S., War Department, Liaison Activities in the U. K. 1943–1945." 20pp.

   SRH-185. "War Experience of Alfred McCormack." 83pp.

SRH-270. "Army-Navy-F. B. I. Comint [Communications Intelligence] Agreements of 1942." 5pp.

SRDJ-113,785–114,000. Japanese Diplomatic Translations. Station "C" Intercept Message File. [10 September 1940–7 April 1941.]

SRS. Diplomatic "MAGIC" Summaries 1943. September, October, December.

—— Record Group 218. Joint Chiefs of Staff. Leahy Papers. Folder 126, Memos to the President from General Marshall.

Franklin D. Roosevelt Library, Hyde Park, New York. Map Room File.

Box 15. Presidential Trips 27 September 1942–28 April 1943. Folders Casablanca Conference Trip, Presidential Trips Hyde Park 6 February–5 April 1943.

Box 16. Presidential Trips 14 May–7 November 1943. Folder Canadian Fishing Trip and Quadrant Conference 31 July–29 August 1943.

Box 192. Map Room Logs— Incoming Dispatches. 1941–July 1943. Folder Log of Incoming Dispatches April May 1942. Folder Log of Incoming Dispatches December 1941 January February March 1942. Folder Log Sheets September 1942.

Box 195. Map Room Logs: 1942–1945. Folder White House Chart Room— Special Log President-Churchill Dispatches. Folder Chart Room Log and Standing Orders [a log of calls and visitors]. Folder 1-A [log of Map Room].

National Security Agency.

Translated solutions of intercepted Japanese diplomatic messages dealing with the accession of Italy to the Anti-Comintern Pact.

Interviews

In person

Carter W. Clarke. Head of Special Branch. 6 December 1963.

Thomas Ervin. Liaison officer in Special Branch. 11 March 1986.

Vincent Fontana. Typist and production manager in Special Branch. 12 March 1986.

C. Roger Nelson. Assistant editor of MAGIC Diplomatic Summary. 12 December 1985.

Benjamin R. Shute. Editor of German military summary. 8 March 1986.

By Telephone

Cletus Beard. Head of Asmara intercept post in 1950s. 20 April 1986.

Carter W. Clarke. 10 January and 19 October 1986.

Arthur Compton. Liaison officer in Special Branch. 27 October 1986.

W. Preston Corderman. Head of Signal Security Agency. 20 April 1986.

George Elsey. Deputy to Leahy in Map Room. 12 February 1986.

Forrest McCluney. Head of Special Branch couriers. 9 March 1986.

John McCrea. Naval aide to Roosevelt. 4 and 12 March 1986.

William Mott. Assistant to Leahy. 13 January and 23 March 1987.

Robert Myers. Assistant in Map Room. 26 April 1987.

William R. Perdue. Editor of Far Eastern Summary. 16 February 1987.

William McKinley Rigdon. Assistant to Leahy. 9 March 1986.

Frank Rowlett. Head of cryptanalytical teams that solved RED and PURPLE. 22 April 1986.

W. R. Smedberg. Head of naval combat intelligence. 12 May 1980.

John A. Tyree. Assistant to naval aide. 19 May 1987.

Letters

Carter W. Clarke. December 1985.

W. Preston Corderman. Commander of Signal Service Agency, 1943–1945. 5 December 1983.

John J. McCloy. Assistant secretary of war. 18 July 1984.

Henry W. Rigby. Editor of MAGIC Summary. 10 February 1987.

Lester R. Schultz. Delivered MAGIC to Roosevelt. 3 and 24 January 1986.

J.C. Sharp. Deputy chief, information policy, National Security Agency. 4 November 1986 (Serial J9420A).

Telford Taylor. Head of Special Branch unit at Bletchley Park. 6 January 1985.

Secondary Sources

(Includes only items cited more than once in the notes or of basic importance)

Adams, Henry H. *Witness to Power: The Life of Fleet Admiral William D. Leahy.* Annapolis, MD: Naval Institute Press, 1985.

Henry W. Rigby. Editor of MAGIC Summary. 10 February 1987.

Lester R. Schultz.

Bell, Ernest L. *An Initial View of ULTRA as an American Weapon.* Keene, New Hampshire: TSU Press, 1977. (A reprint of SRH-005, "Use of [CX/MSS ULTRA] by the United States War Department, 1943–1945," 82pp., and of SRH-006, "Synthesis of Experiences in the Use of ULTRA Intelligence by the U. S. Army Field Commands in the European Theatre of Operations," 29pp.)

Cochran, Alexander S., Jr. "The Influence of 'Magic' Intelligence on Allied Strategy in the Mediterranean." In Craig L. Symonds, ed., *New Aspects of Naval History: Selected Papers Presented at the Fourth Naval History Symposium, United States Naval Academy, 25–26 October 1979* (Annapolis, MD: Naval Institute Press, 1981), at 340–348.

—— *The MAGIC Diplomatic Summaries: A Chronological Finding Aid.* New York: Garland Publishing, 1982.

Hannah, Theodore M. "Frank B. Rowlett— A Personal Profile." *Cryptologic Spectrum* (National Security Agency), 11 (April 1981), 4–22.

Hinsley, F. H., et al., *British Intelligence in the Second World War.* Cambridge and New York: Cambridge University Press, 1979–1988.

Howe, George F. *American Signal Intelligence in Northwest Africa and Western Europe* [Unclassified]. United States Cryptologic History, Series IV: World War II, Vol. 1. [Fort Meade, Maryland]: National Security Agency/Central Security Service, 1980.

Jones, F. C. *Japan's New Order in Asia: Its Rise and Fall, 1937–1945*. London: Oxford University Press, 1954.

Kahn, David. *The Codebreakers: The Story of Secret Writing*. New York: Macmillan, 1967.

Kesaris, Paul, ed. *The MAGIC Documents: Summaries and Transcripts of the Top-Secret Diplomatic Communications of Japan, 1938–1945*. Index compiled by David Wallace. Frederick, Maryland: University Publications of America, 1982.

Lewis, Graydon A., ed. *A History of Communications Intelligence in the United States with Emphasis on the United States Navy*. Denver: Naval Cryptologic Veterans Association, 1982.

Parrish, Thomas. *The Ultra Americans: The U. S. Role in Breaking the Nazi Codes*. New York: Stein and Day, 1986.

Rohwer, Jürgen. "Ultra, the United States and the Battle of the Atlantic 1941." Paper delivered at the 2nd U. S. Army War College International Conference on Intelligence and Military Operations, Carlisle Barracks, Pennsylvania, 12–14 May 1987.

National Archives. Record Group 457. Records of the National Security Agency.

SRH-001. "Historical Background of the Signal Security Agency." Vol. 3 "The Peace." Preface signed by Historian, Army Security Agency. [Assistant Chief of Staff, G-2, 12 April 1946.] 416pp. Reprinted as *The Origin and Development of the Army Security Agency 1917–1947* (Laguna Hills, CA: Aegean Park Press, 1978).

SRH-029 "A Brief History of the Signal Intelligence Service." By William F. Friedman, June 19, 1942. 18pp. Reprinted in Kesaris, ed., 17–31.

SRH-035. "History of the Special Branch, MIS [Military Intelligence Service], War Department, 1943–1944." 63pp.

SRH-041. "M. I. S. Contributions to the War Effort." December 1945. 22pp.

SRH-061. "Allocation of Special Security Officers to Special Branch, Military Intelligence Service, War Department, 1943–45." 33pp.

SRH-062. "History of Military Intelligence Service. Reports Unit." September 1945. 116pp.

SRH-117. "History of Special Branch. M. I. S." June 1944–September 1945. Unsigned. 11pp. Reprinted in Kesaris, ed., 55–67.

SRH-132. "History of the Special Distribution Branch." 7pp.

SRH-146. "Handling of Ultra Within the Military Intelligence Service (M. I. S.) 1941–1945."

SRH-149. "A Brief History of Communications Intelligence in the United States." By Laurance F. Safford, Captain, U. S. N., Ret. 22pp. Reprinted in Kasaris, ed., 1–16.

SRH-152. "Historical Review of OP-20-G." 17 February 1944. [Unsigned]. 13pp.

SRH-154. "Signal Intelligence Disclosures in the Pearl Harbor Investigations." 47pp.

SRH-159. "Preliminary Historical Report on the Solution of the 'B' Machine." By William F. Friedman. 14 October 1940. 10pp.

SRH-305. "The Undeclared War: 'History of R. I.'[radio intelligence]." By L. F. Safford. 15 November 1943. 29pp.

SRH-349. "The Achievements of the Signal Security Agency in World War II." February 1946. 115pp.

SRH-355. "Naval Security Group History to World War II." Prepared and compiled by Captain J. S. Holtwick, Jr., U. S. N., Ret. June 1971. Part I, 464pp.

Notes

1. Rowlett. I know of no evidence that earlier American signals intelligence results— during the Civil War, World War I, or the Washington Disarmament Conference of 1922, to name the three cryptanalytically most likely events— went to the White House.

2. *The Origin and Development of the Army Security Agency 1917–1929* (Laguna Hills, CA: Aegean Park Press, 1978), pp. 8–9.

3. Hannah, 11–14.

4. Rowlett; SRH-001, 303- 04.

5. *Ibid.*, 305.

6. *Ibid.*, 301; Hannah, 14–15.

7. Hannah, 14.

8. Lewis, ed., 12; SRH-305, 020; SRH-149, 8; SRH-355, 161–62; Layton, 79. Rowlett disputes this (Hannah, 15), but the several naval officers' statements suggest that the Navy contributed something, though perhaps more in a general than a specific way.

9. Hannah, 15; Rowlett. On RED and PURPLE, see Cipher A. Deavours and Louis Kruh, *Machine Cryptography and Modem Cryptanalysis* (Dedham, MA.: Artech House, 1985), pp. 211–245. Rowlett says, on p. 2 of a memorandum of 1 March 1980 prepared for author John Toland, that "G2 showed no more than a passing interest in the S. I. S. output [of Japanese diplomatic solutions] until a partially decoded circular message from Tokyo indicated that a secret codicil was being formulated to the tripartite treaty which Japan was negotiating with Germany and Italy." Actually, this intercept could only have concerned not the "tripartite treaty," which was not signed until 17 September 1940, but negotiations for the Anti-Comintern Pact between Germany and Japan. This was signed 25 November 1936, the year in which the A machine was solved; negotiations for Italy's adherence did not begin until 1937. The intercepts reflect this. Italy adhered to the pact on 6 November 1937 but was never told of its secret codicil between Germany and Japan. Parrish, 43, likewise errs in ascribing the army interest to negotiations on a "tripartite treaty." Ironically, the Japanese message of 14 November 1936 that provided a synopsis of the secret codicil was not solved until 13 November 1937 (from solved Japanese diplomatic messages dealing with the Anti-Comintern Pact kindly declassified for me by the National Security Agency). No "partially decoded circular message" was included

in the messages supplied to me. (The agreement between Germany and Italy that in effect created the Axis, the so-called Pact of Steel, was signed 25 October 1936.)

10. Solved Japanese diplomatic messages declassified by N. S. A. In the following citations, the date of the telegram is given first, followed, in parentheses, by the date the codebreakers submitted the translation to the Army G-2. Note the increasing speed of solution. All dates are 1937. Berlin-Tokyo 19 January (8 March) and Berlin-Tokyo 9 March (5 April) for early indications; Tokyo-Rome 15 September (1 October) for start of negotiations; Rome-Tokyo 2 August (23 August) for existing treaty or separate; Berlin-Tokyo 7 October (15 October) for Hitler; Tokyo-Rome 26 October (3 November) for acceptance; Tokyo-Rome 4 November (8 November) for emperor's approval; Tokyo-Rome 31 October, 31 October and 1 November (all 5 November) for part of text. Some of the memoranda to G-2 bear the handwritten initials of Friedman, Rowlett, and John B. Hurt, a translator.

11. *FRUS*, 1937, 1:608. British cryptanalysts likewise seemed to have obtained information about these negotiations only in September–October 1937 (John D. Ferris, "From Broadway House to Bletchley Park: The Diary of Captain Malcolm D. Kennedy, 1934–1946," *Intelligence and National Security*, Vol. 4 [July 1989], pp. 421–450 at 447–448).

12. Rowlett.

13. SRH-145, 001, 008–09.

14. Hannah, 5, 15–19; Kahn, 20–22. Lewis, ed., 14–15 for Navy diplomatic solutions.

15. SRH-001, 308.

16. S. I. S. serial 320 was solved on 12 February, serial 461 on 26 June— 141 messages in 135 days.

17. Kahn, 29.

18. *PHA*, 8:3923, 18:3313–14; Lewis, ed., 15; SRH-270, 024.

19. *PHA*, 2:288, 4:1734.

20. Kahn, 30.

21. *Ibid.*, 26. *PHA*, 11:5475, implies May. But Watson was receiving occasional deliveries of MAGIC in July.

22. Clarke, in reply to my question of 2 December 1985 as to who brought solutions to Roosevelt, wrote: "Navy— always. They never let their poor relation near the old con man." *PHA*, 2:789, which states that from 1 November 1941 intercepts to the president were delivered through the naval aide, may refer only to the time up to Pearl Harbor.

23. *PHA*, 11:5475–76.

24. SRH-200, 184, 198, 042.

25. Howe, 6; SRH-200, 038.

26. SRH-116, 006–07; Henry L. Stimson and McGeorge Bundy, *On Active Service in Peace and War* (New York: Harper & Row, 1947), pp. 454–55.

27. Kai Bird, *The Chairman: John J. McCloy: The Making of the American Establishment* (New York: Simon & Schuster, 1992), p. 142; SRH-185, 77–83; *Who Was Who in America*, 3:572, s. v. McCormack, Alfred;

"Alfred McCormack, Lawyer, Dies; Former Director of Intelligence," *The New York Times*, Vol. 23 (12 July 1956), pp. 4–5; Shute; Nelson, Fontana.

28. SRH-116, 007.
29. Shute; Ervin; Nelson; Clarke (1963), "Carter W. Clarke Dies at 90, An Army Intelligence Officer," *The New York Times*, Vol. A24 (7 September 1987), p. 5.
30. Corderman.
31. Howe, 6; SRH-185, 002.
32. SRH-146, 001.
33. SRH-185, 015.
34. SRH-062, 001, 080; SRH-146, 002. For the 1944 reorganization, see Otto L. Nelson, *National Security and the General Staff* (Washington, DC: Infantry Journal Press, 1946), pp. 526–535.
35. See intercepts in *PHA*, 12:1–248.
36. SHR-116, 008–9.
37. *Ibid.*, 009.
38. SRH-185, 004.
39. SRH-185, 00203; SRH-116, 010.
40. SRH-117, 007, 008.
41. Ervin; Shute; Fontana.
42. SRH-062, 084–85.
43. *Ibid.*
44. SRH-145, 009.
45. SRH-117, 008.
46. SRH-132, 6.
47. Kahn, 575.
48. *Ibid.*; Corderman.
49. SRH-117, 009.
50. Ervin.
51. SRH-113, 010.
52. SRH-132, 6; Ervin.
53. SRH-062, 43.
54. Ervin.
55. *Ibid.*
56. Shute. For the origins of this unit: Howe, 10–12, 90, 123–131.
57. Parrish, 181–2.
58. Fontana.
59. SRH-185, 003, 013; Shute.
60. Bell, 52.
61. SRH-141, 220–23.
62. SRH-116, 015–19; Bell, 55, 58.
63. SRH-146, 1.
64. SRH-062, 087–88; SRH-035, 18; Bell, 50, 52, 56; SRH-062, 049; Perdue, who was in charge from 1942 of what was then called the Japanese Army Supplement; Rigby. Though SRH-062, 038, says that F. A. O'Connell Jr. prepared the Far Eastern Summary, this may refer to a later time.

65. Fontana; SRH-146, 5.
66. SRH-062, 043–44. Anthony Cave Brown, *The Last Hero: Wild Bill Donovan* (New York: Times Books, 1982), pp. 278–286, for Boston Series.
67. SRH-116, 12.
68. SRH-062, 044.
69. Fontana.
70. SRH-146, 5; Ervin; Shute; Nelson; Fontana.
71. The summaries themselves.
72. Fontana; Ervin.
73. Fontana.
74. *Ibid.*
75. Mott; SRH-123, 3.
76. SRH-132, 3.
77. SRH-035, 18.
78. SRH-145, 049.
79. SRH-062, 049.
80. *PHA*, 9:3985.
81. Kahn, 11.
82. *Ibid.*, 30.
83. Mott.
84. *PHA*, 11:5475.
85. *Ibid.*, 5269, 5277.
86. *Ibid.*, 11:5277, 5278.
87. *Ibid.*, 10:4660, 11:5278. He was technically on temporary duty at the White House as communications assistant to the naval aide.
88. *Ibid.*, 10:4660, 11:5280.
89. *Ibid.*, 9:4072.
90. *Ibid.*, 11:5284.
91. *Ibid.*, 11:5278.
92. *Ibid.*, 10:4659–665.
93. *Ibid.*, 5283.
94. McCrea. As an interesting confirmation, Franklin D. Roosevelt Library, Map Room File, Box 195, Folder Chart Room Log and Standing Orders, p. 67, notes that McCrea saw the president in the doctor's office on 14 and 16 May 1942.
95. McCrea.
96. SRH-200, 052.
97. Kahn, 30.
98. Adams, 237. Smedberg said that "probably Leahy brought it [MAGIC] around to him [Roosevelt]." Tending to support this is that Leahy knew of MAGIC since, in the late 1930s, he was chief of naval operations, when a cryptanalyst said of his attitudes to signal intelligence that "We couldn't ask for better. He is thoroughly sold" (SRH-355, 259). On the other hand, Elsey doubted that any MAGIC or ULTRA documents went through Leahy, and Mott said that Leahy did not have access to the intercepts he was bringing to Roosevelt.
99. Mott; inferred from Elsey.

100. Mott; Tyree.
101. Service record, Serial No. 093, National Personnel Records Center, St. Louis, Missouri. Clarke said that the colonel delivering to the White House was not in the Army but was a Marine. This would keep delivery in the Navy Department and eliminates a Colonel Boone who was in Army intelligence at the time—Colonel Joseph W. Boone, O15341 (U. S. War Department, Adjutant General's Office, *Army Directory*, April 20, 1943 [Washington], 174). The only Marine Corps Colonel Boone at the time was Ronald Aubry Boone. Department of the Navy, Marine Corps, Headquarters, History and Museums Branch, Reference Section.
102. Franklin D. Roosevelt Library, Map Room File, Box 15, Folder Casablanca Conference Trip File, Item QMU 171938Z (UTAH 53), and SRS 839, "Magic" Summary No. 490, 19 July 1943.
103. *Ibid.*, Item WHITE 21. Cochran, "The Influence of 'Magic' Intelligence," 348, errs in stating that item WHITE 8 in the above folder is identical to MAGIC Diplomatic Summary of 7/29/43; they are different.
104. Winston S. Churchill and Franklin D. Roosevelt, *The Complete Correspondence*, ed. Warren F. Kimball (Princeton, NJ: Princeton University Press, 1984), 3:321 for "appeared to me," 2:389 for "Much of it," 2:502–503 for "We know." Other references to intercepts at 2:4, 389, 502–503, 666–667, 672–673, 677, 3:229, 256, 321, 341, 388. Kimball says that all the intelligence files have not been declassified and suggests that intercepts sent by Churchill to Roosevelt but not yet published might be found therein. This is reinforced by Martin Gilbert's footnote in Randolph Churchill, then Martin Gilbert, *Winston Churchill* (Boston, MA: Houghton Mifflin, 1966–1988), p. 6 (1983): *Finest Hour, 1939–1941*, at 1260, based on a personal communication, that Churchill told them "Make sure the President knows this" or "Make sure the President sees this."
105. Franklin D. Roosevelt Library, Map Room File, Box 16, Folder Canadian Fishing Trip and Quadrant Conference, WHITE 112.
106. *Ibid.*, WHITE 128.
107. SRH-111; Carl Boyd, "Significance of MAGIC and the Japanese Ambassador to Berlin: (V) News of Hitler's Defense Preparations for Allied Invasion of Western Europe," *Intelligence and National Security*, 4 (July 1989), pp. 461–481 at 472–474; Hinsley, 3:2:32–33, 771–775.
108. SRH-305, 24.
109. Gerhard L. Weinberg, *Reflections on Running a War: Hitler, Churchill, Stalin, Roosevelt, Tojo*, Transcription of the 6th annual Phi Alpha Theta distinguished lecture on history at the State University of Albany on March 20, 1986 (n. p., n. d.), 11, is no doubt correct in observing that Roosevelt got through an enormous amount of paperwork each day and that he "kept track of the 'ultra' materials." Likewise, Cochran, "The Influence of 'Magic' Intelligence," 346, concludes that Roosevelt had "more than a passing interest in intelligence." On the other hand, Adams says, 237, that while Leahy continued to bring ULTRA to the president as it seemed pertinent, "Roosevelt was not much interested in details." None

of these comments answers the significant question of whether he much used the intercepts in running the war. On January 1944, Roosevelt, in a message to Churchill, cited an intercept as a possible answer to a puzzling international incident (Kimball, ed., 2:672–673, 677). This might indicate that he was reading the intercepts voluminously and carefully. On the other hand, his staff might have provided this information to him—an impression reinforced by Kimball's putting a bracketed "WDL?" at the end of the message to suggest that Leahy might have drafted it for him.

110. National Archives, Record Group 218, Leahy Papers, Folder 126, p. 189.
111. SRH-185, 013.
112. *Ibid.*, 004.
113. Corderman.
114. Rowlett.
115. Dallek, 362, 370.
116. SRH-035, 18–19; SRH-116, 014.
117. Nothing in Kimball, ed., 2, checking especially 20, 41–42, 75, 76; *FRUS, 1942*, 2:303–315; *FRUS, 1943*, 2:595–97; W. L. Beaulac (an American diplomat in Spain at the time), *Franco: Silent Ally in World War II* (Carbondale, IL: Southern Illinois University Press, 1986); James W. Cortada, *Two Nations Over Time: Spain and the United States, 1776–1977* (Westport, CT: Greenwood Press, 1978); or in Carlton J. H. Hayes (the ambassador), *Wartime Mission to Spain* (New York: Macmillan, 1945).
118. Franklin D. Roosevelt Library, Map Room Files, Box 167, Naval Aide's File: A/16-Japan and Japanese Islands, 1942–1945, Memo for the President from Marshall, 5 Aug 1942; *FRUS, 1942*, 3:616. I am obliged to Dr. Carl Boyd for this information.
119. McCrea; Mott; Tyree.
120. Gilbert, 6:611, 613, and the numerous references under "Enigma decrypts" in 7 (*Road to Victory*); Martin Gilbert, memorandum, 17 March 1987; Hinsley, 2:4 and entries under "Churchill" in the index.
121. The effort that fails to convince is that of Cochran. He says, at 346, that the decision to get Italy out of the war "could well have been based upon Magic information" about "major strategic differences between the Axis powers, desperate economic and social conditions in Italy, and growing political instability among the fascist elite," citing 17 reports from April to June 1943. But not only did many nonintellingence factors contribute to this decision, not only had the idea been considered even before the North African invasion, but, as Cochran admits, no evidence links the intelligence to the decision, and without evidence his hypothesis remains unproved. The more plausible effort is that of Rohwer. He argues that Churchill knew via ULTRA of Hitler's 21 June 1941 order to U-boats that they not attack large warships whose nationality they did not know, that Churchill passed this information to Roosevelt, and that it encouraged the president to support Britain in the Atlantic more energetically than if he feared German retaliation. Rohwer says that U.S. Navy situation maps show the U-boats dispositions and that this is "clear evidence of the re-transmission of 'Ultra' intelligence from London to

Washington." But National Archives, Record Group 457, SRMN-033, Part I, "Cominch File of Messages on U-Boat, Estimates and Situation Reports October 1941-September 1942," which gives individual submarine positions and estimated positions, does not reach back to June, the Navy's Operational Archives does not have any earlier files, and none of the messages in Kimball, ed., 1:210–281 (21 June to 7 December 1941) deal with any such instructions to U-boats. Thus, plausible as Rohwer's suggestion is, it must await further documentation before winning at least my acceptance.

6

EDWARD BELL AND HIS
ZIMMERMANN TELEGRAM
MEMORANDA*

Edward Bell (1882–1924), the American diplomat who dealt with British intelligence in the matter of the Zimmermann telegram, which pushed the United States into World War I, has been unknown in all but his name. This note offers a brief biography and photograph. It prints two unpublished memoranda that Bell wrote giving his inside story of the telegram, written to explain why an author should not reveal its solution. Also appended are a memo about that solution and its disclosure to the Americans by the telegram's main British cryptanalyst and a note revealing the ignorance of the German minister in Mexico about how the telegram came to Allied knowledge.

Intelligence historians know Edward Bell as the World War I American diplomat in London who liaised with British intelligence in the greatest intelligence coup of all time: the British solution and revelation to the United States of the Zimmermann telegram. This 16 January 1917 message of the German Foreign Minister to the president of Mexico, offering to return to Mexico its former territories of Texas, New Mexico, and Arizona if it would war on the United States, gave a final push to US entry into World War I. But other than his name, and despite his role, the literature of the field gives not even the most basic biographical facts about Edward Bell (Figure 6.1).

I was stimulated to seek additional information by two events. One was my finding, in the National Archives, two Bell letters about the Zimmermann telegram; these provide a firsthand account.[1] They were written to urge that the story not be told by Burton W. Hendrick

---

* From *Intelligence and National Security*, 14(3) (Autumn 1999), 143–159.

Figure 6.1   Edward Bell. (Virginia Surtees.)

in his forthcoming biography of the American ambassador at the time, Walter Hines Page. The story was published anyway. The other event was my accidental discovery that one of Bell's daughters had married the World War II Office of Strategic Services chief in London and later American ambassador to the Court of St James's, David K. E. Bruce. I knew he was long dead, but his address was easy to find. I telephoned Mrs Bruce in Washington. She had passed away a few days earlier. But her secretary suggested that I wait a few months and then write to her sister, Virginia Surtees, in London. I did. She replied at once with a warm and detailed letter.[2] It provided the human portrait that filled out Bell's official chronology and enabled me to give life to a figure who had played a critical role in so significant a drama.

Edward Bell was born in New York City on 9 October 1882 into a family described as 'so Old New York that even before the war some of them were complaining about the nouveau riche invading Manhattan, not a surprising reaction for people who not so long before had kept those *arriviste* Astors off the Social Register'.[3] After Cutler's School in New York, Bell attended Harvard, where he was in the same class as and a close friend of his fellow New Yorker Franklin Roosevelt.

Both were members of the Hasty Pudding Club, the social and literary club Alpha Delta Phi, and the Institute of 1770, an oratorical society and at the time the oldest and largest society at Harvard; Bell was also a member of Sphinx and the Cercle Français.[4]

In their junior year, the two young men toured Britain, celebrating, Roosevelt wrote, 'a most heavenly 21st birthday of Ned's at the Café Royal – just the four of us – goldfish on the table – music, etc. – all in all a perfect little private dining room'.[5]

They graduated from Harvard in 1904, Bell marrying Gertrude Mays Wood immediately thereafter. He worked for a while as a clerk in a brokerage, and from 1909 to 1911 served as vice and deputy consul general in Cairo. On 2 March 1911 he joined the Foreign Service, becoming the secretary of the legation in Tehran on 17 March at a salary of $2,000; 51 weeks later, he became second secretary at Havana. In May 1913, he sought and obtained the second secretaryship of the London embassy.[6] Upon his sailing in the *Lusitania* for the post, Roosevelt wired him on 23 September, 'Goodbye and good luck. Don't acquire an accent with the other things British'.[7]

He arrived there on the 30th, a few days before he turned 32 and a few months after Page became ambassador.[8] A few months later he divorced his first wife, who later joined a group of Paris literary lesbians, and in 1914 married Etelka Surtees, whose father, a member of the elite Coldstream Guards, came from a family long prominent in County Durham, in the north of England.[9]

Bell was about 5ft 9in, with brown eyes and dark hair, always very well dressed. He burst with energy. He walked quickly; he worked hard. A man of keen intelligence and great enthusiasm, he always seemed to be in the center of the group. This likeableness may explain why he got on so well with the British.[10]

A British woman who worked at the embassy, Emily Bax, painted a similar portrait of him. She called him 'a regular cyclone, with flashing black eyes, uncertain temper, brilliant intuitive mind, and a flood of invective that reminded me of the best efforts of a bargee. At first glance', she wrote, 'he looked like the quietest sort of conventional gentleman, perfect in every detail, and his attitude towards Mr Laughlin [Irwin Laughlin, the embassy's first secretary] and the Ambassador was most respectful. But let any little thing happen to disturb him, and off went the lid! Frank Hodson [the embassy messenger] would fly from him, and everybody else gave him a wide berth.' Moreover, she thought, 'There was nothing of the friendly helping hand about him. He believed in leaving people to their fate if they hadn't enough sense to find their own way out of difficulties.' Still, 'apart from boiling up like a bottle of soda water whenever he was crossed, he was one of the most charming as well as amusing men who was ever at the Embassy, so dynamic, so unexpected, so thrillingly interesting!'[11]

'Truth was a passion with him,' wrote a Harvard friend. 'Sometimes impatient of the inaccuracies of those of less exact information than himself he would fairly shout, in correcting them, "Get it right!" '[12]

Bell apparently had a conspiratorial view of the world – 'he seemed to feel that sinister forces were at work to undermine the United States', Bax wrote, including the British Foreign Office – and this perhaps contributed to his being given what Bax called 'one of the most difficult of all jobs in wartime – spies and secret-service activities and the checking-up of many people who were prancing round the world on mysterious errands, mostly unlawful'. As a consequence of this work, 'He used to say that what he had learned had so disillusioned him that after this he would not trust his own mother under oath!'[13]

After he had served in London for a while, his superior reported that 'Mr Bell is exceedingly intelligent, ambitious, and painstaking. He is all that he should be. I have never met... a more efficient Secretary, whether in the Chancery or in Society. He is, in my opinion, the exact type of what a Secretary in the Service should be'.[14]

Still, by mid-1916 eight men had been promoted over him. He resented it and threatened to resign. But a friend at the embassy wrote to Senator Henry F. Lippert of Rhode Island, who forwarded to State the judgment that 'Bell has handled his work with consummate skill and has slaved from early morning until twelve and one o'clock at night, including Sundays for two years, and has taken care of the most important work of the Embassy in connection with Scotland Yard, the Admiralty and the War Office.' Ambassador Page wrote to the Secretary of State that 'I simply cannot afford to lose Bell'. By November, Bell had agreed 'to sit tight', Page cabled. But it took until July for him to win promotion.[15]

The friend's comments were accurate. By mid-1915, Bell had established extraordinarily close relations with Britain's Director of Naval Intelligence, Captain Reginald 'Blinker' Hall, and later with his staff, particularly Claud Serocold, Hall's personal assistant, and Dick Herschell, the Second Baron Herschell, who headed the diplomatic section of Room 40, Hall's codebreaking unit. Bell was 'Ned' to his American friends, 'Eddie' to his British. 'He never betrayed any of the confidences with which he was entrusted, and as a consequence was able to extract a great deal more secret information from Hall and the Intelligence Division than would otherwise have been possible', wrote Patrick Beesly in his *Room 40*.

In August 1915, Hall – already practicing the propaganda that would culminate in the brilliant coup of the Zimmermann telegram – gave Bell some documents for transmission to the US government. These had been taken in Britain from an American journalist who had been given papers of Count Constantin Dumba, who was the Austro-Hungarian ambassador in Washington, of Count Johann Heinrich von Bernstorff, the German ambassador in Washington, and of Captain Franz von Papen, his military attaché. The documents, which referred to fomenting strikes and disruption in American factories, caused a sensation when they were published. They added to anti-German feeling in the United States.[16]

In his most important case, Hall used Bell as a chief interme-diary for the Zimmermann telegram. Room 40 had solved a mes-sage of 16 January 1917 from the German Foreign Minister, Arthur Zimmermann, to the President of Mexico. It revealed that Germany was about to begin unrestricted submarine warfare, warned that this would probably bring the United States into World War I, and proposed that if Mexico would join Germany, Mexico would, upon victory, regain 'lost territories' in Texas, New Mexico, and Arizona.[17]

To satisfy himself that the solution was genuine, Bell, using the Room 40 skeleton solution of German diplomatic code 13040, decoded at least the first part of the cryptogram himself before turn-ing over the tedious job to Nigel de Grey, the chief solver of the mes-sage, whose newly declassified memorandum is printed below.[18]

The solution was cabled to President Woodrow Wilson, who gave it to the doyen of Washington correspondents, the Associated Press's Edwin M. Hood, to be made public.[19] The story appeared in news-papers all over the country on 1 March. It exacerbated anti-German feeling in America and contributed to Congress's declaration of war on 6 April.[20]

The importance of this incident, which underlined the closeness of Bell's relationship with the British, may have been one of the reasons that 'C', the head of the British secret service, gave a dinner for Bell on 23 January 1919. The diplomat was later assigned to Tokyo as counselor of the embassy there; Roosevelt, a former assistant secretary of the Navy, recommended him to the naval attaché, calling Bell 'one of my greatest personal friends'.[21] He acted as chargé from May 1920 to September 1921. Of this assignment, a Harvard friend said that 'In confiding a post of such delicacy and importance to so young a man the State Department could hardly have given a more distinguished mark of its high opinion'.[22]

Bell was assigned to the American delegation to the Conference of Limitation of Armaments in Washington in November 1921. Codebreaking played a role in this: American cryptanalysts solving Japanese cablegrams provided the US negotiators with useful information; it would be interesting to know whether he knew of this. After some eight months as chief of the Division of Current Information, whose duties included intelligence, Bell went, in November 1922, as counselor of embassy, to Peking. At 7.45 a.m. 28 October 1924, he died of a heart attack following a fall on the embassy steps. A high official in the State Department, Joseph Grew, a few days later called him 'one of our most brilliant officers'.[23]

He must have been an attractive and memorable personality. When his daughter Virginia asked people who had known him in the State Department about him, their faces lit up. And when, during World War II, when Bell had been dead for 20 years, Virginia's husband, a Foreign Office official, visited the State Department on business, he was introduced everywhere as 'Ned Bell's son-in-law'.[24] Such was the length of his shadow!

Bell's memoranda follow. The originals may be found in the National Archives, Record Group 59, Entry 346, Office of the Counselor, Leland Harrison's General Correspondence, Box 7, Folder Page-Hendrick. In addition, two other documents of interest in the matter are appended. One is de Grey's memorandum, recently released to the United Kingdom's Public Record Office in London under file number HW3/177. De Grey says that Dillwyn Knox helped him solve the message, not the Rev. William Montgomery, who has been credited with the assistance. The fourth item adds little to the story of the telegram but demonstrates von Eckardt's utter, and somewhat pathetic, lack of knowledge of the matter. It may be found in Leland Harrison's General Correspondence, Box 3, Folder Dr Heinrich von Eckhardt's [sic] Trip Through US to [from] Mexico, Statement dictated by Heinrich von Eckhardt at New York City, on 25 March 1919, to William Neunhoffer, of the Department of Justice, p. 4.

Bell's Memorandum to Hurley

Tokyo, July 13, 1921

Private and Most Secret.

W.L. Hurley, Esquire,[25]
  etc., etc., etc.,
    Department of State,
      Washington

Dear Bill:

Kindly look at the enclosed copy of a letter, from a gentleman I never recall having met [Hendrick], which has caused me to do some pretty hard thinking in the last few days.

Whatever Blinker [Hall] could have been thinking about beats me altogether but at any rate he seems to have spilt the beans. If L.H. [Leland Harrison][26] is within reach you had better get hold of him at once, for he knows more about this matter than you do, or anyone else except myself.

In the first place, Blinker's action (always assuming the Department was not consulted) constitutes a breach of confidence. The arrangement regarding the Z. telegram was not unilateral: it was entered into between the two Governments. Just as Mr Page, L.H., or I would have had no right to give the show away without consulting the parties of the other part, so they have no right to do so without consulting us and obtaining our permission.

You have the London records on tap, and I hope L.H. is there, but in case he is not I shall rehearse the salient points: Z. sent the telegram through the Swedes via Stockholm over the London cable to the Swede at B.A. [Buenos Aires] who turned it over to Luxburg [Count Karl Ludwig von Luxburg, chargé d'affaires at the German embassy there] for transmission to Bernstorff for Eckhardt[27] [Heinrich J.F. von Eckardt,

German minister in Mexico] in Mexico. In the preceeding summer the Bosh had sent out a new table for the cipher code to B. in Washington by the submarine DEUTSCHLAND. It hadn't been used much and Blinker's lads had been able to do little with it so when this message went through London in this new code it yielded very little to their efforts. Luxburg repeated it in the same code to B. As however Eckhardt did not have the new table B. had to decode and recode it to him in the old book. Blinker had a plant in the telegraph office in Mexico who sent back copies of all cipher messages which passed through for Eckhardt, as opportunity offered. This message was sent in January and a copy of the cipher text, in the form in which B. sent it to Eckhardt, reached Blinker towards the end of February. He was able to uncork it, as it was in the old code, and this not only gave him the message itself but also, by comparison with the text that went through London, a start on the new code. It was a kind of Rosetta Stone.

Blinker was torn between reluctance to give away the fact that he could read the Bosh signals and the desire to pin something good right on them. He took me into his confidence and I pressed for the latter. Finally it was agreed that Mr. Balfour (then Secretary [of State] for Foreign Affairs but previously First Lord and consequently acquainted with Reggie's performances) should give a translation to Mr. Page with assurances that it was the goods, as being a stronger move than Reggie's giving it to me. Remember, this was our first offence. Afterwards we dispensed with intermediaries.

Mr. Page came back from his interview with Balfour with the translation in his hand and blood in his eye, and Eugene [Shoecraft, private secretary to Page] and I sat up all night getting off the telegram. The Department published it through the A.P. (being a little new at the game) instead of direct, but admitted responsibility. The resultant sensation is history. Mr. John W. Davis, who at that time was Solicitor-General and very close to the then President and Mr. Lansing [Secretary of State Robert Lansing], told me in London, after he became Ambassador[28] and *before* I disclosed the true inwardness of the affair to him, that no single event contributed more directly to the ultimate declaration of war. (The publication in Washington of the telegram occurred in the twilight zone between 2 February and 6 April 1917.)[29]

Immediately on the publication certain Senators registered skepticism, suggesting it was an English plant. The Department, meanwhile, had obtained from the telegraph office in Washington a copy of the text as B. had sent it to Eckhardt, wired the groups to us in London and gave orders that it should be deciphered by one of the Embassy from the book in the possession of our friends – to make sure! I took it up to the Admiralty and did the job myself and it was all correct, and Eugene and I sent back the true reading (in German) of the decode by telegraph much to the Department's joy. And to make everything just right Z. himself admitted the soft impeachment (and the authenticity of the telegram) a day or two later.

There were two sound reasons why the world should have been led to believe at the time that it was the Americans who had done the trick: First to put the Bosh off the scent. It wouldn't have done at all for him to have known how fly the English were as that might have put ideas in his head (of which he remained innocent to the last) about naval radio messages and the Berlin–Madrid W/T. Second, to throw a scare into him about ourselves; to put the wind up him and cramp his style in the U.S. In both these respects the vaccination worked like a charm, and the world rang with the praise of our wonderful Secret Service. Do you remember how for months afterwards the Treasury and Justice each swore that they had done the job and tried to put each other in the Ananias Club? And Pennoyer's hypothesis that Mrs. Warren Robbins must have worked it in B. A.? [Buenos Aires] (this particularly pleased Blinker).

It was always a most jealously guarded secret and now it has been revealed. It makes no difference, perhaps, to Reggie and the F.O. now; and the latter were always furious that we got the (undeserved) credit. But such childish feelings are beside the point, which is this: the Wilson administration, which was the Government of the day, gained much *kudos* over this affair. It bucked up the public at a critical time and enhanced our national prestige. To give the show away now would probably create a bad impression, not merely of the late administration but of the Government as a whole and as a permanent, continuous and going concern. Political parties mean nothing to me; moreover, if the Department feels that no harm can be done by the publication of this correspondence I am content. But I perceive disquieting elements in the situation and I suggest, therefore, that this matter be at once taken up with Fletcher [Under Secretary of State Henry R. Fletcher] or with the Secretary himself, explained in all its

aspects, and their views ascertained. Then, if they feel that publication would be unwise, every effort should be made to stop this biographer's mouth. If necessary an appeal to Mrs. Page or Arthur [Page,
the ambassador's son] would do it. Tell them, if necessary, that the old
Chief would never have consented to any such thing; that I have often
discussed it with him, and know better than anyone, and I say that.
As a fact, he would loop the loop in his grave at the very idea. In my
mind's eye I can see him now, heels on the brass fender, cigar (unlit)
in corner of mouth, shouting with rage at the very suggestion that he
would ever 'let down' the Government in whose service he laid down
his life. God bless his old heart.

I enclose a letter, unsealed, I have addressed to the biographer. If
the Great Ones approve, seal and send it on. If not, burn. In either
case telegraph what you have done with the letter, and what the
Department decides to do about the whole situation.

The biographer refers to twelve telegrams on this subject. These
must include the cheery exchanges between Z. and Eckhardt as to
whether the latter or B. was responsible for the leak, including the
part about the two conspirators sitting in the dark, reading the telegrams in a low voice, burning them and scattering the ashes. You will
find them all in the Mexico telegram file, 1917. Even at this distance
of time and space I can't help laughing at the thought.

I gather from Enclosure No. 1 that Reggie didn't blow the gaff on our
other transactions, as the writer distinctly states he would like to know of
any other similar incidents. Should the Department be willing to allow
the publication of the Z. stuff there is no reason why they shouldn't
tell how we spoofed Luxburg which might make the Argentines sore
at the British. This would only be fair game as you will remember how
Hirst tried to make us the goat when we were thinking of putting up
a similar game on the Chileans and Erckhert the Bosh Minister there.
(This never came off as I tipped Leland to lay off it. See London files.)

But whatever happens, don't ever let anyone give away the Bolo or
Caillaux business.[30] The French probably to this day believe *we* really
got the goods, and awful complications might result if the complete
truth were known. Also, *in re* Bolo, there was once upon a time a
slight misunderstanding of a group. Leland will remember.

So there you are, my dear old Bill, and go to it. Whatever the
Department decides is good enough for me. But remind Leland that

Reggie said Leland and I would be insane if either of us ever set foot in Germany again as long as we lived. I didn't ask his reasons but he meant it all right; clicked his false teeth, horrid – what price, after this?

Now I am well warmed to the subject, in case anyone high in authority should like to dip into the juicy parts show them the correspondence about the Austrian peace offer of March, 1918, which I got to the President two days before he received it from Riano, the Spanish Ambassador. Also the message sent in October, 1918, to Gen. Kress von Kressenstein[31] by [Wilhelm] Solf, then Secretary for Foreign Affairs, now Ambassador in Tokyo, and touted as the next German Ambassador to Washington.

Before I forget it, if it is deemed advisable, Enclosures 1 and 2 may be copied and sent to Blinker with appropriate explanation, but don't do anything to hurt his feelings.

You will, I know, be sorry to hear that my health is very bad; so bad I am writing to the Department in this pouch that I must leave directly the new Ambassador arrives.

Etelka and the children are at the sea-side and seem to be enjoying themselves. I hope if all goes well that you and I will meet before long.

Yours ever,
Ned

Enclosures [not printed here]:

1. Mr. Hendrick to Mr. Bell, June 17, 1921.
2. Letter addressed to B.T. Hendrick, Esquire, dated July 13, 1921.

Bell's Memorandum to Harrison

Department of State
Division of Current Information
1 May 1922
Memorandum
Most Secret
Mr. Harrison:
Dear Leland:

At your direction, for the preservation of secrecy, this memorandum is written in long-hand.

On Saturday, April 29th, Mr. Secretary handed to you and me an article by Mr. Burton J. Hendrick, which is intended to form a chapter in the book he is writing on the life of Mr. Walter H. Page, formerly Ambassador to Great Britain, under whom I served in London for 5 years. Mr. Hendrick is to bring out parts of the proposed book in the "World's Work" Magazine of which Mr. Arthur Page, the late Ambassador's son, is editor.

Last summer I received a letter from Mr. Laughlin, formerly Counsellor of the Embassy in London, acquainting me that Mr. Hendrick was about to write such a book and telling me that Mr. Hendrick had received from Sir R. Hall and Sir W. Tyrrell[32] information as to the source from which the well-known 'Zimmermann telegram' had sprung. I was horrified and disgusted at this intelligence and wrote and telegraphed Mr. Hurley (U-2) urging that this be suppressed if possible. My reasons for taking this view are easily explained.

1. This information was communicated to our Govt. by the British Govt. (Naval Intelligence Division of the Admiralty) between the time we broke off diplomatic relations with Germany and the time we declared war on that country (last days of Feb. 1917). It was communicated for the obvious reason that if we knew it, we would be more likely to declare war on German that [sic] we otherwise would have been. It was agreed at the time that we should give out this telegram as of our own information for the reasons (a) that it would put the Germans off the track of the true source (British) and (b) that it would put the fear of God into the Germans in their dealings with us, and cramp their style.

   This agreement was made between Sir Reginald Hall (D.N.I., Admiralty) and myself, as you are well aware, and you and I have always known and understood that it, and many similar arrangements, later entered into, stood and were not to be broken save by mutual consent. I may point to the agreement about the German code known as 55515 which we promised never to make known that we had in our possession (retrieved from sunken German cruiser in Baltic). It was subsequently desired to make use of telegrams in this code in the Rumely case,[33] and Mr. Hurley, your successor, telegraphed all over South America in 1920 to find Sir R. Hall to get his permission before we would let the Atty-Gen use them.

2. Mr. Hendrick I know from various sources is unaware that the Luxburg telegrams, the Caillaux telegrams and the Bolo telegrams to say nothing of Bernstorff's cipher *despatches* which have been made public at various times all came from the same (British) sources, but any German, French or other intelligence officer familiar with these matters would, directly he became aware that the "Zimmermann telegram" was sprung from a British source, deduce that these other telegrams also came from a British source. That brings us to the next point. The British gave us the telegrams which we gave the French *as from ourselves* on the basis of which the French shot [?] Bolo and kept Caillaux in jail for 2 or 3 years. Bolo is gone and cannot be recalled, but Caillaux may return to political life one day[34] and I feel that it would be extremely awkward if the question of the source or authenticity of these telegrams should ever be called up by the French. This in my opinion is the reason why Mr. Hendrick's story should never be published, and I think it is a very cogent one.

There is another reason why it should not be published in present form, even if unobjectionable for other reasons: it is stiff with inaccuracies. I shall not attempt to go into them here but will be glad to explain them to you or Mr. Secretary.

Finally, there is one more point. I gathered from what Mr. Secretary said to us on April 29th that Mr. Hendrick had urged as one reason why this should be published that 'it was widely known,' or 'everyone knows it.' This is simply not the truth. When the telegram was first published certain people proclaimed it was an English 'plant.' The Government put the quietus on that in short order and from that day I have never seen that story revived. That alone shows how well the secret was kept. In London Mr. Page, Mr. Laughlin (Counsellor) myself and Mr. Shoecraft (P. Sec.) alone knew about it. Shoecraft and I put up all the telegrams ourselves. Here, the President, Mr. House, Mr. Lansing, Mr. Polk,[35] yourself and (in part) Mr. Salmon[36] were the only ones who knew. Later, others – Winslow, Hurley and one or two more got to know but there has never been a whisper in the papers.

I can well remember other Secretaries in the Embassy in London, my colleagues, in whom I had every confidence, speculating at the time on how our Govt. got the information. They do not know to this day. Under the circumstances to say it is widely known is fantastic.

For the above reasons, I hope Mr. Secretary will decline to give consent to Mr. Hendrick to publish. Indeed, this was settled long ago by Mr. Arthur Page writing that he would not do so without the Dept. consent, which Mr. Fletcher, in an interview, *declined to give*. That ought to have settled the matter for ever and although I am a warm personal friend of Mr. Arthur Page I do not think he ought to have allowed the matter to be brought up again.

E.B.

De Grey Memorandum

Zimmermann Telegram
A Footnote to Friedman's account[37]

31st October 1945

By Nigel de Grey

So much has been written on this subject and so much of what has been written is incorrect in minor respects that the following facts, which are as correct as may be after the lapse of many years, may be of interest.

The version of the telegram upon which we worked was the version in 13040, which reached us from the Cable Office in transit. Although 13040 was an old code book and had been superseded by 18470 before the 1914–18 war, it was still in use in all the smaller Diplomatic posts.[38] In construction it was similar to its successor, which we had secured in the Middle East.[39]

7500 had been too recently introduced for Commander Rotter[40] to have progressed far in its solution It should be remembered that he worked alone or nearly alone on a 10,000 group code which was 'hatted'.[41] It was only in use to Washington and we had had but few messages in it.

By the time that the Zimmermann telegram reached us we had been at work some time on 13040. Only one person worked on it for many months, then two and later three. It was a long code, our experience of book building was at its beginnings and there were many gaps unfilled.

The telegram was sorted first to Knox[42] whose business it was to fill in any known groups. His knowledge of German was at that time too slender for him to tackle any difficult passages in telegrams (and German diplomatic telegrams can be very ponderous) so that the procedure was that if the telegrams appeared from what could be read to have any interest he brought them to me for further study.

We could at once read enough groups for Knox to see that the telegram was important. Together he and I worked solidly all the morning upon it. With our crude methods and lack of staff no elaborate indexing of groups had been developed – only constantly recurring groups were noted in the working copies of the code as our fancy dictated. Work therefore was slow and laborious but by about mid-day we had got a skeleton version, sweating with excitement as we went on because neither of us doubted the importance of what we had in our hands. Was not the American-German situation our daily bread?

As soon as I felt sufficiently secure in our version, even with all its gaps, I took it down to Admiral Hall. It is worth recalling here that although Ewing was nominally our head, Blinker had made a compact with a few of the 'research party' that if ever we dug out anything of real importance we were to take it direct to him without showing it to Ewing whom he mistrusted as a chatter-box (and rightly).

Blinker [Hall] was always accessible to the lads of Room 40, at least he always was to me at that time because I was getting him all the news from Diplomatic Germany.

I was young and excited (so incidentally was Dilly Knox) and I ran all the way to his room, found Seracold [*sic*] (his P/A) alone and Blinker free. I burst out breathlessly 'Do you want America in the war Sir?' 'Yes, why?' said Blinker. 'I've got a telegram that will bring them in if you give it to them.' As may be seen I had all the confidence of my years.

Then came the job of convincing a man who knew no German with a half readable text. And Blinker was no sort of a fool. But he was patient with me and was convinced. Then the three of us talked out all the implications and as I was daily decoding the messages I knew the position between Wilson, Lansing, Bernstorff and Bethmann-Hollweg[43] pretty well. I remember urging D.N.I. to give it to America.

Finally he naturally said he must think it over and sent me off saying, 'But before I do anything I'll tell you what I'm going to do'. That was why we all loved Blinker, he played fair by us.

I think it must have been the next day that he sent for me. He asked for the best version possible that we could produce – in fact we had got only a little further with the help, I feel sure, of Rotter our most experienced man but unfamiliar with 13040. He then discussed with me again the pros and cons. Obviously we had two fears. The first and by far the greatest was that we should 'blow' Room 40 – a crazy risk to run when it is remembered that we read the German Naval codes operationally and always currently. Unrestricted submarine warfare to be declared at once and the shipping position already hazardous. Not the easiest decision for a D.N.I. to make. Secondly we did not want to risk the fact that we took drop copies in London off the cables or reveal that we had bowled out the Swedes in a non-neutral act. The first would have lost us an invaluable source of intelligence if the coup with America failed, the second would have created an unpleasant situation at a pretty critical moment in the war when such things are better avoided.

I remember his saying to me 'Our first job will be to convince the Americans that it's true – how are we to do that? Who would they believe? Is there any Englishman whom they will believe? I've been thinking and the only person I think they would believe is Balfour[44] – Do you think they'd take his word for it?' To all Englishmen at that time Balfour stood head and shoulders above the politicians as the wise man, the elder statesman. He was out of the political arena and no longer tarred with any party brush. I remember plumping without hesitation for him – indeed I thought then and have always thought that Blinker's use of Balfour as his mouthpiece was a stroke of genius (such as he used to exhibit from time to time). Balfour had been First Lord and knew all about Room 40 and was then Foreign Secretary. 'I shall go and see him at once' and he there and then telephoned for an appointment. As I went out Blinker said to me 'You boys think you do a very difficult job, but don't forget I have made use of the intelligence you give me and that's more difficult.'

Most of the rest of the story is now historical but there are a few points more to elucidate. Blinker's plan to cover the source was to get a copy of the telegram from some other place through which it passed – not

London. Moreover the version that went through Bernstorff's office[45] was in 7500 so far as I recollect. This was no use for proving to the Americans that the telegram was genuine. It was a 'hatted' cypher, very little of it was solved and if challenged might well have failed to come up to scratch when applied to another text. Blinker would not have hesitated, in fact did eventually tell the Americans to get a copy from Sayville,[46] but that got him nowhere. Although we had the 13040 version and knew Eckhardt [sic] had no 7500 book, without disclosing our drop copy source, we could not produce it. Nor could we prove that the telegram had actually been delivered in Mexico to the German Legation and had not been faked in London. The only thing therefore was to steal a copy in Mexico City in the form delivered to the German Legation. We had two chances (a) the cable copy (b) the copy sent from Washington by Bernstorff which we banked on being also in 13040.

Hence the delay till the end of February.[47] How we succeeded in stealing the copy I never knew but money goes a long way in Mexico and steal it we did.

The next point worth recording is the true story of Page's telegram of March 2nd, 1917.

Although I remained in charge of the work on 13040 it had been decided that this could be mainly carried out by my two assistants while I was put on either to the Austrian Fleet code or unless my memory plays me false to a new German Naval code introduced about then. Anyhow Zimmermann had simmered down and we in Room 40 had heard no more details. Suddenly I was sent for again and told I was to decypher the telegram for the benefit of Edward Bell of the American Embassy. Needless to say we had worked like beavers on the telegram in the meantime and I knew our by now practically complete version by heart. Being in a hurry I grabbed my own version of 13040 without thinking and went off to D.N.I.'s room. There Edward Bell produced a copy of the telegram and invited me both to decypher it in his presence and to explain the system as I went along. I gaily proceeded and all went well with the first few groups but then on coming to the next I found my book blank and realized with horror that I hadn't done my homework. I had not written up my book and this was by way of being a demonstration to the Americans of the absolute cast iron certainty of our story, good enough to carry firm conviction to their hesitating hearts.

If I stopped and fetched another book he would suspect at once that we had faked it up for his benefit. If I let him see that I was writing it down out of my head he would not believe me. If he did not believe me we should fail and have lost the greatest opportunity ever presented to us. Several seconds of bloody sweat. Then I bluffed. I showed him all the groups when they had been written in my book and passed quickly over those that were not, writing the words into the copy of the telegram by heart.

Edward Bell, most charming man, was thoroughly convinced – the more easily I think in that he wanted to be convinced and anyhow regarded the whole thing as black magic.

A more unconvincing demonstration could never have been given. But it gave Wilson his big stick for the West and South West and America came into the war months earlier than she would otherwise have done.

'Absolutely satisfactory result' as Page said.

The 'Spurlos versenkt'[48] telegrams which afterwards attained notoriety were almost entirely the [decoding] work of Montgomery who succeeded me.[49] His German was excellent and he polished up all our earlier efforts by months of toil.

Many of the statements made by Admiral Hall are incorrect. Some were I think wilfully so – others were due to faulty memory, a thing which never prevented him in after life from making categorical statements, if it suited him, without checking his evidence.

The Zimmermann Note

Mr. von Eckhardt [sic] thinks he should not be blamed by the United States for the Zimmermann note, because it was simply a note of instruction from the Berlin government addressed to him, and was in no way inspired by him; in fact he claimed if he had been able to communicate with Berlin he would have advised his government that the scheme was impracticable and impossible. He further declared that the inception and exposure of the note terminated the plans enunciated, and that he could have only considered carrying out of instructions if he could have been assured of Japan's friendship. In another conversation he stated to me that if the note had not been exposed he was not prepared to say what he would have done in furtherance of the plan suggested. He was most anxious to learn how the Zimmermann note was secured and several times asked me (with the statement if I could not answer him he would not expect me to do so) how the Zimmermann note was intercepted, being particularly anxious to know if it came into the possession of this government in the course of ordinary investigations (which would include, according to his interpretation 'legitimate theft') or whether its exposure was the result of traitorous conduct of a German officer, adding if a German had sold it for money it must have been an officer, and that he suspected a certain German officer. I stated to him I was not in a position to answer his query.

Notes

1. I have since noticed that Friedrich Katz had earlier found and used the first of these letters—under a different archival designation—in his rich and authoritative *The Secret War in Mexico* (Chicago, IL: University of Chicago Press, 1981), pp. 357–359.

2. Virginia Surtees, March 19, 1996. Suttees is the author of more than a dozen books on art and art history. *The Writers Directory, 1996–1998*.

3. Nelson D. Lankford, *The Last American Aristocrat: The Biography of David K.E. Bruce, 1898–1977* (Boston, MA: Little, Brown, 1996), p. 170.

4. Harvard University Archives, HUG300:B12759 (Bell's biographical folder); *Harvard College: Class of 1904*, Secretary's First Report (Cambridge, MA: Harvard UP Printed for the Class), pp. 114, 122, 123, 116, 132; Paul M. Nash and Joseph H. A. Symonds (eds.) *The Harvard Club Book, 1903–1904* (Cambridge: Powell Press, 1904), p. 58.

5. Geoffrey C. Ward, *Before the Trumpet: Young Franklin Roosevelt, 1882–1905* (New York: Harper & Row, 1985), p. 248. Roosevelt, as assistant secretary of the Navy, visited Bell in July 1918 and held an "old fashioned reunion" with his classmate at a London club. See Frank Freidel, *Franklin D. Roosevelt: The Apprenticeship* (Boston, MA: Little, Brown, 1952), p. 349. In 1917, a letter from Bell persuaded Roosevelt to remove a member of the naval attaché's office. And upon Roosevelt's nomination for the vice presidency in 1920. Bell wrote to congratulate him and to predict he would be president one day (National Archives, Franklin D. Roosevelt Library, Bell file).

6. Bell's biographical folder and *Harvard Class of 1904: Twenty-Fifth Anniversary Report June 1929* (Norwood, MA: Privately Printed for the Class by the Plimpton Press, n.d.), p. 49, for pre-London assignments; National Archives, Record Group 59, Bell's personnel file.

7. Roosevelt Library, Bell file (note 5).

8. United States, Department of State, *Register of the Department of State*, 19 December 1917 (Washington, DC: Government Printing Office, 1918), p. 75. (Henceforth, *Register* (1917).)

9. Lankford (note 3), pp. 169–170.

10. Surtees (note 2).

11. Emily Bax, *Miss Bax of the Embassy* (Boston, MA: Houghton Mifflin, 1939), pp. 248–249.

12. *Harvard Class of 1904* (note 6), p. 50.

13. Bax (note 11).

14. Bell's biographical file (note 6).

15. *Ibid.*

16. Patrick Beesly, *Room 40: British Naval Intelligence, 1914–1918* (New York: Harcourt Brace Jovanovich, 1982), pp. 227, 250, 237, 225, 229; Reinhard Doerries, *Imperial Challenge: Ambassador Count Bernstorff and German-American Relations, 1908–1917,* trans. Christie D. Shannon (Chapel Hill, NC: UNC Press, 1989), p. 115; *New York Times*, September 6, 1915, p. 1:1, September 10, 1915, p. 1:6.

17. By far the best source for the origin of the telegram is Katz (note 1), pp. 350–353. He also describes the reaction to the disclosure at pp. 361–378.

18. National Archives, Record Group 59, Department of State Decimal Files 862.20212 1/2. Only the first page and a few lines of the second are in Bell's handwriting. The rest of the eight-page document is in handwriting identified by John de Grey as that of his father Nigel.

19. J Rives Childs says somewhere that the president leaked the story through Hood According to 'Edwin M. Hood Dead', *New York Times*, 10 August 1923, p. 11:3, in 1904 Hood proposed that Secretary of State John Hay dispatch as an ultimatum the lapidary 'Perdicaris alive or Raisuli dead' when a Moroccan chieftain captured the American citizen Ion Perdicans.

20. The best source for the telegram's broader effects is Thomas Boghardt, *The Zimmermann Telegram* (Annapolis, MD: Naval Institute Press, 2012). Cryptologic details and a summary account in David Kahn, *The Codebreakers* (New York: Macmillan, 1967), pp. 282–297.

21. Roosevelt Library, Bell file (note 5).

22. *Harvard Class of 1904: Twenty-Fifth Anniversary Report* (note 6), p. 50.

23. Bell personnel file (note 6).

24. Surtees (note 2).

25. Hurley, whose title was 'drafting officer', was then in charge of intelligence at the State Dept. For his service biography, see United States, Department of State, *Register of the Department of State*, 1 May 1922 (Washington, DC: Government Printing Office, 1922), p. 136. (Henceforth, *Register* (1922).)

26. Harrison dealt with intelligence at State during World War I. For his service biography, *Register* (1917) (note 8), p. 102.

27. Everyone spells his family name with an *h* except him.

28. Ambassador to the Court of St James's 1918–1921. In 1924 he was the Democratic presidential candidate; he lost to Coolidge by a landslide.

29. That is, between the start of unrestricted submarine warfare and the US declaration of war on Germany.

30. Joseph Caillaux (1863–1944), premier for the last half of 1911, was charged in 1917 with treason for his opposition to the war and his friendships with Germans and was imprisoned; he was amnestied in 1924. Marie-Paul Bolo, a businessman crony of Caillaux with a shady past and the honorary title of pasha from the Khedive of Egypt, was convicted of being a spy for Italy and was shot (Jean-Claude Allain, *Joseph Caillaux* (Paris, France: Imprimerie Nationale, 1978–1981), Vol. 1, pp. 439–440, Vol. 2, p. 232).
31. A German commander at Constantinople in Turkish service.
32. Sir William Tyrell, in charge of the British embassy in Washington during part of World War I while the ambassador was incapacitated.
33. Edward Rumely, an American convicted after the war of violating the Trading with the Enemy Act.
34. Which he did, becoming head of the Finance Ministry in 1925 and winning election to the Senate in 1927.
35. Frank L. Polk, in Lansing's absence, acting secretary of state who presented the Zimmermann telegram solution to Wilson.
36. David A. Salmon. As chief of the Bureau of Indexes and Archives (*Register* (1917) (note 8), p. 134), in charge of State's cryptography.
37. This refers to the study by William F. Friedman and Charles J. Mendelsohn, *The Zimmermann Telegram of January 16, 1917 and Its Cryptographic Background*, War Department: Office of the Chief Signal Office (Washington, DC: Government Printing Office, 1938).
38. [De Grey's own note] There were several versions made in which the marginals remained unchanged but with varying page numbers.
39. He apparently refers to the German code wrapped in the underpants of Dr Helmuth Listemann, the German consul in Bushire, Persia, which was seized by the British in March 1915. The story is told in C. J. Edmonds, "The Persian Gulf Prelude to the Zimmermann Telegram," *Journal of the Royal Central Asian Society*, 47 (January 1960), pp. 58–67.
40. Fleet Paymaster Charles J.E. Rotter.
41. A hatted code is, in American nomenclature, a two-part code. One part, the encoding part, has the plaintext elements in alphabetical order and the code elements mixed. In the decoding part, the code elements are in numerical or alphabetical order and the plaintext elements mixed. The term may come from the conceit that the code elements were drawn at random from a hat.
42. Dillwyn Knox. Admiral Sir William James wrote in his *The Eyes of the Navy* (London, U.K.: Methuen, 1956) that de Grey was helped in the solution by the Rev. William Montgomery. Other authors have followed this statement, in part because it has not been contradicted until this statement by de Grey, in part because James headed Room 40 after its founder and first head, Sir Alfred Ewing, left on October 1, 1916, and so had firsthand knowledge of its activities, and perhaps in part because James based his account on Hall's papers. But it is more likely that de Grey knew with whom he was dealing than James did. So I believe that the secondary credit for the solution of this vital message belongs more to Knox than to Montgomery.

43. Theobald von Bethmann-Hollweg, Imperial German Chancellor from 1909 until July 1917.
44. In addition to having been foreign secretary, Arthur James Balfour had been prime minister from 1902 to 1905.
45. This is the version of the telegram mentioned at the beginning of the memorandum.
46. A community on the south shore of Long Island in which stood a radio station used, with the permission of the US government, to receive German Foreign Office messages.
47. This shows that previous historians were wrong in saying that the British government delayed telling Wilson about the telegram in the hope that events might make the disclosure unnecessary. Among those historians are Kahn and Tuchman. The delay stemmed from intelligence reasons, not political.
48. *Spurlos versenkt*, 'sunk without a trace'. The cynical phrase comes from a telegram of Count Luxburg, the German ambassador in Argentina, who said, in a telegram of May 19, 1917, intercepted and solved by the British, 'I beg that the small steamers *Oran* and *Guazu...* may be spared if possible, or else sunk without a trace being left' (United States, Department of State, *Foreign Relations of the United States, 1917, Supplement 1* (Washington, DC: Government Printing Office, 1931), p. 322.
49. This may be the source of Adm. James's belief that Montgomery had solved the Zimmermann telegram.

7

CRYPTOLOGY AND THE ORIGINS OF SPREAD SPECTRUM*

Deep in the guarded labyrinth of the newly constructed Pentagon, an army lieutenant with top security clearance inserts a voltohmmeter probe into a horseshoe-shaped, 7-foot-high panel of electronic equipment. The apparatus is top secret; the room where it sits, with its polished tile floor, is windowless.

Tip to tip with the horseshoe stands a duplicate horseshoe. Each is dominated by its own big railroad clock graduated in 24-hour time and set to Greenwich mean time. Within each horseshoe, ovens hold quartz crystals vibrating at an extremely precise frequency. Near each horseshoe's tips stand two phonographs with some of the most accurate turntables ever made. But they reproduce sounds quite different from such popular songs of the day as "Mairzy Doats."

It was the summer of 1944. World War II was at its climax. In Normandy, the Allied armies had begun to press the life out of Hitler's Third Reich. But the conflict was not over, and the Allied leaders still had to make plans and resolve disputes about tactics and supplies.

Lieutenant Gordon A. Smith, 24, who had recently graduated as an electrical engineer from the Virginia Military Institute, was making routine checks on a pathbreaking radiotelephone scrambler system in the Pentagon in Washington, D.C., that permitted these leaders to confer on high policy in perfect security for the first time in radiotelephone history. The system pushed technology to its limits, maintaining, for example, synchronization of certain elements to a degree then unprecedented in communication. And it pushed technology beyond its former limits, creating, as it did so, some of

---

* From *IEEE Spectrum*, 21 (September 1984), 70–80.

the practical foundations for techniques as broadly useful today as pulse-code modulation and spread-spectrum transmissions.

Suddenly a member of the scrambler unit emerged from one of the side rooms and said, "Okay, let's get on the air. We have a call for London from the White House." Smith put down his probe and moved to an oscilloscope on one of the horseshoes. He picked up a telephone. One of the sergeants radioed the scrambler system's London terminal—at Oxford and Duke Streets, in the subbasement of the annex to Selfridge's department store—with its horseshoes identical to those in the Pentagon. He told the personnel there to begin the operating procedure and to notify Prime Minister Winston Churchill that a call was coming for him.

Secret Telephone in the Cabinet War Rooms

Churchill took and made calls from a closetlike room in the Cabinet War Rooms (Figure 7.1), a vast bombproof warren of offices and dormitories dug between two streets—Whitehall and the Horse Guards Parade—and covered with a thick reinforced concrete slab. To that room an extension had been run inside a steel pipe from the Selfridge annex, more than a mile away. The telephone, which had a ball-shaped high-quality moving-coil transmitter and weighed more than the ordinary handset, stood on a table covered in black baize. On the wall hung a sheet of paper listing London and Washington time. A framed placard gave instructions for the use of the telephone. The door had a simple toilet lock indicating "vacant" or "engaged." Sometimes Churchill puffed so furiously on his cigar during conversations that the smoke leaked out the top and bottom of the door, giving the impression that the room was on fire.

In the Washington and London scrambler terminals—two of a worldwide net—Army technicians put onto the phonograph turntables 14-inch-diameter thin black vinyl records. These disks carried the secret key, generated from white noise, that would mask the voices of the speakers; after a single use, they were destroyed. One record at each receiver was identical to a record at each transmitter; the second turntable was to continue a conversation if it lasted beyond the duration of the first record. The technicians set the stylus at the spiral's start, which, in these disks, was on the inside.

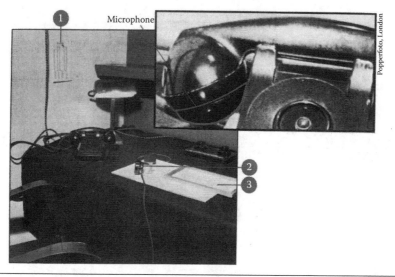

Figure 7.1 This highly secure telephone at the British Cabinet War Rooms underneath the Government Buildings in Whitehall, London, was used by British Prime Minister Winston Churchill during the Second World War to talk with U.S. President Franklin D. Roosevelt. Designed and built by Bell Laboratories researchers in Manhattan 1941, the telephone had a special high-quality, pressure-sensitive dynamic microphone (inset) that responded to frequencies below 200 hertz, important for low-pitched male voices such as Churchill's. A London and Washington time chart (1), an earphone for a secretary (2) and operating instructions (3) were included in the telephone facility.

Both ends agreed when they would start the records. The agreed-upon timing signal from the U.S. naval observatory's radio station WWV, which broadcast time signals, caused the turntables to begin revolving. An ingenious clutch ensured that they accelerated so smoothly that the stylus did not jump out of the groove. The records, a U-boat-infested ocean apart, would be within half a second or so of synchronization. Chirps filled Smith's telephone. Then, watching a counter calibrated in milliseconds the sergeant used a phase shifter to advance or retard turntable speed and bring the two into exact synchronization. As they came into sync, the peeps faded into silence. Smith checked to see if a red light was warning that the extension line to the White House was unbalanced, perhaps from an attempt at tapping; it was not lit. He spoke into the telephone to notify the White House that the scrambler circuit was ready, then replaced the handset with earphones to free his hands.

Suddenly there sounded in his ears not the anonymous tones of some presidential aide but the familiar aristocratic accents of Franklin

(a)   (b)

Figure 7.2   (a) Winston S. Churchill shortly after he became Prime Minister of Great Britain in May 1940, and (b) Franklin D. Roosevelt, President of the United States, during his Aug. 18, 1943, conference in Quebec, Canada, with Churchill. Beginning in 1944 the two conversed freely over the highly secure transatlantic telephone.

D. Roosevelt. "Is it you, Winnie?" Roosevelt asked. And then Smith heard Winston Churchill's voice, somewhat mechanical but instantly recognizable in response. The two conversed, Roosevelt saying that people in America were getting anxious for more military action, and Churchill replying that he needed more ships (Figure 7.2). But Smith, after his initial surprise, paid little attention to the conversation. He was concentrating on keeping green dots on the oscilloscope lined up in the diagonal that showed that the voltages of the noise-masked communications channels were increasing in the proper steps. And, though he was not nervous at handling such a high-level communication, he did keep hoping that everything would work.

The First Unbreakable Scrambler

The call lasted from five to seven minutes. All went well. But after the president and the prime minister hung up, Smith was left with a peculiar feeling: he had been a witness to history—but he could not tell anybody about it.

What was remarkable about the conversation was less its content than that it had been conducted by two of the most powerful men in the world in full confidence that no could overhear them. For the scrambler,

Figure 7.3 This secret telephone receiving terminal in the Pentagon in 1943—about one half of a SIGSALY installation—had two turntables (1) that alternately played recorded key signals. A phase-shifter control (2) allowed terminal operators to manually synchronize these signals with identical ones reproduced off a similar record at a transmitting terminal thousands of miles away to mask the speaker's voice there. Such synchronization was vital for orderly reception. A 24-hour clock (3) was driven, along with the turntables, by the world's most accurate frequency standard at that time (4)—a system that contained a crystal oscillator in a constant temperature oven. Vacuum and gas-tube logic circuits in six racks (5) subsequently quantized signals derived from both the received, completely scrambled voice messages and the record, for further manipulations and subsequent recovery of the message in a synthesizer (6). An oscilloscope (7) allowed a synchronization and quantization level checks. Ten indicating instruments (8) in a similar, U-shaped transmitting terminal, only a portion of which is shown, monitored spectral fluctuations of the transmitted speech.

called SIGSALY by the U.S. Army Signal Corps, was absolutely unbreakable—the first one ever to be so (Figure 7.3).

Earlier scramblers were said to afford only privacy, not secrecy, for though they blocked casual eavesdropping, they could not withstand a determined attack. This weakness perhaps contributed to the Japanese success at Pearl Harbor, for Army Chief of Staff General George C. Marshall refused to use the A-3 scrambler—operated by the American Telegraph and Telephone Co. in New York City—on the morning of Sunday, Dec. 7, 1941. He had wanted to tell the commander in Hawaii that the Japanese were going to submit a note breaking off negotiations at 1 p.m., Washington time, which was 7:30 a.m. in Hawaii. But he feared that the Japanese might have solved the scrambler, in which they had already expressed some interest, and might use the intercept to suggest that the Roosevelt administration had forced Japan's hand, thereby sending the country to war divided.

So he sent his warning by radiotelegraph in code—and it arrived after the attack was over.

The A-3 served also on the transatlantic radiotelephone circuit. Roosevelt had used it before Pearl Harbor to talk with several of his ambassadors abroad, and Marshall had warned him of the danger. Rightly so, for, by the fall of 1941, the Deutsche Reichspost had broken the A-3. The Germans filled a former youth hostel a few hundred feet from the sea at Noordwijk, the Netherlands, with electronic equipment that automatically and instantaneously unscrambled the conversations. These were recorded, transcribed, translated, and sent to Adolf Hitler and other officials. They included wartime talks between Roosevelt and Churchill themselves, as well as conversations between other high officials, such as FDR's advisor, Harry Hopkins, British Foreign Secretary Anthony Eden, and General Mark Clark.

The A-3 was based on 1920s concepts. It divided the voice-frequency band into five subbands, inverted each of them, and then shifted the voice from one subband to another, varying these permutations every 20 seconds. It was a considerable improvement over the first scramblers, which, shortly after World War I, merely inverted the frequencies of the speech band on the radiotelephone circuit between Los Angeles and Catalina Island, about 20 kilometers away. But Bell Telephone Laboratories, which was given a contract by the government in October of 1940 to study speech secrecy, soon recognized that it was inadequate. Consideration of new techniques began. One of these could cover, or mask, the voice with noise. This would be stripped off at the receiver by applying the same noise in opposite polarity, thereby canceling out the noise to leave the original speech. This principle had been conceived earlier, but had not been successfully realized. In 1944 Walter Koenig, a Bell Laboratories engineer studying ciphony, or speech encipherment, pointed out some of the problems.

"Beginners in the study of privacy systems," he said, "never fail to be amazed at the difficulty of scrambling speech sufficiently to destroy the intelligence. The ear can tolerate or even ignore surprising amounts of noise, nonlinearity, frequency distortion, misplaced components, superpositions, and other forms of interference. We can therefore very often obtain partial or even complete intelligence from a privacy system by partial or imperfect decoding."

A high noise-to-signal ratio was therefore needed to conceal the presence of speech, but this in turn made it difficult to recover the voice.

Vocoder Speech Synthesizer Studied

In their studies in the early 1940s, the Bell Labs teams working on speech privacy had looked into the possibility of using the vocoder, a speech analyzer and synthesizer developed by Bell Labs a few years earlier, to investigate reducing the bandwidth needed to transmit speech.

The vocoder's analyzer first filtered the speech frequency spectrum in 10 nearly equal bands of 300 hertz each. Subsequent rectification and low-pass filtering of each of the 10 signals produced by the bandpass filters led to signals at the filters' outputs containing frequencies up to 25 Hz.

A signal corresponding to the pitch, or fundamental vocal-cord frequency, of each voiced sound was also derived. The information in these 11 separate channels, which together occupied a substantially smaller frequency band than the normal voice spectrum does, was transmitted to a receiver. In the synthesizer the fundamental frequency was regenerated from the pitch signal, or, alternatively, a broadband noise generator was activated to produce unvoiced, hissing sounds such as /ssss/. The pitch or noise signals were applied to 10 filters identical to those in the transmitter. The signal produced by each filter was subsequently amplitude-modulated by its corresponding low-frequency signal and the 10 channels were combined to reconstitute the speech, in an attempt to mimic the dynamic acoustic resonances of the human mouth, tongue, nose, and throat.

But the results sounded very artificial, so Bell Labs teams did little with the vocoder. Then, early in 1941, the British Post Office wrote for information about it, hinting that it was to serve in a scrambler system, whereupon the Bell Labs people put the vocoder and the masking principle together to create their own scrambler.

In doing so, however, they were faced with the problem of how to apply the one key that ensures perfect security in any cryptographic system. This key is a sequence of symbols—such as zeros and ones—that is perfectly random and never repeats. These two characteristics preclude any structure that a cryptanalyst can reconstitute and so they determine the "plaintext"—the message in its intelligible form. Even given a portion of the key, the cryptanalyst cannot predict the next symbol and so cannot even begin to solve the next message. Nor will trial and error work, because it would merely generate all messages of the length of the cryptogram with no indication—because the key is random—as to which message is right. This so-called one-time key was devised by a Signal Corps major, Joseph O. Mauborgne, and embodied in a device for teletypewriters that automatically added the electrical pulses of the key to the pulses of the plaintext to produce the cipher-text. This device was well known to Bell engineers, for it had been created in December 1917 by one of their predecessors, an American Telephone and Telegraph engineer named Gilbert S. Vernam.

The Vernam system added in binary. But how could keys that consisted of a series of ons or offs encipher an analog plaintext, as in the vocoder? The leader of the labs' speech-privacy teams, Ralph K. Potter, who held a couple of scrambler patents (Figures 7.4 and 7.5), suggested that the individual vocoder amplitude channels be treated as on-off channels. But the speech was badly mutilated. Each channel was then divided into two to refine the spectral measurement of the speech. This helped, but it was apparent that more amplitude levels would be needed to provide acceptable quality. In the end, 10 voice-amplitude spectrum channels were used plus two channels, for sending the pitch—or "buzz"— and the "hiss" signals. Each of the 10 spectrum channels was sampled 50 times per second—once every 20 milliseconds. At each sampling time, the 10 amplitude samples were each quantized to one of six levels on a logarithmic scale 10 decibels apart, resulting in 10 senary digits. Samples of the pitch-frequency measurement were quantized to a finer scale of 36 levels, represented by a pair of senary digits. Each 20 milliseconds, then, 12 senary digits were generated and transmitted to the receiver. The sampling of an analog signal and its quantization to more than one digit is today known as pulse-code modulation, and SIGSALY marked its first use for speech transmission.

Enter the X-System

Multiple levels in the vocoder channels required multiple levels in the key. But it was not immediately clear how adding senary amplitude

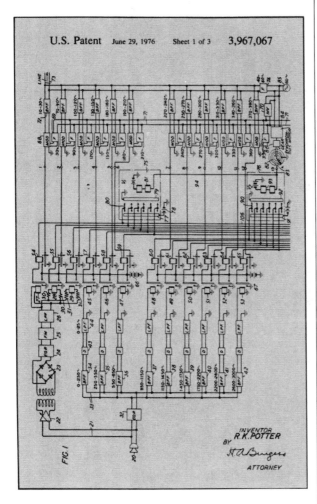

Figure 7.4   In U.S. Patent 3,967,067, issued on June 29, 1976, when secrecy was lifted from it almost 35 years after it had been filed on September 24, 1941, Bell Telephone Laboratories' inventor Ralph K. Potter described a "secret telephony" scheme, not necessarily the one implemented in SIGSALY, that "relates to the transmission of messages with privacy or secrecy." The transmitter shown here spectrally analyzes the speech coming out of a microphone (20), using nine contiguous bandpass filters (34–42), followed by rectifiers (43) and low-pass filters (44). Relays (45–53) quantize the spectrum-defining signals into two levels. Relays 27 to 29 quantize the speaker's pitch, or fundamental frequency signal into three levels. Perforated paper-tape mechanisms (75 and 76, paper not shown) produce a two-level random signal—the encryption key—for each of the spectral and pitch channels. Relays 54 through 65 add these random signals using modulo 2 to the spectrum and pitch signals. Subsequent frequency-division multiplexing by amplitude modulators (68) and filters (72) prepare the signal into an overall bandwidth of 10 to 390 hertz for single-sideband analog transmission.

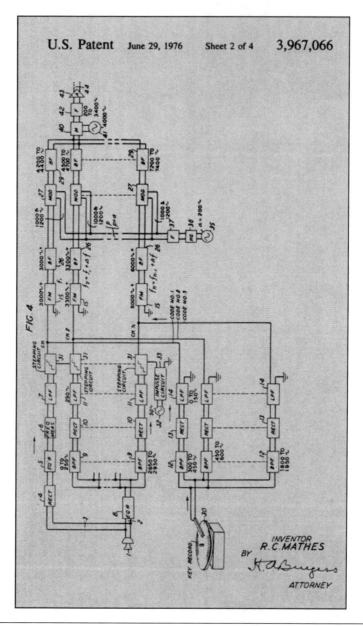

Figure 7.5   In another Bell Telephone Laboratories secret telephone patent filed for and awarded on the same dates as Potter's, Inventor Robert C. Mathes portrays yet another speech-encryption scheme. In its transmitter here the pitch (CH) and spectrum-defining signals are quantized by stepping circuits (31) into typically five levels. A record produces a random masking signal—the encryption key—to each of the channels. Frequency modulators (15) perform modulo addition of the individual spectrum and pitch signals to the masking signal. Amplitude modulators (27) and filters (29) prepare a frequency-division-multiplexed signal for transmission over an analog circuit of a voice bandwidth.

levels, say 4, to a senary key, say 3, could be kept within the senary bound—6—of the vocoder channel. In a discussion on May 27, 1941, Potter and a brilliant theoretician, Harry Nyquist, who was a precursor of Claude Shannon and who himself held patents on scrambler systems saw that the answer lay in modulo arithmetic, though they did not call it that. Sums of message and key that would be greater than the maximum of six amplitude levels of the channel would be "wrapped around" to levels at, or caused to reenter at, the bottom of the amplitude scale. Thus a message level 4 and a key 3 would become 7 minus 6, or cipher 1. That afternoon the idea jelled into a circuit diagram, and the basic building blocks of the scrambler had come into being. Bell Labs began calling it the X-system.

Several refinements followed. Transmission, in full duplex, was by frequency modulation, to combat the fading that afflicted transatlantic radio transmission. Though the vocoder had condensed the total bandwidth, the X-system spaced its 12 channels uniformly across the entire 3-kilohertz telephone band to gain greater ruggedness. This, and the discrete frequency-modulation employed, makes it an early instance of spread-spectrum transmission, if that is defined broadly as any transmission method utilizing a wider band than that used by the information signal itself.

Since the system decomposed and then resynthesized the speech signal, voices did not sound as they did on an ordinary telephone. Recognition depended more on cadence than on timbre. Secretary of War Henry L. Stimson said that the system "makes a curious robot kind of voice" that rendered "the tones [of General Marshall] quite unrecognizable. However, I could recognize the peculiarities of his method of expressing himself." The intelligibility was good and improved as the listener gained experience. And though some users found the voice quality unsatisfactory, most were willing to accept some distortion for absolute security in a telephone call.

To produce a key that had the required randomness, the engineers used mercury-vapor rectifier tubes to generate wideband thermal noise, which was perfectly random. The output of these 14-in.-high, 4-in.-diameter tubes, which emitted a bluish light, was sampled every 20 milliseconds and the samples were quantized nonuniformly into six levels of equal probabilities. These were recorded on vinyl disks that resembled the transcriptions that radio stations then used for music and radio programs—low-noise disks that were larger and revolved more slowly than the then-standard 78-rpm records sold to the public. These masters, made by Bell Telephone Laboratories at the Graybar Varick Building at 180 Varick St. in lower Manhattan, were taken under guard to the World Broadcasting System at 711 Fifth Ave., where two pressings were made. The masters were destroyed and the pressings (codenamed, rather transparently, SIGGRUVs) taken to the army's code-making and code-breaking agency at Arlington Hall, a former girls' school in Arlington, Va., for distribution by courier to the sending and receiving stations.

Synchronization of the records at both ends was made practicable in part by the relatively long sampling interval of 20 milliseconds, in part by the availability of a sufficiently accurate frequency standard. This was provided by a highly stable 100-kilohertz quartz-crystal oscillator that was kept in an oven in the SIGSALY horseshoe to maintain its precision of one part in 10 million—more than sufficient to keep within the plus or minus 1 millisecond required, with only very infrequent manual adjustments.

Telephones Protected against Tapping

An extension, like the one to the Cabinet War Rooms in London, was called an OPEPS—off-premises extension privacy system. Several terminals had them. Washington had two. One ran to the White House, the other to the Navy Department building, an ugly wooden "temporary" structure on Constitution Avenue. The cables were protected by gas pressure and microswitches on the boxes in the Pentagon; any tampering would set off alarms. The OPEPS bay in the White House was in the basement; the telephone connected to it was elsewhere, perhaps in the Oval Office. All OPEPSes added in noise from a strong noise source connected to the receiving end of the line, but balanced out of the receiver by a circuit connected to conjugate arms of a hybrid coil (or bridge transformer). If the wires were tapped, even just within the White House, the circuit would unbalance and activate an alarm. The callers would know something was wrong because the noise they heard would become unbearable.

Eavesdroppers on the SIGSALY transatlantic circuit—mostly a single-sideband channel, called PL-60, of a multichannel, high-frequency installation—would hear a different kind of noise. It sounded rather like Rimsky-Korsakov's bravura violin spectacular, "The Flight of the Bumblebee." Since this was the theme song of a popular radio serial, "The Green Hornet," SIGSALY was sometimes informally called that.

SIGSALY was brought to fruition and terminals were manufactured at Bell Telephone Laboratories at 463 West St. in lower Manhattan by a team of 30 people headed by Paul Blye, an engineer who had been trying to solve scramblers. He began in September 1942, taking over from a research group that had done a lot of work but had been able, in his words, only to "get a whisper," having failed to measure voice pitch well enough. But gradually they overcame one problem after another. Alan Turing, the intellectual father of the computer and the deviser of the universal Turing machine, the exemplar of the computer, who was a top cryptanalyst for Britain, spent two months at Bell Labs, contributing to the work. Claude Shannon, the creator of information theory, checked Potter and Nyquist's reentry algorithm—though he was not told what it was for.

The first terminal was completed early in 1943 in Room L30, formerly the sound movie laboratory. Blye felt that its secrecy was perfect: "We were convinced that we could have dropped a terminal in Berlin and without the records no one could figure it out." Turing finally approved the system, and, on his recommendations, the British declared themselves "completely satisfied" as to its security for transatlantic communications. They were not pleased with the fact that—as Turing put it—"if the equipment is to be operated solely by U.S. personnel it will be impossible to prevent them listening in if they so desire." But the British chiefs of staff concluded that "we could not do anything but agree."

Throughout the war, Blye's group manufactured a dozen terminals. These were installed successively in Washington; London; Algiers; Brisbane, Australia; Fort Shafter, Hawaii; Washington again (primarily for the Pacific); Oakland, Calif.; Paris after its liberation; Guam; on a 250-ton lighter in the Pacific; Frankfurt after Germany's surrender; and Berlin. All could interconnect, and test connections were sometimes made from London through Washington to Australia: they worked perfectly. Several terminals had conference facilities, so that several persons around a table could wear earphones and simultaneously hear the person on the other end of the call, though the telephone had to be handed to anyone who wanted to speak.

Training Conducted in Secret

The Signal Corps ran SIGSALY, and so personnel for it came from the Army. Despite that organization's reputation for assigning men who know one thing to do something else, most of the SIGSALY men had electrical engineering or telephone-company backgrounds. The Army arranged for the Bell Telephone Laboratories School for War Training in New York to teach them how to install, operate, and maintain this new system. The first class, six officers, started on January 5, 1943. Eventually, 186 men were trained there in 10 groups in courses that ranged from 28 to 44 working days. Classes were held in Room 1414 of the Davis Building at 250 Hudson St. in lower Manhattan.

The first students formed the nucleus of a unit set up specially for SIGSALY. The 805th Signal Service Company was activated on Feb. 10, 1943. Its commander was Major Eugene M. Apted, who had come from California's Associated Telephone Co. It eventually comprised 81 officers and 275 enlisted men. Its ratio of one officer to four men was the highest in the U.S. Army. One of its detachments—which averaged four to five officers and six to eight men each—enjoyed another distinction: of all signal units in the Mediterranean base section, together with an obscure postal outfit, for the first half of 1944, it had the lowest rate (no cases) of venereal disease.

Once each detachment set up the equipment, it spent a good part of its time doing routine maintenance. Tests and adjustments had to be made daily, and contact had to be established for an hour with a distant terminal every day.

The first operational terminal that Blye's group manufactured was to go to the White House. The device, the British said, "is clearly intended for the Prime Minister and the President to talk to each other." And, indeed, in the White House late in the afternoon of Jan. 14, 1942, during his first series of meetings with Churchill, Roosevelt had said that he wanted to work out a system of better communications with London. General Marshall told him that secrecy could not be ensured by telephone; the chief of naval operations said that messages could not be sent by telephone, but Roosevelt insisted that a study be made as to the best method of improving communications between Washington and London. Yet, later in the war, perhaps when he got to know Churchill's habits better, Roosevelt seemed less than delighted to be troubled at all hours of the day and night by the Prime Minister, whose late hours and penchant for calling whenever the mood struck him were compounded by the six-hour time difference between London and Washington. So the first terminal was installed not in the White House but in the Pentagon in March 1943. The second went in May to London. The first overseas test call was completed on June 29; opening ceremonies with a formal call to London took place July 15.

Shortly afterward, the OPEPS, or extension, to the underground Cabinet War Rooms was installed in Churchill's tiny telephone room. But as of October, the four calls that had been placed through it had all still been, in the British memorandum's understated term, "ineffective." This, and the likelihood that Churchill had continued to call Roosevelt from the Cabinet War Rooms using the A-3 scrambler instead of going to the SIGSALY at Selfridge's annex, may explain why the Deutsche Reichspost was continuing to intercept his calls. It overheard him talking with Roosevelt on July 29, an interception that suggested to the Germans that the two had been dealing with the new non-Mussolini government in Italy and that hardened Germany's decision to get troops into Italy as quickly as it could. The Germans also intercepted a conversation at 5:05 p.m. Oct. 9 between Churchill and Harry Hopkins, Roosevelt's chief aide. Five days later a test of the London OPEPS proved "satisfactory." However, eventually Roosevelt's objections were overcome and an OPEPS was installed in the White House. The leaders began using SIGSALY instead of the A-3, which is why the chief engineer of the Deutsche Reichspost intercept station got the impression that "there was another telephone connection in use between the United States and England."

For Churchill, a Cigar and Informality

Churchill seems to have been first instructed in SIGSALY in April 1944, by Lieutenant Stephen M. Geis of the London detachment. Before Geis went to the Cabinet War Rooms, he bought the biggest cigar he could find—it cost 10 cents—to present to the prime minister. When Churchill arrived, wearing white coveralls, Geis explained that the system delivered excellent intelligibility but not necessarily the personalities of its speakers. If synchronization failed, he said, Churchill would hear a sound that Geis described as a mad hornet buzzing. If this happened, Geis, who would be waiting outside, needed only to be alerted to restore synchronization. Churchill, to Geis's astonishment, said, "Oh, you may stay here if you wish." Geis replied, "I do not think it proper that I do so, Mr. Churchill." The prime minister accepted the cigar, made the call, which lasted 5 or 10 minutes, and later sent Geis an autographed copy of his book *My Early Life*.

The third terminal was installed in October 1943 with considerable difficulty in the St. George Hotel in Algiers, whose dank basement had 11 irregularly shaped rooms with seven different floor levels and varied ceiling constructions. The air-conditioning ducts, preconstructed for 8-in. walls, would not fit the hotel's walls, which were from 24 to 38 in. thick and merely piles of rocks with sand between them, plastered on both sides. "An attempt to set an anchor," the official history noted, "resulted in making a hole either in a solid rock or in soft sand which runs out the hole." Another problem was that SIGSALY took up so much room that, the hotel owner complained, it cut off air circulation to his wine cellar, causing his champagne to spoil.

Not everybody succumbed to the lure of the telephone, however, even though SIGSALY secured it. General Douglas MacArthur, commander of the Southwest Pacific Theater, refused to talk over SIGSALY because he was not convinced that it was fully secure; he, as well as Colonel Curtis LeMay, chief of staff for the planning of the dropping of the atomic bomb, preferred the teletypewriter system known as SIGTOT that embodied Mauborgne's one-time system in the on-line form invented by Vernam. Eisenhower himself used SIGSALY reluctantly, distrusting its security and complaining that he often could not understand what was said over it.

Not every SIGSALY connection was perfect. A SIGSALY operator noted that a conference from Algiers in February 1944 was "poor." In a connection with London, "some British voices did not actuate our pitch circuits." Delays occurred. Once officials had to wait from shortly after midnight to 4:15 AM. Sometimes circuits were noisy.

But in general, officers and officials liked SIGSALY. And SIGSALY seems to have shielded at least once the greatest secret of the war: the atomic bomb. The superscrambler transmitted what was apparently a discussion of the logistics of the delivery of the two existing weapons to Tinian, whence they were flown to Hiroshima and Nagasaki.

SIGSALY use was probably heavier in the European theater. In its first year of operation, 448 conferences were conducted over the London terminal. Most dealt with the nitty-gritty difficulties of war.

General Strategy by Telephone

Sometimes, however, SIGSALY served aspects of grand strategy.

One instance involved Yugoslavia and whether Britain should support the incompetent royalist, Draja Mihailovic, or the successful Communist, Marshal Tito, in the partisans' resistance against Germany. Into that occupied Balkan nation Churchill had parachuted a trusted envoy, Brigadier Fitzroy Maclean. After dealings there, Maclean got out by air, and in April 1944 he returned to Algiers to report to the prime minister. A cable asked Churchill whether he wanted to confer via teletype or SIGSALY; he chose SIGSALY. At about 2 p.m. on April 17, Maclean, in full Scottish uniform, appeared at what he described as "the brightly lighted and heavily guarded underground room," where "a startlingly pretty WAC sergeant" was ready to record on a Dictaphone what was said. The best link to London was via Washington, and this was established.

Cecil E. Barrette, the 805th's detachment chief in Algiers, conducted Maclean into the conference room, and, after what Maclean called "a series of infinitely disturbing clicks and buzzes, Mr. Churchill's well-known voice came booming and rasping over the ether." Barrette introduced Maclean to the Prime Minister—a technique he used to get the conferees talking. Maclean began by announcing his own identity, as the London telephone book recommended. "At this, the Prime Minister seemed unaccountably annoyed and told me to shut up." Churchill then asked whether Maclean had talked to the "Pumpkin." Maclean asked what he meant. "Good God," exclaimed Churchill, "they haven't got the code!" But soon Barrette and his counterpart in London made it clear that code words were not needed. "Shall we scramble?" asked Churchill gaily though unnecessarily as the conversation resumed—and continued thereafter in plain English. However, after making the meanings of "Pumpkin" and "Pippin" clear as he spoke, he delightedly continued to use these code names. Churchill ordered Maclean to return to London, where his information was instrumental in aligning Britain with Tito.

Another case of the strategic use of SIGSALY took place a few days after the London terminal was opened. Secretary of War Stimson got on to talk to Gen. Marshall in Washington. It included frank talk about Churchill's being "very set on a March on Rome" and, on the other hand, Eden's being "dead set on the Balkans and Greece." Stimson said that Churchill was "overjoyed" at a message indicating Marshall's "approval and interest in a new plan with respect to Naples." When Stimson said that he believed that this "would expedite the taking of Rome so as to leave more time for 'Roundhammer' [his portmanteau code-name for 'Roundup' and 'Sledgehammer,' two plans for the cross-Channel invasion] than otherwise would be left," Marshall interrupted to say, "That was exactly right; you were quite right; that was what I meant."

Summit Conferences Amid Informality

From time to time SIGSALY served the ultimate purpose for which it had largely been conceived: to maintain privacy in conversations between the president and the prime minister. In May of 1944, Lieutenant Raymond Edghill of the 805th was summoned to the annex to 10 Downing Street to arrange for such a call. He arrived at 2 p.m. Churchill, who addressed him as "Raymond," offered him a cigar, which Edghill accepted, and brandy, which he declined because he was on duty. They chatted about the similarity in their last names and about Edghill's collection of coins and stamps. Edghill then set up the conference call at the OPEPS in the underground complex and listened for the first two minutes. It was friendly and cordial. "Hello, Winnie, how are you?" asked Roosevelt. Churchill called Roosevelt, "old pal." They chatted for a bit about Roosevelt's Scottish terrier Fala and then about an Allied surprise attack to be made by moonlight on June 5 or 6. The call lasted perhaps half an hour. At 4, tea was served, Edghill enjoying dainty sandwiches and cakes with Churchill and a British officer.

One of the last talks between the top Allied leaders occurred toward the end of the war in Europe. The president was, however, no longer Roosevelt: Harry S. Truman had succeeded to the post upon Roosevelt's death on April 12, 1945. Churchill called him at 8:10 p.m. April 25, 1945, about an offer by the Nazi SS and Gestapo leader Heinrich Himmler to surrender the German forces on the Western Front separately from the forces fighting the Russians in the east.

"I think he should be forced to surrender to all three governments—Russia, you, and the United States," said Truman. "I don't think we ought to even consider a piecemeal surrender."

"No, no, no," agreed Churchill. And a few moments later, "What we actually sent was [a message] that there could be no question as far as His Majesty's Government is concerned of anything less than unconditional surrender simultaneously to the three major powers."

"All right. I agree to that," said Truman. And, a few minutes later, "All right, then you notify Stalin, and I shall do the same immediately of this conversation between us."

"Exactly," said Churchill. And they rejected Himmler's offer.

Thus, to the very end of the war, SIGSALY played a role of high importance in keeping secret the top plans of key leaders. It concealed so much so well that the older A3 scrambler, which continued in service, carried relatively few communications of importance. A German Foreign Office official noted disappointedly on a sheaf of Deutsche Reichspost intercepts that "There is in general not much to be gotten from them." And Marshall, whose refusal to use the scrambler in the morning of Dec. 7, 1941, had had such dire consequences, was able to say, three years later, probably with SIGSALY in mind, that "we have the very finest equipment now."

To Probe Further

Basic technical information about SIGSALY and its development may be found in M.D. Fagan, ed., *A History of Engineering and Science in the Bell System: National Service in War and Peace (1925–1975)* Bell Telephone Laboratories (Murray Hill, N.J., 1978), pp. 296–317.

The administrative and operational history of the military agency that served SIGSALY is given in the manuscript "Unit History: 805th Signal Service Company," Box 5704, Record Group 447, National Archives Records Center, Suitland, Md., 20746. A larger view, though with fewer details, may be found in Mary Louise Melia's manuscript, "Signal Corps Fixed Communications in World War II: Special Assignments and Techniques," April 18, 1946, War Department Special Staff, Historical Division, in the U.S. Army Center for Military History, 20 Massachusetts Ave., Washington, D.C., 20314.

Anecdotes about the use of SIGSALY and transcripts or recollections of the conversations are in Vol. I of Harry S. Truman's *Memoirs* (Garden City, N.Y.: Doubleday, 1954), pp. 89–94, and Fitzroy Maclean, *Escape to Adventure* (Boston: Little, Brown, 1950), pp. 343–45.

Details about Alan Turing's contribution to SIGSALY and speech encipherment are in Andrew Hodge's outstanding biography, *Alan Turing: The Enigma* (New York: Simon & Schuster, 1983), pp. 245–53, 269–88.

Information about German interception of the transatlantic scrambler is in David Kahn, *The Codebreakers* (New York: Macmillan, 1967), pp. 549–60.

On spread spectrum itself, see *Spread-Spectrum Communications*, ed. by Charles E. Cook, Fred W. Ellersick, Laurence B. Milstein, and Donald L. Schilling (New York: IEEE Press, 1983), a collection of articles; and the forthcoming *Spread Spectrum Communications* by Marvin K. Simon, Jim K. Omura, Robert A. Scholtz, and Barry K. Levitt (Rockville, MD: Computer Sciences Press, 1984), 3 Vols.

Broad invention rights to a basic spread-spectrum method are now claimed by the International Telephone and Telegraph Corp., Nutley, NJ, in Reissue Serial No. 299 469, filed Sep. 4, 1981. This U.S. patent reissue application concerns the original inventions of L.A. deRosa and Mortimer Rogoff.

A receiver, dubbed Rake, that significantly improved the F9C spread-spectrum system by combatting ionospheric multipath interference was described in "A communication technique for multipath channels," by R. Price and P. E. Green Jr., in the *Proceeding of the IRE*, Vol. 46, pp. 555–70, March 1958.

In his book *Bodyguard of Lies*, Toronto, New York, London, 1984, fourth ed., author Anthony Cave Brown says that Churchill was warned by the British intelligence about Germany's breaking of the A-3 scrambler.

Nearly 2000 messages, including letters, telegrams, and transcripts of telephone conversations between Winston S. Churchill and Franklin D. Roosevelt are included in the three-volume book *Churchill and Roosevelt: The Complete Correspondence*, edited by Warren F. Kimball, to be published next month by Princeton University Press of Princeton, NJ The editor mentions SIGSALY in his introduction. The book includes 26 black and white photos and 18 maps.

Appendix 1: A Soviet SIGSALY?

Roosevelt and Churchill were not the only world leaders of their era to take an interest in securing their telephone conversations. Though Adolf Hitler seems not to have used a scrambler (probably because he rarely used a radiotelephone, his conversations going by land line), Josef Stalin had the predecessor of the KGB create a unit to develop a secret telephone apparatus for him to use.

Scientists from the Soviet Union and Eastern European countries were assembled at a research unit, code-named MARVINO, on the outskirts of Moscow. Some of the scientists were prisoners and lived in a guarded dormitory. Like the creators of SIGSALY, they based their work on the vocoder, which they learned about through an article in an American technical journal. This may well have been the vocoder described by Homer Dudley in the *Bell Laboratories Record*, Vol. 18, December 1939, pp. 122–26.

The personnel at MARVINO were told that Stalin took a personal interest in the project, for which at least a prototype was built. Among those at work on the scrambler system was one Aleksandr Solzhenitsyn, a physicist and mathematician jailed for anti-Soviet agitation. He later immortalized the project—calling the unit "Mavrina" and himself "Gleb Nerzhin," a mathematician who programmed experiments in speech reception over telephone circuits, and referring to "the tentacles of cryptography… theories of probability, theories of numbers, theories of error, a dead brain, a dried-out soul" in his novel *The First Circle*.

Appendix 2: Spreading the Spectrum

SIGSALY's employment of more radio bandwidth than was necessary to carry its information links it to a method of transmission that is fundamentally different from the standard kind and that has only recently been gaining widespread recognition and use. This is spread spectrum.

Ordinary forms of radio signals employ a relatively narrow band of frequencies through the modulation of a single-frequency carrier signal. Their success in delivering their message depends on such things as signal power and frequency stability. But they suffer from certain disadvantages. Noise in the transmission band degrades a normal radio signal; the signal is thus vulnerable to jamming. The ease of signal detection can aid unfriendly eavesdroppers in discovering the signal's existence, in finding the direction toward its source, and in intercepting its messages—all sources of military intelligence. And in a crowded electromagnetic spectrum, each signal must compete with those emanating from other transmitters.

But the laws of nature do not decree that ordinary, frequency-limited radio transmission be the only kind. This kind originated first and became common largely because it was simpler. From the 1920s to the 1940s, the idea of a different kind of transmission independently struck people in various parts of the world. In one embodiment of this idea the radio carrier is controlled by a sequence, usually pseudo-random, of numbers or bits. The receiver, which knows this sequence, uses it to reconstruct the original carrier.

One way of doing this is called frequency hopping. The transmitter emits its carrier successively on many different frequencies in rapid short blocks in a controlled order over a wide range. The receiver knows this order, picks up the successive blocks, and assembles them into the original message.

In time hopping—a similar technique in the time domain—the transmitter emits its information-carrying signal during a fraction of a time interval, and where it does so varies from one interval to another. This variation is controlled by the pseudorandom sequence. The receiver, having the sequence, knows when in the block it can find the signal.

The third major form of this kind of transmission is called "direct sequence." For its pseudorandom sequence, it utilizes pulses so much shorter than the bits of the message that they are called "chips." These chips successively multiply fractions of the bits; the result is then transmitted. At the receiver, the incoming signal is multiplied by the chip sequence to recover the original bits.

Because this transmission idea, in all its forms, utilizes a far wider bandwidth in the electromagnetic spectrum than the bandwidth required by the original information signal, it has come to be called spread spectrum. The term was devised in the 1950s by Madison Nicholson and John Raney, two engineers with Sylvania Electric Products Inc.'s Electronic System Division in Buffalo, N.Y., who pioneered in developing the system.

The system enjoys a number of advantages over ordinary radio transmission. The two chief ones attract the military: its relative undetectability, which conceals its transmissions, and its comparative invulnerability to jamming. The latter stems from its wideband nature: a jamming signal, no matter how strong, on a single frequency, or even on a band of frequencies, will blot out only a very small portion of the total spectrum used to transmit the information. Its relative undetectability, at least in its direct sequence form, derives from two facts: an ordinary narrow-band radio would miss nearly all of the transmission, and it would hear the transmission not as signal but as noise. Even if the monitoring receiver were wideband, the signal is so spread that it lies below the level of the noise the receiver hears.

A third advantage arises when channels are lightly used. Spread spectrum permits many transmitters to operate simultaneously over the same wide channel with very little interference. The reason is that the several pseudorandom sequences will coincide only rarely, so each transmitter will add only a low level of noise to the others. But when too many transmitters are sending at the same time, the noise level rises to intolerable proportions. When usage is heavy, allocating individual frequencies to users—as in AM or FM—works better.

The sequence—of frequencies, or time slots, or chips—is the critical element in spread spectrum. If everyone knew it, or if everyone used the same order—for example, sliding up from low frequencies to high—spread spectrum would lose its advantages. Each radio's order must be different, to keep radios from interfering with one another, and that order must—in military applications—be a secret, to prevent the enemy from intercepting or jamming the transmission.

A practicable way of achieving these requirements is to generate a pseudorandom sequence—a sequence that can be recreated but that nevertheless has properties of randomness. Each sequence is characterized by an algorithm in which a secret variable determines the orderly transmission and reception of the signal. If the algorithm and its variable are properly chosen, every such sequence will differ from every other, and it will be virtually unpredictable to an outsider.

The algorithms are often embodied in shift registers with feedback. The initial state of the register corresponds to the variable; its output, to the sequence.

The history of spread spectrum is complex. Many individuals, in many times and places, independently concerned themselves with the problems of detection and jamming and with solutions to these problems. Marconi himself, as early as 1899, had worried about radio interference and experimented with frequency-selective reception to minimize it.

In Poland in 1929, a young engineer and radio amateur, Leonard Danilewicz, a director of AVA, a Warsaw manufacturer of electric and radio equipment, proposed to the Polish Army general staff a device for secret radio telegraphy that, he later wrote, "unfortunately did not win acceptance, as it was a truly barbaric idea consisting of constant changes of transmitter frequency." In Switzerland, in the 1930s, a prolific inventor, Gustav Guanella, devised a radar system that wobbled its transmission frequency "at a high rate between a lower and upper limit" and that employed correlation at the receiver. In Germany, Telefunken engineers Paul Kotowski and Kurt Dannehl applied in 1935 for a patent on a device to hide voice signals under a broadband noiselike signal produced by a rotating generator. And in the United States, movie star Hedy Lamarr and composer George Antheil devised in 1941 a jam-resistant guidance system for torpedoes that controlled the transmission frequencies by means of slotted paper rolls like those used in player pianos [see Appendix 3].

Some spread-spectrum ideas were used in World War II, more perhaps by the Axis side than by the Allied and mostly in radars, where synchronization of the pseudorandom sequences between transmitter and receiver is not a problem. After the war, the military value of the concept led to further research and expansion in spread spectrum in a number of American firms and universities.

At the Massachusetts Institute of Technology in Cambridge, Yuk Wing Lee, Jerome Wiesner (later a presidential science advisor), and Thomas Cheatham collectively developed in 1947 the first high-performance electronic correlators. At about the same time, engineers at the Bayside, N.Y., laboratories of Sylvania utilized spread spectrum for a missile guidance and navigation system. Mortimer Rogoff, an engineer at the Federal Telecommunication Laboratories in Nutley, N.J., a subsidiary of the International Telegraph and Telephone Co., used the Manhattan telephone directory to create a pseudorandom generator.

Meanwhile, early in the 1950s, fundamental research in spread spectrum was beginning at the Lincoln Laboratory of MIT under Robert Fano and Wilbur Davenport.

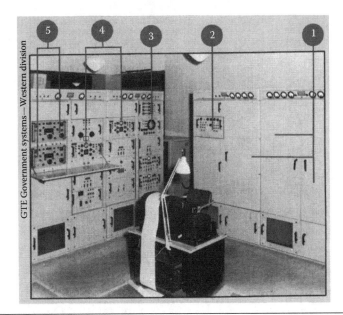

Figure 7.6 This receiving terminal for the F9CA spread-spectrum communication system at the U.S. Army installation in Middletown, Calif., about 1956, had its secret daily transmission codes kept in a group of logic matrices under three safe doors not seen concealed by ordinary cabinet doors (1). The terminal also had a panel for testing digital circuitry (2); an oscilloscope for monitoring ionospheric multipath reflections of the received signal (3); two correlators for improved short-wave reception (4); and two separate short-wave receivers (5) for increasing the reliability.

In 1953 Lincoln Laboratory was developing a spread-spectrum radioteletypewriter for the Signal Corps, using digital pseudonoise generating and synchronizing techniques worked out by Davenport's student, Paul E. Green. Field trials of this long-range, fixed-plant, high-frequency system, called the F9C (Figure 7.6), began in August 1954 between Davis, Calif., and Deal, N.J. By the spring of 1955 it was overcoming jamming. By the end of the year, the U.S. Army Signal Corps let a production contract to Sylvania Electronic Defense Laboratory in Mountain View, Calif., and, in January 1958, an installation near Washington, D.C., became the first in a network with posts in Germany, Japan, and the Philippines. The F9C served a number of years until other systems replaced it.

The value of spread spectrum was emphasized in the summer of 1982 when Israell forces shot down 92 Syrian MIGs in the Bekaa Valley with a loss of only two Israell aircraft. This contrasted favorably with the Israell loss of 89 aircraft in the 1973 Yom Kippur War, when Israell planes, lacking spread spectrum, appear to have been jammed.

Last February, *Military Electronics/Countermeasures* magazine gave one reason for the unheard-of 50:1 kill ratio of 1982: "The positioning of the Israell F-15s and F-16s would not have been possible without secure voice and digital communications. Syrian jammers were unable to degrade the communications of the opposing force significantly," because, it went on, of frequency-hopping radios manufactured by Israel's Tadiran Electronics Industries Ltd.

The advantages of spread spectrum have led to its use in communications between the space shuttle and ground control, in the MILSTAR communications satellite, in the Global Positioning System for navigation, in radar astronomy, and in sideways-looking radar.

Appendix 3: Screen Star Devises a Frequency-Hopping Scheme

In Austria in the 1930s, a lovely young actress named Hedwig Kiesler, who had gained worldwide fame by running nude through the woods in a film called *Ecstasy*, spent hours with her munitions-magnate husband Fritz Mandl and his experts as they tried to solve weapons problems. In particular, he was having trouble controlling his torpedoes: they rarely struck their evasive targets.

In 1938, the year Adolf Hitler occupied Austria, she left her husband and her now Nazi-controlled homeland and came to Hollywood, billed as the world's most beautiful woman. Here she married writer Gene Markey and, under the screen name of Hedy Lamarr, she starred in films—but remained worried about the seemingly irresistible advance of Hitler. Unusually bright, she remembered bits and pieces of the technical information to which she had become privy at her first husband's home and, recalling his problems with his torpedoes, wondered whether a solution could not be found that might help countries opposing Germany. Demonstrating her patriotism in yet another way, Ms. Lamarr, shown in Figure 7.7, mounts a poster calling for purchase of war bonds in her Beverly Hills home (circa 1943).

She knew George Antheil, an American composer who had a fair grasp of electronics, and together they sought to create an effective guidance system. Antheil had, in the 1920s, synchronized player pianos for his opus *Ballet Mecanique* and, as the two sketched circuit diagrams while stretched out on Lamarr's carpeted floor he drew upon

Figure 7.7   Hedy Lamarr mounts a poster for war bonds.

this Idea for a frequency-hopping system of radio control. A transmitter would employ slotted paper rolls like those in player pianos to determine the pseudorandom sequence and duration of signals in the 88 or more frequencies it would use; the torpedo would have an identical roll to receive the transmissions, which would guide it to its target. Without knowing the sequence, a defender could neither deflect the torpedo by fake transmissions nor jam it.

In 1941, Lamarr and Antheil applied for a patent, "Secret Communication System," which, as No. 2 292 387, was granted Aug. 11, 1942, to "H.K. Markey *et al*"; Antheil was the co-inventor (Figure 7.8). Curiously, no secrecy order was imposed on it.

Though only a sidelight in the history of spread spectrum, because it had no direct influence on the evolution of the technology, the frequency-hopping invention did impart to that field its most glittering bit of glamour.

Appendix 4: Putting the Story Together

Spectrum is grateful to Robert Price, chief scientist with M/A-COM Linkabit Inc. in Lexington, Mass., whose support was instrumental in bringing this fascinating story together.

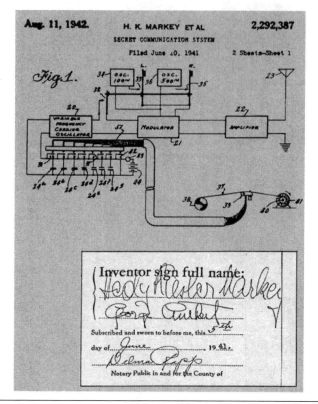

Figure 7.8 In their U.S. Patent No. 2,292,387 invention, August 11, 1942, actress Hedy Kiesler Markey (Lamarr) and composer George Antheil reveal a technique for guiding torpedoes to their targets by varying the frequencies of signals that control the torpedoes left and right movements. Variable oscillator frequencies are determined by switching seven different capactiors (24a through 24g) acoding to a constantly varying pattern controlled by seven perforations along a paper strip similar to those of player-piano rolls. The inventors notarized their patent application on June 5, 1941.

Stimulated by spread-spectrum pioneer Paul E. Green Jr., at present with IBM's Thomas J. Watson Research Center in Yorktown Heights, N.Y., by University of Southern California researcher and teacher Robert A. Scholtz in Los Angeles, Dr. Price undertook about five years ago to study and document the evolution of spread-spectrum technology as many once-secret documents became declassified.

Dr. Price, a dedicated communications engineer and a Fellow of the IEEE, sees his entirely voluntary effort as "repaying a luckily incurred debt" to all those pioneers with whom he worked in the early days of spread spectrum.

Searching for authentic sources, Dr. Price interviewed such U.S. generals as Mark Clark, now deceased, plus others who are still alive.

Civilian interviewees included famous actress Hedy Lamarr, whose torpedo-guidance invention [see Appendix 3] Dr. Price found to be "complete in its potent antijamming concept even before Pearl Harbor." During Dr. Price's interview with her, Ms. Lamarr autographed the accompanying photo, taken at her Benedict Canyon home in California in 1941, during her work there with composer George Antheil on their common invention.

Dr. Price also recalls how Colonel Dorothy L Madsen of Chicago, IL., chief operator of the Pentagon's SIGSALY conference room, volunteered that she had aided President Truman in his transatlantic discussion with Prime Minister Winston Churchill of Himmler's peace offer—another highlight in his research.

Dr. Price says he is indebted to, among others, Amos E Joel Jr. of AT&T Bell Laboratories in Holmdel, N J., Robert M. Fano of the Massachusetts Institute of Technology in Cambridge, and Claude E. Shannon of Winchester, Mass., for their help during his research.

Dr. Price also sees his close work with the late William R. Bennett, important contributor to Bell Telephone Laboratories' SIGSALY secret telephone system discussed in the main article, as well as with author David Kahn and Dr. Scholtz, as an "outstanding privilege."—*Ed.*

PART III
CASES

"The Rise of Intelligence" shows, on the basis of case histories, how defeats drove nations to establish intelligence agencies and then, when armies and navies began using radio, how interception of foreign transmissions enabled armed forces to win battles, thus proving to generals and ministers that intelligence mattered and so deserved recognition and rewards. "Intelligence in World War II" surveys major Allied and Axis victories and defeats in the secret aspect of that conflict. "Why Germany's Intelligence Failed in World War II" digs deep into German history and Nazi sociology and into Hitlers' psyche—as much as it can—to seek answers to that question. "An Enigma Chronology of the Enigma Machine" lists the major events in that legendary device's invention, employment, solution, and exploitation, linked to the major events in world history at the time. "Rommel's Good Source" discloses the intercepts that helped him—until the British stopped them. "Nothing Sacred" lists some of the Curia's codes that the Allies solved. Finland, on the wrong side in the war, had a remarkably good codebreaking agency, a picture of which is offered here. An interview with the head of the Soviet codebreaking and one with a low-level codebreaker provides a picture—unquestionably incomplete but better than anything that has appeared in public before—of the Communist nation's communications intelligence during part of the Cold War. The British and the American chiefs of staff agreed not to reveal that they were solving German cipher machine cryptograms during World War II in part because knowledge of this ability might be useful in the future—perhaps against the Soviets.

8

THE RISE OF INTELLIGENCE*

Intelligence matters today. But for centuries it did not, because it almost never produced victory. This study seeks to show how intelligence rose from superstition and disbelief to a successful and important element of war.

Though generals since Alexander have sought information, for millennia they believed only what they could see: terrain, troops. They distrusted spies. The emblems of foreknowledge were dreams, omens, entrails, the mutterings of the Delphic oracle.[1] So inefficacious did these prove that of Edward Creasy's *Fifteen Decisive Battles of the World: from Marathon to Waterloo,* only one triumphed as a consequence of intelligence. At Italy's Metaurus River in 207 B.C., Rome learned of Carthaginian intentions through an intercepted letter, won the battle, and advanced to rule the Western world. The 14 other victories came from strength and will. History and experience showed that intelligence didn't matter. Generals ignored it. Then, in the 19th century, technology gave armies worthwhile targets for intelligence, mainly railroad lines, which armies would use for mobilization and concentration, and the newly evolved general staff offered intelligence a permanent home. Still, Europe's armies disregarded it—until a defeat had shamed the nation, or fear of a defeat stung it. Defending against such an eventuality requires intelligence because, as Clausewitz says, the characteristic of the defense is "awaiting the blow." This implies foreknowledge. Thus, needing intelligence for defense, each general staff established a section for assembling and evaluating it.

Even so, intelligence did not much affect war and politics until radio interception and codebreaking in World War I enabled generals to win battles. It began at Tannenberg in August of 1914 and rose to the greatest intelligence coup of all time, the Zimmermann telegram of 1917, which helped drive the United States into the war.[2]

---

* From *Foreign Affairs*, 85 (September–October 2006), 125–134.

The powers established agencies to exploit this useful new form of intelligence, demonstrating for the first time that intelligence mattered. In World War II, with voluminous radio transmissions, communications intelligence helped win many military and naval victories. In the Cold War, a defensive war fought with secret agents, intelligence became so important that for the first time its officers received four stars.

Intelligence has thus climbed in three stages. In the 19th century, the general staff institutionalized it. In World War I, radio intelligence gave it importance. In World War II and the Cold War, success and necessity promoted its leaders to equality in rank with combat commanders.

But the combat commanders retain priority, and rightly so. For intelligence works only through force. Even in an age in which information serves as an important element of power, intelligence alone can never win a war. It can help, it can economize, but in the end physical strength wins.

Part I

From ancient times commanders had of course employed advisers – the embryo of a staff. But they exalted fighting and derided thinking. Shakespeare's Ulysses deplored this attitude:[3]

> They tax our policy, and call it cowardice,
> Count wisdom as no member of the war,
> Forestall prescience, and esteem no act
> But that of hand. The still and mental parts,
> That do contrive how many hands shall strike
> When fitness calls them on, and know by measure
> Of their observant toil the enemies' weight,—
> Why, this hath not a finger's dignity.
> They call this bed-work, mapp'ry, closet-war;
> So that the ram that batters down the wall,
> For the great swing and rudeness of his poise,
> They place before his hand that made the engine,
> Or those that with the fineness of their souls
> By reason guide his execution.

Of course, in that time – either Ulysses's or Shakespeare's—no permanent staff existed. Rulers prepared at best generalized war plans; they had no structure for evaluating intelligence about their enemies.

The general staff became that structure. It originated in the quartermasters of the various armies of the 18th century. These men reconnoitered the terrain, planned the routes of march and the encampments, and furnished supplies. Quartermaster corps, like dragoons and hussars, had their own uniforms. Its officers had no authority over the fighting troops. But their planning engendered the future general staff.

Their work required knowledge of the land. But with trade and travel mainly local, few maps existed. Soldiers drew them first. In the mid-1600s, the officers of the army of Frederick William, the Great Elector, surveyed his duchy of Prussia during the summer and reduced their measurements to paper during the winter. In France, military engineers developed contour lines – at first in 1725 for depths in hydrographic surveys, later for the heights and steepness of slopes and mountains.[4] Cartography lay at the core of the general staff.

That staff in its modern form is traced by French military historians to an 1800 pamphlet by adjutant Paul Thiébault, by German, to an 1801 memorandum by Colonel Baron Christian L. A. von Massenbach. Both mention intelligence.

Massenbach, then quartermaster, expressed its importance. "These men [in the service of the king] must know not only their own country, they must also know the neighboring states; they must not only be in the position to indicate those positions that we, under certain conditions, would have to take, but also those which the enemy commander, under these very conditions, would take, and would have to take." And, he concluded, "These means [for obtaining knowledge about the various war theaters] consist in nothing other than in a well organized general quartermaster staff."[5] But Massenbach did not propose a separate unit to assemble and evaluate incoming intellignece.

Thiébault referred to a general staff (état-major) and defined its officers' duties as "to transmit the orders that are addressed to them by the commanding generals." He divided it into four bureaux, of which the fourth dealt with spies, guides, prisoner exchanges. He thus first proposed the institutionalization of intelligence in a general staff. He recounted anecdotes showing that the success of a campaign depends upon good reconnaissance. He declared that espionage "forms an essential part of the work of a chief of the general staff."[6]

The French Revolutionary Wars replaced the small professional armies of absolute monarchies with large armies of civilians. They had to be led by men who knew how to lead such masses and to handle new weapons. A professional officer corps evolved and, within it, growing out of the element whose job was to plan ahead, there emerged the staff.

Commanders had long run spies and gathered intelligence about enemy forces. But not until one critical event had occurred did each staff create a special unit to evaluate intelligence. That event was not the evolution of specific targets from the generalized campaign plans of earlier wars. Railroads indeed constituted such a target, enabling potential enemies to pinpoint assembly places for the first time and thereby infer intentions, thus giving intelligence a *raison d'être*. But their use did not lead to an intelligence-evaluation unit. Nor was the critical event recognition by general staff members of the need for an intelligence-evaluation unit. For while they acknowledged that intelligence might save lives and win battles, they rejected such a unit because of likely dishonor (spies dirty those who deal with them), experience (they had won without it), tradition (no such unit had ever existed), inertia (they would need to change), and economics (more officers would compete for top jobs).

The event that made staffs establish an intelligence-evaluating unit was a defeat. A nation had to lose a war or a battle, or fear that it might, to shake the military establishment into changes that would keep it from losing again. More than anything else, such as tactics or organization, intelligence was central to this concern. Why? Because intelligence inheres in defense. Clausewitz says that the characteristic of the defense is "awaiting the blow."[7] So if armies wanted to defend successfully against another attack, they had to know that an attack was coming. They needed a branch of the general staff to assemble and weigh all kinds of intelligence. They got it after a defeat, or in the fear of one. The role of defeat in establishing such a branch in Western armies is well nigh universal.

Part II

Russia suffered the first of those defeats. A year after Alexander II ascended the throne in 1855, Russia capitulated in the Crimean war.

The liberal new tsar was soon impressed by an instructor in the staff academy. Colonel Dmitri I. Miliutin had in 1847 published a two-volume study of military statistics based on his time in Prussia studying its army. ("Statistical" did not then mean analyzing masses of numbers, as of population and pig-iron production; it meant facts about states, as its etymology shows.)[8] When, in 1861, Alexander named him war minister, Miliutin began modernizing the staff. By 1865, one of its six departments gathered and evaluated information about foreign armies. Miliutin's successors continued his work. In 1903, a reorganization assigned intelligence and mobilization to a new department: the 2nd quartermaster general.[9]

The French monarchy possessed a rudimentary staff that shriveled under the Revolution and Napoleon, but was restored on 6 March 1818 after the monarchy was. It existed alongside the much older *Dépôt de la Guerre*, which did little more than archive maps and statistics.[10] In 1826, France began to dispatch military attachés to its embassies.[11] But Napoleon had so overimpressed the French military that, conceiving fighting to be the job of a single brilliant general, it depreciated the staff. Then, in 1870-71, it lost to an army guided by a general staff. France then hastily created such a staff, which it improved and made permanent on 12 March 1874.[12] Among the six bureaux of this general staff was the 2nd, which became famous as the *Deuxième Bureau*. It dealt with what was at first called military statistics, later intelligence. The staff retained this organization through World War I. France attended to new technologies, staying in the forefront of aviation—seen as airborne scouts—and establishing a number of technical commissions, including one for cryptology, which brought that nation to the forefront of communications intelligence in the years before, and then during, the Great War.[13]

Austria and Prussia mobilized against each other in November 1850 over membership in the Germanic Confederation. Though Prussia yielded at Olmütz, a fearful Austria, on 22 December, following demobilization, combined its staff's intelligence-gathering and intelligence-evaluating elements into a so-called *Evidenzbüro*. The unit later changed its name to the *Nachrichtenabteilung* (intelligence section).[14] Austria also proved more far-sighted than all other powers except France when its army began to intercept and solve foreign military messages in 1911, during the Tripolitanian war, both of whose combatants, Italy and the Ottoman empire, bordered on Austria.[15] In 1912, it began training general staff officers as air observers.

Britain set up a Depot of Military Knowledge in April 1803 during an interval of peace between its wars with France. Modeled along the lines of the enemy's *Dépôt de la Guerre*, two of its four departments provided maps and ran a library. But it degenerated, owing to a scandal and lack of work during Britain's long peace in Europe. A retired Indian Army engineer, Major Thomas Best Jervis, pressed in vain for a topographical department in the Foreign Office. Only when he serendipitously obtained a Russian military map of the Crimea just after the outbreak of the Crimean War in 1854 did the army set up a Topographical and Statistical Department under him. It provided many copies of that map to the British forces in Russia. Russia's advance towards India resumed in the 1860s (the Great Game); that, plus the 1869 opening of the French-owned Suez Canal, raised concerns that India might need to be defended or might be isolated or even lost.[16] The sudden appearance of the victorious Prussians in Paris in 1871 frightened Britain. So though the United Kingdom had suffered no major defeats since Yorktown, these fears perhaps drove the far-sighted, reformist secretary of state for war, Edward Cardwell, to authorize an Intelligence Branch. It was activated on 24 May 1873, absorbing the Topographic and Statistical Department. Demonstrating its importance in terms clear to every military man, Cardwell put a general at its head.[17] It didn't help during the Boer War, however, when British arms at first lost battle after battle. A postwar investigation led Parliament to create a general staff, with intelligence as one of the four subdivisions of its military operations directorate.[18]

The United States neglected intelligence as much as it did its armed forces. Protected by the oceans, the Monroe doctrine, and its potential might, the nation believed it did not need spy intelligence, which in any event its Puritan heritage rejected. And it had won all its wars. But soon after the Spanish-American War ended, Congress and the press exposed the army's embarrassing lack of planning, with its insufficient and rancid rations, its distribution of Civil War winter uniforms for a July campaign in Cuba, its employment of black powder instead of smokeless, its bungled troop embarkations, its inadequate medical supervision. Though not a military loss, these denigrated America's armed forces in almost the same way that a defeat would have.

The country demanded a better system. In 1903, Congress set up a general staff. This included a permanent peacetime unit for intelligence. The army copied the organization of the staff of its oldest ally, France, and made intelligence the second bureau – G-2.[19] As it has remained.

And what did the staff do that was the model for all others? Though in an 1814 memorandum the chief of Prussia's Great General Staff wrote that "The work of the general staff in peacetime is to prepare everything for war; the most exact knowledge of the state and of neighboring states is its main duty,"[20] he and his successors merged intelligence into planning. The staff's branches prepared for fighting in three areas—the east (Russia), the west (France), and the rest (Britain, Italy) – by providing raw information on them directly to the staffers devising campaigns.[21]

A few specialized branches of the staff did deal with particular elements of intelligence. As war with Austria approached in 1866, Chief of the General Staff General Helmut von Moltke established a *Nachrichtenbüro*, an Intelligence Bureau, to gather spy information from that country. The bureau, newly designated IIIb, persisted as a spy agency through World War I.[22] On 31 January 1867, Moltke established another specialized agency, the Geographical-Statistical Branch, to collect what appears to have been publicly available information about other countries. On the British Empire, the annual report began with a study of the Ordnance Survey for the year, abstracted the census, detailed administration and finance and information about mining, agriculture, industry, marine economy, and others, catalogued all publications dealing with the British army published in that year, and reviewed travel guides and maps. The branch bounced from unit to unit until the chief of the Great General Staff, Alfred Count von Schlieffen, abolished it in 1894, distributing its functions to other branches.[23]

The staff established units to watch emerging technologies: on 14 March 1889 one for air—presumably observation balloons—and one for plans for attacking foreign fortresses, possibly with the more powerful new guns, and on 18 January 1908 one about steerable airships, motor vehicles, and radio. During two crises – the Herero uprising in German Southwest Africa in 1904 and the Tripolitanian War in 1911-12 – the staff set up units to collect information. Both were dissolved when the emergencies ended.[24]

For the war that begin in 1870, the Great General Staff mobilized itself into a General Staff at General Headquarters that included an intelligence section. It gathered and evaluated information about the enemy army, which is far more rapid and voluminous in war than in peace. At the end of hostilities, the army demobilized to its peacetime arrangement. The intelligence section was abolished. So the most successful staff of all, the one that others looked up to, never set up a permanent agency for the evaluation of intelligence.[25]

Why not? Because unlike them it had never suffered a defeat. Prussia's losses to Napoleon had come too early in the evolution of the staff to determine its organization. And after the staff did come of age – the date of its separation from the War Ministry on 3 February 1825[26] may be taken for this – Prussia won all its wars. It saw no reason to change. Thus Prussia-Germany negatively proves that defeat engenders intelligence-evaluation units: it never lost a war, so it never established one.

Part III

But other armies did. What did they do with them? Their intelligence staffs dutifully collected documents, paid spies, analyzed railroad maps. They were not an army's best men. Since directing one's own troops is far more important than seeking to determine what an enemy might do, each army puts its leaders not into intelligence but into command.[27] And since a main route to the top – honor and glory—is won not at a desk but on the battlefield, the best men shunned intelligence.

Another fundamental point reduced interest in intelligence. Generals fixated on the offensive. The commanders of the armies in all the major powers of Europe planned that in the next war they would attack.[28] They believed that that offered the best chance of winning. For they agreed with Clausewitz that, while "the defensive form of warfare is intrinsically stronger than the offensive," it "has a negative object" and should "be abandoned as soon as we are strong enough to pursue a positive object."[29] Britain's *Field Service Regulations* of 1909 expressed it forcefully: "Decisive success in battle can be gained only by a vigorous offensive." And since the offense imposes its desires upon the enemy, it doesn't need intelligence: as

Clausewitz said, it is "complete in itself."[30] Intelligence is indeed essential for defense, but not for the offense. And commanders wanted not just to survive but to win. They planned to attack: so they did not need intelligence.[31] Moreover, they might not even have wanted it, because its facts might have discomfited them and required them to redo their plans.[32]

For all these reasons, generals ignored intelligence.

Part IV

World War I differed from previous wars in its unprecedented employment of technology. The airplane, the tank, the machine gun changed the way men fought. In intelligence, airplanes did provide information – armies used them first as scouts – but they could reveal only what was at the front or on the way. The radio wrought the greatest change. For just as railroads gave one's own army new capabilities but furnished the enemy with a new source of intelligence, so did radio. It let armies and navies communicate over great distances without the need to string wire, but it enabled enemies to intercept those messages. Messages can of course be encrypted—but they can also be solved. And this information offered many advantages. It revealed plans before they materialized as troops and guns. It came out of high levels, because only higher headquarters had radios. Its volume, because armies were larger and required much coordination, provided confirmation and detail. It was unmediated, not filtered through a possibly misapprehending brain. It was continuous, unlike agent reports. It was fast, because radio is instantaneous. Above all it was trustworthy, because it consisted of the very words of the enemy. It differed in this way from spy information, which always involved fears that the agent had been turned. (Never have commanders sent fake messages to subordinates – the danger of confusion is too great.) For the first time in history, intelligence became prompt and certain and significant. For the first time, intelligence helped win many battles.

In 1914, as the guns of August began to fire, the kaiser's radiomen overheard tsarist transmissions. These enabled Generals Paul von Hindenburg and Erich Ludendorff to encircle and destroy an advancing Russian army at Tannenberg in one of the great victories of the war.

A key architect of that victory, operations officer Colonel Max Hoffmann, said that "We had an ally that I can only talk about after it is all over – we knew all the enemy's plans.... The Russians sent out their wireless in clear."[33] The same ally helped Germany defeat Russia. "We were always warned by the wireless messages of the Russian staff where troops were being concentrated for any new undertaking," Hoffmann said. "Only once during the whole war were we taken by surprise on the Eastern Front by a Russian attack – it was on the Aa in the winter of 1916-17."[34] The war in the East ended in the establishment of Communist power. It may not be too much claim that that supreme fact of 20th-century history owes its existence in part to communications intelligence.

The same factor was helping the Allies win at sea. Aided by a Kriegsmarine codebook that the Russians found in a stranded German cruiser in the Baltic and loyally presented to their ally, the British read messages of Germany's High Seas Fleet.[35] Foreknowledge of its moves kept the Royal Navy from – as Winston Churchill said – losing the war in an afternoon. In the war against Italy, Austria-Hungary, which had recruited for radio intelligence clever young officers from the several ethnic groups of that dual monarchy, enjoyed great cryptanalytic success. They won a major victory at Caporetto in part, as the Italian postwar commission of inquiry said, because "The enemy had found the keys to almost all our codes, even the most difficult and most secret."[36] On the Western Front, a brilliant young French army officer pushed cryptanalysis to the limit to break the ADFGVX field cipher that Germany had introduced in March 1918 for its supreme attacks in the West. The solution of an ADFGVX cryptogram of 3 June revealed the Germans calling urgently for ammunition, presumably for an attack, and direction-finding disclosed the location. Alerted, the French repulsed Germany's last offensive spasm.[37]

And communications intelligence produced the greatest intelligence coup of all time. The British learned cryptanalysis from the captured codebook and advanced to break Germany's diplomatic codes. In 1917, they solved German Foreign Minister Arthur Zimmermann's foolish, fateful offer to Mexico to attack the United States in return for regaining the "lost territories" of Texas, New Mexico, and Arizona. Britain gave this propaganda weapon to President Woodrow Wilson, and six weeks after he made it public, the United States entered World

War I, with all that that has entailed. Spectacularly and definitively, the episode proved that intelligence mattered.[38]

The powers awoke. They realized that intelligence, and in particular communications intelligence, could win battles. The German troop manual, which before the war listed balloons and dirigibles as sources for intelligence, added enemy communications after it.[39] Countries that did not have cryptanalytic agencies in 1914 but had established them during the war retained them in peacetime – the United Kingdom, Germany, Italy, the United States. And the pattern that defeat engenders intelligence-evaluating agencies recurred. Germany, whose prewar army had never been defeated and had never had a peacetime agency to evaluate intelligence, established one after it lost the war. Intelligence had been institutionalized everywhere.[40]

And it grew more and more significant. During the Washington naval conference of 1921-22, the combined U.S. Army-State Department Cipher Bureau under Herbert O. Yardley helped push Japan to accept a smaller naval force than it wanted.[41] By stopping a naval race this saved many nations millions of dollars. During World War II, intelligence – again chiefly in the form of codebreaking— shortened the war by enabling Allied convoys to avoid U-boat packs, by telling American submarines where Japanese convoys were going so they could be sunk, by helping Allied troops in Europe to win battles big and little. As Army Chief of Staff George C. Marshall said, "... these intercepted codes... contribute greatly to the victory and tremendously to the saving in American lives..."[42]

Many of the battles won by intelligence in both wars were defensive ones; intelligence inheres in the defense. In World War I, Tannenberg, the Royal Navy in the North Sea, the ADFGVX alert, even the Zimmermann telegram warned against proposed attacks. Between the wars, nations that were not preparing aggression built up their intelligence. Poland cracked the German Enigma cipher machine; the United States broke the main Japanese diplomatic cipher machine. Aggressive countries concentrated on weapons of attack – men, tanks, planes—and ignored intelligence. Hitler never combined his half-dozen codebreaking agencies into one, nor did he demand results from his spy agency. And indeed he did not need intelligence during his blitzkriegs. So when the war turned around, forcing him onto the defensive and into a need for intelligence, he did not have it. He never learned where the Allies would attack. The Allies' development of intelligence paid off – at first in the defensive battles, such as Midway and the U-boats, later in the assault on Europe, and the sinkings by American submarines of Japanese convoys.

Part V

These successes empowered the men in charge of intelligence. They contributed to victory just as logistics and manpower and leadership did – though of course indirectly. From 1921 to 1942, of the 10 G-2s in the army general staff, five were colonels and five brigadier generals, while the G-1s, G-3s, G-4s, chief signal officers, and others all ranked as generals.[43] But during that combat, intelligence officers came to wear stars. William Donovan, head of the Office of Strategic Services, rose from colonel to major general. The chiefs of the army and navy intelligence divisions, the heads of the army and navy units producing communications intelligence, Eisenhower's and MacArthur's G-2s – all became general officers or admirals. They did not have the responsibility or the rank of commanders of fighting men, but intelligence work no longer besmirched careers.

And the conflict showed yet again that defeat breeds intelligence. Pearl Harbor spawned the C.I.A. West Germany established the *Bundesnachrichtendienst*. The horrifying start of the war of terror renewed the sequence of defeat and intelligence. 9/11 bred the National Intelligence Community.

Intelligence rose yet more in significance. During the Cold War, both sides feared attack. On the defensive, they intensified their intelligence activity, enlarging their spy, satellite, and interception agencies. The men and women who ran them had to be promoted commensurately. Then, though they proved their ability chiefly in intelligence, they rose to the top of command of fighting troops. For example, Lieutenant General Lew Allen, after serving as head of the codebreaking National Security Agency, was promoted to be the four-star chief of staff of the Air Force. In Britain, Alan West, who served as head of naval intelligence, ended his career as first sea lord, the Royal Navy's top professional officer. Reinhard Gehlen in Germany was a general. Finally, since the intelligence commanders were in a sense fighting the Cold War, and later the war against terror, they rose to four-star rank in their specialty. Admiral Bobby Inman got his fourth star when he became deputy director of the Central Intelligence Agency, as did Admiral William Studeman and General Michael Hayden, former head of NSA, then CIA. All the directors of national intelligence have worn four stars, and in France, Admiral Pierre Lacoste, who became director general of French intelligence, wears five stars. Indeed, so far has the taint of intelligence faded that a former director of central intelligence was elected president of the United States.

Part VI

"Knowledge is power," said Francis Bacon. But that maxim omits two fundamental facts. One is that men cannot know everything and so they cannot foresee everything. They cannot foretell the rise and fall of the stock market, or even who will win the World Series. And these are relatively restricted arenas. So how can intelligence agencies foresee events in so complex a "system" as the world? And even if they could, they would bump against the problem that everyone rejects unpleasant news. People believe what they want to believe. Say a guy is in love with a girl. His friends say she is gold-digging him, two-timing him. Does he leave her? Not if he loves her. Is it different with a leader who has surmounted obstacles and naysayers, who has got to the top in part through his policy, and who believes—often with reasons—that he knows better than his underlings? No intelligence agency can overcome that human obstacle.

And even if it could, it would encounter the other fact that Bacon omitted. Knowledge alone is not power. It needs force to work. It undoubtedly helps commanders because it optimizes resources. It magnifies force by enabling men and guns to be better placed for fighting. It improves psychological resources – will, morale – by reducing anxiety and steadying command. But knowledge, or intelligence, alone cannot win. Strength wins, not brains. The smartest major cannot overpower the dumbest general. If the Axis had the best intelligence and the Allies the worst, the Allies would still have won. Though Odysseus was the wisest of the Greeks, conceiving the Trojan horse that enabled the Greeks to win, he did not use intelligence to recover his kingdom when he came home. He used strength. He slew the suitors with a bow that only he was strong enough to string. The world is physical.

Yet this is the information age. Information is growing in quantity and in quality and so is the form called intelligence. A new idea suggests that perhaps information is itself physical. A physicist has said that "every item of the physical world has at bottom ... an immaterial source and explanation ... that all things physical are information-theoretic in origin."[44] If so, this would link intelligence and strength in a basic way. It would perhaps bring closer to fruition Shelley's poetic hope that knowledge, and its military form, intelligence, could indeed become for all humankind "The trumpet of a prophecy."

Notes

1. Sir Alan Gardner, *The Kadesh Inscriptions of Ramesses II* (Oxford: Oxford University Press, 1960), pp. 28–30; Cicero *De Diviniatio*; Genesis 41; Joseph Eddy Fontenrose, *The Delphic Oracle: Its Responses and Operations, with a Catalogue of Responses* (Berkeley, CA: University of California Press, 1978); Numbers 13.

2. Thomas Boghardt, *The Zimmermann Telegram: Intelligence, Diplomacy, and America's Entry into World War I* (Annapolis, MD: Naval Institute Press, 2012).

3. *Troilus and Cressida.* I.iii.197–210.

4. W. Stavenhagen, "Die geschichtliche Entwicklung des preußischen Militär-Kartenwesens," *Geographische Zeitschrift*, Vol. 6 (1900), pp. 435–449, 504–512, 544–565 at 437; Josef W. Konvitz, *Cartography in France 1660–1848* (Chicago, IL: University of Chicago Press, 1987), p. 167.

5. [Christian Karl August Ludwig] Massenbach, *Memorien zur Geschichte des preußischen Staats unter den Regierungen Friedrich Wilhelm II. und Friedrich Wilhelm III* (Amsterdam, the Netherlands: Verlag des Kunst- und Industrie-Comptoirs, 1809), 3:263, 264.

6. Paul Thiebault, *Manuel des Adjudans-Generaux et des Adjoints employés dans les Etats-Maiors-Divisionnaires des Armées* (Paris, n.p.: An VII), pp. 13, 31n., 124–25.

7. Carl von Clausewitz, *On War,* trans. Michael Howard and Peter Paret (Princeton, NJ: Princeton University Press, 1976), p. 357.

8. Jacob Grimm and Wilhelm Grimm, *Deutsches Worterbuch* s. v. "*statistik*"; Oxford English Dictionary, s.v. "statistic"; Baron de Ferussac, *Plan Sommaire d'un Traiti de Geographie et de Statistique* (Paris, France: Anselin et Pochard, 1821), esp. pp. 21–23.

9. David Schimmelpenninck van der Oye, "Reforming Military Intelligence," 133–50 at 142 in Schimmelpenninck and Bruce W. Menning, *Reforming the Tsar's Army* (Washington, DC: Woodrow Wilson Center Press, 2005).

10. André Corvisier, *Histoire Militaire de La France*, II, *De 1715 à1871* (Paris, France: Presses Universitaires de France, 1992), pp. 245, 426, 431; Dallas D. Irvine, "The French and Prussian Staff Systems before 1870," *The Journal of the American Military History Foundation*, Vol. 2 (Winter, 1938), pp. 198–203 at 202–203.

11. Sébastian Laurent, *Politiques de l'ombre: Etat, renseignement et surveillance en France* (Paris, France: Fayard, 2009), pp. 136–138.

12. Pierre Guinard, *Inventaire sommaire des Archives de la Guerre, Série N 1872–1919*, Ministère de la Défense, État-major de l'armée de Terre, Service historique (Troyes, France: Imprimerie La Renaissance, 1975), pp. 11–12; France, *Journal militaire officiel. Partie réglementaire*, 1874, No. 91 (pp. 230–31). Décret portant réorganization de l'état-major générale du ministre de la Guerre, 12 mars 1874, Art. 1.; Laurent, 330–344.

13. Alexandre Ollier, *La Cryptographie militaire avant la guerre de 1914* (Panazol: LaVauzelle, 2002); Marcel Givierge, "*Étude historique sur la Section du Chiffre*," a photocopy at the National Cryptographic Museum, Ft. Meade, MD.

14. Josef Reifberger, "Die Entwicklung des militärischen Nachrichtenwesens in der k.u.k. Annee," *Osterreichische Militär Zeitschrift*, 14 (Mai–Juni 1976), 213–223 at 214.

15. Otto J. Horak, *Leban und Werke 1873–1967* (Linz: Universitätverlag Rudolf Trauner, [2005, 2006], 1:84–85).

16. Thomas G. Fergusson, *British Military Intelligence 1870–1994: The Development of a Modern Intelligence Organization* (Frederick, MD: University Publications of America, 1984), pp. 18–19, 21–22.

17. William Beaver, "History of British Intelligence in the Victorian Empire" (Oxford D. Phil. thesis, Wolfson College, 1978), p. 15. A copy in the National Cryptologic Museum.

18. Fergusson, 119–121, 251, 252.

19. U.S. War Department, *Annual Report of the Secretary of War, 1903* (Washington, DC: Government Printing Office, 1904), Appendix D.

20. Carl von Grolman in E[mil]. von Conrady, *Leben und Wirken des Generals der Infanterie und kommandirenden Generals des V. Armeekorps Carl von Grolman* (Berlin, Germany: Mittler, 1894–1896), at 2:392.

21. *Ibid.*, 2:390–94, 3:263–266, 28–32 and Maj. Stoerkel, "Die Organisation des Großen Generalstabes,"Bundesarchiv-Militärarchiv,H 3512,6–13,16.

22. Stoerkel, 33–34, 38, 43, 46, 48, 49, 50.

23. Stoerkel, 35, 48, 49; Spenser Wilkinson, *The Brain of an Army: A Popular Account of the German General Staff* (Westminster: Constable, 1895), pp. 140–142.

24. Stoerkel, 43, 59, 56, 60.

25. Stoerkel, 33, 38, 64.

26. Stoerkel, 16.

27. Gen. Friedrich Wilhelm Hauck said he would rather have a good commander for one of his division's three regiments than a good intelligence officer on his staff (interview, 26 April 1970). Gen. Adolf Heusinger,

commander of the postwar Bundeswehr, said that the Wehrmacht used the better staff offices as troop commanders, and that the intelligence spots were filled by second-raters (interview, 8 October 1973).

28. Michael Howard, "Men Against Fire: The Doctrine of the Offensive," 510–526 at 510 in Peter Paret, ed., *Makers of Modern Strategy* (Princeton, NJ: Princeton University Press, 1986).

29. Clausewitz, 358.

30. Clausewitz, 524.

31. See the articles by Norman Stone, Holger H. Herwig, William C. Fuller Jr., Christopher M. Andrew, Jan Karl Tanenbaum, and Paul M. Kennedy in Ernest May, *Knowing One's Enemies: Intelligence Assessment before the Two World Wars* (Princeton, NJ: Princeton University Press, 1984).

32. Jack Snyder, *The Ideology of the Offensive* (Ithaca, NY: Cornell University Press, 1984), pp. 15, 16, 17.

33. Major General Max Hoffmann, *War Diaries and Other Papers,* trans. Eric Sutton (London, U.K.: Martin Secker), 1:41, 18.

34. General [Max] Hoffmann, *The War of Lost Opportunities* (London, U.K.: Kegan Paul, 1924), p. 132.

35. David Kahn, *Seizing the Enigma: The Race to Break the German U-Boat Codes, 1939–1943* (Boston, MA: Houghton Mifflin, 1991), pp. 21–22.

36. Quoted in Horak, 1:118.

37. David Kahn, *The Codebreakers* (New York: Macmillan, 1967), pp. 339–347.

38. Boghardt.

39. Germany, Reichswehrminister, H. Dv. 487, *Führung und Gefecht der verbundenen Waffen*, 1 September 1921, Berlin, Germany: Offene Worte, 1931, §§ 167.

40. Under the Versailles Treaty, Germany was not allowed to have a general staff so had no intelligence section.

41. David Kahn, *The Reader of Gentlemen's Mail: Herbert O. Yardley and the Birth of American Codebreaking* (New Haven, CT: Yale University Press, 2004), pp. 63–80.

42. United States, Congress, Joint Committee on the Investigation of the Pearl Harbor Attack, *Pearl Harbor Attack,* Hearings, 79th Congress, 1st and 2d Sessions (Washington, DC: Government Printing Office, 1946), 3:1133.

43. James E. Hewes, Jr., *From Root to McNamara: Army Organization and Administration, 1900–1963*, Special Studies, Center of Military History (Washington, DC: Government Printing Office, 1975), pp. 389–390, 392–393.

44. John Wheeler, quoted in Hans Christian von Baeyer, *Information: The Language of Science* (Cambridge: Harvard University Press, 2003), p. 233.

9

INTELLIGENCE IN WORLD WAR II*

A Survey

It is appropriate that a new journal on the history of intelligence begin with a survey of its greatest use in the greatest war of all time. This may set the parameters of the field and give future scholars targets to shoot at – and perhaps to shoot down.

The intelligence struggle of World War II was a vast one, vaster even than the shooting war because it reached into neutral countries. So, in an attempt to be manageable, this survey concentrates on the United States, Great Britain, and Nazi Germany. Omitted will be the Soviet Union, Italy, and Japan, because intelligence studies on them are spotty or sketchy or both, as well as the quickly defeated or smaller belligerents, such as Poland, Finland, and France, and the neutrals, such as Sweden and Spain. This survey will attempt to cover the different forms of intelligence, their strengths and weaknesses, intelligence successes and failures, the relative ability of the two sides, and the effect of intelligence on the war.

Two other restrictions should be noted. Intelligence in World War II did not spring full-armed into existence. Rather its faculties developed mainly during World War I, and its organs largely patterned themselves upon those evolved during the earlier conflict. But the details of those institutions and operations cannot be included here. Nor will the World War II intelligence organizations – their constantly changing internal structures and sub- and superordinations – or the flow of paper through them be dealt with except in the sparest way needed for understanding.

---

* From *The Journal of Intelligence History*, 1(1) (Summer 2001), 1–20.

The meat and potatoes of all military intelligence, the least glamorous, often neglected by historians of intelligence but most important to the combat commander, is that obtained at the front by the fighting troops themselves.[1] They see the enemy. They hear him. Sometimes they smell him – his fuel, his cooking. In hand-to-hand combat, they feel him.

This is where military intelligence begins. At its most primitive level, intelligence is targeting. It means a soldier's finding his enemy so he can kill him. A rifleman hears a rustle and throws a grenade at it. An airman finds his target in the cross-hairs of his bombsight and releases his bombs. When, on 14 September 1944, Sergeant Herman Ledford, advancing with other Americans up Mount Altuzzo in Italy, suddenly saw a German emerge from behind two bunkers, he killed him with an accurately aimed shot from his rifle.[2]

Even when not firing at the enemy, soldiers at the front learn a lot about their foe. On the eastern front, for example, German soldiers discovered that Russian troops wearing hats were in a defensive mode, troops wearing helmets in an offensive mode. Russians acting nervous and moving across fields of fire indicated new arrivals and hence a forthcoming attack. Their carrying of gas masks but not packs was defensive, of packs but not gas masks was offensive.[3] Observations of movements – including the noise of tank motors, which troops never missed – reveal a great deal. Hitler himself once analyzed it succinctly: "When I get a report today on a Russian road that leads to a section of the front, in which 36 rifle divisions and armored formations, so many armored regiments and so many other formations are located, and it says that yesterday night 1,000 vehicles traveled on a road, tonight 800 and then 1,200 and 300 vehicles, that is an alarm, then, that runs through the entire eastern front that says, 'Alarm imminent.'"[4]

In addition to this nonspecialized observation, front-line formations established observation posts for a more detailed and protracted study of the enemy and dispatched patrols to obtain close-up views of the enemy's positions and to capture prisoners to interrogate. On 2 March 1940, during the Phony War, a German patrol crossed over the Lauter River, which divides Germany from Alsace, and "discovered a machine-gun position (unoccupied) on the Scheibenhart-Niederlauterbach railroad stretch and a dugout (unoccupied) on the Heidenberg."[5] The information presumably helped the German commander plan his next moves better. And both Germans and Allies employed specialized sound-and-flash ranging units to pinpoint the enemy's heavy guns.

In more fluid situations, units sent out cavalry – mounted or armored – or motorized scouts to feel out the enemy situation – to see where the enemy's main body is, which towns are occupied and which not, what the enemy axis of march is, and the like. In the first days of September 1944, after a spectacular drive across France that ended only when the U.S. Third Army ran out of gas, its XXth Corps sent armored cavalry units east toward Metz. At first they reported that the enemy was panic-stricken, but within a few days German resistance had stiffened and the reports became decidedly less optimistic and more realistic. On 6 September, cavalry units reached the Moselle River, west of Metz, and, though beaten back, reported that no bridges remained.[6] This told commanders what they could expect and prepared them better for the assault.

Sometimes information comes from the enemy himself. Prisoners fear for their lives, especially if they have been captured in combat by men who have just been trying to kill them. Under the threat of death, implicit or explicit, many sing. This elemental method fits the simplicity of the information sought at the front: what units are in the enemy line, where the heavy guns are, whether reserves are present. The intelligence is short-lived, but it can be vital for a company or regimental commander in battle. On 23 March 1943, for example, a prisoner in North Africa reported the presence of three tank companies to U.S. Third Army forces, and others said that the 10th Panzer Division was in the area. This information contributed to the American victory in the Battle of El Guettar.[7] Deserters were similarly useful sources of local information.

Farther from the front, as at divisional headquarters, questions both deeper and wider were asked. What is the organization and armament of your regiment's heavy-weapons company? of its artillery battery? What armor is at your disposal? How good is morale? What do you think of your division commander? In the German army, much of this work was done by specialist interrogators who knew the prisoners' language. Prisoners who were thought to have more information – as about factories at home or other units in which they might have served – were then sent to higher headquarters for yet

more detailed questioning. In the summer of 1944, a German officer captured in southern France provided detailed information about
Germany's defensive Siegfried Line – giving, for example, details
about the field of fire of a machine-gun nest that could not be seen
from the air. He knew so much about it because, years before, he had
helped build the fortifications.[8]

Did prisoners lie? It seemed rare. There was little point, since being
found out risked death, especially at the front.

Longer-range intelligence was elicited from prisoners away from
the front by techniques subtler than fear. The British bugged cells and
recorded inmates' conversations. The Luftwaffe, in its Dulag Luft West
in Oberursel, near Frankfurt, sought to overwhelm prisoners with
its knowledge so that they would feel nothing would be lost – and
something personal might be gained – if they revealed a few more
tidbits of information. For example, from base newspapers, identification papers, and letters found in downed bombers and from scraps of
overheard radio chatter, Dulag Luft built up a picture of, say, a bomber
squadron and its personnel. An interrogator would examine this material before talking to a prisoner. Then, with his apparently inexplicable
knowledge of intimate matters, the interrogator surprised the prisoner
into conceding the truth of some innocuous item, such as his home
address. Once the prisoner was talking, the interrogator got him first
to confirm known material and then gradually to provide new material. Some reports ran to five single-spaced typewritten pages.[9]

"Knowledge of new battle methods of the enemy and the use of
new types of airplanes and weapons," noted an officer of Foreign Air
Forces West, a Luftwaffe intelligence unit, "is won almost exclusively
through questioning of prisoners. Knowledge of this kind is immediately taken into consideration in German battle conduct and in air
defense. It increases our defense success and saves the troops personnel and material."[10]

Captured documents and weapons likewise betrayed information.
In Sicily, a seized Axis map showed defense lines along ridges marked
A, B, and C; then a German order dated 2 August 1943 revealed that
the Hermann Göring Division had been directed to withdraw to ridge
line C.[11] A few days later, an Italian map captured at an enemy headquarters at Gela showed the locations of minefields along the southern
coast of Sicily and along coastal roads. The U.S. Third Army translated

it, reproduced it, and distributed it to all subordinate divisions to help save men and vehicles.

The Germans, too, often seized documents and maps. But it didn't always help. On 7 and 8 June 1944, for example, the Germans defending Normandy from the Allied landings captured, in the briefcase of a dead American officer and in a boat that had drifted ashore, the top-secret operations orders of the two major American assault commands, the Vth and the VIIth Corps. Within 48 hours of the invasion, then, the Germans had the entire order of battle and attack plans for these units. Even aside from the fact that local units had expected the movements, directed toward the south, the information didn't help. Overwhelming Allied air superiority prevented the Germans from countering the Americans' advances, and the need to block a breakout to the east limited defenses in the south in any event. Thus this apparently priceless intelligence did not affect the German reaction in one of the most critical battles of the war.[12]

More valuable than patrols, prisoners, or documents – but also far more difficult to obtain – was aerial reconnaissance, both ocular and photographic. The British sought to make it serve strategic purposes, in determining the effect of area bombing on production and morale. But its optimistic estimates could not be confirmed and that effort was eventually suspended. Aerial reconnaissance served tactics. It chiefly disclosed enemy concentrations and details of fortifications, but it also helped determine specifics of enemy weapons. In comparison with another major source, communications intelligence, aerial reconnaissance consisted essentially of snapshots, which were less useful than the more nearly continuous flow of communications intelligence, and it could only reveal what it could see, whereas communications intelligence could foreshadow events long before they materialized as tanks and troops. On the other hand, aerial photography enjoyed a great psychological advantage over communications intelligence. When a commander looks at a photograph, even with the aid of a photo interpreter, he is seeing the enemy defenses or forces with his own eyes. He trusts the evidence. Communications intelligence, which comes from peepings in earphones and the cerebrations of intellectuals, and spy reports, which may be lies, seem less solid. Nothing convinces like a picture.

When hostilities began, both sides had units for strategic aerial reconnaissance. Soon they expanded their air reconnaissance into lower echelons. They also evolved units at both low and high levels to interpret their pictures. Strategic photographs were evaluated in Germany by the Luftwaffe General Staffs 5th (Intelligence) Branch's Main Photo Branch, working in the reading and hearing rooms of the defunct Prussian legislature in Berlin;[13] in Britain, the R.A.F.'s Photographic Intelligence Unit in a vast neo-Gothic pile, Danesfield House, at Medmenham, evaluated the images.[14]

One typical German strategic reconnaissance flight began on a spring afternoon in 1942. Captain Siegfried Knemeyer lifted his Junkers Ju 88 off a runway in Crete and swung east, then south. He was heading for the harbor of Alexandria, where he intended to photograph the shipping in the harbor. His mission was one of 44 that the Luftwaffe's strategic reconnaissance unit flew against North Africa from 29 May to 17 July; together with one that morning, in which Knemeyer had taken pictures of what looked like splinters in the thin streak of the Suez Canal, it might tell the Germans what the British intended in the eastern Mediterranean. Soon Knemeyer was soaring at 37,500 feet over the historic city founded by the conqueror whom his Führer was attempting to emulate. He ordered the automatic cameras started. One, with a focal length of 12 inches, provided broad cover. The other, with a focal length of about 20 inches, furnished details in a narrower area. They clicked every few seconds, exposing negatives about a foot square. Knemeyer peered out his window. Far below in the clear air, British fighters swung helplessly back and forth, tethered at their ceiling. It was like looking down into an aquarium, Knemeyer thought. He completed his run and turned for home. His two sets of pictures showed 1.5 million tons of enemy shipping assembled in Egypt.[15] When, in June, the British attempted to force a passage to Malta, the Axis was ready: only two of the 17 freighters and tankers got through, and the island remained in jeopardy.

Strategic reconnaissance was complemented by operational, tactical, and battle reconnaissance. Operational reconnaissance, carried out by long-range squadrons, "embraces the surveillance of the enemy's concentration, especially his railroad concentration," German regulations specified.[16] Tactical reconnaissance often concentrated on the strips over which a corps or armored division would advance during the next two or three days – about 20 to 40 miles into enemy territory. The observers in their short-range planes reconnoitered visually at from 7,000 to 15,000 feet. Battle reconnaissance, flown at under 7,000 feet, watched enemy forces, especially reserves, and spotted for artillery.[17] In May of 1943, the Luftwaffe had 377 long-range planes and 402 short-range; the total of 779 constituted about an eighth of the German air force's strength.[18]

For a mission, the airmen would not simply leap into their cockpits, rev up their motors, and take off to see what they could see. They got assignments, as one for the invasion of Greece: "... Where is the enemy effecting resistance? ... Where is the advance battalion of the 50th Infantry Division? Where are roads and bridges destroyed? ..." Upon their return, they reported their observations – sometimes marked on maps—to the intelligence officer. Photographs were evaluated. A sequence would show which way a column of troops was marching. If railroad flatcars headed toward the front were carrying guns or tanks, reinforcements were coming up; if empty, a relief or withdrawal was probably beginning. Artillery positions differed from machine-gun nests.

But the source was far from perfect. Clouds, woods, shadows, darkness, or camouflage concealed troops and installations. Observers mistook one place for another, misspelled place names so that they became unfindable on maps, reported in terms so general – a march column was "large" – as to be useless, and repeatedly confused friend and foe. Compounding this was the occasional refusal of commanders to believe some of the hardest intelligence available. It might seem impossible to ignore pictures that show the actual objects, but Luftwaffe chief Hermann Göring managed it. The photo interpreters might have erred, he would say. Or areas that had not been covered might have furnished different intelligence. Or he simply excluded the pictures from his consideration. Things like this happened at lower levels as well. All of this nullified the results of aerial reconnaissance.[19] Finally, the basic limitation of aerial reconnaissance was that it could not gather information on what it could not get to see. For the first half of the war, Germany's superiority in the air permitted her to reconnoiter from the air. But with Germany's defeats, reconnaissance became more difficult and sparser. Toward the end, it became almost nonexistent. In December 1944, a Luftwaffe officer noted that no air reconnaissance of British industry had taken place for three years.[20] In May 1944, while the Germans were trying desperately to discover where the expected invasion of Europe would come, the Kriegsmarine mourned that "especially on account of the lack of constant comprehensive air reconnaissance, the [enemy's] main transport effort in one sector or another of the Channel coast is not ascertainable."[21]

Allied air reconnaissance, on the other hand, got better as the war progressed. It began poorly enough. In the spring of 1940, French air reconnaissance failed to detect the southward transfer of divisions from Germany's Army Group B to Army Group A,[22] which then unexpectedly cut sickle-like through the flank and rear of the French and British armies, defeating the former and driving the latter to Dunkirk. But a few months later, British reconnaissance planes photographed the Italian fleet in its harbor at Taranto. As the British aircraft carrier *Illustrious* drove through the Mediterranean to her launching position, late photographs were flown to her. These revealed that the anchorage was newly protected by a barrage balloon and the battleships by nets. The British planes, forewarned, avoided the defenses, sank one capital ship and damaged several others, and – in an important victory – drove all Italian war vessels from that harbor in the instep of the boot to more distant ports on the west coast.[23]

Other aids to victory in battle followed. Before the Battle of El Alamein, photo intelligence served as a main source of information on the precise location of enemy units and produced a mosaic of the entire battle line. By photographing German shipyards, it helped raise the Allied estimate of U-boat production to 20 a month, very close to the actual figure. Before the invasion of Sicily, air cover was flown to see if any changes had occurred that would indicate that the Axis was aware of Allied plans; none were found. In 1944, photo evaluation was temporarily baffled by ski-like objects seen in France. With the help of other intelligence, Medmenham discovered that they were launching sites for the V-1 "flying bomb." The Allies bombed them. Likewise, the developmental installation at Peenemünde for the V-2 rocket came under the photographic loupe, leading to bombing raids on it.[24]

In the "wizard war" of radars, photographic intelligence played a determinative role. Dr. Reginald V. Jones, the R.A.F.'s scientific advisor, needed to know the characteristics of a German radar for which the British were seeking countermeasures. Details of its radar dish would reveal them. An installation of this radar was known, from previous small-scale pictures, to be at a large house near the edge of the Boulogne cliffs. But those pictures did not have the necessary detail. A daring British reconnaissance pilot in a Spitfire, timing his shutter work to the split second, raced low over the house and brought back the large-scale pictures needed, permitting the British to blind the radar.[25] In another case, a German vessel that had been converted into a minesweeper by the addition of powerful magnets in its bow to detonate magnetic mines was photographed doing just that. By calculating from successive prints the explosion point and the speed of the ship, the range of the ship's effectiveness could be calculated – and mines built to delay exploding until the sweeper had passed over it.

Photo reconnaissance volume grew to enormous proportions. In August 1944, the U.S. 3rd Army received 3,365,287 air photo prints – more than 100,000 a day.[26] Aerial photos were the only way to assess the damage of bomb raids, and they showed how new navigational aids, such as OBOE, helped improve the accuracy of the attacks. Before the Normandy invasion, they disclosed Germans putting tripods just below the water line to obstruct tanks and landing craft. Oblique photographs by P-38 Lightnings at practically zero altitude, using a camera that compensated for the great fly-by speed, found underwater obstacles and mines attached to stakes between those obstacles. Photo reconnaissance was not perfect. In particular, it failed before the German onslaught that became known as the Battle of the Bulge. Bad weather and German precautions kept Allied air from spotting the German concentrations. But in general air reconnaissance revealed enough about the enemy to help the Allies direct their forces more efficiently and to win battles.

Though no other source could match the dash and excitement of aerial reconnaissance, it itself could not match the value of codebreaking, which, with its associated sorceries, such as direction-finding and traffic analysis, was by far the most important source of intelligence in World War II for both sides. A high German intelligence officer called it "the darling of all intelligence chiefs." Chief of the German General Staff Franz Halder said it was "the most copious and the best source." General Dwight Eisenhower said it was "of priceless value." U.S. Army Chief of Staff General George C. Marshall said its solutions "contribute greatly to the victory and tremendously to the saving in American lives." It owed this preëminence to its trustworthiness, its speed, its volume, its precision, and perhaps its cheapness.[27]

At the start of the war, Poland, France, and Britain were – thanks to Poland's brilliant prewar solution[28] – reading Luftwaffe messages enciphered in the Enigma cipher machine. This provided a few insights into German operations but stukas, panzers, and German enthusiasm spoke louder than Polish and French intelligence. And it was less Enigma solutions than radar and plain-language radiotelephone interceptions that helped the Royal Air Force win the Battle of Britain. But an Enigma solution did reveal in October 1940 that Hitler had disbanded his invasion planning staff – an indication that he was postponing his cross-Channel attack invasion of England.[29]

As the British codebreaking establishment, commonly called Bletchley Park from its location in a Victorian estate northwest of London, gained people, experience, and the electromechanical aids called bombes, and as Axis communication volume increased, the number of solutions – covernamed ULTRA – rose. By the middle of the war, Bletchley was reading tens of thousands of military messages a month. Some of these led to dramatic results. In the Mediterranean, tanker after tanker carrying fuel to General Erwin Rommel in North Africa was sunk because the Allies knew their sailing times and routes; this loss of fuel hobbled Rommel both physically and psychologically.[30] At Anzio, solution of a couple of Führer messages enabled General Mark Clark to ward off a couple of attacks designed to drive his forces back into the sea. In the deception planning for the OVERLORD invasion, intercepts showed how the Germans were responding to the Allied feints. In the Falaise pocket after the Normandy invasion, "unprecedented amounts of Enigma traffic were being intercepted, and most of it was decoded with such rapidity that signal after signal could be prepared so close to German time of origin that each seemed more urgent than the last."[31]

ULTRA was so productive in part because Enigma served the German army at division, corps, and army. But it was not the only German army cipher system solved. Both British and Americans attacked lower-level German army hand ciphers, used at battalion and regiment. The Americans did this with signal intelligence units in the field,[32] while the British centralized all cryptanalytic work at Bletchley. The great bulk of the Enigma and hand-cipher messages dealt with routine matters such as strength returns and situation reports. These must not be disparaged, for they told commanders which units were facing them, how strong they were, and what they were concerned about. This is fundamental intelligence.

Very high level intelligence came from two places. In 1944, the British built a protocomputer called COLOSSUS to solve German army radioteletypewriter on-line encipherment used only between Führer headquarters and the headquarters of army groups and armies.[33] But this source was exceeded in value by the intercepts of Japan's ambassador and its military attaché in Berlin. These produced the highest level intelligence – perhaps reaching the strategic level – obtained by any belligerent in the war. The diplomats enciphered their messages in a cipher machine that had been solved in 1940 by U.S. Army civilian cryptanalysts under the leadership of William F. Friedman and Frank M. Rowlett and that they codenamed PURPLE.[34] The Soviets solved the machine as well – their great codebreaker, Sergei Tolstoy, contributing some of the key ideas.[35] These solutions gave the Big Three entry into the thinking of Hitler as he expressed it to his ally. Much of it dealt with the Eastern Front, the main battlefield of the war. For example, a message of 27 July 1942 from Tokyo to the Japanese ambassador to Germany, General Hiroshi Oshima, disclosed that, despite his urging, Japan was not going to attack the Soviet Union.[36] But some of the intelligence dealt with the West. On 10 November 1943, Oshima reported on German plans to repel the Allied invasion: "… the Germans plan to smash any attempt to land as close to the edge of the water as possible… The Strait of Dover is given first place in the German Army's fortification scheme and troop dispositions…." His military attaché specified that antitank flanking fire would be delivered from two or three casements equipped with 40-millimeter Skoda guns and from two or three others equipped with 50-millimeter guns.[37] It was information like this, of spectacular importance, that led General Marshall to say that the Japanese messages from Berlin comprised "our main basis of information regarding Hitler's intentions in Europe."

Before the war could be won on land, however, it had to be won at sea. "The Battle of the Atlantic was the dominating factor all through the war," wrote Winston Churchill. And the Germans had the edge at first, in part through their originally superior codebreaking. The Kriegsmarine's B-Dienst, short for Beobachtungs-Dienst (Observation Service), its codebreaking unit, was reading, at the start of hostilities, what the British called Naval Cypher but was actually a four-digit superenciphered code; it kept on doing so through the new editions of August 1940 and June 1941. This edition, Naval Cypher No. 3, encoded the Allied U-boat situation report, convoy messages, and communications between the Royal and the United States navies. By early December of 1942, the B-Dienst, with 1,000 men in its Berlin headquarters and 4,000 men, many of them intercept operators, in the field, was reading 80 percent of the messages it intercepted in Naval Cypher No. 3. Admiral Karl Dönitz, commander of U-boats, planned nearly all his U-boat operations on the information from these decrypts. On 30 October 1942, for example, the B-Dienst submitted a report that Convoy SC 107, then east of Cape Race, at the tip of Newfoundland, would steer 45°. At the same time, a U-boat sighted it and reported its exact location. Dönitz ordered his U-boats there. They sank 15 Allied vessels, and the admiral sent a note of appreciation to the cryptanalysts.

Their romp slowed 15 December 1942, when the British changed indicators. But Wilhelm Tranow, the energetic head of English-language cryptanalysis, who matched his technical ability with administrative flair, shifted manpower to the new problem; by February, the B-Dienst was again cracking Naval Cypher No. 3. It sometimes read instructions to convoys 10 and 20 hours before the movements they ordered took place. Its information helped Dönitz position his wolf-packs for what turned out to be the greatest convoy battle of the war: the sinking of dozens of ships from two convoys in March of 1943. In June, however, the Royal Navy abandoned the codebook for a cipher machine. The U.S. Navy had long used machines, and the B-Dienst could not crack either of them. It lost its insight into Allied naval communications.[38]

By the same time, the Allies had fully mastered U-boat communications. It had been a long struggle. The Kriegsmarine's Enigma cryptosystem was more complicated than the army's or the air force's. This prevented the British from learning enough about naval communications to guess often at the probable plaintexts, or cribs, that would allow the bombes to recover the daily keys. A few cribs came from messages transmitted both in Enigma and in lower-level cryptosystems that Bletchley had cracked. The accidental captures of documents from small German warships helped solve a few more naval cryptograms. But this was inadequate. Finally, the planned seizure of some keying documents from an isolated weather ship northeast of Iceland in May 1941 permitted the rapid and voluminous solution of U-boat messages. Knowledge of the locations of the wolf-packs enabled the Allies to steer their convoys around them. But on 1 February 1942, a further Enigma complication put the Allies into the dark. This was overcome in December and, after the B-Dienst lost out on solutions in June of 1943, Allied intelligence again saved convoys. In addition, codebreaking enabled Allied naval forces to go on the offensive against the submarines. It began to pinpoint the locations of U-boats, particularly the U-tankers, sometimes in an oceanic waste the size of Texas. Using this information, airplanes from U.S. Navy escort carriers sank these submarines, throwing Dönitz's plans into disarray and enabling more supplies to reach Britain and the Allied troops stationed there.[39]

There was never a 1:1 inverse relationship between the speed and volume of solutions and the number of merchant ships sunk. Too many other factors – in particular air cover – intervened. But though codebreaking's effect cannot be quantified precisely, no one doubts that it helped win the Battle of the Atlantic.

Communications intelligence helped win the war in the Pacific as well. It contributed significantly to three critical events. The first was the victory at Midway. Naval codebreakers in Hawaii, Australia, and Washington cracked the Japanese naval code that they designated JN25b. Dozens of solved messages revealed to Admiral Chester Nimitz, who commanded in the central Pacific, details of Japan's plans to invade Midway Island and to lure out the U.S. Pacific Fleet. With this information, he disposed his forces to meet the Japanese – and defeated them. The Japanese, who had hitherto only advanced, henceforth only retreated. The battle turned the tide of the war in the Pacific. The second important event was the mid-air assassination of Admiral Isoroku Yamamoto, commander of Japan's navy and its most charismatic leader. Solution of a coded itinerary enabled Marine P-38 fighters to meet him over one of the Solomon Islands and shoot down the bomber carrying him. The effect was as if General Dwight Eisenhower had been killed in the middle of the war. The third event was the blockading of Japan by sinking her shipping. The cracking of the Japanese maru, or merchant marine, code permitted American intelligence to learn the routing of convoys. For example, in the evening of 8 May 1943, a submarine received information that sent it north-ward to Kone Zaki in the Kurile Islands. Early the next morning, it picked up two ships on radar, closed to 1,200 yards and fired three torpedoes at each, sinking a small freighter and a tanker.[40] In some cases the codebreakers could reveal a convoy's expected noon position for the following day – and some sub commanders even complained if the convoy was not on time! By the end of the war, the lack of food and supplies had all but brought Japan to her knees.[41]

The individual episodes that Allied codebreaking made possible, in the European as well as the Pacific theater, were complemented by another effect. The enormous continuous successes of communications intelligence produced a state of mind in the high commanders that enormously facilitated their prosecution of the war. They felt that they knew the enemy's intentions, his capabilities and his preferences, and consequently their own moves were firmer and more assured. That is why communications intelligence was the supreme form of intelligence in the war.

Still, it can't match the appeal of the spy. Perhaps this is because many people have wished at one time or another to possess a spy's essential attribute: not being whom one seems to be, to walk disguised through the wilderness of this world – and to do so in the noble cause of patriotism. These human aspects connect more intimately with people than do the dry mathematics of cryptanalysis. And so spies are more popular in novels than codebreakers. In life, however, they just don't matter as much.

For most of the war, two competing agencies ran spies in Hitler's Germany. One was the Abwehr, the interservice espionage organization appended to the High Command of the Armed Forces. The other was the Nazi Party's SD, or Sicherheitsdienst (Security Service), a branch of Heinrich Himmler's SS. The Abwehr's corruption, failures, and antiparty tinge led Hitler to merge it into the much smaller SD as of 1 June 1944.

The Germans arranged their spies in a hierarchy. At the bottom were the combat agents – those who crossed the lines, little more than scouts, or were parachuted a few miles behind the front. During the height of the war against the Soviet Union, 500 to 800 were behind the lines at any given time. They reported in person or by radio on troop, train, or armor movements. A spy in the West codenamed PAN typified many of these front agents. He was dispatched in December 1944 by the 176th Infantry Division to reconnoiter the forces facing it in Sittard, on the Dutch border. Slipping through the lines in the darkness, PAN saw three English tanks west of the railroad line and 32 medium tanks along the tracks. The next morning, on a friend's bicycle, he counted 300 tanks in the town. Then he returned through the lines and reported to the 176th's intelligence officer. His mission differed from the typical one only in his luck. In the east in the 12 months from October 1942 to September 1943, one Abwehr unit sent 150 agent groups in strengths of from 3 to 10 men behind Soviet lines: members of only two returned.

More consonant with the glamorous image of a spy were the German agents in Latin America, Stockholm, and Ankara. The spy rings in Brazil, which declared war on Germany on 28 August 1942, were quickly rounded up, but those in Argentina, with its antigringo attitude and continuing diplomatic relations with the Axis powers, flourished for much of the war. Under a capable leader, Johannes Siegfried Becker, spies in Argentina gathered information from American newspapers and magazines, from newscasts, diplomats, travelers, soldiers, and government officials, particularly the colonels who really ran Argentina. This information was collated and boiled down into reports sent to Germany by radio – the ring had 33 transmitters – and by courier via ship to Spain. But the radio reports were sketchy and the courier dispatches tardy, and not one of the ships reported as sailing from Latin American ports was sunk by U-boats on the basis of spy intelligence. Despite the energy and dedication of Becker and his men, German espionage in Latin America accomplished nothing for the German war effort except possibly to absorb Allied energy in counterespionage.

In Stockholm, a rangy, energetic Nazi, Karl-Heinz Kramer, ran JOSEPHINE, whose name became almost legendary among German intelligence officers in the West. JOSEPHINE was no single person, however, but a composite of sources in Swedish government circles. Among these were said to be three secretaries in the Ministry of Defense who had access to the reports of Swedish military and air attachés in Britain and whom Krämer allegedly seduced in a classic form of gaining information. He compiled information about British aircraft production that the Luftwaffe called "its most valuable target documents." Krämer ran several other agents as well – or at least he told his bosses that he did – and continued in his cushy post to the end of the war.[42]

The best German spy in Ankara was not an agent trained and inserted but an opportunist in the right place who saw a chance and took it. Elyeza Bazna was the valet of the British ambassador to Turkey. One day in the fall of 1943 he took a wax impression of the dispatch box key that the ambassador had left on his dresser. With a key made from this, Bazna got access to the most secret documents of the embassy. These he photographed and sold to the Germans. So eloquent were they that the Germans codenamed Bazna CICERO. They used them to diplomatically defeat such British measures as a request to station pursuit planes on Turkish airfields and in general to keep Turkey neutral. But one day Bazna saw a new secretary in the German embassy who had spent some years in America with her consul general father. She was with an American who had once chased him and his German contact through the streets of Ankara. He quit at once. Hitler didn't seem to miss his information. And, in a bitter irony, the £20 notes the Germans had given him as pay turned out to be counterfeit.[43]

The Allies, too, used spies. Two of the most useful worked before or just at the start of the war, and one of these proved indirectly to have been the most fateful of all World War II's espionage agents.

He was Hans-Thilo Schmidt, 44, a Nazi who worked in the Reichswehr's Cipher Center. In the summer of 1931, he contacted the French, offering to sell them secret documents, holding out as samples instructions for the Enigma cipher machine. The French accepted and met Schmidt at the Grand Hotel in Verviers in eastern Belgium. He gave them the Enigma documents, enabling the Poles, to whom the French had given copies, to crack the Enigma. Schmidt also supplied useful material about German rearmament and panzer troops. In 1943, he was betrayed by a captured French agent, arrested by the Gestapo, and killed himself. By then, the Allies were reading much Enigma traffic. No other spy in that worldwide conflict came close to matching Schmidt's stupendous, though indirect, effect upon the war.[44]

The other early significant spy, anti-Nazi German physicist Hans Ferdinand Meyer, sent the British naval attaché in Oslo a long report in November 1939 about German scientific developments, such as remote-controlled gliders, radar, torpedoes, and bomb fuzes. This document, one of the most remarkable intelligence reports of the war, was disbelieved by many at first, mainly because it dealt with so many topics. But it proved accurate in almost every detail, and it alerted the British to many developments of which they had previously had no knowledge.[45]

Other spies, though certainly no less brave, did not have the same influence on the struggle. For the United States, at least, this may be attributed in part to the fact that it did not have any spies in place anywhere in the world before hostilities engulfed it and that it is much harder to insert spies during wartime, when every member of the public sees a secret agent whenever a person coughs funny, than in peacetime. And indeed, one of the Americans' best sources was a walk-in.

In August of 1943, Allen W. Dulles, head of the Office of Strategic Services outpost in Berne, Switzerland, was sent a man later code-named GEORGE WOOD who was almost certainly Fritz Kolbe, special assistant to a high official in the German Foreign Office. WOOD claimed to oppose Hitler, and to demonstrate his bona fides produced 186 copies and synopses of documents, most only a few days old. The cautious Dulles sent them for checking to Washington. OSS took seven months to check them and later documents, causing many to become stale. They were eventually accepted as genuine, however, and over 18 months OSS received from WOOD copies of more than 1,600 German diplomatic messages. Some of these came from military and air attachés in the Far East, whose reports included the identification of a number of Japanese divisional commanders in Burma, for example. Donovan later boasted that "OSS took seven months to check them, causing usually skeptical and conservative British intelligence officials to rate this contact as the prize intelligence source of the war." But they may not have been privy to ULTRA.

Dulles actively recruited one of the Allies' best agents in place. This was Hans Bernd Gisevius, a six-foot, four-inch lawyer who had worked for the Gestapo and was, by 1943, serving in the Abwehr. He told about the V-1 buzz bomb and the V-2 rocket, confirming information from other sources. Possibly his greatest contribution was to reveal that the Germans were reading some State Department codes, occasionally used by Dulles, which the mission abandoned, though gradually so as not to raise German suspicions.[46]

Later in the war, the OSS injected agents into Europe – 200 all told. The DUPONT mission, a typical one, consisted of a tall, good-looking dentist, Lieutenant Commander John Taylor, and three anti-Nazi Austrians. In October 1944, they were parachuted onto the marshy eastern shore of the Neusiedlersee, a shallow lake southeast of Vienna. They used bird calls to rendezvous, but their radios fell into the lake. Though the Germans heard the plane, the team escaped, but then spent much of its time moving from town to town to avoid arrest. Taylor observed signs of construction of a major defensive line, but without his radio he was unable to report it. Contacts brought shelter and help only temporarily. And then a gamble failed: a potential contact betrayed two members of the team to the Gestapo. They were arrested, and soon afterward Taylor and the other man were seized after a savage struggle in the hayloft where they were hiding. They were sent to the Mauthausen death camp, but Taylor, at least, survived.

Did the other teams get more information back to headquarters? Yes, but its value was small. The HAMMER group reported from Berlin that the Klingenberg power plant was operating and that one railroad marshalling yard had 26 freight and 18 passenger trains. The most fecund team sent back 52 messages.[47] Though the men were brave, neither in quantity nor in quality was OSS intelligence impressive.

The information collected by these organs was evaluated either by general agencies, such as foreign ministries, or by specialized units, such as the intelligence sections of military formations. The work of both kinds was the same. It consisted of comparing information from one source with that from another to determine whether the data confirmed one another, suggesting that the information was true, or, if the sources did not match exactly, of finding overlaps in which the information was probably true.

The intelligence staffs of the Germans were far smaller than those of the Americans. The Germans believed that small staffs worked faster and more efficiently, cut through to the essentials, kept the intelligence officer's briefings of the commander short.[48] This was not necessarily true. Larger staffs could provide more detail: Americans had a meteorologist on their higher staffs while Germans did not. Before the invasion of Sicily, the American staffs spotted possible enemy mine fields and pillboxes and other defenses – all as the Germans would do – but in addition studied surf and tides at the landing beaches and drew up new tables of daylight and dark. The Germans would have regarded all of this as unnecessary, but in fact these details infused commanders with greater certainty than the approximations the Germans would have used. Nor did the large staff necessarily dissipate the commander's time. In Sicily, General George S. Patton asked his intelligence officer whether he would bring on a major engagement and thus violate his orders if he attacked Agrigento. The officer, who was backed by an immense intelligence apparatus, did not expound on the location and capabilities of the enemy intention. He just said, "No, sir."[49]

Whose intelligence, then, was better? The Allies', by far. Their codebreaking penetrated more deeply, more widely, and far longer into Axis systems than the Axis penetrated into Allied. This helped the Allies win the all-important Battle of the Atlantic and dozens of land operations, from Africa to France. Their control of communications intelligence and of German spies, nearly every one of whom was captured and most of whom were turned, enabled them to fool the Germans, first in the Mediterranean, where the Germans expected the invasion that came in Sicily to come in the Balkans, and then in France, where the Germans thought the Normandy landings merely a feint for a main assault in the Pas de Calais. The latter especially was critical in helping the Allies lodge themselves in Europe so that they could conquer Germany. The chief Allied failures in strategic intelligence – the blindness about Germany's invasion of Norway and about the Pearl Harbor attack – were not as severe as Germany's chief failure – the underestimation of the Soviet Union. A quantitative comparison may sum up the relative abilities of the two sides: Before the Normandy invasion, the Allies' estimate of the number of German divisions was off by only 2 percent. The Germans erred by 40 percent.[50]

The Allies owed this superiority to several factors:

- its communications intelligence, which was far better than the Axis',
- Britain's being an island, which enabled her to capture and imprison or turn all enemy spies who invaded her,

- its original defensive posture as compared to the Axis' original offensive stance, which enabled the Allies to expand the intelligence capability they had built up when they had little more than intelligence early in the war while the Axis neglected intelligence to concentrate on the men and weapons needed for their aggressions,
- the rule of law, which enabled the Allies to concentrate their efforts, while Germany's paladins fought each other for Hitler's favor in part with intelligence as a weapon,
- a more liberal attitude towards intelligence officers, who in the Allied armies were often drafted civilians who entertained no military career plans and so were freer to speak their minds to superiors than the general staff officers the Germans used as many of their intelligence specialists, and
- the turning of the war against the Axis, which gave the Allies the advantages of air superiority for photography and of more prisoners, deserters, and other informants.

Thus ended the secret war. The victory in that, as in the fighting war, was the Allies'.

What effect did intelligence have on the war? It cannot be said to have won it. The war was won by the greater material and human forces of the Allies and by the bravery and spirit of the men and women in combat and in support. But intelligence shortened the war. Thus it contributed to the victory. It saved lives – on both sides. Thousands of men, women, and children who might otherwise have died survived because intelligence had reduced the fighting. That is its ultimate gift to humankind.

Notes

1. Oscar W. Koch with Robert G. Hays, *G-2: Intelligence for Patton* (n.p.: Army Times, 1971), pp. 135–136.
2. Charles B. MacDonald and Sidney T. Mathews, *Three Battles: Arnaville, Altuzzo and Schmidt, United States Army in World War II*, Department of the Army: Office of the Chief of Military History (Washington, DC: Government Printing Office, 1952), p. 150.
3. David Kahn, *Hitler's Spies: German Military Intelligence in World War II* (New York: Macmillan, 1978), p. 102.

4. Helmut Heiber, ed., *Hitlers Lagebesprechungen: Die Protokollfragmente seiner militärischen Konferenzen, 1942–1945* (Stuttgart, Germany: Deutsche Verlags-Anstalt, 1962), p. 750.

5. 98. Infanterie Division, 8159/2, 3. März 1940. Bundesarchiv-Militärarchiv Freiburg i.Br., Germany (henceforth: MA).

6. MacDonald and Mathews, *Three Battles*, pp. 3, 6.

7. Koch, *G-2: Intelligence for Patton*, p. 20.

8. *Ibid.*, pp. 76–77.

9. Kahn, *Hitler's Spies*, pp. 136–142; R. F. Toliver in collaboration with Hanns J. Scharff, *The Interrogator: the Story of Hans Scharff, Luftwaffe's Master Interrogator* (Fallbrook, CA: Aero Publishers, 1978).

10. Oberkommando der Luftwaffe, RL2/558, 6 Dezember 1944, MA.

11. Koch, *G-2: Intelligence for Patton*, pp. 47–48.

12. Kahn, *Hitler's Spies*, pp. 415–417.

13. Wolfgang Schreyer, *Augen am Himmel: eine Piratenchronik* (Berlin, Germany: Deutscher Militärverlag, 1968), pp. 73, 75.

14. Ursula Powys-Lybbe, *The Eye of Intelligence* (London, U.K.: Kimber, 1983), pp. 36, 37; Roy Conyers Nesbit, *Eyes of the RAF: A History of Photo-Reconnaissance* (Far Thrupp: Stroud, Goucestershire, 1996).

15. Siegfried Knemeyer, telephone interview, 27 June 1975.

16. Oberkommando des Heeres, Heeresdienstvorschrift geheim 300/1, *Truppenführung* (1933), I. Teil, §143.

17. *Ibid.*, §§144, 146, 147, 150, 176.

18. "Die Stärke der deutschen Luftwaffe am 5.7.1941, 31.1.1942, und 31.5.1943," *Wehrwissenschaftliche Rundschau*, 11 (November 1961): 641–644.

19. Kahn, *Hitler's Spies*, 132–134, 122.

20. Oberkommando der Luftwaffe, RL2/547, 14.12.44, 1, MA.

21. Oberkommando der Kriegsmarine, III M 1000/57, 392, MA.

22. F. H. Hinsley with E. E. Thomas, C. F. G. Ransom, R. C. Knight and C. A. G. Simkins, *British Intelligence in the Second World War: Its Influence on Strategy and Operations*, Vol. 1 (London, U.K.: Her Majesty's Stationery Office, 1979–1988), p. 130.

23. Andrew J. Brookes, *Photo Reconnaissance* (London: Ian Allan, 1975), pp. 100–101; Hinsley, *British Intelligence*, Vol. 1, pp. 211–212.

24. Nesbit, *Eyes of the RAF*, 76, 142, 197, 156. See also John F. Kreis, ed., *Piercing the Fog: Intelligence and Army Air Forces in World War II*, Air Force History and Museums Program (Washington, DC: Bolling Air Force Base, 1996).

25. R. V. Jones, *The Wizard War: British Scientific Intelligence 1939–1945* (New York: Coward, McCann & Geoghegan, 1978), p. 226.

26. Koch, *G-2: Intelligence for Patton*, 140.

27. David Kahn, "Codebreaking in World Wars I and II: The Major Successes and Failures, Their Causes and Their Effects," first published in *The Historical Journal* in September 1980.

28. David Kahn, *Seizing the Enigma: The Race to Break the German U-Boat Codes, 1939–1943* (New York: Houghton Mifflin, 1991), chapters 4 and 5.

29. Hinsley, *British Intelligence*, Vol. 1, p. 189.

30. *Ibid.*, Vol. 2, p. 423.
31. Ralph Bennett, *Ultra in the West: The Normandy Campaign 1944–45* (London, U.K.: Hutchinson, 1979), p. 119.
32. Joseph S. Schick, "With the 849th SIS, 1942–45," *Cryptologia*, Vol. 11 (January 1987), pp. 29–39; Charles David, "A World War II German Field Cipher and How We Broke It," *Cryptologia*, Vol. 20 (January 1996), pp. 55–76.
33. Stephen Budiansky, *Battle of Wits: The Complete Story of Codebreaking in World War II* (New York: Free Press, 2000), pp. 312–315; F. H. Hinsley and Alan Stripp, eds., *Codebreakers: The Inside Story of Bletchley Park* (Oxford, U.K.: Oxford University Press), pp. 141–192.
34. David Alvarez, *Secret Messages: Codebreaking and American Diplomacy* (Lawrence, KS: University Press of Kansas, 2000), pp. 63, 81–82 and passim. It is sometimes asked why, if the PURPLE machine provided such valuable information during the war, it didn't warn of the attack on Pearl Harbor. The answer is that PURPLE was a diplomatic machine and the diplomats themselves were never told of the attack. Indeed, no message ever specifying an attack on Pearl Harbor was ever transmitted in any code.
35. David Kahn, "Soviet Comint in the Cold War," *Cryptologia,* Vol. 22 (January 1998), pp. 1–24 at 11–12.
36. *Ibid.*, p. 13; Carl Boyd, *Hitler's Japanese Confidant* (Lawrence, KS: University Press of Kansas, 1993), pp. 63, 65.
37. Kahn, "Codebreaking in World Wars I and II"; Boyd, *Hitler's Japanese Confidant*, pp. 105, 112–114.
38. Kahn, *Hitler's Spies*, pp. 213–222; Heinz Bonatz, *Die Deutsche Marine-Funkaufklärung 1914–1945*, Beiträge zur Wehrforschung, 20/21 (Darmstadt, Germany: Wehr und Wissen Verlagsgesellschaft, 1970).
39. Hugh Sebag-Montefiore, *Enigma: The Battle for the Code* (London, U.K.: Weidenfeld & Nicolson, 2000); W. J. R. Gardner, *Decoding History: The Battle of the Atlantic and Ultra* (Annapolis, MD: Naval Institute Press, 1999); Stephen Budiansky, *Battle of Wits: The Complete Story of Codebreaking in World War II* (New York: The Free Press, 2000); R. A. Ratcliff, "Searching for Security: The German Investigations into Enigma's Security," in David Alvarez, ed., *Allied and Axis Signals Intelligence in World War II* (London, U.K.: Frank Cass, 1999), pp. 146–167.
40. Clay Blair, *Silent Victory: The U.S. Submarine War Against Japan* (Philadelphia, PA: J.B. Lippincott, 1975), p. 426.
41. John Prados, *Combined Fleet Decoded: The Secret History of American Intelligence and the Japanese Navy in World War II* (New York: Random House, 1995); Edward J. Drea, *MacArthur's Ultra: Codebreaking and the War against Japan, 1942–1945* (Lawrence, KS: University Press of Kansas, 1992); David Mead, "The Breaking of the Japanese Army Administrative Code," *Cryptologia*, Vol. 18 (July 1994), pp. 193–203.
42. Kahn, *Hitler's Spies*, pp. 302–370; David Alvarez and Robert A. Graham, *Nothing Sacred: Nazi Espionage Against the Vatican 1939–1945* (London, U.K.: Frank Cass, 1997).

43. Richard Wires, *The Cicero Spy Affair: German Access to British Secrets in World War II* (Westport, CT: Praeger, 1999).

44. "The Spy Who Most Affected World War II," in David Kahn, *Kahn on Codes*, pp. 76–88; Sebag-Montefiore, *Enigma: The Battle for the Code*, pp. 15–20, 244–248.

45. R. V. Jones, *Reflections on Intelligence* (London, U.K.: Mandarin, 1990), chapters 10 and 11 and Appendix A.

46. Neal H. Petersen, ed., *From Hitler's Doorstep: The Wartime Intelligence Reports of Allen Dulles, 1942–1945* (University Park, PA: Pennsylvania State University Press, 1996).

47. Joseph E. Persico, *Piercing the Reich: The Penetration of Nazi Germany by American Secret Agents during World War II* (New York: Viking, 1979).

48. Kahn, *Hitler's Spies*, p. 404.

49. Koch, *G-2: Intelligence for Patton*, p. 44.

50. Kahn, *Hitler's Spies*, p. 523.

10

WHY GERMANY'S INTELLIGENCE FAILED IN WORLD WAR II*

Nazi Germany lost the intelligence war. At every one of the strategic turning points of World War II, her intelligence failed. It underestimated Russia, blacked out before the North African invasion, awaited the Sicily landing in the Balkans, and fell for thinking the Normandy landing a feint. Though in operational and tactical situations it often predicted enemy attacks, it sometimes erred grievously, as at Stalingrad and Army Group Center.

The record appears abysmal. But perhaps this is the best that could be done. Every intelligence service strives to realize the words of the evangelist Luke: "For nothing is hid that shall not be made manifest, nor anything secret that shall not be known and come to light."[1] None achieves it. "It will always be a certain tragedy of every intelligence service," wrote General Friedrich Gempp, first chief of the Abwehr, "that even the best results will always lag behind the clients' desires."[2] Is it, therefore, asking too much to expect more of German intelligence? Did it attain the practical, if not the theoretical, limits of any investigation into the dark recesses of other men's minds? Or did other intelligence agencies do better?

Others did. Though the Japanese performed as poorly as the Germans, and though not enough is known of Russian intelligence to evaluate it properly, Anglo-American intelligence far outdid German.[3] It estimated enemy strength more accurately. Throughout the war, for example, the Allies usually knew to within a division the strength of the German forces in France. Their figures were precise[4] when major decisions were being taken at the Washington conference of 1942 and the

* From D. Kahn, "Hubris, Glory, Charisma, Führer," In: *Hitler's Spies: German Military Intelligence in World War II*, New York: Macmillan, 1978.

Casablanca one of 1943, and were off by only one division—58, they said, instead of the actual 59—before the Normandy assault.[5] This error of 2 percent contrasts sharply with the corresponding German error concerning Allied divisions in Britain of 40 percent.[6] And Allied intelligence forecast enemy intentions better. It recognized that Hitler had abandoned his plans to invade Britain and discovered that he intended to attack Russia instead.[7,8] It learned enough about the German rockets and atomic experiments to delay or cripple both by raids. In a host of individual operations, it foretold enemy moves.[9] U-boats rendezvousing with milch-cows in the Atlantic wastes found themselves being depth-charged by Allied planes that suddenly hove over the horizon.[10] The two American divisions at Anzio were saved from overextending themselves and possibly being cut off when an intercept warned them that Hitler was sending nine divisions from Greece to reinforce the defenders.[11]

The Allies were not perfect. They missed at Norway and Arnhem and the Bulge. Their estimates of German aircraft production fell from 79 percent too high to 33 percent too low—a variation of more than 100 percent.[12] The intelligence reports that the Office of Strategic Services handed President Roosevelt were often quite as devoid of inside information about the enemy and his intentions as those Canaris gave Hitler.[13] But still and all the Allies enjoyed considerable success in their intelligence—much of it due to their superiority in verbal intelligence because of their far better code-breaking. The Germans, in contrast, were glaringly inferior.

Five basic factors bred this failure: (1) unjustified arrogance, which caused Germany to lose touch with reality; (2) aggression, which led to a neglect of intelligence; (3) a power struggle within the officer corps, which made many generals hostile to intelligence; (4) the authority structure of the Nazi state, which gravely impaired its intelligence; (5) anti-Semitism, which deprived German intelligence of many brains.

Sometimes thought to be exclusively a product of Hitler's Germany, anti-Semitism had in fact long wrought its deleterious effects on Germany's armed forces and their intelligence agencies. For it excluded many patriotic Jews who might have contributed a great deal. The Prussian army, for example, simply did not commission Jews as regular officers.[14] The Nazis intensified this attitude and its effects. They "coordinated" scientific, technical, and academic organizations with the party philosophy, squeezing Jews out of them. They enacted a law cynically designated as for the "re-establishment of the pro-fessional civil service," which ordered that "Officials who are not of Aryan descent are to be retired."[15] Though this seemed to have little effect on the military establishment because few Jews were there to be fired—in the B-Dienst, for example, none seem to been let go—the impact elsewhere was ruinous.[16,17] The Nazis expelled the Jewish rector of the Göttingen Mathematical Institute, beginning the demolition of the foremost center of mathematics in Germany. Such measures, which stripped many Jewish scientists of their jobs, combined with the street humiliations and the hateful atmosphere to drive them from Germany. Mathematicians, scientists, engineers streamed to Great Britain, Russia, above all the United States. Their quality was high. Though Albert Einstein was in a class by himself, others were highly regarded by their peers: in mathematics alone, about 20% were elected to their host country's foremost honorary societies.[18] The Germany of the 1930s did not miss them. Their departure fed her exhilarating sense of renewal and cleanliness and mission. But even the strongest motivation could not make good the replacement of superb intellects by mediocrities.[19]

Anti-Semitism was not confined to Germany. The American and British military establishments suffered from more than tinges of this malady. But they did not systematically exclude Jews, and they did not refuse their civilian assistance. The most dramatic result came when the Allies, with the help of Jewish brains, built the atomic bomb, and the Germans, without them (and for many other reasons), did not. In intelligence, the Allies gained many speakers of German, who proved valuable as interrogators, and they retained such Jews as William F. Friedman, leader of the team that solved the Japanese PURPLE cipher machine, which provided great insight into both German and Japanese policy. German anti-Semitism both seriously depleted Hitler's intelligence potential and vastly increased the Allies', thus doubly damaging the Reich's intelligence.

Germans have often been accused of arrogance,[20] and in the nation's perception of reality—of which perception intelligence is a small and formalized part—the charge is valid. Arrogance distorted the German view of the world to an unreal one, and so led that coun-try into many harmful decisions.

The flaw seems to have been caused by two linked factors. The sense of national superiority was more exaggerated in Germany than in other countries. And a greater rigidity in thought, an expression of an authoritarianism more pronounced in Germany than elsewhere, blocked its correction by reality. This factor, a psychological one, arose from the teachings of Martin Luther. The excessive chauvinism had its roots in Germany's alienation from the West.

In the High Middle Ages, the emperor Frederick II of Hohen-staufen,[21] the "Amazement of the World" whose biography Canaris was reading the night before his execution, who had been born and bred in Sicily, granted powers to his German princes so he could pursue the Italian and Mediterranean policies that interested him more. These powers helped the princes maintain their separate sovereignties for six centuries against the centralizing force of the Holy Roman Empire, the rising dominance of Prussia, and the urgings of intellectuals for political as well as cultural unity. This particularism distinguished the region now called Germany from England and France, where unified nation-states were forming. In these conditions, Napoleon humbled Prussia,[22] subjugated other German principalities, and snuffed out the Empire—the first Reich, which had lasted for a thousand years.

Napoleon called himself the bearer of the great humanistic ideals of the French Revolution. In rejecting him, the people of the German states also rejected the liberty, equality, and fraternity that had become, in one form or another, the ideals of the democratic West. Setting themselves apart, they praised instead German uniqueness, indeed German superiority. The apostle of this nationalism, Johann Gottlieb Fichte, deprecated "the deadly foreign spirit"[23] in his *Addresses to the German Nation* and declared bluntly that "the German, if only he makes use of all advantages, can always be superior to the foreigner." German pride swelled as Napoleon was defeated, as unification approached with Prussia's 1866 victory over Austria and her absorption of several neighbor states, and finally as it was achieved five years later with the defeat of France and the proclamation of a new German empire—the second Reich. It seemed as if Germany was invincible. Her separate development had succeeded. Everything German was better than anything else.

But this was not so. Booming as her economic expansion had been, astonishing as her military victories were, her population and industry compared with those of all her potential enemies could never have sufficed to make her mistress of the world. Her failure to recognize this separated her from reality. Other countries have suffered from the same problem, among them the United ("One American is worth ten Japs") States. But Germany's distance from reality was greater, chiefly because the tardiness of her nationalism exacerbated her sense of superiority. This was indeed dangerous. What made it fatal, however, was its rigidity, its inability to change, to adapt to reality.

This inflexibility stemmed from an authoritarianism that began in the Reformation.[24] Both Martin Luther and John Calvin freed man from papal authority. But while Calvin's theology also permitted resistance to secular authority, as the Puritan revolution in England showed, Luther's opposed it. His teaching that man is saved not by good works but solely by faith raised the specter of anarchy because no one could really know what a man thought.[25] So he explicitly taught that on earth men must follow the commands of the constituted rulers. "Even if those in authority are evil or without faith, nevertheless the authority and its power are good and from God," he declared.[26] "No insurrection is ever right," he cried.[27] "The answer for such mouths [those of rebels] is a fist that brings blood from the nose." Parents in countries pervaded by Lutheranism, such as Prussia, willingly assimilated these ideas to increase and facilitate their control in the family.[28] The authoritarian personality became established to a greater extent in Germany than elsewhere.[29] Revolution never succeeded there.

The dynamics of an authoritarian person include a need to contain, or at least not to aggravate, an underlying anxiety. One mechanism for this seeks to exclude anxiety-causing events by rigidly controlling the environment. Such a person consequently holds views that meet his needs. And because these views are anchored deep in his psyche, no mere external data can change them. They will not yield to actuality.

It was that way among many Germans with their exaggerated feeling of superiority. Their authoritarian rigidity kept reality from moderating the excesses of that feeling, which reigned unstinted. The result was arrogance. This extreme and stiffnecked overestimation of self skewed Germany's perception of the world far more than the chauvinism of other countries warped their views of the world. Consequently, when she finally collided with reality, the effects proved much more damaging, and sometimes disastrous.

In 1917, considering America as too weak and too far away to do anything, she began unrestricted submarine warfare, which led to America's declaration of war on her. "Germany's policy towards the U.S.A. shows in particularly crude colors the fundamental traits of Germany's world policy at the beginning of the twentieth century," wrote Professor Fritz Fischer, the foremost scholar of the period.[30] "Dazzled by confidence in their own strength, the Germans underestimated the economic and organizatory capacities of America." It cost them the war.

Even after the failure of Germany's supreme offensives in the spring of 1918, however, arrogance kept the German generals from recognizing that they had lost the war. Nor, finally, did the actual capitulation teach them anything. They refused to believe that other armies had beaten the German on the field of battle.[31] To sustain their overestimation of self, they embraced instead the legend that they had been stabbed in the back by Jews and Communists.

Twenty-one years later, arrogance again took its deadly toll. Hitler, with the concurrence of his generals and without even investigating the matter, decided that Germany could quickly conquer the Soviet Union. A few months later, pooh-poohing America's industrial might, he declared war on the United States.

These losses of contact with reality affected the very life and death of the nation. They encompassed and overshadowed anything intelligence could do and arrogance made itself felt in small things as in great. Albert Speer recognized that Germany could not match Allied production. He held, however, that the qualitative superiority of German weapons outweighed the Allied quantities.[32] It was a delusion. The OKW Operations Staff, in discussing the strategic situation after the Allied landing in North Africa, spoke of equaling the enemy's strength and of the possibility of "a victorious ending of the war."[33] Reinhard Gehlen's irrational view that Germany could not lose the war, which so resembled that of his World War I predecessors, sprang—as did theirs—largely from arrogance.[34]

Arrogance thus predetermined the whole German attitude and directed all German actions. It consequently preëmpted intelligence. It foreclosed the German mind from even thinking that intelligence might be necessary. In 1914, the army was so certain of success that many units left their intelligence officers behind.[35] In 1941, Hitler invaded Russia with no real intelligence preparation. Arrogance, which broke Germany's contact with reality, also prevented intelligence from seeking to resume that contact. The other factors that affected German intelligence did not have an impact that, like this, transcended intelligence. They merely damaged intelligence as such.

Hitler decided to solve what he saw as his nation's problems by warring upon other countries. Germany would strike the first blow. She would be—despite grievances, despite rationalizations—the aggressor.

Now offense and defense enjoin different attitudes toward intelligence. It exists, of course, in both. But it is essential to victory only in the defense. The difference between intelligence in the two modes is that between an accompanying and a defining characteristic. All elephants may be gray, but grayness is not a defining characteristic of elephants, merely an accompanying one. Intelligence is a defining characteristic of defense; it is only an accompanying characteristic of offense.

"What is the concept of defense?" asked Clausewitz.[36] "The parrying of a blow. What is its characteristic feature? Awaiting the blow." Now an army can await a blow only if it believes that a blow is planned, and such a belief can be created only by information about the enemy. Defense requires intelligence. There can be, in other words, no defense without intelligence.

Defense also acknowledges that the initiative will come from the enemy. And indeed the offense acts, the defense reacts. The offense prescribes to the enemy; it makes the basic decisions. It is "complete in itself," said Clausewitz.[37] Thus information about enemy intentions, while helpful and to a certain degree always present, is not essential to an offensive victory. (What is essential, Clausewitz said, is surprise, or denying information about one's own plans to the enemy.[38] This further implies that intelligence, meaning knowledge of enemy intentions, is necessary for success in defense.) In other words, while intelligence is integral to the defense, it is only contingent to the offense. As a result—and this is the crucial point—emphasizing the offensive tends toward a neglect of intelligence.

An example will make this clear: the German invasion of France in 1940. According to the plan, a powerful armored force, driving southwest out of the Ardennes Forest, would curve like a sickle to the northwest to strike the Allied armies from the side and then crush them against the Channel and against other German forces. The greatest danger lay in a counterattack by the French reserves. So the Germans protected their long and vulnerable flank by lining it with outward-facing forces. The point is that they did not make these dispositions on the basis of intelligence, of knowing that French reserves were to the south. They made them of their own volition. Where the enemy reserves were or would be was naturally of interest, but it was not essential to German planning. Planning omitted intelligence.[39]

The same conditions held, on a vaster scale, for Hitler's overall planning for his war. He intended to impose his will on other countries. Their fate would lie in his hands. For this he needed no intelligence. He concentrated on what he did need: men, guns, tanks, planes, fuel. "The war will be won with tanks and airplanes, antitank and antiaircraft guns," he said.[40] He poured his energies, his money, and his men into armaments but not into intelligence.

Neither he nor his high commands ever lashed the Abwehr into serious activity, or supported it with the resources and manpower that would allow it to mount serious espionage campaigns against the countries of Europe. Nor did the Abwehr itself seem to feel that it had to dig hard. It lazed along. It sowed some agents here and there, but it implanted none in the high government circles of nations whose attitudes might be critical to Germany—Poland, Czechoslovakia, Belgium, Sweden, Turkey, France itself. Its effort against Britain was tardy, feeble, and utterly ineffective. In other areas, it did gather a few tidbits—mobilization and troop identifications in France, airfield locations along the Soviet Union's frontier, the Norden bombsight, some coastal gun positions in Norway, a minor French naval code.[41] But never once did it score a coup.

Contrast this with Allied espionage. It had its failures, too, but it nevertheless obtained some documents that indirectly but importantly affected the war. French espionage won as a spy a weak and lazy member of the Reichswehr's Cipher Center who sold the operating instructions and some actual keys for the main German cipher machine, the Enigma. With the help of these, Polish cryptanalysts reconstructed the mechanism.[42] When war came, Allied solutions of Enigma messages contributed greatly to the victories of the battles of Britain and the Atlantic, to the control of German spies in Britain, with the deception that that made possible, and to the winning of many combat actions in Europe in 1944 and 1945.[43]

The espionage stroke that ultimately made all this possible was not a fluke, either. France watched Germany carefully, and in particular informed herself in accurate detail about German rearmament: she was concerned about German aggression.[44] The same fear never actuated the Germans into investigating their neighbors. And so they never achieved the same success.

The organization of German intelligence depicts the same negligence. The OKW for years before and during the war did not have an I c branch. On the other hand, the British chiefs of staff established a Joint Intelligence Committee at the very start of the war. Well before the war, the Admiralty established an Operational Intelligence Center that during the conflict became adept at predicting U-boat moves, thus enabling the Allies to sink them and to reroute their own convoys to safety.[45] The OKM never had one.

In the euphoria of Hitler's early triumphs, however, none of these omissions mattered. Poland, Denmark and Norway, France and the Low Countries, Yugoslavia—all justified Hitler's belief that it was the offensive and its armaments that counted. The armed forces naturally had intelligence agencies to tell them where the enemy was, but this information was not essential for victory, since German armies went where they wanted to go anyway. One student has brilliantly epitomized this by commenting that during the first few years of the war the Wehrmacht carried the Abwehr along like a "happy parasite."[46] All German experience in the first part of the war confirmed the insignificance of intelligence.

Then Hitler attacked Russia. He thereupon began losing the strategic initiative. The whole war flopped over. Soon Germany was forced onto the defensive. At once intelligence assumed importance. In a host of ways, Germany began seeking it. Censors, who had previously only spot-checked mail transiting Germany, began in mid-1942 to open it all.[47] Ribbentrop had previously instructed his diplomats to gather information; now it became their "main duty."[48] Halder decided he could no longer afford the lackadaisical work of Kinzel in Foreign Armies East and replaced him with the dynamo of Gehlen. The OKW Operations Staff added an intelligence officer. In their situation conferences, Hitler and his generals and admirals, who earlier had seldom said much about the enemy, talked about him more and more.[49]

But it was too late. Their information remained low-level and sparse. Germany's spies sat in no high councils. Her codebreakers pounded ineffectually upon impregnable walls. The disdain of the previous years had taken its toll.

The situation was just the opposite with the Allies, in particular the British. Their original defensive posture had compelled them to build up their intelligence to warn them of the designs of the aggressor. They put more men into the intelligence agencies and spent more money on them than others did. Intelligence helped them optimize their few resources—especially after Dunkirk, when Britain seemed to have little else but her intelligence. Then, when the German tide of war ebbed, and the Allies seized the offensive, they reaped all the advantages that this extensive organization and greater experience gave them. Their information, in contrast to Hitler's, was high-level, voluminous, and reliable. And they used it to speed their victory.

Germans, however, cannot blame Hitler alone for this disregard of intelligence. The attitude had a long history. Prussia-Germany recognized that her location between potential enemies and her inferiority in natural resources and population made it impossible for her to win a war of attrition. These factors, together with difficult domestic problems most easily suppressed by unification through an aggressive foreign policy, decreed the strategic offensive as her military doctrine.[50,51] The Schlieffen plan for smashing France in 1914 by sweeping through neutral Belgium formulated this in its most brutal terms. Germany's defeat in 1918 after four terrible years seared the necessity for a quick offensive victory in the next war into the national consciousness—and into Hitler's. As a result, he created the blitzkrieg, with its dire consequences for intelligence.[52]

In the same way, the World War II leaders of Great Britain do not deserve all the praise for building up their intelligence agencies. Britain's circumstances had given them a big head start. Her island position made it difficult for her to dominate Europe directly, by land forces, as France, for example, had done. She did so indirectly, by being the nation whose strength, thrown to one side or the other, could decide a continental conflict. This balance-of-power policy, which is a reactive, or defensive, technique, requires intelligence to succeed. Intelligence also contributes to economic expansion, which was Britain's other source of power. And so, beginning with Sir Francis

Walsingham under Queen Elizabeth I, or, some say, as far back as Edward III in the late Middle Ages, Britain cultivated intelligence.

In a sense, then, each nation's attitude toward intelligence may be seen as an expression of its geography and its internal dynamics. Britain was a sea power, essentially defensive: the Royal Navy is called, not the spear of Britain, but her shield. She needed intelligence. Germany was a continental power with severe domestic tensions. Her armies, attacking, did not require intelligence. And so she failed to develop it.

This fundamental neglect of intelligence perfectly suited the élite of the German officer corps. They believed that the aggressiveness from which it stemmed protected Germany and thus their livelihoods from foreign dangers. Inside Germany, however, in the army, they did not merely ignore intelligence. They fought it. For intelligence threatened their jobs.

The advance of technology naturally creates technicians. In the military, for example, there evolve artillerists, railroad men, and specialists on foreign armies. Their knowledge gives them a certain power.[53] Basically, this consists of the threat of withholding their knowledge, thereby weakening the military forces of their country. Such power enables them to demand at first merely work within the military establishment, then officer posts, then access to the top. The existing officers resist this incursion, for it robs them of jobs once their own.[54]

The Prussian-German officer corps was far more adamant than others.[55] Its Junkers feared displacement more, for, unable to subsist on their lands and unwilling to enter trade, they had no place else to go. Moreover, ever since the Great Elector of Brandenburg had given these rebellious aristocrats commissions in his army to bring them under his control in the late 1600s, they had enjoyed a virtual monopoly of the officer posts.[56] All they had to do to get a job was be born. They contended that only fear of loss of honor prevented cowardice among commanders, that only noblemen had honor, and that consequently only noblemen were entitled to lead troops; bourgeois artillerymen, no matter how well trained, could never do more than lay guns. In fact the Junkers were seeking to ban competition for commissions and to keep it as easy for themselves as possible. In sociological terms, they opposed any shift from an ascriptive to an achievement system of authority.[57]

Like the officer corps as a whole, the general staff fought the threat of specialist competition within its own prestigious domain.[58] In some cases, the pressure of technology proved too great, and it yielded: the railroad expert is a case in point. It opposed intelligence more successfully. Through the nineteenth century, it appeared to have some right on its side. Four millennia of military history had taught that intelligence had played virtually no role at all in war. The staff believed, with some validity, that men, fire, and will won battles.[59] But while the French, the British, and the Americans[60] saw that the French and industrial revolutions were changing things and established special intelligence sections within their general staffs, the Germans did not. Their general staff continued its old and self-serving opposition to intelligence.[61]

It rationalized this view by holding that, since information about the enemy was merely part of the whole, the commander should handle it as part of his overall duties. Intelligence was subsumed under operations. And since the general staff ran operations, it controlled intelligence questions. One of these was whether intelligence should separate out as a speciality, and this possibility the general staff precluded. It required no intelligence courses of students at the War Academy; matters dealing with information about the enemy were amalgamated into the instruction on tactics.[62] It expostulated on the importance of standing above the particular problems of individual branches and seeing them as part of the broad operational picture.[63] When questionable situations concerning the enemy arose during battle, it maintained, energetic operations would clarify them. It ostracized officers who dealt with spies on the ground that association with these deceivers had tainted them; it preferred, one student has said, "honourable ignorance rather than useful knowledge gained by devious means."[64] It belittled intelligence and, in compensation, overemphasized the role of the commander.[65,66] Thus Chief of the General Staff of the Army Alfred Count von Schlieffen declared that it is "difficult to ascertain where the enemy will go from his assembly area. What cavalry and airships can report about it will generally come in too late. The commander must guess or calculate the intentions of the enemy."[67]

Not even German officers, however, could continue to suppress intelligence after its breakthrough in World War I. To do so, they saw, would jeopardize the nation and hence their position. So they created intelligence officers at the field staffs and an intelligence branch at headquarters. But they did so grudgingly. Their greater conservatism both compelled and enabled them to hang onto as much of their old power as possible. This they did by continuing to refuse intelligence the full status that it had long had in other armies. They institutionalized this attitude by placing the chief intelligence officer (Ic) under the chief of operations (Ia).[68] They safeguarded it by teaching almost no courses on intelligence methods.[69] And they propagandized it when they thought it necessary. The progress of the specialists increased their nervousness and made the army commander of the 1920s, Hans von Seeckt, sharpen Schlieffen's point. "Uncertainty and chance are inseparable characteristics of war. No understanding can control them, no beam out of the brightest and sharpest intellect can illuminate them. Only the will of the commander can dominate them…. The clarity of the will is the only light in the darkness of doubt and the future."[70] What was really nagging him was the fear that, if intelligence could win wars, no one would need generals.

Now there is no doubt that intelligence is merely part of the whole and that control of one's own men and resources by the Ia is more important than the knowledge of the enemy provided by the Ic.[71,72]

But the German system automatically impaired the quality of its own intelligence. Because the Germans felt that intelligence was part of tactics, they used general staff officers for Ic posts, but because the Ia was the more responsible job, they put the better men into those posts—and this filled the Ic posts with second-raters. A different philosophy would have enabled them to fill the intelligence slots with trained specialists, whose information the operations officer would have fitted into the entire tactical picture. The Allies, for example, used drafted civilians as intelligence officers even of army groups with great success.[73] First-class minds became expert on the enemy; with no worries about a career, they could both be kept in a post for the duration of the war and express their opinions more forcefully. The Germans, with their disdain for technicians and what they called "the burden of technology," which they felt gummed operations (laying telephone wire, for example, delayed commanders and cost them initiative and momentum), did not realize what the collecting and sifting of intelligence detail could yield.[74] The subordination of Ic to Ia further harmed German intelligence by forcing information to fight through an extra level of command and by reducing the authority with which the Ic would express his views to the chief of staff if they differed from those of the Ia. The whole German system undervalued intelligence as compared to other armies, in which the G-2 was as much the immediate subordinate of the chief of staff as the G-3.

Two factors somewhat ameliorated this situation. Wartime shortages of general staff officers drove the army to fill many divisional intelligence posts with reserve officers,[75] who developed in effect into intelligence specialists. And Gehlen pressed for making chief intelligence officers at least equal in rank to their chiefs of operations.[76] But the first was always regarded as a deviation from the norm and never affected posts from corps upwards, and the latter did not rectify the chief of operations-chief intelligence officer subordination. Only later, when the defensive situation enabled Gehlen and chief intelligence officers time and again to help commanders save men and material, did the army begin to change its attitude to intelligence—slowly, reluctantly, and partially.[77] But this was too little, and by then it was too late.

A quite different factor crippled the high-level organs of intelligence in the Nazi state. This was its authority structure. The Nazis called it the "Führer-Prinzip,"[78] but the great sociologist Max Weber had earlier identified it as "charismatic authority."[79] It damaged intelligence by reducing both its quantity and its quality.

The sole source of power in Nazi Germany was Adolf Hitler. It was a purely personal power: his word was law. It emanated from the devotion placed by the masses and the leaders in him as the embodiment of a revolutionary mission.[80] Weber contrasted this authority with two other kinds. Traditional authority maintains the sanctity of immemorial tradition; ancient Egypt and mandarin China typify it. Legal authority strives rationally to fulfill enacted norms; this authority is exerted through specialist officials assigned particular areas of competence—a bureaucracy.[81] The western democracies best exemplify the type.

Charismatic authority is fueled by faith, and Hitler's charisma released torrents of emotional energy among the Germans—far more than either traditional or rationally legal governments would have done. Believing in their Führer, the Germans held gigantic rallies, built autobahns, paraded by torchlight, recreated an army and an air force, conquered most of Europe, and purified the continent of subhumans. Often Hitler boasted of how much his policies had achieved.[82] Devotion to him kept exhausted soldiers fighting even in the hopelessness of 1945.

Charisma thus accomplished much. But it had its disadvantages. Charismatic authority was inefficient and, in the end, ineffective.

From the outside, the principle of strict adherence to the Führer made Nazi Germany appear to be a highly unified state, tightly controlled by an organization whose chain of command ran clearly from Hitler to the lowliest block leader—the cliché was "monolithic." Inside, however, it was a teeming nest of snakes, each seeking to devour the other, with no clearly defined tasks or authority, intent only—and this aspect of the Führer-Prinzip was real enough—on winning the approbation of Hitler and thus enhancing his own power.

For the remission of power by the masses to Hitler had freed him of the restraints of legal or traditional authority. He could arrange his personnel and his organizations as he wanted. And he wanted, basically, to replicate them and to let his subordinates fight among themselves, for two possibly contradictory reasons.[83] First, he believed that competition brought the best man to the top. He employed this social Darwinism within the party and between party and government.[84] Second, by multiplying organizations he would guarantee his power and facilitate his control. To allow any subordinate exclusive authority in an area would cede to that subordinate the power that knowledge confers; Hitler would become the captive of the subordinate in that field. On the other hand, distributing the authority of that function by giving similar duties to several subordinates would force them to come to him for their power.[85] To these ends he assigned Göring to head the four-year plan while Funk was minister of economics, appointed Dietrich his press secretary and Goebbels his propaganda minister, made the OKW into a rival of the OKH, let Ribbentrop set up his own spy service next to the existing ones of the armed forces and the party.

But this technique was inefficient. In intelligence, it dissipated the precious limited expertise of the political cryptanalysts in three agencies. It drove rival organizations, such as the three spy services, to waste time and energy intriguing, backbiting, and defining competencies in the jostle for Hitler's favor instead of concentrating on the enemy. It choked off the very intelligence that was supposed to help agencies make decisions. Hitler refused to allow Speer to transmit information to the OKH; when Dönitz wanted to see the documents of the Foreign

Office, he had to get special permission.[86,87] Hitler decreed in his "basic order" of 11 January 1940: "No one, no post, no officer, may learn about a matter to be kept secret if he does not unconditionally need to know about it."[88] All this diminished the quantity of intelligence.

Charismatic authority was, in addition, ultimately ineffective. It judged policy and information on the basis not of reason but of (Nazi) faith. Himmler told the Abwehr officers at Salzburg that an intelligence service must rest, not upon honest and objective evaluation of the facts, but "upon a race, upon a people of the same blood."[89] Boetticher's reports from Washington seemed right because of his views about Jewish control. The Nazi state practiced such irrationalism. The priority of ideology, which stemmed from its greater emotional force, ensured that, when disputes occurred, the most ideological authority invariably won.[90] Thus Ribbentrop, head of a party post for foreign affairs, ousted the career diplomat von Neurath as foreign minister. Thus the anti-Hitler chief of the general staff, Halder, was replaced by the pro-Nazi Zeitzler. Thus Speer displaced Thomas. Thus Himmler's SS expanded first into foreign policy at the expense of the less ideologically committed Foreign Office, and then into military affairs, with Himmler becoming chief of the replacement army and commander of an army group, at the cost of the unpolitical army. And thus the SD swallowed the Abwehr.

Though this may have worked, at least for a while, within the closed system of Nazi Germany, it failed outside it. Intelligence is better the closer it fits reality. But charismatic authority turns from the most valid route to external reality: reason.[91] It thus becomes dysfunctional. Even a Hitler Youth's perfect trust in the Führer could not keep Allied bullets from killing him. Even the deepest ideological convictions about Slavic inferiority and Communist weakness did not defeat Soviet Russia. Charismatic authority reduced the quality of German intelligence.

Now charismatic authority no more attained its pure form under Hitler than it did anywhere else in the world. A strong element of legal authority persisted, as Germany's vast bureaucracies made manifest. When disputes occurred within this sphere, as between the Abwehr and the Foreign Office on sending agents to North Africa, they were settled in a reasonable way.[92] Moreover, charismatic authority was not confined to Nazi Germany. Under the Kaiser,[93] the heads of three high army offices and several commanders in the field all had direct access to him as supreme war lord; the same situation existed with the navy.[94] During the early New Deal, Franklin Roosevelt's administrative techniques included overlapping jurisdictions and competitive assignments.[95]

But authority in the democracies was basically legal. This enabled them to shape a unified organization. The Anglo-American coalition is the supreme example. Of course, men wrangled, withheld information, and built empires, but the battles were not the battles to the death that they were under Hitler because law ruled, not men.[96] This increased efficiency. At the same time, the rule of rationality in legislative authority led the Allies to see the world more as it is, despite some wishful thinking, and so to take more effective actions.[97] The contrast is striking between the effect on intelligence of this form of government and that of Nazi Germany.

Charismatic authority fragmented the German intelligence effort and so reduced quantity. It screened the intelligence output in irrational and unreal ways and so reduced quality. Hitler's charisma devastated German intelligence.

For all these reasons, the intelligence that was delivered to the Führer was flawed and insufficient. But suppose it had been perfect. Would he have made better use of it? Would he have exploited its insights to maneuver more effectively?

For Hitler was the ultimate consumer. He stood at the apex of the intelligence pyramid. While he made sure that subordinates saw only part of the intelligence picture, he himself had access to all of it, and he alone evaluated it, making the final decisions on its meaning. More important, he alone decided whether the armed forces would act on it, and so in the last analysis he alone determined its impact on the German war effort.

Hitler wore five hats. He was head of state, head of government, party chief, commander of the armed forces, and acting commander in chief of the army. In one or another of these capacities, quantities of information flowed to him. Every morning the Reich press chief laid not only the German and party papers before his door but also press reports from abroad, such as those from the *Daily Mail*, from Tass, from Swiss and Swedish newspapers.[98] Every day, the Foreign

Office liaison to the Führer headquarters, Walther Hewel, submitted three to five documents.[99] On Friday, September 19, 1941,[100] for example, he gave Hitler a telegram from the embassy in Rome, one from the legation in Lisbon, an intercepted Turkish message solved by Pers Z, and a report from an agent of the Foreign Office's Inf III spy service. On other days Hewel gave him reports of the Forschungsamt, memoranda from Ribbentrop and Likus, one of Ribbentrop's chief aides, and clippings from the Foreign Office's press branch.[101] He also reported orally,[102] passing on, for example, the report of a Foreign Office liaison man in North Africa telling how American soldiers had only gone to war to earn money.[103] In addition, Hitler held situation conferences twice a day.[104] At these Jodl and, after the start of the Russian campaign, the chief of the general staff presented the military situation in almost suffocating detail.[105] During the battle for Stalingrad, for example, Zeitzler reported to him:

> At the Fiebig Group is a little town, it's called Kiryevo; enemy cavalry in a strength of about 1,000 men came in there. The following is interesting about this. Prisoners were made from the 40th Guard Division and the 321st Division. These two divisions were formerly on the northwest corner of the [German] 6th Army. The prisoners stated they were brought up in speedy marches for three nights in a row. From this one can conclude that he [the enemy] is now weakening the front of the 6th Army in order to press in this point near Chir. A further indication for this is that the 6th Army was only very weakly attacked today.[106]

Often army commanders reported in person;[107] often Hitler telephoned them for information.[108] Beyond this, Hitler got oral and written reports on various matters from the greatest variety of sources[109]—Göring, Goebbels, gauleiters and other party functionaries, special emissaries such as Philip, Prince of Hesse, or Constantin von Neurath,[110] son of the former foreign minister, who told Hitler how bad the Italians in Sicily were, industrialists, foreign statesmen and diplomats whom he received, even occasionally anonymous letters. In all, he said, he spent eight hours a day just reading reports and memoranda.[111]

Hitler understood a lot about intelligence. He recognized the difficulty of identifying troops from airplanes and knew that intercept operators could recognize individual enemy radiomen.[112,113] Unlike most laymen, he realized that there was no such thing as "the" English code but that several existed of different strengths and times of service.[114] He knew exactly how intelligence officers put together details into a complete picture: "When I get a report today on a Russian road that leads to a section of the front, in which 36 rifle divisions and armored formations, so many armored regiments and so many other formations are located, and it says that yesterday night 1000 vehicles travelled on a road, tonight 800 and then 1200 and 300 vehicles, that is an alarm, then, that runs through the entire eastern front: that says 'Attack imminent.'"[115] He was alert to the possibility of deception, commenting that one report was "too good to be true" and asking of another before the Allied invasion, "Must they do that so ostentatiously?"[116,117]

He not only understood intelligence, in tactical and operational areas he made good use of it. In October 1942,[118] he deduced from "extensive enemy movements" and "the bridging of the Don" that the Russians would "launch a major attack... across the Don in the direction of Rostov." He sent in three divisions. A few weeks later, Luftwaffe aerial photographs showed "that the number of new bridges built across the Don in the sector of the Rumanian 3rd Army is steadily growing. The Führer therefore still expects a major Russian attack across the Don in the direction of Rostov." He ordered the bridges bombed.[119] When in February 1941 the German attaché in Ankara warned that Turkey would go to war with Germany unless German troops in Bulgaria stayed 50 kilometers from the frontier Hitler issued the necessary orders.[120] When British newspapers announced that American Flying Fortress bombers would "pulverize" Germany, Hitler built up his flak positions and stocked them with quantities of ammunition.[121]

But his use of intelligence ceased at the borders of his strategy. For this issued from his basic conceptions, which had made him what he was and had brought him to where he was. Any admission of error in his racism or anti-Semitism or sense of geopolitical mission would have undermined not only his political power but his very personality. Consequently, these tenets were inaccessible to reason, excluded from argument. No facts could ever have convinced Hitler that he was wrong.

On the other hand, some reassured him that he was right. He had constructed his picture of the world from aspects of reality, and whenever he detected these aspects again, or corollaries of them, he

accepted them as confirmation of his views. The impoverished farm-
ers of the motion picture *The Grapes of Wrath*,[122] which he viewed as
a documentary rather than fiction, verified for him his image of a
"decayed country."[123] These selective corroborations occurred frequently in the years of victory. He had always held that America
would eventually absorb the British empire.[124] So he seized upon all
reports of friction between the Allies as bearing out his vision and its
effects.[125] Feedback intensified this distortion. His subordinates knew
what he liked, and supported him with innumerable substantiations
of his views.[126] They submitted favorable reports and seconded his
remark during conferences.

But other, less comforting aspects of reality nevertheless impinged.
Hitler's mind defended itself from them mainly by denying them.
It lightened the burden on itself by selecting a staff that blocked off
many of the items before they ever came to Hitler's attention. Reich
Press Chief Dietrich censored much of the press material.[127] Keitel
prevented Thomas from submitting his reports.[128] These men believed
that they were protecting their leader. Once Seifert, head of the evaluation bureau of the Forschungsamt, sent up a report with unpleasant
news.

> "How can you submit such a report to the Führer at this time?" an
> adjutant asked him.
>
> "If I hadn't submitted it, you should have had me put up against a
> wall and shot," replied Seifert.
>
> 'No," came the response. "When the Führer has made a decision, we
> must no longer disturb his intuition."[129]

At the situation conferences, Jodl emphasized minor German successes and soft-pedaled German retreats so that an observer would
scarcely realize that major offensives were pounding Germany back.[130]
On November 6, 1944, after the Germans had lost a bridgehead over
the Moselle, Jodl told Hitler about it like this: German skirmishers
south of the Moselle "were suddenly attacked very strongly. It became
a very bitter close combat around these little villages. Three [enemy]
tanks were shot up. He [the enemy] finally threw our skirmishers back
across the Moselle. The southern bridgehead was then given up."[131]
Elsewhere the talk stressed the Russian attacks that were thrown
back, the German counterattacks under way, the brave resistance of

units in tactically meaningless situations. Occasionally, when the soldiers had to admit to a withdrawal, they never spoke of a defeat—the enemy "pressed in,"[132] his overwhelming forces compelled the brave troops to yield a little ground. In such ways did Hitler's staff protect him from unpleasant news.

But sometimes bad news did reach him. In some cases, he neutralized it beforehand. If the report showed a preponderance of enemy strength, he charged the submitter with "defeatism"—lacking confidence in Germany's victory.[133] This eliminated him from serious consideration. Or Hitler could tax the report-writer with being an "expert,"[134] meaning usually a general staff officer or a diplomat. During his years of diplomatic and military triumphs, the diplomats and the general staff had warned him of dire consequences if he took a certain action; he had dared it anyway and, succeeding, had proved once again his genius and their incompetence. Consequently he could presume their statements to be as wrong now as they were before.

When this procedure was not available, he distorted the information to fit his views. Though Germany had 75 million people and the United States 135 million, Germany was ahead in population because only 60 million of the Americans were of decent racial stock.[135] Sometimes Hitler changed figures to make them more agreeable. A month after the navy had reported to him that the Americans would build 300,000 tons of shipping a month, he was basing arguments on a figure in his head of 70,000 tons.[136,137] When Jodl told him that a German unit advancing on Rome to arrest the king and the post-Mussolini government was 100 km from the city,[138] Hitler exclaimed: "One hundred? Sixty kilometers!" This process included "underestimation of enemy possibilities," which Halder saw as early as 1942 as becoming "dangerous."[139]

Most often, however, Hitler simply rejected unwelcome news. When England refused to make peace, he "could not conceive of anyone in England still seriously believing in victory."[140] The naval attaché in Russia reported to him about Russian ship construction figures, based on the time ships spent on the ways, obtained from aerial photographs. The size of the figures surprised Hitler, and he concluded, "What we can't do, the Russian can't do either."[141] Across a Pers Z intercept that told him about good agricultural results in Russia, he scrawled, "This cannot be."[142] When an aide wanted to give him information on the destruction of Hamburg from the awesome Allied raids in July 1943, Hitler cut him off: "You don't have to report that—I've already gotten the pictures."[143] Jodl's statement that Allied armor had rolled up part of the Westwall in March 1945 was contradicted: "That's also not so certain. It can be only two or three tanks."[144] Nor was this occurrence rare at his situation conferences. When Guderian submitted Gehlen's figures on Russian troop concentrations, he raved that they were "completely idiotic"[145] and that Gehlen ought to be committed to an insane asylum. When a Luftwaffe officer laid before him a giant composite aerial photograph showing that the Russians had assembled the greatest artillery concentration of all time before Army Group Center, he swept it furiously from the table.[146]

As matters worsened, as the evidence for defeat loomed more and more, Hitler shielded himself from it not only psychologically but also physically, encapsulating himself more and more in his own world.[147] He curtained his railroad car and traveled at night. During situation conferences he darkened the room. He visited the front only once after 8 September 1943, and refused to inspect bombed cities. He would not receive officers who had been in combat. He forbade "pessimistic" and "defeatist" talk.[148]

In a few isolated cases, he seemed to apprehend the true nature of the situation: "We are constantly losing industrial areas";[149] "The V-1 unfortunately cannot decide the war"; "Our own measures depend upon them [the enemy operations goals]." But in fact these were mere obeisances; they marked no confession of basic error. Nothing, but nothing, could turn him from his Nazi views. While the British bombed German cities and the German British, he envisioned a postwar "durable friendship" between Nazi Germany and England.[150] With Soviet tanks approaching his capital, he saw nothing wrong in his conception of Russian weakness, only in the timing of his attack.[151]

No evidence could penetrate obstinacy like that. So even if Hitler had been served with perfect intelligence, it would have had no essential effect upon him. He would have selectively absorbed what he liked and denied the rest. In the tactical area perfect intelligence might have helped; strategically it would have mattered not a jot.

The more basic question about Hitler and intelligence is not whether better information would have helped him. It is this: Why did the man who had handled reality so effectively in the 1920s and 1930s that he became the master of Germany and of Europe turn into a creature who petulantly swept unwelcome papers off his desk?

The answer lies less within Hitler than without. External circumstances effected the change. They stripped his defenses from him bit by bit and exposed his neuroticism more and more. The results could be seen not only in intelligence, but in all his actions.

During the early years, Hitler acted largely as he wished, relatively untrammeled by outside forces. His talents—in particular his fierce determination, his rigid will—enjoyed free play. They enabled him to become head of his party and of his country. Expanding these talents onto the world stage, he manipulated other nations to make Germany, and consequently himself, the dominant power in Europe. Hitler acted, molded, led; other men and nations reacted, bent, followed. In psychological terms, he was accommodating to reality by alloplastically altering reality. He was reshaping the world to satisfy his needs. In all this, outside of a few tactical reversals, he was not checked.

Then, in 1939, Britain refused to acquiesce in his program any longer. Her declaration of war seriously limited his freedom of action for the first time. The most direct, simplest, and surest way of resolving this frustration, after Britain spurned his peace offers, was to invade and conquer the island. But Hitler shied from this. He chose instead a solution that promised less to reshape reality than to meet his needs. He attacked Russia. Instead of battling a nation he really did not want to fight, he could destroy one he hated. Instead of fighting at sea, he could fight on land. Instead of sweating in the fear of defeat, he could wallow in the certainty of victory. And all this, he thought, came in addition to depriving Britain of her last hope and thus bringing her to her senses. So instead of facing the objectively more effective solution, he reverted to the subjectively more gratifying one. For the first time in a vital matter, he accommodated autoplastically. Instead of his changing the world, he let the world change him. In psychological terms, he regressed.

Britain's intransigeance was but the first external force to bar him from fulfilling his wishes. As it so often does, an immature response led to greater difficulties. His attack on Russia eventually cost him the strategic initiative, and thereafter events increasingly frustrated him. Increasingly, he responded with regressive behavior. When his blitzkrieg in Russia failed, he declared war on America. When he lost

France, he ordered the destruction of Paris. When the enemy occupied Germany, he directed Speer to destroy the country. And when, near the end of the war, generals laid intelligence before him that set forth nothing but more frustration, he swept it out of his sight.

Hitler was not the only leader in the history of the world to prefer preconception to uncomfortable intelligence, though his greater power enabled him to assert his more global prejudices much more completely than the others. Long before he arrived, chief of the general staff Schlieffen had analyzed the phenomenon: "The higher commander generally makes himself a picture of friend and foe, in the painting of which personal wishes provide the main elements. If incoming reports appear to correspond with this picture, they are laid by with satisfaction. If they contradict it, they are discarded as entirely false."[152] A few years later, his countrymen repeated the paradigm like sleepwalkers. The Kaiser's government wanted Belgium in 1914 to submit to a temporary occupation—and was surprised when she refused. It overlooked evidence that Britain would not remain neutral in what one scholar has called "a miscalculation bordering on blindness."[153]

Such blindness does not impair only Germans. In 1681, Louis XIV paid no heed to the repeated reports of his ambassador at The Hague that the Swedes were seeking a Dutch alliance because he wanted one with them instead; when the treaty was signed, he refused to take it seriously.[154] Later he dismissed information on Austrian weapons and military successes in order to maintain his previous conclusions.[155] In 1937, Japanese intelligence teams studying the Red army after losing a border clash with Russia found essentially what they wanted to: the fighting was atypical, no conclusions could be drawn, the Russians were as strong as expected, the Japanese had not underestimated them.[156] Next year the Russians sent them reeling again at Khalkhin Gol.

But what about Hitler's opponents? How did Churchill react to bad news? He too was a strong leader; he too not only believed but had to demonstrate his belief in victory; he too could not passively accept obstacles but had to overcome them. Did he then reject unpleasant intelligence?[157] No. He didn't like it. He fumed at it. But he accepted it. He took it into account in his planning.

In part it might be that it was easier for him to do so. The war situation presented him with really bad news less often than it did

Hitler. Even in the dark days after Dunkirk, Churchill could hope. Hitler, when the tide turned against him after years of triumph, could not. As he saw his destruction approaching, the psychological pressures became so great that the wonder is not that he swept papers off his desk, but that he did not crack earlier. The different experiences of the two further contributed to their divergent attitudes toward unpleasant information. Churchill had fought elections and, as a child of parliament, had sometimes submitted to opposing views. Hitler had never held office before he became chancellor; opponents, such as Rohm, the SA leader, he assassinated. The whole pattern was far more extreme and unaccommodating. It reflected the basic difference between the two men. Hitler's personality was essentially neurotic, deriving its strength—the inflexible will that enthralled everyone within its range—from its need to maintain its defenses. Churchill, born in a palace, the grandson of a duke, victor over early failures to become an early success, possessed an inner security and confidence that Hitler never had. What clinched their different ways of receiving bad news was their different sources of power. The House of Commons had accorded Churchill his position. If he did not do well—and disregard of reality rapidly leads to inadequate functioning—it would take the prime ministry away from him. Hitler, on the other hand, had total control and was not subject to easy removal, no matter what he did. Only a threat of loss of confidence by the mass of people could perhaps have held him to account, but faith and fear alike precluded that.

In the end, reality overwhelmed Hitler. Unable to avoid any longer the recognition that his life and all that it had stood for had been annulled, he at last annihilated himself. Three weeks later, what was left of his government, the wickedest regime of all time, capitulated. And with it there passed into history the feeble, and rightfully doomed, efforts of German military intelligence in World War II.

Notes

1. "For nothing is hid": *Luke* 8:17.
2. "It will always": Fritz Gempp, "Geheimer Nachrichtendienst und Spionageabwehr des Heeres," Im Auftrag der Abwehrabteilung des Reichswehrministeriums (photocopy in National Archives, T-77:1438–40, 1442, 1507–09) at II: 7:162.

3. Japanese poor: United States Strategic Bombing Survey (Pacific), Japanese Military and Naval Division, *Japanese Intelligence Section, G-2* (Washington, DC: Government Printing Office, 1946).

4. Figures precise: comparing United States, Department of State, *Foreign Relations of the United States: Diplomatic Papers: The Conferences at Washington, 1941–1942, and Casablanca, 1943* (Washington, DC: Government Printing Office, 1968), pp. 431, 584, with Germany, Oberkommando der Wehrmacht, Wehrmachtführungsstab, *Kriegstagebuch ... 1940–45*, ed. Percy Ernst Schramm, *Kriegstagebuch...1940–1945*, (Arbeitskreis für Wehrforschung), Frankfurt am Main, Germany: Bernhard & Graefe, 1961–64), 2:1377 and 3:8.

5. 58, 59: Harry C. Butcher, *My Three Years with Eisenhower* (New York: Simon and Schuster, 1946), p. 544; Chester Wilmot, *The Struggle for Europe* (New York: Harper & Bros, 1952).

6. 40 percent: dividing the 79 of German estimates into the 47 actual and subtracting from unity.

7. Abandoned plans to invade Britain: Frederick W. Winterbotham, *The Ultra Secret* (New York: Harper & Row, 1947), pp. 57–58; Patrick Beesly, *Very Special Intelligence* (London, U.K.: Hamish Hamilton, 1977), p. 41.

8. To attack Russia: Winston Churchill, *The Second World War* (Boston, MA: Houghton Mifflin, 1948–1953), Vol. 3, pp. 354–56.

9. German rockets: Churchill, 5:226–40.

10. U-boats: Beesly, passim.

11. Anzio: General Mark Clark, telephone interview, 20 November 1974.

12. German aircraft production estimates: Charles Webster and Noble Frankland, *The Strategic Air Offensive Against Germany, 1939–1945*, United Kingdom Military Series, Vol. 4 (Her Majesty's Stationery Office: 1961), p. 498.

13. Office of Strategic Service reports: Franklin D. Roosevelt Library: PSF: Boxes 167–170.

14. Did not commission Jews: Demeter, 224.

15. "Officials who are not": Germany, *Reichsgesetzblatt* (1933), 175.

16. Little effect on the military: Hans Mommsen, *Beamtentum im Dritten Reich*, Schriftenreihe der Vierteljahrshefte für Zeitgeschichte, 13 (Stuttgart, Germany: Deutsche Verlags-Anstalt, 1966), p. 57.

17. None let go from B-Dienst: Heinz Bonatz, letter.

18. Göttingen, 20%: Max Pinl and Lux Furtmuller, "Mathematicians Under Hitler," Leo Baeck Institute, *Year Book XVIII* (London, U.K.: Secker & Warburg, 1973), pp. 129–82 at 132, 142–43.

19. Replacement of superb intellects by mediocrities: Joseph Needham, *The Nazi Attack on International Science*, The Thinkers Forum, 14 (London, U.K.: Watts, 1941); Alan D. Beyerchen "The Politics of Academic Physics in the Third Reich: A Study of Ideology and Science," PhD dissertation, University of California at Santa Barbara, 1973; Dietrich Orlow, *The History of the Nazi Party, 1919–1932*, Vol. 2 (Pittsburgh, PA: University of Pittsburgh Press, 1969–73), pp. 487, 492; E. W. B. Gill, "German Academic Scientists and the War," Field Information Agency, Technical, 28 August 1945.

20. Arrogance distorted: Fritz Fischer, *Germany's Aims in the First World War* (New York: Norton, 1967), p. 92.

21. Effect of Frederick II of Hohenstaufen: Geoffrey Barraclough, *The Origins of Modern Germany* (Oxford, U.K.: Blackwell, 1947), pp. 232–33.

22. Napoleon's effect: *Ibid.*, 407; Karl Dietrich Bracher, *The German Dictatorship: The Origins, Structure, and Effects of National Socialism*, trans. Jean Steinberg (New York: Praeger, 1970), p. 17.

23. "deadly foreign spirit," "German": Johann Gottlieb Fichte, *Addresses to the German Nation*, ed. George Armstrong Kelly (New York: Harper & Row, 1968), pp. 101, 60; Bracher, 22–28.

24. authoritarianism that began in the Reformation: Erik H. Erikson, *Young Man Luther: A Study in Psychoanalysis and History* (New York: Norton, 1958), p. 252.

25. solely by faith: Martin Luther, *On the Freedom of a Christian*, §§8, 10.

26. "Even if those": quoted in Erich Fromm, *Escape from Freedom* (New York: Holt, Rinehart and Winston, 1941), p. 82.

27. "No insurrection," "The answer": quoted in Erikson, 235, 236.

28. parents assimilated: My assumption. But studies show that German families are authoritarian and more so than American: Donald L. Taylor, "The Changing German Family," *International Journal of Comparative Sociology*, Vol. 10 (1969), pp. 299–302; Donald V. McGranahan, "A Comparison of Social Attitudes among American and German Youth," *The Journal of Abnormal and Social Psychology*, Vol. 41 (July, 1946), pp. 245–57.

29. dynamics of an authoritarian person: These tend to make such a person a poorer intelligence officer than the egalitarian or tolerant personality (Norman Dixon, *On the Psychology of Military Incompetence* [London, U.K.: Jonathan Cape, 1976], 258, 264–66, 274). Consequently, German Ics [Ic was the German designation for the officer in each unit's staff that handled intelligence; Ia dealt with the German army's own operations] may have been poorer intelligence officers than Allied G-2s. But I have no evidence on this point, and the number of variables is so great in the raw data that I do not see how any evidence for or against this hypothesis could be collected. Nevertheless, the authoritarian's desire to control his environment and the consequent rigidity in thought, which in effect means a preference for theory over the uncertainties of reality, may explain what Ralf Dahrendorf called "The German Idea of Truth" and the desire for ultimate solutions in his *Society and Democracy in Germany* (New York: Anchor Books, 1967), pp. 129–71.

30. "German policy towards": Fischer, 307.

31. refused to believe: John W. Wheeler-Bennett, *The Nemesis of Power: The German Army in Politics 1918–1945* (2nd edn.: London, U.K.: Macmillan, 1967).

32. qualitative superiority: Alan Milward, *The German Economy at War* (London, U.K.: University of London, 1965), pp. 100–106, 129–30.

33. Förster, Gerhard et al., *Der preussisch-deutsche Generalstab 1640–1965* (Berlin, Germany: Dietz, 1960), p. 105.

34. resembled World War I: Hans-Heinrich Wilhelm, *Die Prognosen der Abteilung Fremde Heere 1942–45* in *Zwei Legenden aus dem Dritten Reich,* Schriftenreihe der Vierteljahrhefte für Zeitgeschichte, 28 (Stuttgart, Germany: Deutsche Verlags-Anstalt, 1974), pp. 7–75.

35. left their intelligence officers: Kenneth Strong, *Men of Intelligence* (London, U.K.: Giniger, 1970), p. 34.

36. "What is the concept": Clausewitz, *Vom Kriege,* bk. vi, ch. 1, §1. Repeated in the German army manual for Troop Command, Heeres Dienstvorschrift [H.Dv.] 300, §41.

37. "complete in itself," active: *Ibid.,* bk. vii, ch. 2. Also in H.Dv. 300, §39.

38. surprise, superiority of numbers: *Ibid.,* bk. iii, chs. 8, 9.

39. planning omitted intelligence: Erich von Manstein, interview, 2 August 1970.

40. "The war will": *Staatsmänner und Diplomaten bei Hitler, Vertrauliche Aufzeichnungen über Unterredungen mit Vertretern des Auslandes,* ed. Andreas Hillgruber (Frankfurt am Main, Germany: Bernard & Graefe, 1967–1970), Vol. 2, p. 299. Somewhat similar quote at *Documents on German Foreign Policy,* 9:122.

41. French naval code: Bonatz, 93.

42. French espionage: G. Bertrand, *Enigma* (Paris, France: Plon, 1974), pp. 26–28.

43. contributed greatly: Winterbotham; Beesly.

44. French watched Germany: Georges Castellan, *Le Réarmement clandestin du Reich, 1930–1935, vu par le 2e Bureau de l'état-major français* (Paris, France: 1954).

45. Admiralty Operational Intelligence Center: Beesly, passim.

46. "happy parasite": H. R. Trevor-Roper, *The Last Days of Hitler* (New York: Macmillan, 1947), p. 24.

47. censors: Germany, *Akten zur Deutschen Auswärtigen Politik 1918–1945,* 3:21.

48. "main duty": *Ibid.,* 3:75–76.

49. more and more: My observations from *Hitlers Lagebesprechungen* and the *Lagevorträge.*

50. difficult domestic problems: Michael R. Gordon, "Domestic Conflict and the Origins of the First World War: The British and the German Cases," *Journal of Modern History,* Vol. 46 (June 1974), pp. 191–226.

51. decreed the strategic offensive: Franz Halder, former chief of the German general staff, saw this as a basis of the undervaluing of intelligence in the German army, letter, 20 January 1972.

52. created the blitzkrieg: Milward, 12–14.

53. power of specialists: Victor A. Thompson, *Modern Organization* (New York: Knopf, 1961), pp. 6, 12–13; Rosemary Stewart, *The Reality of Organization* (London, U.K.: Macmillan, 1970), pp. 69–70; Seymour M. Lipset and Reinhard Bendix, *Social Mobility in Industrial Society* (London, U.K.: Heinemann, 1959), pp. 3, 11.

54. officers resist: Morris Janowitz, *Sociology and the Military Establishment* (New York: Russell Sage Foundation, 1959), pp. 18, 20; Thompson, 14, 46, 96–97.

55. more adamant: Friedrich Hayn, "Aus der täglich Kleinarbeit der Abteilung Ic," in his *Die Invasion: Von Cotentin bis Falaise*. Die Wehrmacht im Kampt, 2 (Heidelberg, Germany: Vowinckel, 1954), p. 133; *German General Staff Corps*, 3.

56. Great Elector, monopoly: Otto Büsch, *Militärsystem und Sozialleben im Alten Preussen 1713–1807*, Veröffentlichungen der Berliner Historischen Kommission…,7 (Berlin, Germany: Walter de Gruyter, 1962), pp. 30–31; Herbert Rosinski, *The German Army*, ed. Gordon A. Craig (New York: Praeger, 1966), pp. 24–25, 36; Howard in Karl Demeter, *The German Officer-Corps in Society and State 1850–1945*, trans. Angus Malcolm, (London, U.K.: Weidenfeld & Nicolson, 1965), p. ix; Waldemart Erfurth, *Die Geschichte des deutschen Generalstabes von 1918 bis 1945*, Studien zur Geschichte des Zweiten Weltkrieges, 1 (Göttingen, Germany: Musterschmidt, 1957), p. 5; Weber, 3:981, 1:225–226.

57. ascriptive to achievement: Janowitz, *Sociology*, 27–28.

58. general staff fought: Erfurth, 213.

59. men, fire, and will: Michael Howard, interview.

60. J. D. Hittle, *The Military Staff: Its History and Development* (Harrisburg, PA: Military Service, 1944), passim.

61. intelligence under operations: Rosinski, 299; cf. Thompson, 76, 143; Stewart, 78.

62. amalgamated into tactics: [Louis A.]von Schafenort, *Die Königliche Preussische Kriegsakademie: 1810–15. Oktober 1910* (*E. S. Mittler*), 391; Hansgeorg Model, *Der deutsche Generalstabsoffizier: Seine Auswahl und Ausbildung* in *Reichswehr, Wehrmacht und Bundeswehr* (Frankfurt am Main, Germany: Bernard & Graefe, 1968), saw this as a basis of the undervaluing of intelligence in the German army), 13, 15; Kord Konus, "Ic Dienst bei Höheren Kommandobehörden des Heeres im Ostfeldzug," *Wehrwissenschaftliche Rundschau*, Vol. 2 (1952), pp. 394–401 at 395.

63. standing above, part of whole: *German General Staff Corps*, 95.

64. "honourable ignorance": Dixon, 293.

65. belittled intelligence: P-041i, 43; Geyr, 7, 8; D-407, 55; Strong, 34; Ulrich, Liss, "Der entscheidende Wert richtiger Feindbeurteilung," *Wehrkunde*, Vol. 8 (November 1959), pp. 592, 643–644; cf. Thompson, 116.

66. overemphasized commander: Rosinski, 305–309.

67. "difficult to ascertain": Generalfeldmarschall Graf Alfred von Schlieffen, *Gesammelte Schriften* (ESM: 1913), 1:8.

68. I c under I a: Germany, Heeresleitung, HDv.g.92, 18; HDv.g.89, 11; D-407, 5, 19–20.

69. no intelligence courses: Model, 34, 48, 78–79; P-04H, 43.

70. "Uncertainty and chance": [Hans] von Seeckt, "Die Willenskraft des Feldherrn," *Militärwissenschaftliche Rundschau*, Vol. 1 (15 December 1935), pp. 2–6 at 6.

71. I a more important than I c: Rudolf Hagemann, adjutant in 102d Infantry Division, interview, 7 October 1973; Siegfried Westphal, chief of staff to Rommel and Rundstedt, interview, 11 May 1970; Friedrich Wilhelm

Hauck, commander of an infantry division, interview, 26 April 1970; cf. Karl W. Deutsch, *The Nerves of Government* (London, U.K.: Free Press of Glencoe, 1963), pp. 159–160.

72. I c second-raters: Adolf Heusinger, head of operations branch, interview, 8 October 1973.
73. civilians as intelligence officers: Edgar "Bill" Williams, Montgomery's intelligence officer, interview, 15 December 1972.
74. did not realize: *German General Staff Corps*, 95.
75. reserve officers: *German General Staff Corps*, 113; P-018a. 12.
76. equal in rank: Gehlen, 37.
77. army attitude changes: Heusinger, interview.
78. "Führer-Prinzip": Otto Dietrich, "Der Nationalsozialismus als Weltanschauung und Staatsgedanke," 5, in H.-H. Lammers et al., eds., *Die Verwaltungs-Akademie: Handbuch für den Beamten im nationalsozialistischen Staat* (Berlin, Germany: Industrieverlag Spaeth & Linde, n.d.), 1:1:2.
79. "charismatic authority": Weber, 1:215. I am indebted to Joseph Nyomarkay's fine book, *Charisma and Factionalism in the Nazi Party* (Minneapolis, MN: University of Minnesota Press, 1967), for the illuminating insight about charismatic authority.
80. devotion: Weber, 1:242–43.
81. traditional, legal authority: *Ibid.*, 215.
82. Hitler boasted: Example in [International Military Tribunal], *Trial of the Major War Criminals before the International Military Tribunal, Nuremberg* [1947–1949], 37:547.
83. replicate, let his subordinates fight: Nyomarkay, 28, 33; Bracher, 212.
84. social Darwinism: Peter Hüttenberger, *Die Gauleiter: Studie zum Wandel des Machtgefüges in der NSDAP*, Schriftenreihe der Vierteljahrshefte für Zeitgeschichte, 19 (Stuttgart, Germany: Deutsche Verlags-Anstalt, 1969), pp. 198, 212; Jeremy Noakes, *The Nazi Party in Lower Saxony, 1921–1933*, Oxford Historical Monographs (Oxford, U.K: University Press, 1971), pp. 96–97.
85. distributing the authority: Victor A. Thompson, *Modern Organization* (New York: Knopf, 1981), p. 87.
86. Hitler refuses Speer: Albert Speer, *Inside the Third Reich: Memoirs* (New York: Collier, 1981), p. 316.
87. Dönitz special permission: *Lagevorträge*, 521.
88. "No one": Grundsätzliches Befehl, printed on the inside front cover of many official army manuals.
89. "upon a race": National Archives, Washington, National Sozialistisches Deutsche Arbeiter Partei, BA, EAP 161-b-12/278:4–5.
90. most ideological authority won: Weber, 3:1115–17; Hans Gerth, "The Nazi Party: Its Leadership and Composition," *The American Journal of Sociology*, 45 (January 1940), pp. 517–40 at 539.
91. charismatic authority rejects reason: Max Weber, *Economy and Society*, ed. Guenther Roth and Claus Wittich, Vol. 1 (New York: Bedminster, 1968), p. 244.

92. Abwehr-Foreign Office dispute: *Akten zur Deutschen Auswärtigen Politik 1918–1945,* Vol. 2, pp. 240, 357–59.

93. under the kaiser: Craig, 230; Rosinski, 240; Walter Hubatsch, *Der Admiralstab und die Obersten Marinebehörden in Deutschland 1848–1945* (Frankfurt am Main, Germany: Bernard & Graefe, 1958), p. 111.

94. Jonathan Steinberg, "Germany and the Russo-Japanese War," *American Historical Review,* Vol. 75 (December 1970), 1965–86 at 1968.

95. Roosevelt techniques: Arthur M. Schlesinger, *The Coming of the New Deal* (London, U.K.: Heinemann, 1960), pp. 516–23.

96. not battles to the death: Cf. Popov, 69.

97. rationality in legal authority: Weber, 1:244.

98. press reports to Hitler: Dietrich, 154; Speer, 298: *Hitlers Lagebesprechung,* 709; *Hitlers Tischgespräche,* 441.

99. Hewel submitted: Average of AA: Vorlagen beim Führer for September, 1941.

100. 19 September 1941: AA:Vorlagen beim Führer, 431792.

101. other days: *Ibid.,* 431776–99.

102. reported orally: Speer, 299.

103. liaison man: *Hitlers Lagebesprechungen,* 170.

104. situation conferences: Heiber in *Hitlers Lagebesprechungen,* 12; Warlimont, 219–25; Keitel. 146–47.

105. chief of the general staff: Halder, 3:52, 497; *Hitlers Lagebesprechungen,* passim.

106. "At the Fiebig": *Hitlers Lagebesprechungen,* 58.

107. in person: *Ibid.,* 369–83, 537, 621.

108. telephoned: Gersdorff, interview.

109. greatest variety of sources: Hans-Adolf Jacobsen, *Nationalsozialistische Aussenpolitik 1933–1938* (Frankfurt am Main, Germany: Metzner, 1968), pp. 47–52.

110. von Neurath: *Hitlers Lagebesprechungen,* 221–28.

111. 8 hours a day: *Ibid.,* 608.

112. difficulty of identifying troops: *Ibid.,* 106.

113. intercept operators: *Ibid.,* 761.

114. several existed: Militärarchiv: III M 1006/6:169.

115. "When I get": *Hitlers Lagebesprechungen,* 750.

116. "too good": *Ibid.,* 535.

117. "Must they do that": *Ibid.,* 557.

118. October 1942: OKW, *Kriegstagebuch,* 2:864–65.

119. ordered bridges bombed: *Ibid.,* 889.

120. issued necessary orders: Martin L. Van Creveld, *Hitler's Strategy 1940–1941: The Balkan Clue* (Cambridge: University Press, 1973), pp. 122–23.

121. built up flak: *Hitler's Table Talk,* 182.

122. *The Grapes of Wrath*: *Hitlers Lagebesprechungen,* 170–71.

123. "decayed country": *Hitler's Table Talk,* 188.

124. Americans would absorb: *Hitlers Zweites Buch,* 173; *DGFP,* 13:692.

125. seized upon reports of friction: *Staatsmänner,* 2:306.

126. National Sozialistisches Deutsche Arbeiter Partei.

127. Dietrich censored: Jacobsen, 349.

128. Keitel prevented: Keitel, 183; Thomas, 160, 270.

129. "How can you": Seifert, interview, 7.

130. Jodl softpedaled retreats: Boldt, 6.

131. 6 November 1944: *Hitlers Lagebesprechungen*, 703.

132. "pressed in," yield ground: *Ibid.*, passim.

133. "defeatism": *Ibid.*, 493; *Staatsmänner*, 2:237.

134. "expert": *DGFP*, 12:940–41; *Hitlers Lagebesprechungen*, 816–17; *Hitlers Tischgesprache*, 238, 396, 443; Gehlen, 23: Speer, 305; Kersten, 83–87.

135. Germany ahead in population: Weinberg, "Hitler's Image of America," 1013.

136. 300,000 tons: OKM, *Denkschriften*, 222.

137. 70,000 tons: *Hitlers Tischgespräche*, 201.

138. 100 km: *Hitlers Lagebesprechungen*, 316–17.

139. "underestimation," "dangerous": Halder, 3:489.

140. "could not conceive": *DGFP*, 10:82.

141. "What we can't": Baumbach, interview.

142. "This cannot be": Kahn, 445–46. Possibly the 1942 Yugoslav intercept cited by Gehlen, 64.

143. "You don't have": *Hitlers Lagebesprechungen*, 201.

144. "That's also not": *Ibid.*, 901.

145. "completely idiotic": Guderian, 387.

146. swept it from table: Primavesi, interview; Warlimont, 1st interview.

147. encapsulates himself: Fest, 925–26; Speer, 245, 299–300, 304.

148. forbade "pessimistic" and "defeatist" talk: Speer, 423; *Staatsmanner*, 2:237; *Hitlers Lagebesprechungen*, 493.

149. "We are," "The V 1," "our own": *Hitlers Lagebesprechungen*, 847, 818, 836, 824.

150. "durable friendship": *Hitler's Table Talk*, 12.

151. timing of the attack: *The Testament of Adolf Hitler*, 97.

152. "The higher commander": Schlieffen, 1:188.

153. 1914: Jonathan Steinberg, "A German Plan for the Invasion of Holland and Belgium, 1897," *Historical Journal*, Vol. 6 (January 1963), pp. 107–19 at 118.

154. 1681: Andrew Lasky, "'Maxims of State' in Louis XIV's Foreign Policy in the 1680s," in *William III and Louis XIV: Essays 1680–1720 by and for Mark A. Thompson*, ed. Ragnhild Hatton and J. S. Bromley (Liverpool: Liverpool University Press, 1968), at pp. 12–13.

155. dismissed information: Richard Place, "The Self-Deception of the Strong: France on the Eve of the War of the League of Augsburg," *French Historical Studies*, Vol. 6 (Fall 1970), pp. 459–73.

156. 1937: Alvin D. Coox, "The Lake Khasan Affair of 1938: Overview and Lessons," *Soviet Studies*, Vol. 25 (July 1973), pp. 51–65 at 64.

157. Churchill attitude toward intelligence: Cavendish-Bentinck, interview.

11

AN ENIGMA CHRONOLOGY*

In view of the importance of ULTRA to the history of intelligence, and in view of the errors in dating that appear in so many accounts, I thought it would be worthwhile to establish a list of important dates in the story of the Enigma cipher machine and its solution. Most deal with the naval machine.

This chronology comes mainly from my book, *Seizing the Enigma* (New York: Houghton Mifflin, 1991), which is based as much as possible on primary or on solid secondary sources, chiefly F. H. Hinsley et al.'s magisterial *History of British Intelligence in the Second World War* (Cambridge: Cambridge University Press, 1979-1988). For my book, the Naval Historical Branch in London made available to me a key primary source for much naval dating, but I promised not to cite it by name, a promise that I am honoring. Information about the times of naval solution comes from analyses of intercepts in the Public Record Office, London, and in the National Archives, Washington. To avoid burdening this list with a heavy bibliographical apparatus, I have given as sources the page numbers in Hinsley or in *Seizing the Enigma* that specify these dates or detail those incidents. Notes in the form 2:659 refer to Hinsley; those in the form 140 or 31 to Kahn, in which the notes to the text cite the source. "GC&CS" is the Government Code and Cypher School, the British codebreaking agency at Bletchley Park. Names in capital letters of colors, insects, and birds are GC&CS's covernames for Enigma keys.

An important element in the history of the solution of Enigma is that the Luftwaffe Enigma was solved more easily by GC&CS than the naval Enigma, though until 1 February 1942 both used the identical machine with identically wired rotors. One reason is that the air force (like the army) chose the three rotors inserted into its machines from a set of five rotors while the navy chose its three from a set of eight.

---

* From *Cryptologia*, 17(3) (July 1993), 237–246.

In addition, air force key settings could often be recovered in the first few months of the war from the key indicators at the head of the cryptograms and later from blunders by the ciphering clerks in making up their part of the key. This gave GC&CS insight into Luftwaffe messages, providing enough cribs for a daily recovery of keys. The naval settings, on the other hand, were taken from books and permitted neither the indicators nor the blunders approach; without some early solutions, GC&CS could not at first get enough messages to yield future guesses of plaintext for cribs. Captures of the books were thus the necessary first step for solution of the naval Enigma. The Enigma keys used by the army were seldom solved because the army cipher clerks, more experienced than those of the Luftwaffe, seldom made blunders.

Solution of the Enigma consisted of guessing an intercepted cryptogram's plaintext (either from knowledge of the traffic previously passed between posts or from solutions of the same messages in other cryptosystems) and then seeing whether the bombes (which were in effect multiple Enigmas) found a setting of the Enigma rotors that would produce such a ciphertext from the assumed plaintext. If they did, that setting was the key for the day on that cipher net and permitted the reading of other messages on the net. The process had to be repeated for each net each day.

Not included here are minor matters, such as the dates of early improvements in Enigma construction or keying, of techniques the Poles used to overcome these changes, or of the solution of secondary keys, such as the Luftwaffe's practice key. (I consider keys minor if they did not contribute significantly to the fighting. Some people may of course differ with my judgment.) A full list of solution dates is given in Hinsley, 2:658-668, 3:1:483-487, 3:2:855-857. In some cases, Hinsley does not state for how long the solutions continued. The date of 24 May 1943 at 2:667 is a misprint for 24 May 1945, Hinsley told me.

DATE		ENIGMA	THE WORLD
1918	Feb 23	Arthur Scherbius files for a patent for the Enigma cipher machine (Patentschrift Nr. 416291)	
	Apr 15	Arthur Scherbius offers the Enigma to the German navy (31)	
1918	Nov 11		World War I ends

DATE	ENIGMA	THE WORLD
1921 Feb 19		France and Poland sign accord for "concerted measures for the defense of their territory"
1926	German navy begins using Enigma (40-41)	
1928 Jul 15	German army begins using Enigma (51)	
1931 Nov 8	Hans-Thilo Schmidt betrays army Enigma instruction manual and keying methods to the French, who give them to the Poles (59)	
1932 Dec	With the help of keys betrayed by Schmidt and given by the French to the Poles, cryptanalyst Marian Rejewski reconstructs the wiring of the three Enigma rotors, enabling the Poles to begin solving German army Enigma messages (65-66)	
1933 Jan 30		Führer of the Nazi party, Adolf Hitler, named chancellor of Germany
1938 Dec 15	Two new rotors (making a total of five) go into service on army Enigma; Rejewski recovers wiring, but tenfold increase in number of keys overwhelms Poles, requiring them to ask aid from their allies (77)	
1939 Mar 30		Britain and France guarantee to help Poland if she is invaded by Germany as Czechoslovakia was
Jul 24	Poles reveal success to British and French (79)	
Sep 1		Germany invades Poland
Sep 3		Britain and France declare war on Germany
1940 Jan 6	British break into Luftwaffe Enigma using hand methods (1:108, 2:659)	
Feb 12	British seize two of the three unknown rotors used in the naval Enigma from a crew member of the U-33 captured after the submarine was sunk (114; 3:2:957) (see Figure 11.1).	
Apr 9		Germany invades Denmark and Norway
May	First bombe installed at GC&CS (1:494, more likely than August installation date given at 1:184 because regular solution of RED began May 22)	
May	First break into naval Enigma: using documents salvaged 26 April from the trawler *Polares* (303, 3:2:957), GC&CS solves April messages (117) (Figure 11.2)	

DATE		ENIGMA	THE WORLD
	May 10		Germany opens massive offensive against France; Winston Churchill, a long-time supporter of communications intelligence, named prime minister
	May 22	GC&CS begins solution of Luftwaffe general purpose key (RED) continuing virtually uninterrupted to end of war (1:109, 144)	
	Jun 10		Last Norwegian troops surrender
	Jun 22		France surrenders
	Aug	The last unknown naval rotor obtained from a naval capture (3:2:957)	
	Aug 12		Adlertag (Eagle Day): Germany attempts to win air superiority over England as invasion preparation
	Sep 15		Battle of Britain Day: it becomes clear that Germany's attempt to win air superiority has failed
	Oct 12		Hitler postpones invasion of Britain until spring
	Dec 10	SS (Schutzstaffel) general-purpose key (ORANGE I) first broken by GC&CS (2:668)	
1941	Jan 28	Luftwaffe operational key for Africa first solved by GC&CS; solutions end 31.12.42 with introduction the next day of separate Fliegerkorps keys (2:660)	
	Feb and Mar	2 U.S. Army and 2 U.S. Navy American cryptanalysts visit GC&CS and learn Enigma cryptanalysis (235-237)	
	Feb 15		General Erwin Rommel named commander of German forces in North Africa
	Mar 12	Documents seized from patrol ship *Krebs* permit reading of some March and all April and May naval messages in the Home Waters key net, also used for U-boat messages (137)	
	Jun 1	GC&CS reads Home Waters (and U-boat) messages for a month with keys seized from weather ship *München* and U-110 (169) (Figure 11.3)	
	Jun 22		Germany invades the Soviet Union
	Jun 27	GC&CS breaks German army Russian front key (VULTURE I); solutions last until spring 1944 (2:662)	

DATE		ENIGMA	THE WORLD
	Jul 2	GC&CS reads Home Waters (and U-boat) messages for a month with keys seized from weather ship *Lauenburg* (182) (Figures 11.4 and 11.5)	
	mid-Aug	Home Waters key (DOLPHIN), then also used by U-boats, begins to be solved daily in 36 hours without seized keys on bases of knowledge gained in two preceding months; solutions continue to 7 May 1945 (1:338, 2:663-664)	
	Sep 6	Churchill visits GC&CS at Bletchley Park (184-185)	
	Oct 5	TRITON key net for U-boats separates U-boat keys from Home Waters key (205); solutions continue on both nets in times ranging (in January) from 12 to 120 hours	
	Dec	GC&CS first solves Enigma of the Abwehr, the armed forces espionage service; solutions, called ISK (Intelligence Service [Dillwyn] Knox), continue to end of 1944 (2:668)	
	Dec 12		Germany declares war on the United States
1942	Jan 1	Keys for Luftwaffe's Fliegerkorps IX (WASP) and Fliegerkorps X (GADFLY) broken on day of first appearance and continue to end of war; key for Fliegerkorps IV (HORNET) broken to December 1943 (2:660)	
	Early	New Short Weather Key goes into service (2:750), ending GC&CS's ability to use meteorological messages as cribs to read naval Enigma (189-190)	
	Feb 1	4-rotor Enigma goes into service on TRITON; U-boat solution blackout begins (2:179)	
	Apr 3		Rommel begins offensive against British
	Apr 22	GC&CS breaks the Luftwaffe key for ground-air cooperation in Africa (Fliegerführer Afrika, or SCORPION); this ends February 1943	
	Jun 30		Rommel halts offensive at El Alamein
	Fall	U. S. Navy liaison officer starts at GC&CS	
	Oct 23		British attack at El Alamein begins German rout
	Oct 30	New Short Weather Key captured from U-559 (220, 226)	
	Nov 8		Americans and British invade North Africa

DATE	ENIGMA	THE WORLD
Dec 13	GC&CS, using new Short Weather Key to get cribs, breaks 4-rotor Enigma keys (SHARK); blackout ends (226, 2:667) but solutions irregular and at first slow (sometimes 8 days), by end of month much faster (around 12 hours)	
1943 Jan and Feb	SHARK solutions stutter, but when working some are fast enough to be of operational value (229)	
Mar 10 -Jun 30	90 SHARK keys solved in 112 days (230)	
Mar 14-20		Greatest convoy battle of the war, in which 21 ships are sunk, leading Allies to fear that the Atlantic lifeline to Britain could be cut
May 24		Commander of U-boats Admiral Karl Dönitz withdraws his submarines from the North Atlantic, signifying a major Allied victory in the Battle of the Atlantic
Aug	SHARK being read almost solid and fast (242)	
1944 Jun 6		Allies invade Normandy
Nov	Individual U-boat keys end SHARK solutions, but so great is Allies' strength in ships and airpower that this no longer matters much (262)	
1945 May 8		Germany surrenders

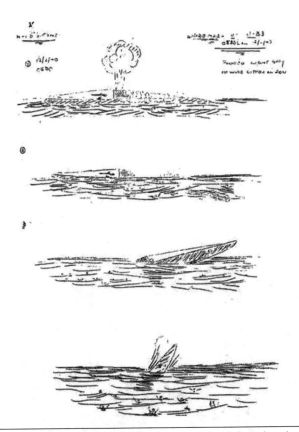

Figure 11.1 12 February 1940: A series of sketches — artist not indicated — showing the end of the U-33 after it surfaced in a vain attempt to escape the minesweeper *H. M. S. Gleaner* in Scotland's Firth of Clyde 12 February 1940. The sketches show (1) a shower of sparks from the coning tower; (2) crew members in the water as they abandon ship; (3) more in the water as the submarine starts to sink; (4) the U-boat in her final dive with survivors swimming away from her. Three rotors were recovered from a crew member who forgot to take them from his pocket and drop them in the ocean (Public Record Office, ADM 199/123, p.54).

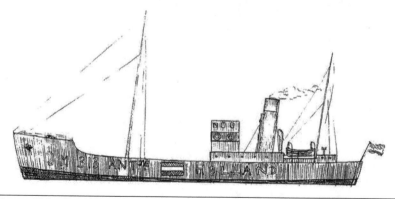

Figure 11.2 May 1940: The former trawler *Julius Pickenpack,* now a German attack vessel disguised as the Dutch ship *Polares*. From one of its canvas bags, thrown overboard on the approach of British warships but saved by a British sailor, the British obtained cryptographic documents useful in solving German naval Enigma traffic. (From Public Record Office, ADM 199/476, p. 243.)

Figure 11.3 1 June 1941: The officers and crew of the U-110, in port, await an approaching inspecting officer while the skipper, Lieutenant Fritz-Julius Lemp, 28, approaches the gangplank to greet him. On patrol, the submarine was seized by the British and, before it sank, yielded an Enigma machine and keying documents. These enabled the British to read U-boat messages for June 1941. Lemp was lost during the action. (From David Kahn collection.)

Figure 11.4   2 July 1941: Hinrich Gewald, 58, skipper of the *Lauenburg,* whose capture by the British led to the seizure of Enigma keying documents that enabled the British to read U-boat messages for July 1941. (From David Kahn collection.)

Figure 11.5   2 July 1941: The *Lauenburg,* just before being boarded on 28 June 1941. (From David Kahn collection.)

12

THE BLACK CODE*

While keeping Washington informed, an American military attaché inadvertently gave Erwin Rommel vital information about Allied forces in north Africa.

Colonel Bonner Frank Fellers may have been the most important American military attaché of World War II. President Franklin Roosevelt read his dispatches and acted on them, and Fellers once reported to the president in person. From his post in Cairo, he provided details of armor and air that would help American forces when they invaded North Africa, the place where Germany threatened to cross the Suez Canal, seize the Middle East's oil, and shake hands with the Japanese to control most of the world. Yet, in a curious situation entirely beyond his control, he became, for a while, a major informant of Germany's great general, Erwin Rommel, the Desert Fox.

As attaché, Fellers was extremely energetic, conscientious, intelligent, and knowledgeable. A native of Illinois and a West Pointer, he had served three tours in the Philippines, where he adored the head of the American military mission, General Douglas MacArthur. In 1936 he sycophantically called MacArthur's speech on taking command "a Sermon on the Mount, clothed in grim, present-day reality. I shall never forget it." His passion for English—when assigned to teach mathematics at West Point, he transferred to the English department—shows in the clarity and precision of his "Psychology of the Japanese Soldier," a paper he wrote after his second tour on Corregidor. As MacArthur's liaison to the president of the Philippines, Manuel Quezon, Fellers accompanied the chief executive on his Atlantic crossing to the coronation of Britain's King George VI. Then, in mid-1940, while he was teaching English at the Point for the second time, the army selected him as an assistant military attaché

---

* From *MHQ: The Quarterly Journal of Military History*, 18 (Autumn 2005), 36–43.

to Spain, possibly because he had learned Spanish in the Philippines. However, before he set out for Madrid, the War Department ordered him to Cairo as attaché in Egypt. For in September, from its colony of Libya, Italy had invaded Egypt, a former British protectorate.

European armies first established attachés in the 1840s to keep up with developments in military technology. The United States sent its first attaché—a naval expert—to London in 1882; military attachés went in 1889 to London, Paris, and Vienna to "examine and report upon all matters of a military or technical character that may be of interest and value to any branch of the War Department and to the service at large." In the pre- and post-World War I years, when the United States did not employ spies and could not intercept military cryptograms of foreign nations (the naval cryptograms of Japan being the sole exception), attachés provided America with most of its intelligence on foreign military and naval establishments.

When Fellers arrived in Cairo on October 31, 1940, he was one of about 125 American military attachés in fifty stations throughout the world. After obtaining approval from the British foreign minister, Anthony Eden, to visit British installations and forward positions in Egypt and after completing his protocol calls upon Egyptian officials, Fellers was taken to the desert by the leading British commander, General Henry Maitland ("Jumbo") Wilson, and introduced to the British officers and men there.

"From that time on I had free access to the desert," Fellers said. "I just lived with them and I was very close to the Tommy."

The theater of war was the sandy desert of the Mediterranean coast, where mobile, mechanized forces dominated. Fellers was an artillerist, not a cavalryman or tanker. Still, he charged energetically into the assignment. He felt that if his work was to be accurate, usable, and acceptable to his superiors, he had to do his own observing and reporting. He went where he wanted with his own driver and car—a camouflaged van with a bunk in the back that he called his hearse. Fellers sensed that Washington believed the British were feeding him material, but he insisted that was not the case: "The British were courteous and friendly to me, but they did not educate me. I educated myself." After one battle he reported, "I saw the Germans withdraw through minefields and except for artillery and medium tank fire the British were too weak to attack." Later that day, "I talked with tank commanders who claimed eight German tanks to their credit whose tanks had been hit by 88 mm and as high as 12 times with 50 mm."

Washington, 4000 miles away, needed to know what was happening on the Allied (then almost exclusively British) side of the North African theater. Fellers was the man on the ground. Working from an office in the American legation decorated with maps and photographs, he dictated his reports in what one visitor called his "colorful, downright way." Fellers and his assistants sent back volumes of reports—two, three, sometimes five a day by the middle of 1941 (Figure 12.1). They dealt with the greatest variety of topics: daily operational summaries, German plywood gasoline tanks, British tropical uniforms, one-man explosives-carrying boats, the defense of a British troopship while at sea, supply and administrative lessons from the operations of the British 7th Armored Division in the Libyan campaign, maps of the El Katrit Station and of Port Fouad, the technique Germans used in aviation attacks, the contents of captured documents. He kept this up—he could hardly have intensified it—after the United States entered the war.

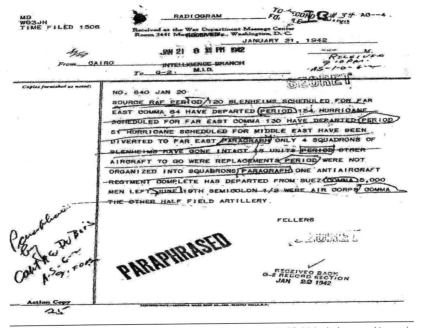

Figure 12.1 Colonel Fellers gave specifics about the movement of British airplanes and troops in this January 21, 1942 message to the War Department.

Many of Fellers' reports offered technical details intended to improve American equipment and tactics. Others were of direct value to men in combat. "Absence of direct ground-air and air-ground radios in forward areas and failure of army to devise distinctive marks or signals so that their tanks can be identified by RAF [Royal Air Force] are believed responsible for lack of tank-air cooperation," he warned on February 2, 1942. On February 24, he replied to two War Department messages: "American 37mm guns can penetrate all Axis armor but effect[ive] range much less than that of Axis tanks weapons and antitank guns. This fact is terrific handicap to American light tanks and must be corrected." On June 12, 1942, he alerted Washington that the "greatest single tank destroyer is German 88mm dual purpose guns with which British appear unable to deal."

He gave a concrete example: "At 8 a.m. May 27th after having enveloped Hacheim 60 German tanks struck British 22nd Brigade in square 36-41. A regiment of 50 American medium and light tanks was committed against the 60 Panzer tanks. Immediately it was apparent that the British regiment was being worsted. Brigadier General Carr ordered a 2nd regiment of 50 tanks to assist the one engaged. In 10 minutes the 2nd regiment lost 8 American medium tanks from 88mm dual purpose guns."

Other reports dealt with larger issues. Fellers sometimes appeared critical of the British and pessimistic about their chances. He blamed the disunified British command structure in part for Britain's loss of Crete to German paratroops. On January 31, 1942, as Rommel and his *Panzergruppe Afrika* were moving eastward, Fellers gloomily predicted: "There is nothing to prevent Rommel moving as far east as Hacheim.... Although the RAF has numerical superiority the British army in Cyrenaica is tired, depleted, their strength negligible, their supply problem colossal. Believe personally only sound plan to retire into the Tobruk-Bardia-Maddalene triangle, which can be supplied and held."

Though Fellers sent bulky or nonurgent items to Washington by ship, he radioed important messages. His clerks encoded them with the code book given to military attachés, officially named Military Attaché Code No. 11 but usually called—from the color of its binding—the "Black Code." So many and so frequent were these messages that as early as January he complained that the "code book through fair wear and tear is falling to pieces, being used day and night." His staff concealed the code groups by enciphering them, and then took the cryptograms to the offices of the Egyptian Telegraph Company, which radioed them to Washington.

Fellers was careful about security: The code was kept in a safe with a combination lock inside a room with a barred steel door locked with a Yale padlock, to which he kept the sole key in his possession. Although not a signals officer, he was alert to cryptologic violations. He told Washington on February 1, 1942: "So many mistakes are occurring in cable messages from Washington DC that there may be danger of compromising the code.... Improper use of cipher indicators throughout paragraphs in general.... Sometimes 35 to 40 groups occurring without change of cipher table." In addition, the next day he wrote: "Your cable number 491 encoded but not enciphered. Believe that code compromised. Will not use confidential code book until advised by you."

Apparently, Washington advised Fellers that the code had not been compromised, for he resumed using it. His caution did not avail him—both European Axis powers already had the Black Code. The Italians had stolen it from the American embassy in Rome. Though Fanny Patrizi, an American-born marchesa who was the mistress of the American military attaché there, was suspected of the theft, the real story involves less romance. Around September 1941, two specialists of the *Servizio Informazione Militare* who had copied keys to embassy offices entered the military attaché office, opened the safe, and, after carefully noting the shelf position of the Black codebook, removed it and rushed it by car to SIM headquarters. There, agents photographed it and then returned it to its location in the safe. SIM perhaps photographed the encipherment tables—although stripping the superencipherment it not very difficult if the cryptanalyst has the underlying code—and possibly the State Department cryptosystems as well. Soon the Italian foreign minister was gloating, "everything that [U.S. Ambassador William] Phillips telegraphs is read by our decoding offices."

The Italians did not give the code to their allies, the Germans. In January 1942, the Germans solved it themselves. A cipher branch lay within the *Oberkommando der Wehrmacht*, or OKW, the High Command of the Armed Forces. In this *Chiffrierabteilung*, or Chi, at Tirpitzufer 80 in central Berlin, dozens of codebreakers—many of them mathematicians or linguists—attacked the cryptosystems of the Allies and the neutrals. The Black Code resisted their efforts but weakly. Its system of enciphered code was antiquated; it had been widely used in the 1920s, and was easily solved even then.

Moreover, the volume of American military attaché messages worldwide eased the cryptanalysts' task. They got their raw material—the intercepts they sought to solve—from radio listening posts scattered across Europe. On January 19, 1942, Berlin ordered: "As complete as possible interception of messages between Cairo and Washington and vice versa is extremely important.... Primarily of interest: Cairo-Washington with addresses AGWAR [Adjutant General War Department] Washington and MILID [Military Intelligence Division] Washington; Washington-Cairo MILATTACHE Amlegation S.N."

The post that captured many of Fellers' radiograms lay in a broad field in the lovely medieval town of Lauf-an-der-Pegnitz near Nuremberg. Here 150 radiomen in low, tree-shaded stucco buildings encircled by six radio towers tuned their receivers to the foreign transmitters that they could pick up best: Italy, the Vatican, Argentina, the United States, and Egypt, among others. The post at Treuenbrietzen, near Berlin, backed up Lauf. As the dots and dashes raced overhead, the radiomen copied the enciphered Black Code gibberish. The intercepts were teleprinted to Chi in Berlin. Here the cryptanalysts stripped Fellers' encipherment off and rapidly converted the underlying code groups into the original English. Translators then turned that into German. Specialists at Foreign Armies West, the intelligence branch of the OKW, edited the reports into dispatches giving their essence. The reports disguised their cryptanalytic origin by saying that they came from a "reliable source" or a "good source." Cipher clerks enciphered them on the Enigma cipher machine, and radiomen transmitted the mumbo jumbo into Morse code and spewed it into the ether. The whole process sometimes took less than two hours.

They sent the messages to North Africa, to the man who could use them best: General Erwin Rommel (Figure 12.2). Fellers was so excellent, so energetic an observer and reporter that, inadvertently, his information helped not only those he intended to aid but also his enemies. As Rommel was rebounding across the desert early in 1942, throwing the British back three hundred miles in seventeen days, he was getting information like this from the Fellers intercepts:

Figure 12.2   German General Erwin Rommel, who regularly led his panzer units into battle.

January 23: Two hundred seventy airplanes and a quantity of antiair-craft artillery being withdrawn from North Africa to reinforce British forces in the Far East.

January 29: Complete rundown of British armor, including number in working order, number damaged, number available and their loca-tions; location and efficiency ratings of armored and motorized units at the front.

February 6: Location and efficiency of the 4th Indian Division and the 1st Armored Division; iteration of British plans to dig in along the Acroma–Bir Hacheim line.

February 7: British units stabilized along the Ain el Gazala–Bir Hacheim line.

By then the Germans and Italians were sharing information. On January 29, the Italian *Commando Supremo* gave the German military liaison officer a long Fellers intercept of January 19 dealing with Axis activity. On February 3, the Foreign Office gave a German embassy official two Fellers messages dealing with air matters. The intercepts continued during the spring, while Rommel was resting and gathering strength for his next attack. A German intelligence appreciation of May 20 depicted the enemy situation well, listing the British units and sharply evaluating them and their commanders; it was based largely on Fellers' own evaluations.

On May 26, when Rommel rolled forward once again, the intercepted messages told him about British plans to anchor their defensive line, and then about their later changes of mind. With these messages building his confidence and his knowledge, and with plentiful gasoline to fuel his armored vehicles coming from tankers that the inadequate British forces on Malta could not block, Rommel drove the British back—toward Egypt, Suez, and the Middle East's oil.

However, the Germans and Italians were not the only ones able to break codes. Since the spring of 1940, the British codebreaking establishment at Bletchley Park, some 60 miles northwest of London, had been reading German messages enciphered in Enigma, the electromechanical cryptosystem widely used by the German armed forces (Figure 12.3). However, these were *Luftwaffe* messages,

Figure 12.3 Arthur Scherbius invented this German cipher machine, code-named "Enigma," in 1919. German armed forces used it into World War II. Polish cryptanalysts cracked the ULTRA crypto system in the 1930s.

encrypted sloppily. Not until September 17, 1941, did the British occasionally break into a more carefully handled German army system, which Bletchley called CHAFFINCH. Solving it required either the discovery of German carelessness in an encipherment or guessing that a CHAFFINCH message had been re-enciphered in the easier-to-solve *Luftwaffe* system and then using one of several copies of an electromechanical device called a "bombe." The bombes were in very short supply. It was not until April 1942 that conditions again permitted Bletchley to read CHAFFINCH messages. On the 14th, Bletchley read a CHAFFINCH intercept that turned out to be an intelligence appreciation to Rommel. It said it based its information on a "reliable source." At the end of May 1942, another message to the intelligence officer of the German air commander in Africa said: "From a particularly reliable source, the following report was made on 16/4 [April 16].... The R.A.F. in Egypt is making no use of the technical courses established by the Americans," because the British mechanics were incompetent.

This message attracted the attention of Prime Minister Winston L.S. Churchill, who noted on it in red ink: "C.A.S. [chief of air staff] What action? WLC 31.V." (Figure 12.4). Investigation showed that the allegations might "have some element of truth," but more important was the fact that the message "bears striking resemblance" to the text of a signal received by the American mission in Egypt. The report concluded, "Dope given in German report suggests information was obtained in Washington as signal AMSEG 540 not decoded here until 17th. Breaking of American code another possibility."

On June 10 Churchill was advised that "a good source reported on 8/5" about a visit to several British units: "Battle morale of officers and men excellent, training inferior according to American ideas." The chief of the secret service, Sir Stewart Menzies, who oversaw Bletchley, wrote on a cover sheet in his own hand: "Prime Minister: I am satisfied that the American ciphers in Cairo are compromised. I am taking an action." He signed it "C," the initial traditionally used by the secret service chief. The chief of air staff then told Churchill, "Action has already been taken to rectify this."

This did not satisfy the prime minister. In 1914 as first lord of the Admiralty he had accepted a seized German code book from the Russians that set Britain on its codebreaking path; he later called

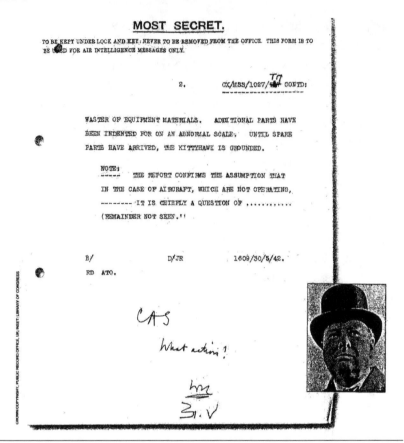

MOST SECRET.

TO BE KEPT UNDER LOCK AND KEY: NEVER TO BE REMOVED FROM THE OFFICE. THIS FORM IS TO
BE USED FOR AIR INTELLIGENCE MESSAGES ONLY.

2.   CX/MSS/1027/ CONTD:

WASTER OF EQUIPMENT MATERIALS.   ADDITIONAL PARTS HAVE
BEEN INDENTED FOR ON AN ABNORMAL SCALE.   UNTIL SPARE
PARTS HAVE ARRIVED, THE KITTYHAWK IS GROUNDED.

NOTE:
        THE REPORT CONFIRMS THE ASSUMPTION THAT
IN THE CASE OF AIRCRAFT, WHICH ARE NOT OPERATING,
-------- IT IS CHIEFLY A QUESTION OF ....
(REMAINDER NOT SEEN.''

B/   D/JR   1609/30/5/42.
RD ATO.

CAS

What action?

31. V

Figure 12.4   This message attracted Churchill's attention.

this the best "means of forming a true judgment of public policy." In his tiny, neat writing, Churchill directed Menzies to "report what steps you have taken about the cipher."

Meanwhile, Menzies investigated further, and found that "there has arisen an element of doubt as to whether the Germans are reading an American cipher, and there is a possibility that a traitor is providing the Germans with the contents of certain American messages." He told Churchill: "The investigation which I am conducting with the American cryptographers is not completed. There are at least three American ciphers in use between Cairo and Washington, and until the Americans inform me which cipher was used for the messages in question, it is impossible to determine whether the Germans have broken a cipher, or whether there is a traitor who is betraying information and transmitting it to the enemy by a secret channel. Both we and the Americans appreciate the urgent necessity of stopping the leak, and will report our finding."

Churchill circled the word "report," wrote "Yes" in unusually large letters, and scrawled his paraph next to it. Churchill's concern was valid.

Although Washington had ordered the Black Code replaced on June 3 after recognizing Germany was intercepting and decoding messages, rectification had not in fact taken place, although the air chief had assured Churchill. It had been delayed by the U.S. Army's stubborn adherence to a cryptologic truism: No one wants to believe that his own cryptosystem can be broken.

Fellers continued sending messages in the Black Code, and the Germans and Italians continued to read them. On June 1, he reported pessimistically that the British "air ground liaison was poor and the RAF repeatedly bombed own forces. The ground units of the armored division were never present to occupy the ground captured by the tanks." Pointing out that the British "supply problem is considerably relieved by railhead in vicinity of El Adem," he predicted that "the British will undoubtedly attack as they have adequate replacements in men and materiel." On June 4, he told Washington, "A British counter-attack is expected to start by June 8." On June 12, he told Washington after visiting two British corps headquarters and three armored units, "As certain armored units in particular are behind in their training, a British offensive in Cyrenaica is not likely at present." The Axis almost certainly intercepted many of these messages and forwarded them to Rommel, who indicated their value by referring to them as his "good source." Nor was he the only one who found them useful.

Adolf Hitler himself hoped that the American representative in Cairo "would continue to tell us about the English military planning through his badly enciphered cables." The *Seekriegsleitung*, the naval war staff, heard about one message as it considered the situation on Malta. The logistical struggle of the desert war centered on that island. Airplanes and warships based on it constantly attacked Axis convoys bringing armor and supplies to Rommel, who, having just captured Bir Hacheim, was rolling fast and needed fuel. To help prevent the Allies from throttling his supply line, Rommel ordered Axis airplanes to sink Allied ships strengthening Malta. The island desperately needed relief.

The British planned to destroy those Axis airplanes, either by para-chuting saboteurs onto the Axis airfields or by inserting them with the Long Range Desert Group. Fellers communicated details of these plans to Washington with the comment, "This method of attack offers tremendous possibility for destruction, risk is slight compared with possible gains." The Germans and Italians intercepted and solved this message—and massacred the saboteurs. The operation failed, and Axis airplanes saved by this foreknowledge attacked a pair of convoys heading for the island, crippling one and forcing the other to turn back.

Fellers was unaware that his reports had fallen into enemy hands. He has been slandered as "Colonel Garrulous." This is unfair; he was doing his job well and properly. Should he have restrained himself, not reported on future operations? Only if he suspected that his messages were insecure. Yet, he had no proof that they were. He was not a code officer. Communications security was the job of the Signal Corps. Fellers could not have been expected to know that the Black Code had been compromised.

On June 11, the British intercepted and solved a German message reveling in the "Good source reports" that had compromised the parachuted saboteurs and the Long Range Desert Group. Messages flew between Bletchley and Washington. On June 16, Menzies told Churchill: "Washington informs me that it is now clear that the cipher of the American Military Attaché in Cairo is compromised, and I have asked that this should be changed immediately to a cipher providing the highest security, but without furnishing any reason for the change-over. Should the Germans obtain any information dispatched on the new cipher, we shall then know for certain that there is a traitor in Cairo. In my opinion, the Germans have succeeded in photographing the American cipher book; as this is held at a number of stations abroad, it is impossible to determine where the treachery occurred. We cannot, moreover, rule out the possibility of a traitor in U.S.A., where the books are printed."

When the British continued to read Axis messages citing the "good source," as they did on June 23, Churchill asked Menzies, "Is this still going on?" He replied: "U.S. Authorities having now changed their cipher, no further leakage should occur as from 25th July 1942. If leakage continues, then there must be a traitor with access to American telegrams in Cairo, transmitting by Secret Wireless from Egypt, but available evidence does not support this likelihood."

Because the cryptographic change was being dealt with at this high level, the delay came to the attention of the chief of the general staff, General George C. Marshall. On June 21, he fired off a cable to Cairo, stating: "Our message ... effecting changes ... not complied with. Matter of greatest concern. Contact military attaché and direct his immediate compliance with changes."

That Olympian thunderbolt had its effect. The Army put its SIGABA cipher machine, which the Axis never cracked, into Cairo, blacking out Rommel's good source. On June 29, the German High Command's Foreign Armies West mourned, "Unfortunately, we will not be able to count on these intercepts, which gave us immediate information about almost all enemy measures, for a long time to come."

A story circulated to explain the blackout that recalled the stab-in-the-back legend after World War I, which sought to exonerate the German armies from their defeat in the field by saying that they had been betrayed at home by Communists and Jews. It did not consider that perhaps the Allies had recognized the weakness of the Black Code and replaced it, and certainly not the possibility that the Allies had broken Axis cryptosystems. Rather, the story went that the Fellers intercepts had been leaked to underground Communist cells, the *Rote Kapelle* (Red Orchestra), which somehow got the *Reichssender* Berlin to broadcast a radio play, *Behind the Scenes of World Politics*, late in June 1942. Relating the espionage struggle in the Middle East, it quoted Fellers' reports. Within a week, his cryptosystem had been changed, and the Axis went blind. However, no record of such a broadcast can be found, either in the German files or in those of the British Broadcast Corporation's monitoring service.

Of course, the Fellers intercepts were not Rommel's sole source of information. He had air reconnaissance, ground patrols, a few Arab agents, and a tactical communications intelligence company, *Horchkompanie* 3/N.56, which until it was captured on July 9, 1942, had produced much valuable information. He also had momentum. On June 21, Rommel captured Tobruk, with 28,000 prisoners, great quantities of stores that he could use in his advance, and a port through which he could more easily bring in the fuel and other supplies he needed. The next day, Hitler promoted him to field marshal. On the 23rd, he crossed the Libya-Egypt border, and continued rolling.

Fellers continued sending his reports back to Washington—this time unintercepted. His influence at this critical moment was perhaps greater than that of any other American military attaché. At least one of his messages went to President Roosevelt. No. 1156 of June 23, 1942, recommended that the American air forces in India be sent to the Middle East and that a corps of two armored divisions, one infantry division, and two tank-destroyer battalions likewise be sent to the Middle East—proposals that he had voiced as early as March 9. However, the situation was much more critical now. When Roosevelt commented on it to Marshall, the chief of staff rejoined, "Fellers is a very valuable observer but his responsibilities are not those of a strategist and his views are in opposition to mine and those of the entire Operations Division."

Marshall had set out those views in a memorandum for the president earlier that day: "The matter of locating large American ground forces in the Middle East was discussed Sunday night…. It is my opinion, and that of the Operations Staff, that we should not undertake such a project…. You are familiar with my view that the decisive theater is Western Europe. That is the only place where the British forces can be brought to bear on the Germans. A large venture in the Middle East would make a decisive American contribution to the campaign in Western Europe out of the question. Therefore, I am opposed to such a project." Still, twenty-three B-24 heavy bombers, already in India and destined to bomb Japan from China, were sent to Egypt.

A week later, Rommel's spearheads planted the swastika in the desert sands only sixty miles west of Alexandria, at El Alamein. Here they prepared to punch through Palestine and perhaps join with Hitler's forces in Russia, which were just then opening their massive summer offensive. Gigantic northern and southern pincers then could seize the Middle East oil, block the Mediterranean, choke off the supply line to Russia, and link with the Japanese to conquer the world. Could the British hold out?

A worried Roosevelt had his aide, Harry Hopkins, ask Marshall whether the United States could make any moves "that might favorably affect situation in the Middle East?" The president also wanted Marshall's personal analysis of the situation and his judgment on what kind of air and land forces were needed in Syria "that would tend to hold Turkey in line?"

Marshall replied at once, sending his three-page typewritten reply by hand to Roosevelt's country home at Hyde Park, New York. He pointed out that "Rommel is greatly extended and if checked by destruction of his supply bases and interruption of his supply lines, he would be in a difficult position." Nevertheless, he said, "Army G-2 estimates Rommel may reach Cairo in one week; Army operations say two weeks." There were, he said, no moves "that can affect the immediate situation."

At this juncture, Fellers was recalled. On June 19, 1942, the army had established the U.S. Army Forces in the Middle East to replace the nine-month-old North African Military Mission. Storm clouds lowered. The head of USAFIME, Maj. Gen. Russell L. Maxwell, who knew of Fellers' criticisms of the British command structure, equipment, and personnel, proposed restricting the attaché to discussing Egyptian affairs only. Maxwell would provide Washington "with my personal estimation of the situation and enemy activities from time to time."

Fellers was named as the acting chief of staff of USAFIME while retaining his position as attaché. Soon he was complaining that his messages, which previously had been seen only by his "most trusted code clerks," some not even by his assistants, would thenceforth be seen by USAFIME code personnel "over whom I have no control" and "some of whom I suspect of loquaciousness." And they did talk. Apparently, word had gotten back to the British about Fellers' criticisms, and they asked Maxwell whether Fellers would continue as the War Department liaison officer for intelligence. Though Maxwell said that Fellers "has followed his own concept of his mission in a most courageous manner," he cabled Marshall on July 7 (referring to himself in the third person): "It is regretted that due to unfortunate disclosures Fellers finds it most difficult if not impossible to gain access to the kind of information Maxwell must have for operational purposes. Therefore Maxwell has relieved him as his acting chief of staff and does not feel justified in assigning him as his GEE two [intelligence officer]." He felt that Fellers' "return to the United States for full report to War Department is most desirable."

The American envoy, Alexander Kirk, an experienced diplomat who thought highly of Fellers' "marked ability, experience, and special knowledge," acknowledged that his overzealousness might have antagonized the British. Not everybody liked Fellers. General

Dwight Eisenhower, who knew him from their work together in the Philippines under MacArthur, once said, "Any friend of Bonner Fellers is no friend of mine."

Although Kirk asked that Fellers' return be postponed "until the existing emergency has ended," the War Department said, "It is imperative for Colonel Fellers to come immediately to Washington so that first hand information may be obtained on the military situation in the Middle East." He was ordered home for temporary duty in the British empire branch of the Military Intelligence Service.

Fellers may have been persona non grata in Cairo, but Washington eagerly awaited his arrival. A member of the staff of the Office of Strategic Services raved to Major David Bruce: "I am informed that the brilliant and thoroughly informed Colonel Fellers is returning here from Cairo. Every report from every source is lyrical in praise of this officer, some going so far as to say that he should be C in C in Egypt. In view of his profound knowledge of everything in the Middle East, I suggest the possibility that you and Colonel [William J.] Donovan may wish to see him."

Upon his return, Fellers reported on the situation to Roosevelt, at the president's invitation, on Thursday, July 30. Fellers expressed his pessimism about the ability of the British to hold the Nile Delta and the Suez Canal, believing Rommel would penetrate British lines by the end of August. The president asked what could be done. Fellers said ten planes a month would help, though he pointed out that the air forces alone could not stop German operations in the desert, where vehicles move in ones or twos and not always on roads or in defiles. At Roosevelt's meeting at 8:30 that evening with the chief of the Joint Chiefs of Staff, the chief of the Army Air Forces, and the naval aide, Roosevelt—with Fellers' comments in mind—asked that the joint chiefs see what could be done for air reinforcements.

Two months later, the former attaché was awarded the Distinguished Service Medal. While awaiting his next permanent assignment, the army tapped his expertise as it prepared for America's first European offensive: its landing in North Africa. Fellers attended the armored force maneuvers at the desert training center in California from October 13 to 15, 1942. He remarked that the terrain, climate, and the "going" of the California desert were almost identical to Libya and complimented the officers and men on their spirit and conduct, but criticized some "erroneous concepts" held by some commanders. Marshall commended his perceptive report to General Lesley J. McNair, commander of the Army Ground Forces. His information may have helped those first American army troops landing in North Africa.

Fellers was then sent to where he had started his career: the staff of Douglas MacArthur. He became one of the few men to whom the autocratic commander would express personal sentiments. MacArthur gave him a brigadier general's star, and he served as his chief of psychological operations. Fellers retired in 1946 and died in 1973.

13

NOTHING SACRED

The Allied Solution of Vatican Codes in World War II*

Vatican codes were regularly broken during World War II by American and British cryptanalysts, a document[1] released into the National Archives reveals. It shows that, when engaged in total war, even the powers that honored religion stopped at almost nothing, not even at prying into matters spiritual. To them, as to the Germans who also broke into Vatican messages,[2] there was nothing sacred.

Both Axis and Allies wanted to glean from the intercepts indications about the policies of the Vatican and intelligence about enemy or neutral activities that the curia or the nuncios may have obtained. Perhaps based on a romantic image of cardinals scurrying through frescoed corridors and informants whispering, confession-like, secrets of state into clerical ears, the report referred to the papal representatives' "unparalleled position in the diplomatic corps" and "the intelligence reports which help to make the papal secretaries so well informed on world affairs." Unfortunately, the document includes no solved messages, and this writer knows of none yet made public, to show exactly what information the intercepts provided.

According to the 60-page report, the British began attacking Vatican cryptosystems in June of 1942. The cryptanalysts of Britain's so-called Government Code and Cypher School eventually identified two Vatican cryptosystems, determined the meanings of 2,824 of one codebook's estimated 11,000 codewords, and recovered large parts of the tables for enciphering those codewords in the Vatican's two-step system. At this point, early in September 1943, after the fall

---

* From M. Wala, *Gesellschaft und Diplomatie im Transatlantischen Kontext: Festschrift für Reinhard R. Doerries zum 65. Geburtstag.* Wiesbaden: Franz Steiner Verlag, 1999, pp. 217–220.

of Italian dictator Benito Mussolini led to Italy's withdrawal from the war and a decline in Italian diplomatic traffic, the United States joined the assault.

Three youngish Americans were assigned to it: Genevieve Grotjan Feinstein, who had made a critical breakthrough in 1940 in the solution of the Japanese diplomatic cipher machine,[3] Albert Small, an experienced cryptanalyst who had also helped solve that machine,[4] and Dr. Martin Joos, who became a noted philologist and lexicographer, writing the definition of cryptologic terms for *Webster's Third New International Dictionary of the English Language Unabridged.*[5] Later they and others were transferred; by May of 1944 a team of three cryptanalysts was dealing with Vatican and Italian diplomatic systems.

To begin with, the three original Americans had several thousand intercepts from after the Pearl Harbor attack and a handful from before. They and their successors began by separating out the messages in the system solved by the British, which—for reasons not now known—the British called the E system and the Americans, KIA. This gave the codebreakers a set of messages all in one system. They then corrected and expanded the British-reconstructed table for enciphering the codewords. This enabled them to strip off that encipherment and get to the codewords. By guessing at the meanings of unsolved codewords in somewhat the same way as a crossword-puzzle solver fills in blanks, they added 3,051 plaintext values to the 2,824 the British had given them. Though these totaled only about half of the code, the values were the more frequently used, enabling the Allies to read 99 percent of the texts of the 6,700 intercepted KIA messages.

KIA was the basic Vatican code, officially called *il cifrario rosso,* the red cipher, from the color of its cover; it was assigned to virtually all stations. It seems to have been put into service before 1936, the date of the earliest intercepted traffic and of the German-Italian Pact of Steel, since its vocabulary lacks the word for *Axis.* It included tables for specifically clerical matters, such as lists of dioceses and vicariates apostolic, terms of canon law, and titles of heads of orders.

The cryptanalysts, who did not know that the curia had used Italian in its communications for some 300 years, held the romantic notion that "Latin might have been expected as the basic language of Vatican codes." But, they conceded, "thus far in the experience of the

SSA [the U.S. Army's Signal Security Agency] no Vatican code has been found which is not in Italian." The reason, they observed, is that "With the single exception of Paschal Robinson, the Nuncio to Eire, every diplomatic representative of the Holy See speaks Italian as a native." This enabled them to bring to bear their experience gained in the solution of Italian diplomatic codes "since, in spite of striking differences from the cryptographic point of view, the linguistic problems in both kinds of traffic are fundamentally the same."

The second most important Vatican code was the yellow, called KIB by the Americans. It was more secure than the red and was used by nearly all the important stations, excluding only some distant posts, such as Peking, Tokyo, and Sydney, probably because of the difficulty of delivery during wartime. It was not solved. After the KII was found to be the KIA with a different encipherment for the codewords, it became up to 90 percent readable. Other codes were the KIC (the green code, in Vatican terms), the KIF, the KIG, and the KIH, all of which were investigated but none of which were solved, mainly because the traffic volume did not suffice. "In this respect then Vatican policy is far different from that of the Italians who failed to provide enough systems for the heavy traffic sent and sent so many messages that adequate traffic [for solution] was inevitable in almost all systems and keys," the report said.

The document also praised the Vatican code clerks for showing "much more care in the preparation of messages than do those in the employ of the Italian government.... This high standard of accuracy is probably to be explained by the use of ordained priests, men of high education, as code clerks.... Moreover, the central office never commits such a blunder as the establishment of a new system through a message in an older system."

In a few sentences that provided some historical depth, the report alluded to the 1906 study of papal cryptology by Professor Aloys Meister of the university at Münster.[6] Meister published the epochal manuscript of the Renaissance humanist Leo Battista Alberti, who wrote it around 1466 at the request—made during a stroll in the Vatican gardens—of Leonardo di Piero Dati, secretary to Pope Paul II. Except for the invention of public-key cryptography in the 1970s, it is the most important single work in the history of cryptology, for in it Alberti explained cryptanalysis for the first time in the West, set out his invention of polyalphabetic substitution, for many years the most important and the most widely used cryptosystem, and proposed enciphered code for the first time.[7]

While these three great practical and theoretical feats placed the curia at the pinnacle of the cryptology of the time, Vatican cryptology enjoyed a more broadly general excellence, to which the notebooks of the Renaissance papal cipher secretaries of the Argenti family attest. Alas, it declined in succeeding centuries, as David Alvarez, a professor of government at St. Mary's College of California, the pre-eminent specialist in the history of Vatican cryptology, has demonstrated in four important articles.[8] During World War I, for example, the Italians, the Germans, and perhaps the Swiss read Vatican crypto-grams, including traffic to and from the nuncio Eugenio Pacelli, later Pope Pius XII. This weakness also enabled the cryptanalysts of the German Foreign Office to break Vatican codes during and perhaps before World War II. As for the United States, Herbert O. Yardley, head of the American codebreaking establishment of the 1920s, the so-called American Black Chamber, decided not to attack Vatican cryptosystems when the director of military intelligence, who controlled much of the unit's money and was a Catholic, turned white after Yardley said he was considering targeting them.

"You are quite right, Yardley," he said. "I wouldn't bother with the Vatican code telegrams. I'm glad to see that you recognize that there are certain limits that we can not exceed in the espionage necessary for the successful operation of your bureau."[9] That reticence vanished in the era of total war.

An error in the newly released document has disappointed historians of cryptology, who would like to have numbered a future pope among the world's outstanding cryptologists. The reports lauds a monsignor of the Secretariat of State whose job title in 1943 was "deputy for ordinary business and code secretary." Before World War II, a visitor to Rome had been told that this man was "the Vatican's expert in cryptography; so apparently this prelate is not an ecclesiastic nominally at the head of the cryptographic bureau but actually one of its experts. If so, he is a cryptographer of no mean ability." The official was Giovanni Battista Montini, better known to history as Pope Paul VI. In fact, Professor Alvarez says, Montini was far too busy—consulting once or twice a day with the pope, meeting regularly with diplomats, reading incoming dispatches, and drafting outgoing ones—to deal with the technicalities of codes and ciphers, though they lay within his purview. Moreover, his still unexplained order to use the red code, suspected even by the curia to have been compromised, to send a warning about the German attack in the West in 1940 to one nuncio in the Low Countries and a different code to send the same warning to the other nuncio—a practice that gives codebreakers a crib to the unknown code—shows that he did not know this subject. Professor Alvarez, who has been trying for some time to identify the "cryptographer of no mean ability," thinks that the Allies believed that Montini was this man because his title included the term "code secretary," when in fact his subordinates handled cryptology.[10]

The texts of the solved Vatican cryptograms ought to exist somewhere, probably in the as-yet-unreleased files of the National Security Agency, the government codemaking and codebreaking organization that descended from the World War II cryptologic bodies. They may well shed further light on Vatican activities during World War II. Historians await their release.

Notes

1. "Vatican Code Systems in the SSA [Signal Security Agency] 1943–1944," Washington, September 1944, in Folder Vatican Code Systems, Box 1284, Record Group 457, National Archives (NA II), College Park, Maryland. All information not otherwise footnoted comes from this document.
2. Affidavits of Adolf Paschke and Kurt Selchow, Exhibits 55 and 54, Case 11, *United States of America vs. Ernst von Weizsäcker et al.*, Trials of War Criminals before the Nürnberg Military Tribunal under Control Council Law No. 10, NA II.
3. David Kahn, "Pearl Harbor and the Inadequacy of Cryptanalysis," *Cryptologia*, Vol. 15 (October 1991), pp. 273–94 at 293.
4. *Ibid.*, p. 282.
5. David Kahn, *Plaintext in the New Unabridged* (New York: Crypto Press, 1963), reprinted in David Kahn, *Kahn on Codes* (New York: Macmillan, 1983), pp. 120–38 at 121.
6. Aloys Meister, *Die Geheimschrift im Dienste der Päpstlichen Kurie* (Paderborn, Germany: Schöningh, 1906).
7. *Ibid.*, 125–41. This has been superseded by the collation of all known manuscript copies by Augusto Buonofalce published in 1994 in the sumptuous *Dello Scrivere in Cifra* by Galimberti Tipografi of Turin.

8. David Alverez "A Papal Diplomatic Code," *Cryptologia*, Vol. 16 (April 1992), pp. 174–75; "The Papal Cipher Section in the Early Nineteenth Century," *Cryptologia*, Vol. 17 (April 1993), pp. 219–24; "Faded Lustre: Vatican Cryptography, 1815–1918," *Cryptologia*, Vol. 20 (April 1996), pp. 97–131; "Vatican Communications Security, 1914–1918," *Intelligence and National Security*, Vol. 7 (October 1992), pp. 443–53.

9. Herbert Yardley, *The American Black Chamber* (Indianapolis, IN: Bobbs-Merrill, 1931), pp. 332–34.

10. Alvarez, personal communication.

14

FINLAND'S CODEBREAKING IN WORLD WAR II*

During World War II, Finland's codebreakers solved some of the cryptosystems of the Red Army, the U.S. State Department, and the Turkish Foreign Ministry, among the major targets, and cryptosystems of Romania, Brazil, and the Vatican as minor targets. But the results, though successful technically, had but little effect either upon Finland's military tactics during her two wars with the Soviet Union—the Winter War of 1939–1940 and the Continuation War of 1941–1944—or upon her foreign policy toward the United States, which until 1944 maintained diplomatic relations with her although she was a co-belligerent of America's enemy, Nazi Germany.

The heart, soul, and father of Finnish codebreaking was Reino Henrik Hallamaa, born 12 March 1899, in Tampere,[1] an industrial city 100 miles northwest of Helsinki. A radio amateur, Hallamaa was 18 when Finland declared its independence from Russia. But on 28 January 1918, Finnish Communists supported by the Bolshevists, seized government offices in Helsinki, starting a civil war. Three days later, Hallamaa was drafted into the government army.[2] After a year of fighting, these Whites, supported by a German force, drove out the Reds. In the spring of 1919, Hallamaa and other members of Finland's sole radio battalion were ordered to the island of Suursaari in the Gulf of Finland to take over a radio station that the Russians had left there.[3]

"The air was full of Russian naval radio messages," he recalled—some probably originating in a new war with Russia over Karelia that lasted from June to October 1919. "I began trying to solve these, and

* From B.P. Hayden and H. Samuel (eds.), In: *The Name of Intelligence: Essays in Honor of Walter Pforzheimer.* Washington, DC: NIBC Press, 1994, pp. 329–347.

once when the Russians sent the same message enciphered and in clear, it was easy to solve other messages. The systems were monoalphabetic substitution, sometimes with homophones, sometimes using bigrams, always with numbers. So it began.

"I sent the results to the battalion staff, where they caused a sensation, and I was promoted to sergeant, which for draftees at the time was a giant step forward. All this interested me greatly, and I remained in the army after my conscription service was up. In 1921 I became a reserve officer, continued my studies in civilian schools and then entered officer candidate school, from which I emerged two years later as a lieutenant. I was soon appointed to the general staff. There I was assigned to set up a radio intelligence service for the Finnish army. It was 18 June 1927.

"I sat alone in an office with a pencil in my hand and a sheet of paper on the desk. What followed then was a desperate struggle for men, equipment, and money. The results appeared very slowly. I visited Germany and managed to do some systematic work in the German High Command of the Armed Forces Cipher Branch[4] under then Government Counselor [Wilhelm] Fenner. I had the opportunity to visit several outposts; in Stuttgart I even stayed a couple of weeks. In Halle an der Saale I visited the signal school and saw then, for the first time, a motorized radio reconnaissance detachment. And I returned home, with a head full of new ideas, to the General Staff building, Korkeavuorenkatu 21, Helsinki, where I worked the entire time on the fifth floor under the cover name of 'Statistical Office.'

"After three years I had gotten far enough that about a dozen people were working in six rooms and the number [of people] grew from year to year. The outposts, under the command of Lieutenant Lotsari, worked satisfactorily intercepting messages, and traffic analysis gave very good results, especially for the naval traffic—Captain Pakarinen at the head. As for cryptanalysis, our experience in this area grew over time.

"In the meantime we began to cooperate with Poland [which had also been invaded by the Bolsheviks] and learned a lot from her. One of my cryptanalysts worked for a long time in Warsaw, which received solved Russian naval systems from us in return. The Germans apparently knew nothing about this cooperation. A very great help for us was the Estonian Captain Kalmus; this head of the Estonian intelligence service was himself a first-class cryptanalyst and now and then he came to us to learn from our experiences....

"Soon my organization was so big that I had no time anymore to do cryptanalysis myself. I merely organized the whole thing and developed it further. In fact I was not a good codebreaker; my first apparently good results were simple Russian systems, and afterward I devoted myself to the problems of development and administration. And it was certainly better that way: we were ready when the war began in the fall of 1939."[5]

Hallamaa's small group had already solved some Russian codes. But he realized that he would need additional help. Earlier in 1939, Captain Åke Rossby, head of the cryptanalytic unit of Sweden, of which Finland had for centuries been a part, came to Hallamaa for help. The Swedes had been reading the four-digit Soviet naval code but had suddenly lost out. Hallamaa knew what had happened: the Soviets had changed the encipherment key. He gave Rossby the information needed, and Rossby returned home satisfied. Then, in September 1939, as the Soviet Union thundered out its demands upon its small neighbor, Hallamaa flew to Stockholm with a proposal. He explained it to the head of Swedish intelligence, and 10 minutes later was talking to the Swedish commander-in-chief. He offered the Swedes a suitcase full of Soviet codebooks and other intelligence material in exchange for American radio receivers and diplomatic intercepts from the Swedish post and telegraph office. The deal was struck, and, he recalled, "Within half an hour the Swedes had advanced 10 years in the development of their radio intelligence." Soon thereafter, Rossby and a young mathematician, Arne Beurling, came to Finland to work for a while with the Finnish cryptanalysts; Beurling developed into an extraordinarily successful codebreaker.[6] The cooperation thus laid down proved useful to both countries in the next years.

When the Soviets invaded Finland on 30 November 1939 to start the Winter War, Hallamaa was a major. He was a big man with a prominent nose, slicked-back dark hair and a serious expression. He was energetic, ambitious, ruthless, always thinking ahead.[7] Perhaps most important, he had the confidence of his chiefs, Colonel Aladar Paasonen, the head of Finnish army intelligence, and Field Marshal Baron Karl Gustaf Mannerheim, the commander in chief.

Hallamaa's first need was manpower. One man he recruited, Erkki Pale, became one of his chief deputies. A small, lively, cheerful man, Pale, born in 1906, had been sent by his parents to a military school in St. Petersburg to get a better education than that available in Raivola, where his father was the stationmaster. So he knew Russian. At the University of Helsinki, he studied mathematics, later becoming a life insurance actuary. Pale thus had the rare combination of knowing both Russian and mathematics. Though he and Hallamaa had known each other since about 1936 from the Helsinki Tennis Club, where they played billiards together,[8] it was only after a professor of mathematics whom Hallamaa had asked for recommendations said that Pale was the best—take him, that, a month after the war began, Hallamaa pulled Pale out of the coastal artillery, where he was a reserve lieutenant, and installed him as a cryptanalyst. Others were recruited in similar fashion. Pentti Aalto, a soft-spoken linguist who was to become the effective head of those who broke American codes, had a friend who was a cuneiformist and translator of the Koran, had been ahead of him in officer candidate school, and had gone on to Hallamaa's unit. He called Aalto and said that this is work he should be doing. "Remember me," said Aalto for when he got out of the school. The friend did. Big, raw-boned Kalevi Loimaranta was recommended by a friend and became the sole, and badly needed, mathematician among the diplomatic codebreakers.[9]

The rapid expansion of cryptanalysis during Finland's two wars led first to a dispersion and then to some consolidations. The diplomatic cryptanalysts stayed in the General Staff building, a former headquarters of the Russian gendarmerie with long, winding corridors, only until they moved some time in 1940 to Mikkeli, the seat of Mannerheim and his staff, about 125 miles northeast of Helsinki, where they installed themselves in the attic of an elementary school.[10] The cryptanalysts solving middle- and low-level Soviet military codes—those using 2-, 3-, and 4-digit codes—and NKVD (secret police) systems went to quarters near Savonlinna, a few miles northeast of Mikkeli. Those attacking the 5-digit strategic Soviet codes worked out of a two-story wooden journalists' club, Syväranta, in Tuusula, 20 miles north of Helsinki. In 1942, these two merged into a headquarters at Sortavala, a town on the northern shore of Lake Ladoga in territory that, though ceded to the Soviet Union in the peace treaty of 1940, had been captured in the army advances of 1941. Pale headed the combined unit, which attacked all Soviet military systems and was quartered in a semiclassical structure that had once been a home for disabled children called Vaalijala. The Red Navy traffic was worked on first in Tuusula and, after 1941, in Kaunianen, just west of Helsinki, where diplomatic radio messages were intercepted. Scattered along the front were the detachments of a motorized radio interception company, called MOTO, which provided combat communications intelligence.[11]

Hallamaa's unit was a part of the Tiedustela Jaosto, or Intelligence Group, of General Headquarters. It was designated Tiedustela 2, or Intelligence 2. (Tiedustela 1 dealt with all nonradio intelligence.) In addition to the cryptanalysts, Tiedustela 2 included an intercept battalion that had five companies distributed over Finland. The agency was sometimes called RTK, short for Radio Tiedustela Keskus, or Radio Intelligence Center.[12]

At the start, the diplomatic cryptanalysts consisted sometimes only of Pentti Aalto and Mary Grashorn. But gradually their numbers grew. Their first chief, Yrgö Somersalo, proved incompetent and was removed, apparently by the codebreakers themselves, who then ran their organization as kind of a democracy under the nominal leadership of Grashorn but with Aalto as a leading light. Their organization included the translators[13] and a pair of secretaries. In 1944, at its largest, it comprised 38 cryptanalysts, divided into five sections: the United States, with 19 codebreakers; Turkey, with 12; what was called Serbia but which attacked Yugoslav partisan systems, with 3 cryptanalysts plus 1 shared with Romania, which then had 1½; Brazil, with 2; and the Vatican, with 1.[14]

Their day began around 9 a.m., when Aalto picked up at Tiedustela 1 the intercepts sent in from the intercept companies, from the post office, where the censors copied the 5 to 10 diplomatic messages transmitted each day, and from Sweden[15] and Hungary. These he gave out to the codebreakers specializing in the various languages.[16]

Among the simplest codes to crack were those of the Vatican. In the 16th century the papal curia led the world in cryptology, and Aalto thought that they had not advanced beyond that level, as described in a couple of studies of nomenclators of that period in a Finnish journal by H. Biaudet in 1910.[17] Vatican codes were attacked by O. Nikulainen because he was the only cryptanalyst who knew Italian. However, the results had little value.[18] The Yugoslavian systems of General Draja Mihailovich's Chetniks and of Josip Broz Tito's Communist partisans were likewise weak and enabled the Finns to follow the confused and bloody fighting between and among these irregulars and the German and Italian occupation forces in the Balkans.[19] The Brazilian codes had been given to the Finns by the Hungarians, who had some good cryptanalysts, in part owing to a tradition reaching back to the Austro-Hungarian monarchy.[20] The Finns also attacked some British consular systems. One was solved relatively easily because a consul in Petsamo, the port for nickel on the Arctic Ocean, broke the basic encryption rules—his coded messages were sometimes enciphered, sometimes not—and because the messages dealt with information the Finns knew, such as the traffic in and out of Petsamo. The Germans gave the Finns a 5-digit one-part British consular codebook (a one-part code has the codenumbers in numerical order next to the plaintext words and phrases in alphabetical order) that apparently they had captured in Norway, and the Finns themselves cracked a two-part code (one that has plain and code elements mixed relative to one another, requiring one section for encoding and one for decoding) that was also enciphered (keynumbers were added to the codegroups to further conceal them). But none of these solutions yielded much information.[21]

Why did the Finns devote almost a third of their cryptanalysts to the relatively insignificant country of Turkey? Turkey, a World War I ally of Germany and a hereditary enemy of Russia, stayed neutral all the time Finland was in the war. As a consequence, Turkey had, in the major capitals of the world, diplomats who listened to what was going on and reported it to Ankara. This gave the Finns interesting gossip and illuminating details. Turkey had many cryptosystems, but the Finns could break all of them. A common type was a 4-digit code in which the last two digits of each 4-digit codegroup gave the page in the codebook and the first two the line on that page in which the plaintext word or phrase stood. To the successive codegroups, the Turks would add numbers—the encipherment key—to disguise them. They would then separate the sum, which was the ciphertext, into 5-digit groups for transmission. But in some systems the encipherment key consisted of only five digits. It seemed to take the Finns only 10 minutes to strip off this encipherment, laying bare the basic code, which they had long ago reconstructed. The codes on the next higher level used a 10-digit key, and the most secret codes used an encipherment key of 40 digits—a sad contrast with the keys thousands of digits long used by other countries. Moreover, when the Turks "changed codes," they rarely produced an entirely new codebook but more often merely changed the numbers on the pages and columns. All of this greatly facilitated the work of the codebreakers.[22]

Finland expended her greatest diplomatic codebreaking effort on the systems of the United States. Americans liked Finland. They knew that she had been the only country to pay back her war debt, and they admired her heroic underdog stand in 1939 against the bullying Soviet Union. So, although Britain declared war on her in December 1941 because she persisted in fighting the Soviet Union, the United States retained diplomatic relations with her. The Finns were glad not to have another enemy and, to keep themselves as well informed as possible about American moves, they read as many coded American messages as possible. These included not only messages to and from the American legation in Helsinki, but messages to and from American embassies in Moscow, Stockholm, Berne, Ankara, and perhaps elsewhere.

Three basic systems were cracked. One was the gray code—so named from the color of its binding. It dated from around World War I and was so familiar to American diplomats that one gave his farewell speech in it. When its codewords were enciphered, the State Department called it "special gray." The brown code, a more modern one, was not enciphered.[23] The most secret system was the strip cipher, formally known as the M-138. The State Department selected it, for example, for a triple priority message between President Franklin D. Roosevelt and British Prime Minister Winston S. Churchill just after the Atlantic Conference of August 1941. The M-138 was based on a cipher device invented, interestingly enough, by the first secretary of state, Thomas Jefferson.[24] M-138 consisted of a set of 50 numbered cardboard strips, each bearing a different mixed alphabet printed twice. To begin, the clerk chose the 30 strips that that day's key designated, arranged them in the order that the key specified, and set them out horizontally. Using the letters on the strips, he spelled out the first 30 letters of his message by sliding the strips back and forth until the letters stood in a single vertical line. Next, he chose any other column as the ciphertext for those 30 letters. He wrote the 30 ciphertext letters down, then repeated the process with the next batch of 30 plaintext letters. He continued this way to the end of the message. The recipient of the cryptogram would know, from that day's key, which he had been previously given, which 30 strips should be used and the order in which they were to be laid out. He would arrange the first 30 cryptogram letters in a vertical line and would then scan the other vertical lines. Only one would be English: this would be the plaintext. Each post had its own set of strips; the key changed daily but was the same for all posts. This cryptographic weakness was probably permitted for logistical reasons. One set of strips, called O-1, served for intercommunication among the posts.

The Finns got their break into the strip system when the German military espionage agency, the Abwehr, whose chief, Admiral Wilhelm Canaris, was a friend of Hallamaa, gave them photocopies of instructions for the strip cipher and of the strips for Washington's communications with the posts at Riga (which had been closed since June 1940) and Helsinki, as well as the O-1 set. The source of the instructions and the strips is not known.[25] The daily keys were, however, not provided, so to read the messages the Finns had to reconstruct these. Some of the first work on this was done by K. E. Henriksson. He guessed that some telegrams began with the word "Secret" and, since the strip cipher has the peculiarity that no letter can represent itself, he was able to identify correctly some cases of "Secret" and so begin the solution.[26] As he became more familiar with the telegrams' phraseology and signatures, he gained speed. He and the others were also helped by the fact that messages in codes that Helsinki could read were also transmitted in strip—a crib that simplified their work. Later, Kalevi Loimaranta and others, using State Department circular telegrams of which he knew the text from a known set of strips, reconstructed the alphabets of strips at other posts,[27] such as Moscow, and began reading U.S. cablegrams from there. (The Germans helped them in this, giving them the successors of the O-1 strips, namely O-2, O-3, O-4, and O-5, which they apparently got by cryptanalysis.)[28] The Finns discovered that strip sets no longer in use at one post would turn up in service at another. This further eased their work. Eventually, they were able to break each day's American transmissions the day they were sent.[29]

Solutions were sent to the translators, whence they were to be typed up in four copies. Grashorn looked them over and dispatched one copy to the president of the republic, Risto Ryti, one to the foreign minister, who for much of the time was Henrik Ramsay, the third to Mannerheim, and the fourth to Hallamaa.[30]

United States policy sought to pull Finland out of the war. This would relieve pressure on the Soviet Union and stretch Germany's resources by forcing her to take over the fronts on which Finland had been fighting. It never worked. Indeed, one incident in 1943 involving codes increased American suspicion of Finland and perhaps sped the ultimate rupture of relations.

On 19 March 1943, Secretary of State Cordell Hull cabled the American chargé d'affaires in Helsinki, Robert M. McClintock, to call on Foreign Minister Ramsay and inquire "if the Finnish Government is disposed to accept the good offices of the United States Government in establishing contact between the Finnish Government and the Soviet Government with a view to the initiation of discussions between them for the cessation of hostilities and the restoration of peace."[31] Six hours after he had received this cable, McClintock delivered an aide-mémoire based on it to Ramsay. The Finns knew that the Germans could read the strip system, in which Hull's message had been enciphered. They apparently feared that the Germans, upon solving Hull's message might think that the Finns were considering betraying them and might take punitive measures. So the Finnish government decided to preclude this by sending Ramsay to Berlin to demonstrate that Finland was not doing anything behind Germany's back.[32] He was treated to a harangue by the German foreign minister, Joachim von Ribbentrop.[33] Nothing was said on either side about broken codes, nor did anything have to be, since McClintock had given Ramsay the substance of Hull's message and Ramsay had given the aide-mémoire to Ribbentrop. The word got out about Ramsay's trip and, when McClintock had an interview with Mannerheim on 11 May 1943, he complained that it was "not pleasing to us" to have Ramsay tell Ribbentrop of "our most secret conversations." Mannerheim replied that the Germans "had other means of finding out what was going on."[34] McClintock understood. He had previously reported his suspicions that the Germans had broken the codes of his mission.[35] The next day, he replaced his strips with a substitute set, which the Finns could not read until they discovered they were the same as had been previously used between Washington and Teheran.[36] The episode probably reduced American confidence in Finland, and perhaps contributed to the U.S. rupture of diplomatic relations on 30 June 1944.

What was the effect of the diplomatic solutions on Finland's conduct of the war? It appears to have been minimal.[37] The cryptanalysts may not have read the most secret messages, which would have reduced their usefulness.[38] More to the point, Finland's freedom of action was so limited that even the best intelligence could not much expand her options. But if codebreaking information did not lead to any striking results, it may at least have let Foreign Ministry officials learn in advance of other countries' proposals and gain some time in thinking out responses to them. Limited though this help may have been, the Finnish government evidently thought it valuable enough to keep the codebreakers producing their intelligence to the end of the war.

The war was fought, however, less in the carpeted salons of foreign ministries than in the muddy trenches of front lines. And here codebreaking helped the Finns somewhat.

The Red Army employed an almost bewildering variety of codes. The simplest, for front-line use, were the 2-digit codes. They changed daily. They consisted of a 10 × 10 table filled with letters and common words; an element was enciphered by picking the numbers of the row and column in which it stood. The 3-digit codes served, apparently, battalion and regiment for tactical purposes; 4-digit, division and corps, also for tactical purposes. All changed at various intervals. Most important of all were the 5-digit systems, which concealed the messages of the high command to army groups and armies. Though the 4-digit codes permitted a vocabulary of 10,000 plaintext words, phrases, place names, and so on, and the 5-digit codes a vocabulary of 100,000, neither ever approached their maximum possible sizes. (The reasons were probably that such codes would take too long and cost too much to construct and that code clerks would not optimally use all the available plaintext elements.) The 4-digit codes rarely exceeded 5,000 elements; the 5-digit, though the number of plaintext elements grew as the war went on, never exceeded 25,000. Both the 4- and 5-digit systems were enciphered (as with the Turkish codes) by adding key numbers to the codenumbers; the length of the encipherment key varied from 1,500 numbers to what amounted to infinity: no key numbers were ever repeated—the so-called one-time pad, the only theoretically and practically unbreakable cryptosystem. (The Finns recognized these latter because messages in them always ended with a group of the form 37730 or 58850, from which the Finns called it the ABBA system. Recognizing that it was unbreakable, they simply put these messages to one side.) Moreover, while the codes remained in service for several months, the encipherment tables were often changed daily.[39]

To solve Russian military messages, Erkki Pale had under him in the Sortavala children's home some 300 people, divided into three sections: traffic analysis, which teased information out of message volume, location of transmitters, message routing, and other noncryptanalytic material; the cryptanalytic section;[40] and the so-called tactical section, which translated, evaluated, commented upon, and distributed the solutions. Solving the enciphered codes required that the encipherment be removed, which was a mathematical task, before the underlying code could be reconstructed, which was a linguistic job. Pale had divided his 100-man cryptanalytic group accordingly. They worked around the clock, in part because the 2-digit codes had to be solved at once or not at all. Both Loimaranta and Pale liked their work: they found it fascinating and felt that it was important.

The cracking of the most valuable of the codes, the 5-digit, began slowly. The Finns succeeded only after the Winter War in reading the first edition of what the Russians called the 011-A. But thereafter they continued to read messages in this code and its successors—as the 023-A and the 045-A—and other 5-digit codes with fair regularity. They were helped because, in the sometimes fluid warfare of the Eastern Front, the codebooks and the encipherment keys were occasionally captured: the second edition of the 011-A, which served from January to October 1941, was captured in June 1941. Friends helped, too. Information from Sweden's Arne Beurling enabled Pale and his team once to achieve a minor technical triumph: establishing the true values of codenumbers instead of the relative values usually obtained when an encipherment is removed; this was the only time in the war they managed this. The Japanese once delivered a three-foot-high stack of 5-digit intercepts from the Far East. The Finns cracked the code—and then, a few months later, discovered that the Russians were now using it for units fighting the Finns and the Germans. Likewise, the Germans sent over a package of intercepts that gave the Finns the depth that Pale and Captain Oun, a brilliant Estonian cryptanalyst working with the Finns, needed to strip the encipherment. But ingeniousness was the Finns' greatest ally. They knew that, in the captured second edition of the 011-A, the last two digits of each codegroup were either both odd or both even. So they went through the intercepts and noted whether the final two digits were both odd, which they marked with a 0, or both even, marked with a 1. They compared the strings of 0s and 1s in several cryptograms with one another. Two alike meant that the same portion of the encipherment table had likely been used to encipher the codenumbers. This gave them the depth they needed to strip the encipherment.[41]

All this effort meant that, on a good day, a fifth of the intercepts were fully solved, about three fifths were partly solved, and the remaining one fifth was unsolved.[42] The solutions helped the Finns in some tactical matters. During the Winter War's battle of Suomussalmi, the codebreakers solved a message of the Red Army's 662nd Battalion, in which its commander complained that his men lacked boots, snow-suits, and rations. Another message disclosed that a political officer had been killed by his own men. Both messages revealed a lot about Soviet morale. Still another revealed to Mannerheim the advance of the crack Russian 44th Division; he sent five battalions that severed the division's column and destroyed the parts in detail, assuring his victory. Temperatures during the battle dropped to 56 degrees below zero, and the Finns overheard some pitiful messages from isolated Russian units. One encircled group radioed that they were burning their papers and were going to shoot their last horse for food and that this was their final message. Silence followed: Finnish forces had crushed them. A Russian battalion sent a coded message that it was desperately short of supplies and would build three fires in a triangle to show the Red air force where to parachute desperately needed food and ammunition. The Finns solved it and passed it to their forces on the ground, who built the triangle of fires and watched with bitter satisfaction as the packages floated down into it. Still other intercepts gave warning of air raids on Helsinki, giving the authorities ample time to sound air-raid alerts.[43]

But these results were at best tactical. Even the solution of the higher-level codes did not always help. When the Soviets began their massive offensive against the Karelian Isthmus on 9 June 1944, Oun, the Estonian, recognized that the 4-digit messages raining down were encoded with the same code as he had solved several months earlier. He began reading the messages—to the accompaniment of hammering to pack crates to pull back. But the information the Finns got was useless because they had no forces, no resources to stop the onslaught. "We only learned that we couldn't do anything," said Pale.[44]

The episode is emblematic. The codebreaking results had little effect on the war either because the Soviets were too powerful, or the fronts too static to yield intercepts, or the information too insignificant. Whatever the reason, it cannot be claimed that Finland's codebreaking, despite the heroic and often brilliant work of her cryptanalysts, contributed in any important way to her military plans and actions in World War II.

Postscript: On 19 September 1944, the day that Finland signed the armistice with the Soviet Union, Hallamaa, fearing an occupation, moved many of his subordinates and his files to Sweden. This was Operation Stella Polaris. In the years since then, some of the files have disappeared, the microfilms made of some have also disappeared, and many files were burned. As a consequence, virtually none of the records survive, except for some of the diplomatic intercepts now in the Valtionarkisto, or National Archives of Finland. At the end of July or the beginning of August 1944, Hallamaa revealed to Wilho Tikander, an officer of the American Office of Strategic Services, that the Finns were reading secret State Department messages. In return, he was paid 200,000 Swedish crowns—money apparently not for himself but to keep his organization alive. On 28 October 1944, Henriksson, the strip cipher cryptanalyst, explained his solution to Tikander and Randolph Higgs. A month later, Loimaranta and Pale met with four Americans, one named Ericson, to provide additional confirmation, which Loimaranta supplied. In November, the O.S.S. bought 1,500 pages of material about the Soviets from the Finns. But Secretary of State Edward Stettinius thought that this information was not worth risking the grand alliance with the Soviet Union, and ordered it returned, which, by 15 February 1945, it was. After the war, Hallamaa, all but exiled for his anti-Soviet activities, retired to Spain, where he called himself Ricardo Palma. There he raised carnations and there, on 11 August 1979, the *spiritus rector* of Finland's radio intelligence service died.[45]

Notes

1. Joppe Karhunen, *Reino Hallamaa Salasanomasotaa* (Helsinki, Finland: Weilin+Göös, 1980), p. 263.
2. *Ibid.*, p. 265.
3. Reino Hallamaa, letter, 21.2. 1970.
4. At the time actually the Cipher Center of the Army Command. The High Command of the Armed Forces did not come into being until 4 February 1938 and the Cipher Center, though part of it, did not rise to a branch until 1939.
5. Hallamaa, letter.
6. Hallamaa, letter, 2 December 1969; David Kahn, *The Codebreakers* (New York: Macmillan, 1967), pp. 479–480, 482, 541, 644–645— but see footnote 43; Wilhelm M. Carlgren, *Svensk Underrättelse Tjänst 1939–1945* (N.p.: Liber Allmännä Förlaget, 1985), pp. 66, 68.
7. Erkki Pale, interviews, 17 and 18 November 1978, 11 November 1993; Pentti Aalto, interview, 11 November 1993, and interview, 1990, with Rhoda Amon and others. Henceforth as Pale and Aalto.
8. One billiard game led to a dispute, which only ended a year later when Hallamaa offered to shake hands and make up. Pale, who was tennis champion of the club three times, said disdainfully that Hallamaa was not a very good tennis player because he wasn't flexible enough.
9. Pale; Aalto; Kalevi Loimaranta, interview, 10 November 1993.
10. Aalto.
11. Pale, *Enclosure II to Letter* (15 February 1988).
12. Pale; Aalto; Loimaranta.
13. Aalto.
14. List compiled by Aalto.
15. When Beurling requested reciprocity for this, Hallamaa refused it, sending Pale to do the dirty work of telling him.
16. Aalto.
17. "Sixte-Quint et la candidature de Sigismond de Suède au trône de Pologne en 1587," *Suomolainen tiedeakatemia*, Série B, 2 (2), pp. 1–22, and "Un chiffre diplomatique du XVIe siècle," *Ibid.*, Série B, 2 (3), pp. 1–16.
18. Aalto.
19. Jukka L. Mäkelä, *Im Rücken des Feindes: Der Finnishce Nachrichtendienst in Krieg* (Frauenfeld: Huber, 1967), p. 156.
20. Aalto.
21. Mäkelä, pp. 162–163.
22. Mäkelä, pp. 161–162; Aalto.
23. Aalto.
24. Silvio A. Bedini, *Thomas Jefferson: Statesman of Science* (New York: Macmillan, 1990), pp. 235–238; Louis Kruh, "The Genesis of the Jefferson/Bazeries Cipher Device," *Cryptologia*, Vol. 5 (October 1991), pp. 193–208; U.S. Patent 2,395,863.
25. Pale and Aalto think that it may have come from the Finnish passenger Avro-Anson airplane named the *Kaleva* that two Soviet SB-2 airplanes

shot down on 14 June 1940 as it was flying from Reval to Helsinki. The crew of two plus all seven passengers, including an American, Henry William Antheil, were killed. See *The New York Times* (16 June 1940), 34:5. A Soviet submarine, which had been loitering in the area for several days, gathered 100 kilograms of mail from the sea. If Antheil was a courier, this might have included the cipher material. It would have gone to the Soviet Union, but since the Molotov-Ribbentrop pact of 1939 was in effect at this time, Stalin might have given the material to Hitler, perhaps in return for something else. It all sounds far-fetched to me. Simple espionage seems more probable.

26. Aalto.
27. Loimaranta.
28. Pale, Enclosure B to letter, 28 April 1988, states that Henrikson visited the Cipher Branch of the High Command of the Armed Forces from 9 to 18 January 1943. A topologist there, Wolfgang Franz, had reconstructed the strips, apparently on the basis of intercepts from Berne (David Kahn, *Hitler's Spies: German Military Intelligence in World War II* (New York: Macmillan, 1978), pp. 192–193.
29. Aalto.
30. *Ibid.*
31. United States, Department of State, *Foreign Relations of the United States: Diplomatic Papers, 1943* (Washington, DC: Government Printing Office, 1963), 3:250. Henceforth *FRUS.*
32. In a portion of his memoirs quoted in Mäkelä, p. 161, Mannerheim says that Finland had for some time been considering quitting the war and that Ramsay was sent to Berlin to urge Germany voluntarily to pull her troops out of Finland. The former seems more like a wish than a possibility and the latter a total lapse of memory on the part of the field marshal, for Ramsay never mentioned anything like that.
33. Germany, Auswärtiges Amt, *Akten zur deutschen Auswärtigen Politik, 1918–1945*, E:5 (Göttingen, Germany: Vandenhoeck & Rupprecht, 1978), Document 248.
34. *FRUS*, p. 277. Three weeks earlier, Hull had reported to President Franklin D. Roosevelt that "we had unmistakable evidence that Germans learning of our approaches brought increased pressure on Finns not to enter into any discussions with us with a view to any contact with Soviet Government." *Ibid.*, p. 269.
35. *Ibid.*, p. 275.
36. Pentti Aalto, "Sotasyyllisyyslaki ja ministeri Ramsayn matka Berliiniin," *Sotahistoriallinen Aikakauskirja*, Vol. 11 (1992), pp. 177–187, using the English summary, "The Bill of Indictment and the Visit of Foreign Minister Ramsay to Berlin," at pp. 187–188.
37. Aalto says he rarely read the text of the telegrams for their content and does not know what effect the solutions had on Finnish policy.
38. I have cursorily checked the several hundred pages of diplomatic intercepts— American, Turkish, and others— that the Valtionarkisto, the Finnish national archives, sent me from the records of President Ryti,

Foreign Minister Ramsay, and the Foreign Ministry against documents that seemed to me especially sensitive or secret from *FRUS*. None of the latter seem to be present in the photocopies sent me.

39. From a document dealing in part with Red army and air force cryptosystems; Mäkelä, pp. 17–21; Pale.

40. Salakirjoitusjaos, for those who wish to improve their Finnish.

41. Pale. For techniques of stripping an encipherment, see Kahn, *The Codebreakers*, pp. 440–444.

42. Pale.

43. William R. Trotter, *A Frozen Hell: The Russo-Finnish Winter War of 1939–1940* (Chapel Hill, NC: Algonquin Books, 1991), pp. 151–152; Kahn, *The Codebreakers*, p. 645. Several Finns, including some of the cryptanalysts, have pointed out, sometimes with asperity, that my ascription of these solutions to the Swedes' Arne Beurling errs; in fact, they were Finnish cryptanalyses that the Swedes reproduced or were given. Finland's help to the Swedes is acknowledged in C. G. McKay, *From Information to Intrigue: Studies in Secret Service Based on the Swedish Experience, 1939–1945* (London, U.K.: Frank Cass, 1993), p. 29.

44. Pale.

45. Jörgen Cederberg and Göran Elgemyr, "Operation Stella Polaris—Nordic Intelligence Cooperation in the Closing Stages of the second World War," in Wilhelm Agrell and Bo Huldt, eds., *Clio goes spying: Eight Essays on the History of Intelligence*, Lund Studies in International History, 17 (Malmö: n.p., 1983), pp. 120–149; Pale, Enclosure B to letter, 28 April 1988; McKay, pp. 243–244; Carlgren, pp. 159–160; Bradley F. Smith, *The Shadow Warriors: O.S.S. and the Origins of the C.I.A.* (New York: Basic Books, 1983), pp. 353–355.

15

SOVIET COMINT IN THE COLD WAR*

Part I

The great intelligence lesson of World War II is that the best information comes from codebreaking. Not from spies, who more often than not err or lie. Not from aerial reconnaissance, which merely photographs forces in place or on the way. And not from prisoner-of-war interrogations, which yield mainly tactical data. More than any other source, codebreaking furnishes trustworthy, high-level, fast, unmediated, voluminous, continuous, cheap information.

It helped to win the battle of the Atlantic and turn the tide of war at Midway, led to the midair shootdown of Admiral Isoroku Yamamoto, disclosed defensive details of Hitler's Atlantic Wall, made possible dozens of tactical victories during the Allied invasion of Europe, enabled American pigboats to strangle Japan by sinking her convoys.[1] Near the war's end, American solutions of French and Latin American codes helped the United States shape the United Nations the way it wanted.[2]

The Cold War revalidated the lesson. Communications intelligence – comint – again furnished the bulk of and the best American secret information. Officials newly cleared for material supplied by the National Security Agency often exclaim "They're getting all that!?" in astonishment at its quantity and quality. While satellite photography of missile silos showed what the Soviet Union had and where, it could not say what it would do with the weapons. Reading other countries' messages revealed foreigners' plans and helped the United States during disarmament talks, the Gulf War, and negotiations on auto imports with Japanese ministers.

But in all these episodes about how codebreaking helped shorten World War II and stabilize the international system afterward by

---

* From *Cryptologia*, 22 (January 1998), 1–24.

reducing surprises, one great dimension was missing: Soviet comint. How good was it? Had the Soviet Union enjoyed successes during the Cold War? If so, what were they, and what effect did they have on such events as the Cuban missile crisis?

These key lacunae, which had troubled historians, embarrassed me. When I lectured on codes and their history, audience members frequently asked how good the Soviets were in codebreaking. I had to confess that I didn't know. But, I said, trying to recover, it's widely believed that, to the extent that ability in cryptanalysis can be forecast, it parallels excellence in chess, mathematics, and music. And who, I would ask rhetorically, was good in all three fields?

But this was hypothesis. I wanted facts. Hoping that some Soviet codebreakers might have defected and boasted of their triumphs, I questioned Dr. Louis Tordella, then retired as the longest serving deputy director of the U. S. National Security Agency about it. He told me – and, from our relationship and the then more open attitude of the NSA, I don't believe he was concealing anything – that, to his knowledge, no such defection had ever occurred. Tordella knew nothing about Soviet cryptanalytic successes.[3] Likewise, a formerly top secret Allied study of "Russian Cryptology during World War II," recently declassified, included no specifics of such successes.[4]

But then things began to open up. One day I received a call from a former member, then in Britain, of the Soviet communications intelligence agency, a branch of the KGB. He gave his name as Victor Makarov and said he had served in the agency for five years, translating intercepted Greek telegrams (Figure 15.1).[5] He wanted to write a book with my help. I interviewed him for two days in his flat and in Room 222 of the Hotel Highcliff in Bournemouth.[6] He was a slender, fresh-faced young man, with a fairly good command of English and a detailed, worm's-eye view of Soviet cryptologic activities. Overflowing with his information and eager to please, he spoke rapidly, his ideas pushing his words out so fast they tumbled over one another. He had clear and specific memories of his work and the agency that did it, and he admitted ignorance when he had no first-hand knowledge. Though Greece was obviously no great power, it did deal with those powers, gaining more insights than its apparent insignificance suggested. Makarov's information was new and detailed and filled with fascinating incidents. But, for a number of

Figure 15.1   Victor Makarov, translator of Greek intercepts for the KGB's 16th Directorate.

reasons, no book ensued. Nor did I have the overview of Soviet cryptology that I was seeking.

The end of the Cold War had deprived both the Soviet and the American comint agencies of much of their chief raison d'être: cracking one another's codes. Soviet codebreakers were discharged; the NSA shrank. Both bodies faced the same bureaucratic imperative: the self-preservationist need to gain public, and therefore budgetary, support in a time of a downsizing. It was time to try Russia. Makarov had told me the name and some of the work of the head of the KGB codebreaking and codemaking units, Nicolai Nicolayevich Andreyev. In 1993 in Moscow, where I obtained his home address, I had a letter in Russian handed to him as he was getting into his car to go to work. But he declined to see me. I came home empty-handed.

Then, early in 1996, a Russian whom I had befriended at an international cryptology conference telephoned me. Would I like to meet General Andreyev? (Figure 15.2)

Part II

I flew to Moscow. After the details of such matters as interpreters (both theirs and mine) had been arranged, I was picked up on the morning of 13 June 1996 by a chauffeur and driven to 19 Pryesnyensky Val, a low undistinguished modernistic office building with horizontal lines of gray stone and gray steel (Figure 15.3). I was escorted in, took an elevator up

Figure 15.2   The author and General Andreyev at their meeting in Moscow, 13 June 1996. (Photo by David Kahn.)

Figure 15.3   19 Pryesnyensky Val, where the interview with Andreyev took place. (Photo by David Kahn.)

a floor or two, and was shown into a long room with curtained windows on one side and a long table down the middle; almost certainly no Westerner had ever stepped into it. It was an exciting moment. I was about to obtain, for the first time, a high-level view of the recent history of Soviet endeavors in the field that almost certainly produced more intelligence than all the Burgesses and MacLeans and Philbys and fourth and fifth men, perhaps more even than the atomic spies.

I was greeted near the door not by the burly Soviet thug of film and legend but by a grandfatherly man with flyaway gray hair wearing a gray suit. Andreyev was a skier, a badminton player, a puzzle solver.[7] His serious but relaxed demeanor belied a toughness that had enabled him not merely to survive in the vicious infighting of one of the most powerful and ruthless organizations in history but to seize a key job from other bureaucrats, raise his section to a directorate, shift to the command of a chief directorate, and win promotion to general. He was, at the time of his entry into the KGB, not an electrical engineer or a mathematician, two obvious sources of comint recruits, but a geologist; his devising of improved bugging methods, particularly against Americans, had given him an early success.

Andreyev offered me a chair. My translator sat to my left. Andreyev, his translator, and another official sat across the table, their backs to the window. Andreyev welcomed me in his quiet voice, and we began.

The essence of what I learned from him and Makarov was twofold – and this, it must be emphasized, is incomplete, preliminary, nondocumentary, and certainly not error-free. First, the Soviet Union seems to have gained most of its communications intelligence, not from cryptanalysis, but from bugs and traitors. The presence of Andreyev, a bugging expert, at the top of Soviet comint supports this belief. The American embassy in Moscow, as well as at least the consulate in Leningrad, was for years riddled with electronic listening devices. High-level American cryptosystems appear not to have been solved by analysis, but some were read because traitors had sold them to the Soviet Union. By contrast, the United States and the United Kingdom appear to have obtained most of their signals intelligence from cryptanalysis. The founders of the American and British comint organizations after World War I were codebreakers, though agency chiefs after World War II were managers.

Second, Soviet communications intelligence did not fundamentally change the course of the Cold War. Nor, in fact, did any intelligence. It would be nice for intelligence historians and spy buffs if it had, but in fact the Cold War was won by economic factors. People did not know this in advance, however, and since communications intelligence, among other forms of information gathering, had helped guide Soviet leaders through the murk of world affairs, they devoted a quantity of resources to it.

An annual report stated that, in 1967, the KGB read 188,400 cables of 152 cryptosystems of 72 capitalist states, broke 11 codes and "obtained" seven others, planted microphones in 36 locations, and intercepted cryptograms from 2,002 radio transmitters in 115 countries.[8] (These figures exclude the results of the comint unit in the GRU, the military intelligence agency.) In 1985 the KGB reported to Soviet leader Mikhail Gorbachev that "Secret documentary information of the capitalist states and their political-military blocs is regularly obtained by means of interception and decoding of messages transmitted by various channels of information."[9] These may have influenced some individual events during the Cold War.

Part III

Among the fruits of this effort, Andreyev said, were Soviet Premier Nikita Khrushchev's better understanding of the American position during the Cuban missile crisis, thus helping him avoid war. The Soviets, for example, intercepted some U. S. Navy communications indicating that it was tracking the Soviet vessel *Aleksandrovsk*, which was taking the nuclear warheads that were at the heart of the crisis to Cuba.[10] Likewise, Andreyev's units contributed bits and pieces during the SALT and START disarmament talks. On the other hand, the Soviets learned nothing in advance – at least not from comint – of one of the most shocking events in American history, the assassination of President John F. Kennedy, Andreyev said.[11]

Makarov substantiated Andreyev's generalities with some fascinating anecdotes and specifics.[12] During the Israeli siege of Beirut in August of 1982, the Greek ambassador in the Lebanese capital cabled Athens about his meeting with Yasser Arafat, chairman of the Palestine Liberation Organization. Arafat had told the ambassador that there was almost no hope that the Arabs could hold out and asked that the Greek prime minister, the socialist Andreas Papandreou, use all his influence, particularly in the international socialist movement, to get Israel to call off its offensive. Athens sent a copy of this telegram to its embassy in Moscow. The Soviet Union obtained a copy, which was sent to Makarov for translation. Cryptanalyzed intercepts arrived on individual sheets of paper giving the number of coded groups[13] but this came in on a long roll of teleprinter paper, which told Makarov that it been gotten by bugging. Not all telegrams had to be translated in full, but Makarov's chief said this one had to be. An hour later he came back and told Makarov that it had to be done at once – the generals are waiting. Makarov complied. His chief told him the next day that the Soviet Union had had no information on the situation in Beirut and that this telegram had become the only source.

In October, 1981, the Greek ambassador to the United States reported on his meeting with representatives of the State Department and the National Security Council to discuss the future of Lech Walesa and his anti-Communist Solidarity movement in Poland. The State man was optimistic about its success, but the NSC representative said that the suppression of Solidarity was inevitable because of the collapse of the Polish economy, pressure from the Soviet Union, and the ideological character of the Polish leadership. The message, which was repeated to Moscow, was read by the Soviets and gave them insight into the varying American evaluations of one of the most important events of the times.

Another Greek telegram out of Washington that Makarov read dealt with a split at the top of the Reagan administration about whether the president should attempt to improve relations with the Soviet Union by attending the funeral of Soviet leader Leonid Brezhnev and meeting his successor, Yuri Andropov. Among those in favor were Vice President George Bush, Secretary of State George Shultz, and Director of Central Intelligence William Casey. Opposed were Secretary of Defense Caspar Weinberger, Ambassador to the United Nations Jeane Kirkpatrick, and Assistant to the President Michael Deaver. The opponents won; Ronald Reagan stayed at home. But the intercept told the Soviets about factions within the Reagan administration and implied the future course of American policies toward the Soviet Union.

While the Khomeini regime in Iran was holding American diplomats hostage in Teheran, United States interests there were being represented by Switzerland. That neutral encrypted at least some of its diplomatic messages with a Hagelin cipher machine. This was named for a Swede, Boris C. W. Hagelin, who had devised its ancestor in 1934 and had moved his firm to Switzerland after World War II to avoid Swedish controls. The Soviets were cracking these messages— either by cryptanalysis or with stolen keys but not by bugging—the day they were intercepted. The messages were in French, and the translators, who reported to the deputy chief of section in the same room as Makarov, were impressed by the wide knowledge of the Swiss ambassador in Teheran, in particular by the fact that he knew the name of the governor of Moscow in 1812 who started the fire that helped drive Napoleon out of the capital. In the intercepts in the latter part of 1980, the Swiss complained about delays and sudden difficulties in their talks with the Iranians. Makarov believed that these resulted from the higher Soviet leaders' using these intercepts to somehow compromise the Swiss and, out of hostility to President Jimmy Carter, to slow down the hostages' release.

Other countries' messages were also solved. Makarov listed some of the country results he knew about from his duty as a destroyer of documents:

- Germany. Penetrated via bugs on its teleprinters, the TX-20, in Budapest.
- Israel. Results apparently sparse and only military, not diplomatic, since only one interpreter worked on them, and in a unit specializing in military matters. Because the Soviet Union and its allies did not have diplomatic relations with Israel, embassy bugging in the Communist capitals was not possible.
- Syria. Messages were read, whether by bugging or cryptanalysis Makarov did not know.
- Iraq. Same.
- Iran. Cryptanalyzed extensively.
- Palestine Liberation Organization. Read, at least around 1982.
- Algeria. Bugged, through the Siemens teleprinter T-1000.

- Portugal. The Soviets read intercepts about politician Mario Soares's electoral goals. They could have obtained much of this from the newspapers, but in their conspiratorial way they trusted the intercepts more. The Soviets hated Soares, who, though a Socialist, had fought the Communists and, to reduce his chances in the presidential election of 1986, they received him at a lower protocol level than they otherwise might have done.
- Italy. Telegrams of the counterintelligence service, perhaps encrypted in the Hagelin HC machines, were solved. Makarov knew of no comint about the attempt on Pope John Paul II's life.
- Vatican. Worked on in the Italian cryptanalytical group. Only lower-grade ciphers were solved. The higher-grade ciphers were strong—stronger than the Italian ciphers. Some of the messages may have listed the bishops who would be named cardinals.
- Switzerland. Its Hagelin machines were solved.
- China and North Korea. While in 1980 one could not enter the room where Chinese messages were worked on, in 1981 one could go in freely, indicating to Makarov that material in it had declined in value to where it no longer had to be kept secret. Both nations used what Makarov said were "block notes." These were hand ciphers, perhaps one-time pads, a theoretically and practically unbreakable cipher. Neither country used machines.
- Japan. Cryptanalyzed solid up to 1983 because of weak points in their cryptosystems. After that, the Soviets got their Japanese information only by bugging.
- Indonesia. The deputy chief of Makarov's section said that ancient tradition had made the Indonesians into good codemakers—but not good codebreakers (though how one could be the former without being the latter is questionable). They tested the Hagelin machines, concluded that they were not secure enough for them, and did not use them. This showed Makarov that at least this third-world country was shrewder in cryptology than Switzerland and Italy. Consequently, the Soviets had to bug the Indonesians.

- Zaïre: The Russians read then-President Sese Soku Mobuto's intelligence service reports, some of which dealt with his enemies' attempts to harm him through magic, attempts that the Russians took seriously.

The Soviet Union gave its targets the names of plants and animals as covernames. Germany was BOXTREE; France was FLAX. But the United States was often referred to as Special Target No. 1.

Part IV

Russian comint has a long history.[14] It began in the 1740s under the Tsarina Elizabeth with the establishment of a black chamber in the St. Petersburg post office for the perlustration, or opening and reading (including cryptanalyzing and translating, if necessary), of letters, both diplomatic and personal. Specialists slid hot wires under wax seals to open the missives; others forged seals as needed. One of its more talented directors, Christian Goldbach, is remembered in the history of mathematics for stimulating work by Fermat and Euler.[15] Elizabeth paid particular attention to the work of the black chamber, having its intercepts read to her and using them to make policy. In 1913-14, when it was a branch of the Ministry of Foreign Affairs and the telegraph made it easier to obtain messages, its dozen employees read 2,939 intercepted diplomatic telegrams[16] of such countries as England, France, Germany, Austria, Turkey, Persia and Japan.[17]

The Communist grab of power in 1917 changed little more than organization and some personnel. (Among those who fled was tall, stolid E. C. Fetterlein, who went to Britain and solved codes wearing on his index finger a large ruby, which he said had been given him by Nicholas II for his codebreaking exploits.) The Spets-Otdel, or Special Section, of what was at first the Cheka, later the OGPU and then the NKVD, continued the older agency's tradition.

World War II led to great advances. Toward the end of 1941, Soviet cryptanalysts solved the top Japanese diplomatic cipher machine, called the 97-*shiki o-bun In-ji-ki* or Alphabetical Typewriter '97 by the Tokyo Foreign Office, for the Japanese date of its introduction (A.D. 1939). They thus surpassed the British and the Germans, neither of whom

ever cracked the machine, and matched the Americans, who had succeeded a year earlier, covernaming the machine PURPLE. In both
cases, the work was accomplished by teams – directed in Washington
by the boyish-looking Virginian Frank Rowlett, in Moscow by one of
the Soviet Union's greatest cryptanalysts, Sergei Tolstoy (no relation
to the novelist), who had the key ideas for the solution.[18]

Though no intercept warned either the Russians or the Americans
of Pearl Harbor (because no Japanese diplomat was ever messaged
about the attack), the Tolstoy solutions did tell the Soviet Union that
Japan was going to advance southward, toward the oil and rubber of
the Netherlands East Indies, and not north, to stab the USSR in the
back as it was fighting for its life against Hitler. This eased Stalin's
decision to withdraw troops from the Far East and throw them into
the battle for Moscow, stopping the blitzkrieg and saving the capital of Mother Russia. (The Communist spy in Japan, the German
Richard Sorge, who is sometimes credited with making this possible,
had been arrested in October 1941 and, Andreyev said, did not play
as important a role as codebreaking had done.)[19]

Later in the war, the cracking of the Alphabetical Typewriter
'97 provided the Soviet Union with enormously useful information. Possibly the most important was a message of 27 July 1942
from Tokyo to the Japanese ambassador and former military attaché
Lieutenant General Hiroshi Oshima, telling him that, in spite of his
urging, Japan was not going to attack the Soviet Union.[20] During
the summer of 1942, Oshima toured the eastern front for 10 days
and wrote a detailed, 11-page report on the situation. He encrypted
it using the Alphabetical Typewriter and radioed it to Tokyo.[21] The
Soviets presumably intercepted and solved messages like this, which
disclosed German conditions and intentions. They did not, however,
pass them to the western Allies, probably for the same concerns about
security that kept the British and Americans from giving the Soviet
Union much information gleaned from their solutions of German
cryptosystems.

Perhaps the greatest remaining mystery of World War II is whether
the Soviet Union was able to break the chief German cipher machine,
the Enigma. The British had been able to do so, gaining quantities of
extremely valuable intelligence. But their success, which built upon
brilliant prewar Polish work, had required the incisive idea of a genius,

Alan Turing, the intellectual father of the computer, and the clever electromechanical cryptanalytic device that he invented to implement it. Historians did not know whether the USSR had had the same idea as Turing and, if it had, they questioned whether Russians, not famed for precision mechanics, could have built the ingenious electromechanical cryptanalytic devices that Turing had invented to implement his idea.

But it was known that the Red Army had captured Enigma machines from time to time. Mere possession would not have sufficed, however. Indeed, the Germans premised their adoption of the Enigma in the 1920s on the belief that, even given a machine, so many rotor orders, rotor ring settings, rotor starting positions, and cable pluggings were possible that no enemy could run through them all in less than many eons.[22] The recipient of an incoming message was told how to set up his machines by keys, which were distributed on sheets of paper to all the members of a communications network. Normally, each sheet contained a month's worth of keys. It seemed probable that the Red Army had captured some of these key lists. This would have enabled the Soviets to read that net's messages for that month. But Western historians believed such seizures had been too infrequent to permit continuous, or almost continuous, reading of Enigma messages.

In fact, the Soviets knew how to solve the Enigma.[23] But they did not have the technology to make the Turing devices.[24] It might have been possible to organize people to replicate the mechanisms' work.[25] But manpower was in very short supply and anyhow the Soviet military cryptanalysts were solving German hand cipher systems, which, though they did not yield the higher-level intelligence that Enigma solutions did, generated quantities of tactical information. Later in the war, however, as the Red Army advanced more than it retreated, it captured increasing numbers of Enigma key lists. These enabled the Soviets to read a growing percentage of the valuable Enigma traffic.[26]

Part V

Determining whether the United States and its allies were planning a nuclear war against the Soviet Union was the primary task of Soviet comint during the Cold War. In striving to accomplish this task, did it crack any or many American cryptosystems?

The United States enters the known history of Russian cryptology in 1905. The American minister in St. Petersburg handwrote President Theodore Roosevelt on July 5 that "I have discovered beyond a doubt that the Russian Government have in their possession our entire cable code.... Instead of having one of the secretaries or the clerk copy the letters it was the custom to allow the chasseurs [uniformed attendants] to do it in another room by themselves. These men were in the employ of the Russian Government & all was too easy."[27] His report came as TR was preparing to negotiate the treaty of Portsmouth ending the Russo-Japanese War; no doubt the Russians wanted whatever information about those discussions they could get. In 1930, while its chief was the energetic Gleb I. Bokiy,[28] the Spets-Otdel began attacking American cryptosystems,[29] and in that very year the Communists were reportedly reading a U.S. code. After President Franklin D. Roosevelt recognized the Soviet Union in 1933, opportunities expanded for that nation to intercept more messages. And the Soviet cryptanalysts, like their counterparts in other countries, had almost certainly cracked the frail old State Department codes. But during World War II, the Soviet Union did not solve American systems, because the United States was an ally.[30] These scruples may have been reinforced by such down-to-earth problems as insufficient manpower and by the use of all-but-unbreakable machines for high-level U.S. Army and Navy use and, from 1944, for the State Department.

Soviet hesitation vanished with the start of the Cold War. The loss of cryptanalytic contact probably hampered its efforts, as it usually does, but it did not prevent the Soviet Union from breaking a widely used cryptosystem of the United States and the North Atlantic Treaty Organization called the KW-7, perhaps helped by captures in Vietnam.[31] Andreyev thought that NSA, which creates all American and at least approves all NATO cryptosystems, had overlooked some weaknesses in the KW-7, which utilized wired codewheels. Though the field advances on a broad front, with both sides often working on things simultaneously, "Sometimes one organization goes ahead a few years, then the other," he said.[32]

But codes do not always need to be broken. They can be stolen. And codes are an especially attractive target because obtaining one will grant access not to just a single secret, as a military plan, but to a whole range of information. And theft can be quicker and cheaper than cryptanalysis – though it more risks losing the source. Around the turn of the century, when the 1905 compromise took place, American codebooks were said to have been bought by the agents of the tsar for tens of thousands of rubles.[33] In 1913, the American vice consul general in Moscow wrote the State Department "that the 'Larrabee Cipher Code' referred to in the above instruction as being 'transmitted herewith,' was not to be found in the envelope."[34] The technique persists, though with modern cryptosystems consisting not of codebooks but of integrated circuit chips embedded in computers it is harder to do nowadays. A succession of agents have sold instead manuals for the machines and key lists. As just one example, a U.S. Army sergeant, Jack E. Dunlop, lived well with a cabin cruiser and a blonde mistress on the gains of his betrayals – until, realizing he was about to be caught, he committed suicide.[35]

The Soviet Union succeeded most spectacularly in this field with John A. Walker Jr., his brother, his son, and his best friend. As a Navy warrant officer who handled Navy cryptosystems, Walker and his fellow spies photographed the documents needed to read messages. This went on for more than 17 years, until he was arrested in May 1985 after his ex-wife turned him in. Soviet defector Vitaly Yurchenko, saying that this information enabled the Soviet Union to read "millions" – probably an exaggeration – of American messages and gain insight into naval strategy and tactics, claimed that his chiefs called it "the greatest case in KGB history." And Andreyev endorsed as accurate a 1989 *Washington Post* article illuminating the seriousness of the Walker case and contending that the United States hadn't caught all the Soviet code spies.[36]

Other back doors were unlocked by electronics. A conversation overheard by Makarov suggests that the American consulate in Leningrad was penetrated through such a back door. He was in an office dealing with American matters when a KGB employee came in and said to a superior, "Paul, we have done Leningrad so we'll be having work soon." Paul turned to Makarov and said, "Victor, we'll soon be getting work to which you don't have access, so you must leave now."

Probably the oldest of such backdoors are hidden microphones. As early as May 14, 1937, the embassy in Moscow reported finding in the ambassador's residence, Spaso House, "two fine wires almost directly over the chair behind the Ambassador's desk" where he "was accustomed to dictate a large portion of his correspondence" and to receive visitors. An embassy electrician had observed fresh cigarette butts and "several piles of human excrement" in the attic, which led to a hidden attic compartment in which the eavesdropper lay, the wires, and, later, the microphone, with the manufacturer's stamp "Leningrad Telephone Factory." One of the diplomats and the electrician thought that "during recent months some person has used the portion of the attic in which the wiring was found, in order, with the assistance of a microphone, to overhear conversations taking place in the Ambassador's office. In this connection, it should be pointed out that Mr. Davies [the ambassador] was accustomed to dictate a large portion of his correspondence while sitting at the desk in the office in which the microphone equipment was apparently suspended, and also there to receive members of his staff, foreign diplomats, journalists and other persons." Wires were also found in the apartment of the ambassador's secretary and in another building, where they seemed to lead to the apartment of embassy official George Kennan. Various indications pointed to one of the embassy's Russian doormen, Samuel Lieberman.[37] Presumably he was discharged and precautions taken.[38] A special value of overheard conversations is that they not only reveal information directly but, by providing clues to the texts of telegrams, help cryptanalysts break cryptosystems.

The bugging continued or resumed after World War II. By 1960, more than 100 bugs had been found in American embassies and residences in the Soviet bloc. One was discovered in Spaso House in 1959 shortly before Vice President Richard Nixon was to stay there. Proof of its presence emerged when American officials, having referred in a conversation to a colleague as having a higher rank than he actually did, next morning heard Soviet officials speak of him by that rank. The best known Soviet bug was that hidden in the wooden carving of the Great Seal of the United States, presented by the Soviet Union in 1945 as a gift to the US embassy in Moscow and hung behind the desk of the successive ambassadors. The Soviets flooded that office with microwaves; a metal box in the belly of the bird modulated the ambassadorial speech; a Soviet antenna picked up the affected microwaves and converted them into speech. It was discovered during a routine check in 1952. The United States exposed it at the United Nations after the U-2 was shot down in 1960 to show that the Americans were not the only ones spying.

This merely drove the Soviets to greater subtleties. In 1983, a few years after the United States began building a new embassy in Moscow with Soviet labor, a security detachment found it riddled with eavesdropping devices. Some were concealed within the prefabricated columns the Soviets provided for the construction; others, such as cables that seemed to connect nothing, were excused as shoddy Soviet workmanship; the very reinforcing rods were said to have been arranged to facilitate transmitting the eavesdropping. The building was justly called "the world's largest microphone." Work was stopped. In 1992, the United States and Russia agreed that Americans could build the structure. Work is under way. For security, the diplomats use the old embassy.[39]

An especially clever electronic back door taps the pre-encryption circuits of cipher machines to access the original, uncoded message. One of the most striking Soviet successes lasted more than half a decade. It only ended when, on January 11, 1983, the red-faced counselor of the French embassy in Moscow wired his horrified foreign minister that "In the course of work done this day by the cipher chief of this embassy of fixing a teleprinter (CJG347758) of the cipher service put into service in January 1977, it appeared that the body of the condenser, from which emerged four wires instead of two, contained a complex electronic apparatus, evidently intended to transmit telegraphic information in clear onto the exterior electricity grid." The telegram added that the five other teleprinters were similarly "equipped." An investigation showed that the Soviets had installed the bugs during the 48 hours that the apparatus was being shipped by train from Paris to Moscow unaccompanied by guards. The freight car's contents were indeed designated as diplomatic baggage, but that nicety had not stopped the Soviets, who had little difficulty in counterfeiting the official French seals.[40] For six years, therefore, the KGB had obtained the content of all teleprinted messages from Moscow – including the ones dealing with a then forthcoming meeting in Warsaw between Soviet leader Leonid Brezhnev and French President Valéry Giscard d'Estaing soon after the Soviet invasion of Afghanistan. Knowing the French intentions, Brezhnev was helped in maneuvering Giscard into renewing the East-West dialogue at a time when the Soviet Union was diplomatically isolated.[41]

Other bugs were better hidden. Tiny sensors on Western teletype-writers transmitted the plaintext messages before they entered the encryption circuits. The Siemens T-1000, used by several countries, was a favorite target. If the machines were being trucked to a nation's missions in the USSR, the KGB sometimes applied the bugs while young women distracted the drivers. Or, in the unlikely case that that didn't work, it authorized a team to crash a car into the truck. The KGB tapped Germany's TX-20 teleprinter with sensors so small they could barely be seen. Called "ants," they had to be "dusted" onto the printing block by a KGB agent, sometimes, apparently, at the factory or in the embassy, which naturally had to be broken into. Their weakness was their very short range, which is why the Soviets preferred to insinuate their antennas as close as possible to the tele-printers. Often this was in embassy walls, though one antenna in the American embassy was snaked into a radiator. In the Canadian embassy once, just as a Soviet wire was discovered and was being yanked out, the Soviets felt the pull and tugged back, leading to a bug tug.[42]

Still another electronic back door exploits the fact that every time an electric circuit opens or closes mechanically, the contact spark emits electromagnetic radiation. Such a spark is created whenever a typist keyboards a letter into a teleprinter, a computer, or a cipher machine. This radiation is that of the letters of the original message before being encrypted. Faint though it may be, the radiation can be picked up by a sensitive radio receiver; sometimes its echo can be detected on the power supply circuit. An interceptor can tape-record the radiation. The waveform of the radiation for, say, the letter "a" will differ from that for "b." Using the same method of frequency analysis that a cryptanalyst would utilize for solving a monoalphabetic sub-stitution, the interceptor can determine which letter each waveform represents. The result yields the original messages without having to break the far more complex encrypted version.

A final back door utilizes the fact that cathode ray tubes generate magnetic fields. So, therefore, do cipher machines that have computer screens to show the message being input. A modified television set can detect such a field and reproduce it, thus revealing the original message without any need to crack the cipher. To prevent this, as well as spark radiation interception, the cipher machines and their connections to the outside are shielded; the United States has code-named this protection TEMPEST. But sometimes leaks remain, and in those cases the Soviet Union has been able to circumvent America's generally excellent cryptography.[43]

Part VI

While the Soviet Union's vast 6th Directorate of the military intelligence agency, the GRU, was assigned armed forces codemaking and codebreaking, the KGB worked on domestic (police) and foreign communications. Its 8th Chief Directorate dealt with communications; its Department D handled codebreaking. Then, in 1973, under Andreyev's impulsion, the cryptanalysis was hived off into a new directorate, the 16th. It never rose to a chief directorate – Makarov thought the reason was that, to the KGB, foreign signals intelligence was never as important as surveillance of the population. When Andreyev was promoted to head the 8th Chief Directorate, he was succeeded as head of the 16th by KGB General Igor Vasilovich Maslow, who had been granted a Lenin award for the French embassy coup.[44]

The 16th's headquarters was in a yellow, nine-story, 1950s apartment house-like structure in Moscow at Samotechnaia 9, about 10 minutes' drive from the Kremlin (Figure 15.4). Each floor or floors housed a department, with sections and desks divided into smallish rooms of four or five individuals. The directorate housed many of its computers – including the most powerful computer in the Soviet Union, called SWORD – in a handsome modernistic 21-story white skyscraper on Prospekt Vernadskogo near Moscow University in a large, overgrown field under which lies a hidden KGB city (Figure 15.5).[45]

The directorate was divided into Service No. 1 – there were no other Services – and multiple departments. Service No. 1 was responsible for the bugging and other technical penetrations of foreign embassies; it was the directorate's most important element. Service No. 1, located at 24 Zamorevnova Street, is itself divided into several departments.

Its First Department develops the methods of technical penetration. Specialists analyze teletypewriters for points that can be bugged and devise methods to pick up cipher-machine radiation. The Second Department obtains this radiation from points near the embassies

Figure 15.4   The apartment-house-like building at Samotechnaia 9, Moscow, housed the KBG'S 16th Dictorate, for communications intelligence.

and wires it to secret apartments, where it is turned into the original messages. The Third Department deals with the customs agency and other directorates of the KGB to insert and remove the bugs. Makarov did not remember the function of the Fourth Department, but the Fifth cleans the intercepted signals by removing static and other interference.

The directorate's First Department, with about 100 people, broke codes. There was no Second Department. The Third translated. The Fourth polished the translations, added needed references, and selected from the directorate's output the material to be distributed. It then printed two booklets each day whose contents differed according to their subscribers' needs. Brochure No. 1, usually of less than a dozen pages, went to selected members of the Politburo. Brochure No. 2 went to the chiefs of the KGB's First and Second Chief Directorates, for espionage and counterespionage respectively. In addition, the 16th Directorate sent its information, though without specifying its source, to the heads of government departments. The Fifth Department, the most mathematical, analyzed ciphers

Figure 15.5   The skyscraper on Prospekt Vernadskogo that housed the SWORD supercomputer, used by the KGB for cryptanalysis. (Photo by David Kahn.)

and liaised with the Soviet Union's East European allies. The Sixth Department handled finances. Makarov did not know the functions of many of the other departments but believed that several were subsections of the directorate's Scientific Research Institute.[46]

Part VII

This arrangement ended in 1991. After the putsch of August 1991, Soviet leader Mikhail Gorbachev dissolved the KGB. The 8th Chief Directorate and the 16th Directorate were formed into a new Federal Agency for Government Communications and Information, called FAPSI from the initials of its Russian name, Fyedyeral'noye Agyenstvo Pravitelstvyennoi Svyazi i Informatsii.[47] Modeled on the U.S. National Security Agency, which combines codemaking and codebreaking and, in effect, controls the export of cipher devices and algorithms, it was intended to similarly control Soviet cryptology. Andreyev became its first head. When the Soviet Union was disbanded, FAPSI became an agency of the Russian republic.

With the end of the Cold War, the comint targets of the great powers shifted from one another to drug traffickers, other organized criminals, terrorists, and insurgents. These types work internationally, and international cooperation is needed to subdue them. This exists among police forces, and even among the CIA and the remnants of the KGB – in October 1992, the then director of central intelligence, Robert Gates, visited Moscow to initiate joint efforts. But because comint is easier to lose than most other sources, and because such loss would hurt more, the agencies of communications intelligence are more reluctant than other agencies to risk such cooperation. Andreyev told me, however, that he might be interested in cooperating with the United States in attacking the cryptosystems of these malefactors. The National Security Agency declined comment when asked about this.[48] How remarkable – and how useful – cooperation would be with the NSA! Two great engines of war would turn their efforts at last from dueling one another in darkness to brightening a world at peace.

Notes

1. See, for example, F. H. Hinsley *et al.*, *British Intelligence in the Second World War* (Cambridge: Cambridge University Press, 1979–1988); Ralph Bennett, *Behind the Battle: Intelligence in the War with Germany, 1919–1945* (London, U.K.: Sinclair-Stevenson, 1995); Clair Blair, *Hitler's U-Boat War: The Hunters 1929–1942* (New York: Random House, 1996); John Prados, *Combined Fleet Decoded: The Secret History of American Intelligence and the Japanese Navy in World War II* (New York: Random House, 1995); David Kahn, *Seizing the Enigma* (New York: Houghton Mifflin, 1991).
2. Stephen Schlesinger, "Cryptanalysis for Peacetime: Codebreaking and the Birth and Structure of the United Nations," *Cryptologia*, Vol. 19 (July 1995), pp. 217–235.
3. Interview, 6 June 1993.
4. National Archives, Record Group 457, Historical Cryptographic Collection, Box 256, Folder 15.
5. Makarov also gave an interview to the *Moscow Express Chronicle* (19 February 1992), pp. 4–5, which provides additional background on him; published also in Russian in the Russian edition (10–17 February 1992), pp. 4–5.
6. Interview, 14 and 15 October 1992.
7. United States, Foreign Broadcast Intelligence Service, *Daily Report, Central Eurasia, Russia*, National Affairs, FBIS-SOV-99-185, "Work of KGB Eighth Directorate Described" (24 September 1990), pp. 64–68, at 64.

8. Raymond L. Garthoff, "The KGB Reports to Gorbachev," *Intelligence and National Security*, Vol. 11 (April 1996), pp. 223–244 at 228.

9. *Ibid.*

10. Aleksandr Fursenko and Timothy Naftali, *One Hell of a Gamble* (New York: W. W. Norton & Co., 1997), p. 254. But see also Note 1, p. 388.

11. This and all other information from Andreyev comes from the 13 June 1996 interview.

12. This and other information from Makarov comes from his interviews, 14 and 15 October 1992.

13. These were distributed – perhaps after being retyped – on onion-skin paper bound in large volumes called Red Books, which the recipients could read but were not permitted to retain or to take notes on. Christopher Andrew and Oleg Gordievsky, *KGB* (New York: HarperCollins, 1990), p. 455.

14. Except where otherwise noted, all information on the history of Russian cryptology comes from the badly needed, scholarly, and extremely useful book by T[atiana]. A. Sobolyeva, *Tainopis v Istorii Rossii* [Secret Writing in the History of Russia] (Moscow, Russia: Myezhdynarodnieye Otnoshyeniya, 1994).

15. For the contributions of Goldbach and of other mathematical crypt-analysts, see Sobolyeva's "ForgottenNames," *VIP: International Magazine About and For Decision-Makers* (No. 14), pp. 44–46.

16. Sobolyeva, 233.

17. Union of Soviet Socialist Republics, Komissiya po izdaniyu dokumentov epokhi imperializma, *Die Internationalen Beziehungen im Zeitalter des Imperialismus: Dokumente aus den Archiven der Zaristischen und der Provisorischen Regierung.* Kommission beim Zentralexekutivkomitee der Sowjetregierung, M. N. Pokrowski, ed. Otto Hoetzsch, German ed. (Berlin, Germany: Reimar Hobbing, 1931–1936), prints solutions from those countries and others at (roman numerals for Reihe, arabic numerals for Band, arabic numerals preceded by colon for Halbband (where used), arabic numerals preceded by comma for page) I:1, 83, 162, 241, 249; I:2, 243, 244; I:3, 5; I:4, 15, 51, 120, 128, 197, 253; I:5, 2, 3, 147, 171, 196, 150, 163, 183; I:6:1, 11, 51, 54, 89, 92, 151, 163, 166, 193,195, 225, 239, 243, 250, 290; 1:6:2, 393, 404, 406, 423, 429, 439, 448, 453, 460, 472, 481, 493, 499, 509, 522, 523, 532, 561, 584, 630, 643, 647, 654; II:7:1, 201, 217, 282, 291, 299, 306, 310, 324, 325, 333, 352; II:7:2, 434, 445, 496, 502, 541, 597, 652, 658; II:8:1, 31, 84, 86, 189; II:8:2, 475, 587, 568, 574, 584, 671, 678; III:1:2, 819, 868; III:2:1, 165; III:4:1, 191, 206, 264, 176, 277, 313, 332, 349, 362, 416, 417. No American solutions are given. Some additional information in Christopher Andrew and Keith Neilson, "Tsarist Codebreakers and British Codes," *Intelligence and National Security*, Vol. 1 (January 1986), pp. 6–12 and R. Ye. Shchyegolyeva, ed., *Padyeniye Tsarskogo Ryezhima* (Leningrad, Russia: Gosudarstvyennoye Izdatyelstvo, 1925), 3:264–265, 268–269, 5:134–137. For some anecdotes, see Germany, Auswartiges Amt, Abteilung A, "Die Sicherheit der Chiffre-Correspondenz in Russland (Russland Nr. 100)," in U. S. National Archives, Microform T-139, Roll 308.

18. Andreyev. Andrew and Gordievsky, pp. 271–272.

19. *Ibid.*

20. The American version of this solution is given in Carl Boyd, *Hitler's Japanese Confidant* (Lawrence, KS: University Press of Kansas, 1993), pp. 60, 62, 63.

21. *Ibid,* 65.

22. Ray Miller, "The Cryptographic Mathematics of Enigma," *Cryptologia,* Vol. 19 (January 1995), pp. 65–80, calculates the number of Enigma configurations as 3×10^{114} – more than the estimated number of atoms in the universe.

23. Andreyev interview.

24. Andrew and Gordievsky, 307.

25. Andreyev said this might have been possible. Erkki Pale, a Finnish World War II cryptanalyst specializing in Soviet cryptosystems, did not think it was.

26. Andreyev interview.

27. George von Lengerke Meyer to Theodore Roosevelt, 5 July 1905. Theodore Roosevelt Collection, The Houghton Library, Harvard University, Cambridge, Massachusetts.

28. On Bokiy, see the biography by Sobolyeva, *Dovveryeno Zashchishchat Revolyutsivu* (Moscow, Russia: Izdatyelstvopolitichyeskoi literaturi, 1987). See also David Kahn, *The Codebreakers* (New York: Macmillan, 1967), p. 640.

29. Sobolyeva, 334.

30. Andreyev interview. Andreyev criticized the United States for attacking Soviet cryptosystems in 1943 in a project codenamed VENONA that later showed that Julius Rosenberg was spying on the atom bomb project for the Soviet Union.

31. Tordella interview.

32. Andreyev interview.

33. Sobolyeva, 235.

34. Vice Consul General in Moscow Alfred V. Smith to Department of State, 13 September 1913, Department of State Decimal File 119.25/117, Record Group 59, National Archives. The Larrabee was indeed just a Vigenère, and the table was used with a keyword, which may not have been in the envelope, but the removers of it did not know that before they stole the system, and in any event knowledge of the system would have saved the cryptanalysts at least a little time.

35. Kahn, pp. 696–697.

36. On the Walkers, see John Baron, *Breaking the Ring* (Boston, MA: Houghton Mifflin, 1987), Howard Blum, *I Pledge Allegiance ...* (New York: Simon & Schuster, 1987), and Pete Early, *Family of Spies* (Bantam, 1988). For a more conservative view, see David Kahn, "Year of the Spy: Was U.S. Hurt?" *Newsday* (27 July 1986), Ideas, 1 ff. The *Washington Post* article is by William Scott Malone and William Cran, "Code Name Catastrophe: How Moscow Cracked Our Secret Cipher Systems" (22 January 1989), p. Dl.

37. National Archives. Record Group 59, Department of State Decimal File, 124.61/111, -/112, -/114.

38. The documents are silent on these points.

39. A good summary of this issue, which generated many news stories and much Congressional rhetoric, is Dick Nelson and Julie Koenen-Grant, "A Case of Bureaucracy 'in Action': The U. S. Embassy in Moscow," *International Journal of Intelligence and CounterIntelligence*, Vol. 6 (Fall 1993), pp. 303–317. John Ziolkowski, a former Senate staffer who had worked on this matter, was most helpful.

40. Thierry Wolton, "Comment le KGB avait piégé l'ambassade de France." *Le Point* (8 avril 1985), pp. 64–66.

41. *Ibid.*, 65; Julie Malcom Newton, "Soviet Policy Towards France, 1958–1991: A Case Study of the Soviet Union's Westpolitik," D. Phil. Thesis, St. Antony's College, Oxford University (Michaelmas Term, 1993), p. 137.

42. All Makarov interview.

43. Andreyev interview.

44. Makarov interview.

45. Makarov interview; David Kahn visits.

46. All Makarov interview.

47. United States, Foreign Broadcast Intelligence Service, *Daily Report, Central Eurasia Russia*, FBIS-SOV-91-001, "Communications, Information Agency Created" (2 January 1992), p. 57; FBIS-SOV-92-054, "Communications Agency Future Pondered" (19 March 1992), pp. 49–50.

48. Telephone call from NSA spokeswoman, 14 November 1997.

16

How the Allies Suppressed the Second Greatest Secret of World War II*

The greatest secret of World War II was the atom bomb. The second greatest was the British and American solution of messages encrypted in Germany's Enigma and other cipher machines. This was code-named Ultra. It gave the Allies insight into important German plans and activities and enabled them to foil those intentions, helped them dodge U-boat wolfpacks to bring more supplies to Britain, permitted them to learn of and sink tankers bringing fuel to General Erwin Rommel in North Africa, and let them feed the Germans false information that aided the Allies' lodgement in France. Yet the Allied official histories of World War II do not discuss this great intelligence coup, which had so great an impact on that struggle.[1]

The postwar reports of General George C. Marshall and Admiral Ernest J. King say nothing about the breaking of German codes.[2] The green books, that extraordinary series of official histories of the *United States Army in World War II*,[3] which deal not just with the fighting forces but also with support elements, do not mention Allied solution of high-level enciphered German messages. Nor do the volumes of Samuel Eliot Morison's official *History of United States Naval Operations in World War II*.[4] Likewise the official Army Air Forces history.[5] The official United Kingdom Military Series has suppressed signals intelligence against Germany.[6] Winston Churchill's magisterial *The Second World War* has been cleansed of all mention of signals intelligence.[7]

---

* From *The Journal of Military History*, 74 (October 2010), 1229–1241.

Yet the 1945–1946 Congressional investigation into the Pearl Harbor disaster dealt intensively and extensively with the American solution of Japanese diplomatic codes before the attack and, to a lesser degree, with wartime military solutions.[8] So the official histories referred to these, though sometimes obliquely. In addition, shortly after the war newspaper and magazine articles and books appeared dealing with the effects of American cryptanalyses—the victory at Midway in 1942 and the midair assassination of Admiral Isoroku Yamamoto in 1943, to name the most striking.[9] The official histories relate these, though usually not with great specificity about the cryptanalyses. But about Allied solution of German cryptosystems—nothing, with one exception. In a secret 1944 letter published in the Congressional hearings, U.S. Army Chief of Staff General George C. Marshall, urging Republican presidential candidate Thomas E. Dewey not to make a campaign issue of pre-Pearl Harbor codebreaking, revealed with startling particularity the value of Allied cryptanalyses of both Japanese and German messages.[10] Though the press picked this up,[11] and knew about the import of codebreaking in the Pacific, no one—not the press, not Allied or former Axis popular or scholarly historians, not the official historians—followed through to the scope or impact of codebreaking in the European theater.

Why not? Probably because the known explanations satisfied them. World War II in Europe was won—to oversimplify—by Soviet manpower and American production, preceded by British fortitude. Codebreaking was not necessary to this. The Allies would have won without it. And the historians had plenty to do. They had to gather information about battles, manpower, organization, supplies, tactics, personalities, command, intelligence (as prisoner interrogations and aerial reconnaissance, though not cryptanalytic). They had to organize their histories, decide what to put in and what to leave out, and write them. They had to argue with former commanders who did not like their conclusions and with supervisors who disagreed with their presentations. In the end, they satisfactorily answered the questions of why the Allies won the war.

Reminiscing over beers at a conference after the Enigma revelations, some Army historians said that while everyone knew about the Japanese intercepts, and used them in their books, the thought never occurred to anyone that the Allies were breaking major German cryptosystems. Some said that they suspected that something was going on in the intelligence field because the military decisions being made were just too good. But they concluded that the British had infiltrated an agent into Adolf Hitler's headquarters. Hugh Cole, author of *The Ardennes: Battle of the Bulge* (1965), in the green book series, said that during the war he had shared his tent with the Third Army's Ultra briefing officer and that, though he thought it strange that every so often his tentmate and General George S. Patton would go to the middle of a field and talk, he never suspected that they were discussing codebreaking. Forrest Pogue once said that, while he was writing *The Supreme Command* in the 1950s, a number of senior officers even told him that a source was missing. He thought that they were referring to espionage. That an unknown element—particularly one as technical, as unfamiliar, as exotic as cryptanalysis—might have played a pervasive role simply did not occur to him or the other historians in that pre-computer, pre-internet era.[12]

One may also ask why the Germans didn't guess the Allied cryptanalytic success during the war. They had greater need to do so than the historians and greater experience. Indeed, Admiral Karl Dönitz, suspicious about some unexpectedly clever Allied moves, asked his cryptologic experts three or four times whether the Allies might be reading his radioed instructions to his U-boats. They repeatedly reassured him it wasn't possible: the complexity of the Enigma and the Kriegsmarine's ability to quickly change any keys suspected of being compromised precluded extensive solution. Moreover, they believed that the Allies' own messages—which the Germans were reading—would reveal these solutions. But the Allies never mounted an operation based on codebreaking without having a cover story to explain it, such as an airplane sighting of the target. The Germans also thought that if the Allies were reading German cryptosystems, they would have improved their own, and finally that radar, not codebreaking, was telling the Allies of U-boat locations.[13]

Most significantly, none of the several German codebreaking agencies ever envisioned the extent and effectiveness of the Ultra enterprise. In the first place, it rested upon the stroke of genius of British mathematician Alan Turing. He and others invented an electromechanical device that so vastly improved upon a Polish predecessor, called a "bombe," as to practically constitute a new method of solution. His own bombe solved Enigma messages by rapidly testing guessed (often stereotyped) plaintexts against intercepts to find the correct setting from among the millions possible. It didn't always work, but when it did the British could use that setting to read other intercepts. The Germans, though they had some simple cryptanalytic machines,[14] never conceived of a bombe, with its speed and capacity. In the second place, while they did pay lip service to the possibility that the Allies could expend "extraordinary mechanical outlay" to produce cryptanalytic intelligence from the Enigma, they never imagined that what would come into being was a huge organization of thousands of people using scores of bombes that would test hundreds of messages a day, find some Enigma keys, use these to rapidly decipher intercepts on many Enigma replicas, turn them into usable intelligence, and distribute them to higher commanders for use in battle—all in total secrecy and without a single leakage.

Nothing like this had ever existed in history: even the newest Axis foreign cryptanalytic organizations employed at best a few hundred people turning out a few score solutions each day. So if the Germans, pressed more urgently and knowing more cryptology, could not imagine this,[15] how could the Allied historians do so?

The British Chiefs of Staff did not know about the German suspicions. But they feared that, once the captured German documents[16] became available at the end of the war, historians, comparing them with Allied moves, would guess that codebreaking had played a role in the victory. So, even while the Allies were still fighting Japan, they considered steps to prevent the historians from revealing this capability.

The British Joint Intelligence Subcommittee began a report of 20 July 1945 to its joint chiefs with:[17] "In this paper we discuss the problem of ensuring the security of our Special Intelligence organisation during the post-war years, having special regard to the production of official histories upon which work has already commenced." ("Special Intelligence" was the euphemism for the product of high-level cryptanalysis.) The report goes on: "It is vital, in our opinion, that the strict security precautions regarding the existence of this organisation and the results of its work, which have been observed during the war, should continue in the future." It offers no reason. It observes that

"A great number of German official archives… will, in due course, be made available to the official historical sections" and that "It will be undesirable and indeed impossible to suppress the German records."

Then it touches the core issue:

When our official historians eventually study these German records they will analyse them in comparison with the relevant British documents with regard to operations and the employment of new weapons and techniques. It will then be revealed to them that the Naval, Army and Air staffs have, throughout the war, been in possession of information concerning enemy movements and operational and technical information which could not have been received from agents or other means slower than Special Intelligence. Obvious instances are the re-routing of convoys to avoid submarine attacks by orders issued immediately after the issue of German orders to their U-boats: the countermeasures to meet the G.A.F. [German Air Force] attacks on this country and the routing of our deep penetration raids into Germany: the employment of our forces in the field in the face of German disposition.…

The subcommittee goes on:

5. It will be undesirable to warn the large number of officials engaged in the preparation of official histories, as disclosure of the most secret sources of Special Intelligence on such a scale would defeat its own object. Unless, however, some indication is given to the historical sections concerned, the comparing of the German and British documents is bound to arouse suspicion in their minds that we succeeded in reading the enemy's ciphers. A solution of this difficulty might be the issue of a carefully worded warning to the head historian of each Service Ministry incorporating a general directive to all personnel of their departments. They should not, in any case, be given access to original Special Intelligence material.

6. In case, in spite of this warning, the existence of a Special Intelligence Organisation is unwittingly betrayed, it will be necessary for all such histories to be scrutinised by staff already indoctrinated. We therefore consider that all official histories should be submitted to the Intelligence Directorate at the relevant Ministry before publication.…

We have no knowledge of the action the Americans propose to take in this matter, or if indeed they have yet considered it. We suggest however, that it will be necessary for an approach to be made to the U.S. Chiefs of Staff with a view to obtaining an agreed policy on the action to be taken.

So on 4 August 1945, the Representative of the British Chiefs of Staff wrote a memorandum to the Combined Chiefs of Staff (American and British) on "Use of Special Intelligence by Official Historians."[18] It read:

The British Chiefs of Staff are concerned about the possibility of leakage of information regarding special intelligence when official historians start to analyse German Archives and compare them with relevant Allied records. A great number of German official Archives are now in the process of being sorted and translated and the British Chiefs of Staff feel that it will be quite impracticable to try and suppress them....

3. If it is agreed that official histories should not reveal the existence of special intelligence material, the problem arises as to how far it is necessary and desirable to go in producing complete histories using all available material including that obtained from most special sources. The British Chiefs of Staff would propose only to write up important battles, using personnel already indoctrinated.

4. The British Chiefs of Staff would like to coordinate their policy on this matter with the United States Chiefs of Staff and would welcome their views on the following proposals:

a. The Head Historian of each Service Historical Section should be warned by means of a directive. A Draft of this is enclosed.

b. The fighting Services, using personnel already indoctrinated, should write up certain important battles showing what extra information was given to our Commanders by Special intelligence to complete the knowledge they already had of the enemy.

c. Official Historical Sections should not in any case be given any special intelligence material.

d. All histories prepared for publication and all Staff Studies prepared for official circles should be submitted to the relevant security authority to ensure that no unwitting compromise of source has occurred.

On 10 August, the American Joint Chiefs set up an ad hoc committee that reported three days later, in part that[19]

a. The proposal to safeguard special intelligence is sound. Essential uniform measures should be taken by the British and the United States. b. The measures taken must be realistic. To deny that Signal Intelligence sources produced valuable information would be naïve. The objective should be to maintain security as to the degree of success attained, the techniques and procedures employed and the specific intelligence produced. c. Exact procedures will vary due to difference in the organization of military forces of the two nations and difference in the arrangements for production of war histories. d. Coordination of procedures should be effected informally between representatives responsible for the preparation of history by British and United States army, naval and air authorities respectively. e. Specific recommendations applicable to the Signal Intelligence aspects should be furnished by the Army-Navy Communications Intelligence Board [a subsidiary of the Joint Chiefs of Staff] to the United States War and Navy Departments. f. The language used in the British memorandum and proposed draft directive is not sufficiently precise to have exactly the same meaning in British and American military and naval terminology. Certain clarification is essential.

General Marshall proposed minor changes in wording; Admiral William D. Leahy, chairman of the Joint Chiefs, approved these; and on 7 September the U.S. Joint Chiefs of Staff approved a memorandum for the representatives of the British Chiefs of Staff that "Appropriate agencies in the United States Army and Navy are being charged with responsibility that special intelligence sources are protected" in official histories.[20]

A British document of 17 March 1948 states that "copies of the revised General Directive and Indoctrination Brief have been passed to the appropriate authorities in Canada, Australia, New Zealand and the U.S.A. for consideration and concurrence."[21] All apparently followed the recommendation.

But unofficial leaks sprang. In 1950, the historian Hugh Trevor-Roper, who had had access to British cryptanalytic results during the war, wrote in a review of a biography of Admiral Wilhelm Canaris, the 1935–44 chief of German armed forces espionage, that "all Abwehr hand-cyphers were read by the British from the beginning of 1940 and machine-ciphers—which were clearly thought to be invulnerable—from 1942."[22] In 1967, Wladyslaw Kozaczuk, a retired Polish officer, disclosed for the first time in his book *Bitwa o Tajeminice: slubzby wywiadowcze Polski i Rzeszy Niemieckiej 1922–1939* that the Poles had solved the German Enigma machine in the 1930s.[23] A retired Luftwaffe colonel, Herbert Flesch, an amateur cryptologist, heard of this,[24] and probably others did as well. But the book was in a language few western scholars of cryptology read and was published in a country behind the Iron Curtain, and its remarkable disclosure did not attract much notice. But the story appeared elsewhere as well. In his 1967 *La Guerre secrète des services spéciaux français 1935–1945*,[25] former French intelligence officer Michel Garder wrote that a spy gave the French information about a German cipher machine, but he never named the spy and he wrongly stated that this had enabled a French cash register company to reconstruct it. A German historian of intelligence, Gert Buchheit, wrote in *Die Anonyme Macht* that Polish cryptanalysts had analyzed the German cipher machine.[26] British turncoat Kim Philby, in his 1968 memoir *My Silent War*, mentions codebreaking without giving details.[27] Trevor-Roper, by then Regius professor of modern history at Oxford, reviewing this in 1968, wrote that "The breaking of the 'Enigma' machine was made possible by the Polish Resistance and S.O.E."—not quite right, but he had revealed very specifically that the Allies were reading Enigma messages (Figure 16.1).[28]

Then, in 1973, Gustave Bertrand, a retired French intelligence officer, perhaps stimulated by Garder's story, which had mentioned him by name, published *Enigma: ou la Plus Grande Énigme de la Guerre 1939–1945*.[29] He gave personal details about running the spy early in the 1930s who had provided the information that led to the Polish and then the French and British solution of the Enigma. He reported the trilateral meeting in Warsaw in July 1939 in which the

Figure 16.1 Men and women at work on German cryptograms at Bletchley Park.

Poles disclosed to their allies their cryptanalytic bombe and presented them with reconstructed Enigmas. He said that, after the Germans defeated Poland in 1939, its cryptanalysts fled to France to continue their work and that French cryptanalysts solved Enigma messages. With this story—though Bertrand knew almost nothing about the British work—the cat was out of the bag.

A Briton, Group Captain F. W. Winterbotham, had been pressing for several years to tell the Enigma story. He had had a merely peripheral role in the work—he managed the highly restricted distribution of the solutions, far less important than those who solved the intercepts or who evaluated the results—but he wanted money.[30] Bertrand's publication enabled him to press the authorities even harder. So did his fear that popular author Anthony Cave Brown would publish much of the story in his *Bodyguard of Lies* before he did.[31] By this time, the Enigma machines that Britain had given its former colonies in Asia and Africa for their secret communications had worn out and been replaced by electronic cryptosystems; that they had been solved during World War II no longer needed to be kept secret.[32] Sir Arthur "Bill" Bonsall, head of Government Communications Headquarters (GCHQ), the British cryptologic agency, felt that so many other indications of the

Allied solution of Enigma had appeared that he could no longer block Winterbotham's importuning.[33] But Winterbotham was not allowed to see any of the original documents. This led to several errors in his text, chiefly his story that Churchill let Coventry be bombed to save Ultra, which was false.[34] Though thousands had maintained their oath of secrecy, forswearing the fame and fortune that revealing the story would give them, Winterbotham won Her Majesty's Government's permission to publish his book. In 1974, *The Ultra Secret* revealed the greatest untold secret of World War II. It exploded in headlines around the world. It helped explain why some decisions had been taken and how codebreaking helped win the war faster than otherwise. It possessed the always fascinating element of secret knowledge, of hidden control. The book became a best seller.[35] Some sensationalizers claimed that Ultra, as the solutions were called, won the war. This is nonsense. But the codebreaking did shorten the conflict.[36] And knowledge of it would have deepened the official British and American war histories by helping explain *why* things happened as they did.

In a way, though, it didn't matter whether the historians did or did not mention Ultra. What happened happened. The historians indeed had not told the whole truth, perhaps allowing readers to conclude that some commanders were brighter or luckier than they really were. But they did not lie.

After the revelation, an army historian, chatting with Pogue and Cole, asked them whether the codebreaking disclosures meant that the green books would have to be rewritten. Both replied, in effect, No, the histories were accurate even without the Ultra knowledge. But they conceded that telling *how* things happened would have added to the story.[37]

Still the two nations had kept their communications intelligence success secret for years after the war had been won. Why? A 1951 British file, the "Indoctrination into Special Intelligence," explained that

> Although the war has ended, it is still a vital necessity that no hint concerning the extent or the value of this source of information should be given. There are two main reasons for this: (i) Other enemies may arise in the future. Were they to know what successes were achieved in this war as a result of this special source, they could ensure that this source

would not be available to us. (ii) No possible excuse must be given to the Germans or Japanese to explain away their complete defeat by force of arms. Knowledge that this source of information was available to us would provide such an excuse.

Further on:

The time-limit for reticence about Special Intelligence never expires and although from time to time reports of alleged activities in connection with Special Intelligence may be broadcast or published, it is of the utmost importance that complete and absolute silence on such matters should be maintained by those, both past and present, who have been authorised to have access to Special Intelligence unless they are freed from this obligation by unmistakeable and categorical order.[38]

Indeed, though the story was out, Britain could have refused to acknowledge Winterbotham's tale, could have maintained an official silence upon something that it and the United States had kept secret for so long and whose secrecy had benefited them. And other, unstated reasons existed to keep the Allied cryptanalytic success secret even after hostilities ceased. Probably the main one was that the Cold War began soon after the hot war ended in 1945. The Allies did not have to reveal their capabilities in this field to the Communists. They had not done so fully even while they were allies in the war against Germany, giving the Soviet Union only some results through a liaison unit in Moscow.[39] Why do so now, when they were all but fighting foes? In addition, the United States was reconstructing its defense organization—creating an independent air force, setting up a unified defense department, establishing a central intelligence agency, consolidating its cryptologic agencies, in general trying to repair what had permitted Pearl Harbor. The codebreaking revelations might have delayed this effort. Moreover, such a revelation might also remind other countries about cryptology: maybe they should solve or steal American codes; maybe they should improve their own. The United States and the United Kingdom had developed strong cryptologic capabilities. Why should they confirm and thus jeopardize this enormous military and political advantage? To set the record straight? Not worth it. To help academics? Certainly not worth it. What was worth it were social and political advantages, the uplifting of the pride of a nation that had once ruled the earth and that had saved freedom. Critic George Steiner has said that "Increasingly, it looks as if Bletchley Park is the single greatest achievement of Britain during 1939–45, perhaps during this century as a whole."[40] Telling the world about this—that was worth it.

Acknowledgments

The authors thanks Ralph Erskine, David Hatch, and Edward S. Miller for carefully reading a draft of this chapter. Mr. Erskine provided essential information about the inadequate German testing of the Enigma. Dr. Hatch offered a valuable historical observation. Mr. Miller made helpful suggestions.

Notes

1. Later histories, published after the revelations of Group Captain F. W. Winterbotham in 1974 (see below), do mention the codebreaking. In particular, the magisterial five-volume official *British Intelligence in the Second World War: Its Influence on Strategy and Operations*, by F. H. Hinsley et al. and Michael Howard (London, U.K.: Her Majesty's Stationery *Office*, 1979–90).

2. [U.S. War Department, General Staff], *General Marshall's Report. The Winning of the War in Europe and the Pacific. Biennial Report of the Chief of Staff of the United States Army, July 1, 1943 to June 30, 1945, to the Secretary of War* (Published for the War Department in Cooperation with the Council on Books in Wartime by Simon and Schuster, n.p., 2 September 1945). Nothing about the successful deception for Operation Overlord, based in part on codebreaking. *U.S. Navy at War 1941–1945: Official Report to the Secretary of the Navy by Fleet Admiral Ernest J. King, Commander in Chief United States Fleet and Chief of Naval Operations* (Washington, DC: U.S. Navy Department, 1946). Silent about convoy reroutings to dodge wolfpacks, which were based largely on cryptanalysis of intercepts of Kriegsmarine radiograms.

3. *United States Army in World War II* (Washington, DC: Department of the Army, 1947–98): 78 volumes, plus a reader's guide. All bound in green cloth.

4. Samuel Eliot Morison, *History of United States Naval Operations in World War II*, 16 vols. (Boston, MA: Little, Brown, 1947–62).

5. Wesley Frank Craven and James Lea Cate, eds., *The Army Air Forces in World War II*, 7 vols. (Chicago, IL: University of Chicago Press, 1948–58).

6. Among these are the multivolumed J. R. M. Butler's *Grand Strategy* (1956–76); L. P. Ellis's *Victory in the West* (1962-68); Charles K. Webster's *The Strategic Air Offensive against Germany* (1961); Ian Playfair's *The*

Mediterranean and the Middle East (1954–84); and Stephen Roskill's *The War at Sea* (1954–61), though on 2:208 (1956), after referring to German naval cryptanalytic successes, he slyly says, "The reader should not, of course, assume that we British were meanwhile idle in achieving the opposite purpose."

7. David Reynolds, "The Ultra Secret and Churchill's War Memoirs," *Intelligence and National Security*, Vol. 20 (2005), pp. 209–24. This useful article offers a detailed picture of how officials purged those memoirs of any hints of Allied codebreaking.

8. United States, Congress, Joint Committee on the Investigation of the Pearl Harbor Attack, *Pearl Harbor Attack*, Hearings, 79th Cong., 1st and 2d sess., 1946, 39 parts. Even before the war had ended, the military tried but failed to keep these solutions secret. Bills were introduced to do this: H.R. 2711 of 21 March 1945 and S. 805 of 30 March 1945. Both were supported by a letter of 10 March 1945 from the secretaries of War and the Navy and other high officials. Files on those bills, both 79th Congress, 1st Session, National Archives and Records Administration (NARA). I am grateful to Rodney Ross of NARA for spelunking through House and Senate files and finding this and other information. See also "Navy Opposes Disclosure of Full Pearl Harbor Data," *New York Times*, 9 September 1945, 1:2. But the secretaries' wishes could not withstand the desire of Congress and the nation for full knowledge of the Pearl Harbor disaster — knowledge that was thought to depend in large part upon cryptanalysis of Japanese messages. The joint committee's hearings and exhibits dealt extensively with those solutions. The records of the International Military Tribunal for the Far East also contain some references here and there to Allied codebreaking of Japanese messages. The Nuremberg trials did not mention Allied codebreaking of German messages, even though one of the chief American prosecutors, Telford Taylor, had worked as a liaison at Bletchley Park, the British codebreaking center northwest of London. For pre-Pearl Harbor and some wartime solutions of Japanese messages, see citations in David Kahn, *The Codebreakers* (New York: Macmillan, 1967), pp. 977–85, 1069–75.

9. Of American foreknowledge of the Japanese advance on Midway, based on codebreaking, King speaks only of the "best estimate of the situation" *(U.S. Navy at War 1941–1945*, p. 47). Morison writes that Nimitz deduced "a large part of his enemy's plans" and that "He foretold that his enemy would employ two to four fast battleships" (Morison, *History of United States Naval Operations in World War II*, vol. 4, *Coral Sea, Midway, and Submarine Operations* [1949], pp. 93–94). He does not mention Commander Joseph J. Rochefort's codebreaking activity in Pearl Harbor, which had provided this information and had been mentioned in the Pearl Harbor hearings. Of the spectacular midair assassination of Admiral Isoroku Yamamoto, made possible by intercepting and solving his coded itinerary, Morison says only "As had been predicted...." (Morison, *History of United States Naval Operations in World War II*, vol. 6, *Breaking the Bismarcks Barrier* [1954], p. 128). The *New York Times*

series on the Yamamoto shootdown, written by Army Air Forces Captain Thomas G. Lanphier, Jr., one of the pilots, says only that Yamamoto arrived at the time and place that "the White House cablegram had promised" (15 September 1945, p. 5). Craven and Cate, eds., write in *The Army Air Forces in World War II*, vol. 4, *The Pacific: Guadalcanal to Saipan, August 1942 to July 1944* (1950), pp. 213–14, that "The decoders in Washington had precise information on Yamamoto's itinerary." In fact, an American naval cryptanalyst in the Pacific, Marine Corps Major Alva B. Lasswell, had solved the Yamamoto itinerary message and Nimitz ordered the assassination to proceed (Edwin T. Layton with Roger Pineau and John Costello, *And I Was There* [New York: Morrow, 1985], p. 475). Moreover, King's report never mentions either the codebreaking that largely enabled American submarines to sink many Japanese troop convoys and freighters or the solutions that enabled Allied convoys to dodge U-boat wolfpacks; of the latter, he writes only that the Allies "made available the latest intelligence" (207). A story on 7 June 1942 in the *Chicago Tribune* about Midway indeed stated that "the strength of Japanese forces…. was well known in American naval circles several days before the battle," but it never specified cryptanalysis; in any event, the Japanese never saw it. Gabriel Schoenfeld, *Necessary Secrets: National Security, the Media and the Rule of Law* (New York: Norton, 2010), discusses this case but with several errors.

10. *Pearl Harbor Attack*, 3: 1132–33.
11. Reprinted in *New York Times*, 8 December 1945, p. 5; *Time, 17* December 1945; *Life*, 19 December 1945; and perhaps other publications as well.
12. Hugh M. Cole, *The Ardennes: Battle of the Bulge*, U.S. Army in World War II (Washington, DC: Department of the Army, 1965); Forrest C. Pogue, *The Supreme Command*, U.S. Army in World War II (Washington, DC: Department of the Army, 1954). For reminiscing historians, including Cole: Memo, Frank R. Shirer, chief, Historical Resources Branch, U.S. Army Center of Military History. Pogue made his statement at the National Security Agency after the Ultra revelations. Memo, David Hatch, historian, National Security Agency.
13. David Kahn, *Seizing the Enigma: The Race to Break the German U-boat Codes, 1939–1943*, 1998 corrected edition (New York: Barnes & Noble, 2009), pp. 234–45; R. A. Ratcliff, "Searching for Security: The German Investigations into Enigma's Security," *Intelligence and National Security*, Vol. 14 (Spring 1999), pp. 146–67, esp. 157–61. This issue is a special one on *Allied and Axis Signals Intelligence in World War II*, edited by David Alvarez and later reprinted as a separate book (Portland, OR: Frank Cass, 1999). See also Timothy P. Mulligan, "The German Navy Examines Its Cryptographic Security, October 1941," *Military Affairs*, Vol. 49 (April 1985), pp. 75–79.
14. Some are described in Willi Jensons withdrawn dissertation, "Hilfsgeräte der Kryptographie" (Flensburg, Germany, 1955). A copy is at the National Cryptologic Museum, Fort Meade, Maryland. Walther Seifert, head of evaluation for the Forschungsamt, said that that agency used

Hollerith machines for cryptanalysis (David Kahn, *Hitler's Spies* [New York: Macmillan, 1978], pp. 181, 575). And though a German naval cryptanalyst, Lieutenant Hans-Joachim Frowein, broke messages with a crib using a punched-card mechanism in 1944 (TICOM Report I-38, "Report on Interrogation of Lt. Frowein of OKM/4Skl/III, on his work on the security of the German naval four-wheel Enigma"), his organization seems to have regarded this as merely a curiosity and never envisioned the mass testing of intercepts against supposed plaintexts that the Turing bombe did. A Kriegsmarine report of 10 July 1944 on cipher security, "Marineschlüsseldienst und Marinefunkverfahren": OKM: Sk1 2329/44, in captured German naval records PG 17626: PRO: ADM 223/505, The National Archives (TNA), Kew, United Kingdom, says that the Cipher Section (Chi) of the Oberkommando der Wehrmacht (the High Command of the Armed Forces) found that the Enigma was vulnerable if three things were assumed. The first supposed that an intercept ran 300 letters — not uncommon in naval traffic. The second involved a complicated condition that had little importance for naval traffic. The third factor supposed "extraordinary mechanical outlay on the part of the enemy" for cryptanalysis. The B-Dienst (Beobachtungs-Dienst, the German naval codebreaking organization) observed that, though it could conceive of a machine to do this, "we have none here or under consideration." I am obliged to Ralph Erskine for these references. For a general overview, see Ralph Erskine, "Enigma's Security: What the Germans Really Knew," in *Action This Day*, eds. Michael Smith and Ralph Erskine (London, U.K.: Bantam Press, 2001), pp. 370–85.

15. Of course, the German cryptologists may have unconsciously resisted facing the possibility of Allied solution of the Enigma. For if they admitted it, they would have had to scrap familiar mechanisms and years of experience, invent a new system, test it, win approval for it, manufacture thousands of machines, distribute them, train personnel in their use, and put them into service, preferably all at once (to avoid compromises), with commanders likely to rage at them over the inevitable delays and blunders. This would require an immense amount of work. Everyone would hate them for it. And they would have to admit to themselves, their colleagues, and their superiors that they had been incompetent and that their error had led to the deaths of many of their countrymen. They would have to face the wrath of Dönitz—and possibly of Hitler. They might not have wanted to look very hard at the possible insecurity of the Enigma.

16. David Kahn, "Secrets of the Nazi Archives," *Atlantic Monthly*, Vol. 229 (May 1969), pp. 50–56, tells about the seizure, processing, and historians' exploitation of these documents.

17. J.I.C. (45) 223 (O) (Final), 20th July 1945, File Number 70/27, CAB 103/288, TNA. Henceforth only by CAB number.

18. C 103089-90, Folder CCS 337 (9-12-43), Sec. 1 to CCS 350.05 (1.1.45), Box 251, Central Decimal File, 1942-45, Record Group 218 (Records of the Joint Chiefs of Staff), NARA. Henceforth just by serial numbers beginning with C, all in this file.

19. C 103099.

20. C 103111.

21. J.I.C. 553/48, CAB 103/288.

22. The biography is by Karl Heinz Abshagen. The review appeared in the *Cornhill Magazine* (Summer 1950), but this and later references to his review of Kim Philby's autobiography, published in *Encounter* (April 1968), are to their reprints in H. Trevor-Roper's *The Philby Affair* (London, U.K.: William Kimber, 1968), "all Abwehr hand-cyphers", 116. Hints and oblique references are in J. C. Masterman, *The Double-Cross System in the War of 1939 to 1945* (New Haven, CT: Yale University Press, 1975).

23. Wladyslaw Kozaczuk, *Bitwa o Tajeminice: slubzby wywiadowcze Polski i Rzeszy Niemieckiej 1922–1939* (Warsaw, Poland: Ksiazka i Wiedza, 1967), pp. 126–28.

24. Flesch told me this during a visit in Bad Godesberg in 1969.

25. Michel Garder, *La Guerre secrète des services spéciaux français 1935—1945* (Paris, France: Plon, 1967), pp. 77–79.

26. Gert Buchheit, *Die Anonyme Macht* (Frankfurt am Main, Germany: Athenaion, 1968), at 110, 229. In his later book *Spionage in zwei Weltkriegen* (Landshut, Germany: Verlag Politisches Archiv, 1975), Buchheit gave, at 94-95,96-99,101, part of the name of the spy who betrayed details of the Enigma to the French: Hans-Thilo Schmidt, which I independently and fully but later discovered (David Kahn, "How I Discovered World War IIs Greatest Spy," *Cryptologia*, Vol. 34 [January 2010], pp. 12–21).

27. Kim Philby, *My Silent War* (New York: Grove Press, 1968), pp. 55, 57, 105–8, 111.

28. Trevor-Roper, *The Philby Affair*, p. 74.

29. Gustave Bertrand, *Enigma: ou la Plus Grande Enigme de la Guerre 1939—1945* (Paris, France: Plon, 1973).

30. Michael Herman, a former official at Government Communications Headquarters (GCHQ), and his "Secret Intelligence in an Open Society," not yet published. I am grateful to Mr. Herman for letting me see this article in draft form.

31. Sir Michael Howard, letter, 19 March 2010.

32. Interview with Sir Joe Hooper, a former head of GCHQ, undated.

33. Telephone interview with Sir Arthur "Bill" Bonsall, 30 April 2010.

34. Howard, letter.

35. F. W. Winterbotham, *The Ultra Secret* (London, U.K.: George Weidenfeld, 1974). For some of the publishing details of Winterbotham and other revelations, see Robin Denniston, "Three Kinds of Hero: Publishing the Memoirs of Secret Intelligence People," *Intelligence and National Security*, Vol. 7 (April 1992), pp. 112–25. Denniston, then a publisher, now a priest of the Church of England, is the son of Robin Denniston, head of British codebreaking from World War I to World War II. His biography of his father is *Thirty Secret Years: A. G. Denniston's Work in Signals Intelligence*

1914–1944 (Clifton-upon-Teme, U.K.: Polperro Heritage Press, 2007). For Winterbotham as a best-seller, at least in the United States, see the *York Times Book Review* best-seller lists for the fall of 1974.

36. For a knowledgeable view of the value of codebreaking, see Sir Harry Hinsley, "The Counterfactual History of No Ultra," *Cryptologia*, Vol. 20 (October 1996), pp 308–24.
37. Shirer memo.
38. CAB 103/288, pages not numbered.
39. Hinsley, et al., Vol. 2, pp. 59–62, and Bradley F. Smith, *Sharing Secrets with Stalin: How the Allies Traded Intelligence, 1941–1945* (Lawrence, KS: University Press of Kansas, 1996). The Russians were also sometimes reading Enigma messages. A German report of a conference of radio specialists, 17 January 1943, states: "It has been determined with certainty that in individual cases the Russians have succeeded in solving radio messages that were enciphered with the Enigma. The reason for this, aside from general key failures, is that too great a number of messages were encrypted with the same key. Therefore from now on thrice daily key changes for machine encryption." Frame 7108489, Roll 83, T-311, Microfilm of captured German records, NARA. See also David Kahn, "Soviet Comint in the Cold War," *Cryptologia*, Vol. 22 (January 1998), pp. 1–24 at 13–14.
40. "Machines and the man," *Sunday Times* (London), 23 October 1983, p. 42, a positive review of Andrew Hodges's excellent *Alan Turing: The Enigma* (London, U.K.: Burnett Books, 1983).

PART IV

A THEORY, CLAUSEWITZ, AND MORE

"A Historical Theory of Intelligence" starts with the biology of threat assessment, progresses to the mechanical and electrical enlargement of human senses, discusses the human resistance to often unwanted information, and concludes with the value of correct information to humankind. "Clausewitz on Intelligence" shows why Clausewitz disdained intelligence—it was often late or wrong—and how modern technology has somewhat invalidated his view but why in the larger sense it remains true. "Surprise and Secrecy" suggests that surprise is a consequence not of insufficient information but of insufficient time to digest it and that secrecy can be divided into binary digits and so analyzed mathematically. "Intelligence Lessons in Macbeth" shows that even the strongest leaders sometimes dodge unpalatable information. "Garbles" narrates how errors in encryption or transmission can sometimes have history-altering effects. "The Cryptologic Origin of Braille" reveals how an encryption inspired Louis Braille to invent his writing for the blind. "The Only Fake Message I Know Of" tells of a German case in World War I. "The Prehistory of the General Staff" finds parallels in political (including military) and commercial activity.

17

AN HISTORICAL THEORY
OF INTELLIGENCE*

Intelligence has been an academic discipline for half a century now. Almost from the start, scholars have called for a theory of intelligence. None has been advanced. Although some authors entitle sections of their work 'theory of intelligence', to my knowledge no one has proposed concepts that can be tested. I propose here some principles that I believe warrant being called a theory of intelligence because they offer explanations or predictions that can be seen to be true or untrue. I believe that the facts I give validate the theory; other scholars may adduce facts that disprove it.

I define intelligence in the broadest sense as information. None of the definitions that I have seen work. It is like the term 'news'. Though all but impossible to define, every journalist knows what it is: when something newsworthy is said in a court or a legislative hearing, all the reporters start taking notes.

My principles seek to deal with the past, the present, and the future of intelligence by accounting for the rise of intelligence to its current importance, explaining how it works, and specifying its main unsolved problems.

The Past

The roots of intelligence are biological. Every animal, even a protozoan, must have a mechanism to perceive stimuli, such as noxious chemicals, and to judge whether they are good or bad for it. At that level intelligence is like breathing: essential to survival, but not to dominance. To this primitive capacity for getting information from objects, humans have joined the ability to obtain it from words.

* From *Intelligence and National Security*, 16(3), Autumn 2001, 79–92.

This verbal ability has led to a form of intelligence far more powerful than the kind used by animals or men to hunt prey or flee predators. It has driven the rise of intelligence to its present significance.

For intelligence has not always been as important or as ubiquitous as it is today. Of course, rulers in all times have used it, and have even paid tribute to it. Rameses II beat prisoners of war to make them reveal the location of their army.[1] The Hebrews spied out the land of Canaan before entering it.[2] Sun Tzu wrote, 'Now the reason the enlightened prince and the wise general conquer the enemy wherever they move and their achievements surpass those of ordinary men is foreknowledge.'[3] Ancient India's Machiavellian treatise on kingship, the *Arthasastra*, declares: 'My teacher says that between power (money and army) and skill in intrigue, power is better [...] No, says Kautilya, skill for intrigue is better.'[4] Caesar's legions scouted their barbarian foes.[5] In the age of absolutism, ambassadors paid informants, while specialists in curtained, candle-lit black chambers slid hot wires under wax seals to open diplomats' missives – and then decoded them.[6] Before the Battle of Prague, Frederick the Great observed his enemies' dispositions from a steeple.

But these and similar episodes were sporadic. Most did not stem from an organized effort to gain intelligence. Usually, generals won battles without much more information about their foes than seeing where they were. Cannae, the classic victory of warfare, in which Hannibal encircled a larger Roman force and annihilated it, owed nothing to intelligence. Though rulers outlined campaigns, they did not detail mobilization and battle plans, leaving intelligence little to discover. That is why, in fourteen out of Sir Edward Creasy's *Fifteen Decisive Battles of the World: from Marathon to Waterloo* (1851), victory was decided by strength, brains, and will – with knowledge of the enemy playing an insignificant role. The exception was the Battle of the Metaurus River in Italy in 207 B.C. The Romans, having intercepted a Carthaginian message, were able to concentrate their forces, defeat Hasdrubal before his brother Hannibal could reinforce him[7], and become the chief power of the Western world.

The French and industrial revolutions begat new conditions. In shaping the modern world, they created modern intelligence. The desire of Frenchmen to defend their new democratic nation against the invading armies of monarchist states, and the need to counter the professionalism of these states' forces with a superiority in numbers, led to armies far larger than those of the past. By 1794, France had a million men under arms. The *levée en masse* called for a war economy to support it. Crops were requisitioned. Industrial output was nationalized. Suddenly, factors that had never counted in war became significant. It mattered little to a medieval king how much coal and iron his enemy could produce; such knowledge was vital to a modern head of state. Railroads made possible the rapid mobilization, concentration, and supply of large bodies of troops. These deployments called for war plans far more detailed than any ever envisioned by Caesar or Frederick. At last, intelligence had targets that gave it a chance to play a major role in war.

The industrial and political revolutions also expanded the sources that enabled intelligence to gain access to these new targets. I divide these sources into two kinds.

One consists of information drawn from things, not words. It is seeing marching troops, fortifications, supply dumps, campfire smoke; hearing tank-motor noise, smelling cooking, feeling ground vibrations. I call it physical intelligence. For centuries it came only from the observations of the common soldier, patrols, the cavalry. But the balloon, the Zeppelin, the airplane provided more physical intelligence more quickly than the deepest-driving horsemen. The camera saw more than the eye and reproduced its vision for others. Radar detected oncoming bombers long before humans, even aided by searchlights, could spot them. In addition, larger armies meant more prisoners who might report on, say the supply situation or artillery positions. All these sources provided more physical intelligence than armies had ever been able to get before.

But this increase was greatly outstripped by the growth of the second source, verbal intelligence. This acquires information from a written or oral source, such as a stolen plan, a report on troop morale, an overheard order, even a computerized strength report.[8] Verbal intelligence made intelligence as important as it is today.

Verbal intelligence had long been relatively sparse. But the two revolutions engendered new sources. Larger armies yielded more documents for seizure. Parliamentary government, with its debates and public reports, exposed many specifics about a nation's military strength and programs. A daily press reported on these as well as on the economic situation. The tapping of telegraph wires and the interception of radio messages furnished far more verbal intelligence than the occasional waylaying of a courier ever did.

This growth is significant because verbal intelligence can furnish more valuable information than physical. Understanding this must begin with an acknowledgment that war has both a material and a psychological component. The material elements consist of such tangibles as troops, guns, and supplies. The psychological comprises such matters as a commander's will, his tactical ability, and the morale of his troops. The material factors dominate: the most brilliant, most determined commander of a regiment cannot withstand an army.[9] And this factor is served by verbal intelligence, while the less important psychological component is served by physical intelligence. The reason is this: the men and weapons that are the sources of physical intelligence affirm the likelihood of an encounter with greater probability than a plan, for men cannot move guns or troops as easily as they can rewrite orders. Greater probability is another way of saying less anxiety, and anxiety is a psychological factor. Physical intelligence, by lessening anxiety, steadies command. On the other hand, verbal intelligence deals with intentions, and just as the enemy needs time to realize those plans, so a commander who knows about them gains time to prepare against them. He can shift his forces from an unthreatened flank to an endangered one, for example. In other words, verbal intelligence magnifies strength – or, in the current jargon, is a force multiplier. Thus it serves the material component of war, and because that component is the more decisive, verbal intelligence influences more outcomes than physical.[10]

For the first 4,000 years of warfare, up to the start of World War I, nearly all information came from physical intelligence. That is why intelligence played a relatively minor role: physical intelligence does not often help commanders to win battles. Then, when the guns of August began firing, radio, which in effect turns over a copy of each of its messages to the foe, and the trench telephone, which lets indiscreet chatter be easily overheard, generated enormous quantities of verbal intelligence. These two new sources helped important commanders win important victories.

In August 1914, Germany's interception of a radioed plain-language Russian order told General Paul von Hindenburg and his deputy, General Erich Ludendorff, that they would have time to shift troops from a northern front in East Prussia, where the Russians were advancing slowly, to a southern one, where the Germans could outnumber them. The Germans made the move – and won the Battle of Tannenberg, starting Russia into ruin and revolution.[11] In 1917, Britain's cryptanalysis and revelation of the Zimmermann telegram – in which Germany's foreign minister, Arthur Zimmermann, promised Mexico her 'lost territory' in Texas, New Mexico, and Arizona if she would join Germany in a war against America – helped bring the United States into the war, with all that that has entailed.[12] It was the most important intelligence success in history. Britain's knowledge of Germany's naval codes enabled the Royal Navy to block every sortie of Germany's High Seas Fleet – and so, some have argued, keep it from winning the war in an afternoon.

Verbal intelligence served on the tactical level as well. It helped the Germans when, in 1916, the British fought to take the adjoining villages of Ovilliers and La Boisselle on the Somme. The British suffered casualties in the thousands. In a captured enemy dugout, they found a complete transcript of one of their operations orders. A brigade major had read it in full over a field telephone despite the protest of his subordinate that the procedure was dangerous. 'Hundreds of brave men perished', the British signal historian related, 'hundreds more were maimed for life as the result of this one act of incredible foolishness.'[13]

At last the admirals and generals understood. Intelligence had made its influence clear to them in the way they knew best. Despite their reluctance to share power and glory with intelligence officers, they realized that to spurn intelligence might cost them a battle or even a war – and their jobs. They and their governments drew the appropriate conclusions. Britain, Germany, Italy, and the United States, none of which had had codebreaking agencies before the war, established them after it. Germany, the most conservative state, whose General Staff had long subordinated intelligence to planning, created for the first time in its history a permanent peacetime military agency to evaluate all information.[14] Intelligence had arrived as a significant instrument of war.

And in the next war, verbal sources made intelligence even more useful to commanders. It sped victory, saving treasure and lives. The reading of U-boat messages enciphered in the Enigma machine shortened the Battle of the Atlantic, the most fundamental struggle of the war, by months. Other Enigma solutions disclosed some of the Wehrmacht's tactical plans, particularly in France in 1944. Cracking the Japanese 'Purple' machine enabled the Allies to read, for example, the dispatches of the Japanese ambassador in Germany, giving them what US Army Chief of Staff General George C. Marshall called 'our main basis of information regarding Hitler's intentions in Europe'.[15] The Battle of Midway, which turned the tide of the war in the Pacific, was made possible by intelligence from codebreaking. Marshall described its value:

> Operations in the Pacific are largely guided by the information we obtain of Japanese deployments. We know their strength in various garrisons, the rations and other stores continuing available to them, and what is of vast importance, we check their fleet movements and the movements of their convoys. The heavy losses reported from time to time which they sustain by reason of our submarine action largely result from the fact that we know the sailing dates and routes of their convoys and can notify our submarines to lie in wait at the proper points.[16]

Generals actually praised intelligence. Marshall said the solutions 'contribute greatly to the victory and tremendously to the saving in American lives'.[17] General Dwight D. Eisenhower wrote to the head of the British secret service, whose best information came from codebreaking, that 'the intelligence which has emanated from you [...] has been of priceless value to me'.[18] Their tributes crowned the ascent of intelligence from its humble biological origins as a mere instrument of survival to its supreme capability: helping a nation win a war.

The Present

The theory of verbal and physical intelligence explains, I believe, how intelligence grew – its past. But it also describes the present, by showing how physical intelligence steadies command and verbal intelligence magnifies strength. So I believe it can be incorporated into the principles that a theory of intelligence should offer. Indeed, it forms the first of three. This first principle defines the function of intelligence. Magnifying strength and steadying command may be compressed into this: Intelligence optimizes one's resources. I call it O'Brien's Principle, after Patrick O'Brien, an economic historian, who casually remarked to me before lunch one day at St Antony's College, Oxford, 'Well, David, isn't all intelligence just about optimizing one's resources?' This is the fundamental, the ultimate purpose of intelligence.[19]

O'Brien's Principle, like any logical proposition, may be obverted. A unit may not have intelligence and thus may not optimize its resources. It may be overwhelmed or, in intelligence terms, surprised. Surprise is the obverse of O'Brien's Principle.

Another corollary of O'Brien's Principle explains what a commander does when he has no intelligence, or faulty intelligence: I have dubbed this the null hypothesis. In the physical realm, he creates a reserve. The purpose of a reserve, Clausewitz said, is 'to counter unforeseen threats [...] Forces should be held in reserve according to the degree of strategic uncertainty.'[20] In the mental realm, the commander must remain firm in his decisions. He 'must trust his judgment and stand like a rock on which the waves break in vain [...] The role of determination is to limit the agonies of doubt.'[21] In other words, when a commander lacks the information that can optimize his resources, he must replace it with force and will. These are the counterparts of intelligence in the physical and psychological components of war.[22]

The second permanent principle of intelligence holds that it is an auxiliary, not a primary, element in war. Some writers say loosely that intelligence has won this battle or that, but this is hyperbole. Battles and wars are won by men and guns, brains and will. Intelligence merely serves these. It is secondary to disposing one's forces, obtaining supplies, inspiring the troops. When I asked a general once whether he would rather have a good intelligence man on his staff or a good commander for one of his division's three regiments, he laughed, and his wife said that even she knew the answer to that one. The regimental commander, they said, was far more important. Colonel David Henderson, one of the first military men to study modern intelligence, declared in *The Art of Reconnaissance* (1907) that information cannot be classed with such matters as tactics, organization, discipline, numbers, or weapons because 'its influence is indirect, while theirs is direct'.[23] It is indeed a force multiplier and facilitator of command, but it cannot always make up for insufficient strength or inadequate leadership. It is a service, not an arm.

The third principle is perhaps the most interesting. It came to me when, while working on a book, I was looking for cases in which intelligence helped win battles. I noticed that I was finding many more defensive victories than offensive. These ranged from battles of world-wide importance, such as those of the Metaurus, Tannenberg, and Midway, to smaller operational clashes, such as the German Ninth Army's rebuff of a Soviet offensive south of Rzhev in November 1942 on the basis of all-source intelligence,[24] down to tactical actions, such as the repulse of a Soviet counterattack out of Sevastopol on 21 January 1942, to which wiretaps had alerted the German 24th Infantry Division.[25] In all of these, intelligence helped award victory to the defenders. On the other hand, when intelligence helped win offensive victories, it rarely served directly, as by ascertaining enemy strength or intentions. Rather, as at D-Day, it aided deception – a doubly indirect service. Wondering why intelligence seemed to play so much more significant a role in the defense than in the offense, I looked up the definitions of these two modes to see if they offered a clue. Clausewitz's seemed to, and eventually I propounded a hypothesis. It maintained that intelligence is essential to the defense but not the offense. This theory seemed to explain several phenomena, suggesting that it might be valid.

Intelligence exists, of course, in both the offense and the defense, but in different ways. The difference is that between an accompanying and a defining characteristic. All elephants are gray, but grayness is not a defining characteristic of elephants, merely an accompanying one. Intelligence is a defining characteristic of the defensive; it is only an accompanying characteristic of the offense.

'What is the concept of defense?' asked Clausewitz. 'The parrying of a blow. What is its characteristic feature? Awaiting the blow.'[26] Now, an army can await a blow only if it expects one, and it can expect one only on the basis of information or belief, right or wrong, about the enemy. There can be, in other words, no defense without intelligence. And Clausewitz says the same thing contrapositively when he asserts that surprise is needed for an offensive victory.[27]

To defend is to acknowledge that the initiative comes from the enemy. And, indeed, the offense acts, the defense reacts. The offense prescribes to the enemy; it makes the basic decisions. It is 'complete in itself,'[28] said Clausewitz. Thus, information about enemy intentions, while helpful and to a certain degree always present (an army must see its enemy to fight it), is not essential to an offensive victory.

An invading force can march about the countryside, imposing its will, without needing to know where the enemy is. If it learns that the enemy plans to counterattack, it shifts to a defensive mode – and then it requires intelligence. Military theorist Barry Posen has observed, in the terms of information theory, that the offensive, by seizing the initiative and thereby structuring the battle, reduces uncertainty[29] (one reason commanders love it). And less uncertainty means less need for intelligence – which, in one of its functions, steadies command.[30]

What all of this says is this: while intelligence is necessary to the defense, it is only contingent to the offense. The validity of this principle[31] is demonstrated, I believe, by two data. One is the relative frequency of defensive intelligence successes over offensive ones – the phenomenon that started me on the search. The second is that the nations that are aggressive tend to neglect intelligence, while nations in a defensive posture emphasize and rely on it. A clear example is Poland between World Wars I and II. Her fear of being gobbled up by one or the other of her powerful neighbors motivated her – alone of all the powers – to crack the German Enigma cipher machine. Another case is Britain. She long based her foreign policy on the balance of power, which is a reactive technique; it needs intelligence to succeed – and Britain's secret services were legendary. An example that proves the irrelevance of intelligence to the offensive is Nazi Germany. Hitler expected to dictate (and for a while did dictate) to others as he began to conquer the world; for this he did not need intelligence, so he neglected his espionage and cryptanalytic organs to concentrate instead on Stukas, Panzers, and elite divisions – and when the war came, his inadequate intelligence failed him.[32] During the Cold War, the United States, worried about Soviet aggression, enormously extended its intelligence agencies. And the Soviet Union, almost paranoid about encirclement and subversion, developed the largest intelligence system on earth.

The Future

These three principles of intelligence – it optimizes resources, it is an auxiliary function in war, and it is essential to the defense but not to the offense – seek to explain intelligence's operation and its place in the universe, just as the theory of the rise of verbal intelligence seeks to explain how intelligence became as important as it is.

But what must intelligence do to improve? What problems must it resolve? What is its future?

I ask this in the largest sense. It is not a question of whether the end of the Cold War will decrease intelligence activity or whether the need to watch a multiplicity of nations, ethnic groups, economic institutions, and terrorists will increase it. Nor is it a question of techniques and their constant seesaw struggle with countermeasures. In response to the pervasiveness of this century's intelligence, a technology of stealth – the silent submarine, the bomber almost invisible to radar – has emerged. This, in turn, has given rise to ever more refined techniques of detection, such as instruments that spot the gravitational anomalies created by a mass of metal underwater. But none of these issues raise fundamental questions about the future of intelligence – nor does the perennial difficulty that these sensors collect far more raw data than the agencies can evaluate in usable time.

Intelligence faces two all-encompassing, never-ending problems. Both are ultimately unsolvable. But intelligence must strive for a solution in the way that a graphed function reaches for – but never actually meets—its asymptote. The first problem is how to foretell what is going to happen. The goal, of course, is to predict everything. And certainly prediction is better in many cases that it ever was before. The new ability springs from the growth in intelligence tools. During World War II, Allied codebreaking revealed many more U-boat operations than it did in World War I. Wellington said, 'All the business of war... is... guessing what is at the other side of the hill'.[33] Today, the near blanketing of the theater of war with Buck Rogers collection devices – over-the-horizon radar, television cameras in the noses of drones and smart bombs, wide-ranging and detailed surveillance by satellite – renders the other side of the hill almost as visible as this side. It is hard to imagine an invasion like that of D-Day surprising any nation possessing today's observation tools. Still, not everything can be known in advance. Camouflage conceals men and weapons. Commanders change their plans. Accidents happen. These hindrances are multiplied a thousandfold in dealing not with a confined though complex activity like a single battle but with the major events of the post-World War II world, such as, for example, the fall of the Shah of Iran. Many more factors, many more people come into play than in a limited action. Even without secrecy, the interaction of these elements is all but incalculable. As Clausewitz said of the difficulty of evaluating another state's capabilities and intentions, 'Bonaparte was quite right when he said that Newton himself would quail before the algebraic problems it would pose.'[34]

This is why intelligence did not foretell North Korea's gamble in attacking South Korea, the Soviet emplacement of nuclear missiles in Cuba, the end of the Cold War itself. Prediction may be getting better, but it can never be perfect.

Even if it were, it would confront intelligence's other basic problem: how to get statesmen and generals to accept information that they do not like. This problem – which may be called the Cassandra complex – is as old as mankind. Pharaoh slew the bearers of ill tidings. Stalin ignored dozens of warnings that Germany was about to attack his country. Hitler swept aerial photographs from his desk when that indisputable evidence showed overwhelming enemy strength. The problem was clearly seen by Germany's pre-World War I Chief of the General Staff, Field Marshal Count Alfred von Schlieffen: 'The higher commander generally makes himself a picture of friend and foe, in the painting of which personal wishes provide the main elements. If incoming reports appear to correspond with this picture, they are accepted with satisfaction. If they contradict it, they are discarded as entirely false.'[35] When Secretary of the Navy Frank Knox was told that the Japanese had bombed Pearl Harbor, he exclaimed, 'My God, this can't be true. This must mean the Philippines.'

This condition, which psychologists call denial, is not limited to military or political affairs. People often reject reality. An investor does not want to hear all the reasons that a project may fail. A husband insists that his wife, coming home late, is faithful. As Rod Stewart sings, 'Still I look to find a reason to believe.' Shakespeare long ago set out the phenomenon in *Troilus and Cressida:* '... yet there is a credence in my heart,/An esperance so obstinately strong,/That doth invert th' attest of eyes and ears.'[36] Edna St. Vincent Millay asked her readers to 'Pity me that the heart is slow to learn/What the swift mind beholds at every turn.'[37] And a little boy begged of Shoeless Joe Jackson, upon hearing that he had betrayed a World Series for money, 'Say it ain't so, Joe.'

Can this very human disposition be changed? Can the facts and logic of intelligence ever overcome wishful thinking? At present, they can only do so if the feelings are not deep-seated. If the consequence of facing the facts is too painful, the evidence will be ignored, suppressed, denied.

Where then is intelligence headed? A new factor darkens its future. Intelligence owes its success to the growth of verbal information. But as the cheap, miniaturized, unbreakable systems of cryptography proliferate, they will increasingly deprive cryptanalysts of the opportunities that data banks and the Internet and cellular telephones offer. As America's first modern cryptologist, Herbert O. Yardley, said in 1929 of AT&T's unbreakable one-time tape cipher machine, 'Sooner or later all governments, all wireless companies, will adopt some such system. And when they do, cryptography [codebreaking], as a profession, will die.'[38] The amputation of intelligence's right arm will cripple it. Just how serious this problem will be, however, no one yet knows.

But other factors counter this one and brighten the promise of intelligence. People see the advantage of permitting intelligence – in both its politico-military and its personal meanings – to rule emotion. They know that reason usually produces better solutions to problems than feelings do. This explains the growth of psychotherapy. This is part of what St Paul meant in his profound statement to the Corinthians: 'For we cannot do anything against the truth, but only for the truth.'[39] This is why intelligence is so useful. As David Hume wrote in *An Enquiry Concerning Human Understanding*: 'We may observe, in every art or profession, even those which most concern life or action, that a spirit of accuracy, however acquired, carries all of them nearer to that perfection.' He calls this 'the genius of philosophy', making intelligence a branch of that high domain, and says that from this accuracy, 'the politician will acquire greater foresight and subtlety, [...] and the general more regularity in his discipline, and more caution in his plans and operations.'[40] Reason also produces technologies superior to those stemming from tradition or charisma, and these technologies allow their societies to dominate others. Witness the subjugation of China at the turn of the twentieth century, the conquest of Native Americans, Europeans' grab of colonies in Africa, the rise of post-Perry Japan. The very establishment of intelligence agencies indicates a tendency toward greater reliance on facts and logic. The trend's success suggests that it will continue.

Accentuating this trend is an aspect of man's nature. Aristotle opened his *Metaphysics* by stating, 'All men by nature desire to know.' The first man is the first example. Adam wanted to know what God told him he should not know, so he ate of the fruit of the tree of the knowledge of good and evil, and thus brought death, sin, and sorrow into the world. Like Adam, like Faust, every intelligence service strives to realize what the evangelist Luke put into words: 'For nothing is hid that shall not be made manifest, nor anything secret that shall not be known and come to light.'[41] None achieves it. 'It will always be a certain tragedy of every intelligence service', wrote the first head of Germany's post-World War I spy service, 'that even the best results will always lag behind the clients' desires.'[42] But the absence of perfection does not keep leaders, political and military, from letting intelligence serve them, any more than they let the absence of perfection keep them from using any other resource they have. Evidently they believe intelligence's results are worth its costs. Should they always follow its sometimes implied advice? No. It may be wrong. It is almost certainly incomplete. But they should at least take it into account.

The universal tendency toward least effort[43] will further enlarge intelligence. As an optimizer of resources, intelligence saves money by reducing the need to buy military equipment – though, as merely an auxiliary element of war, it cannot reduce this need to zero. Since it is integral to the defense, intelligence will be increasingly seen as essential to nonaggressive nations. Yet it must improve its predictions and must convince leaders to accept them if it is to fully realize its potential.

That potential spreads beyond the military. Like the benefactions of knowledge, of which it is a form, the benefactions of intelligence touch all humankind. In war, intelligence shortens the struggle, sparing gold and blood. In peace, it reduces uncertainty and so relaxes tensions among states, helping to stabilize the international system. These are the ultimate human goods of intelligence; these are the ways this servant of war brings peace to man.

Notes

1. Sir Alan Gardiner, *The Kadesh Inscriptions of Ramesses II* (Oxford, U.K.: Oxford University Press, 1960), pp. 28–30.
2. Numbers 13.

3. Sun Tzu, *The Art of War,* trans. Samuel Griffith, Vol. xiii: 3 (Oxford, U.K.: Clarendon Press 1963), p. 144.

4. R. Shamasastry, trans., *Kautilya's Arthasastra,* 4th edn. (Mysore, India: Sri Raghuveer, 1951), p. 637 (Bk IX, Ch.l).

5. Julius Caesar, *The Gallic War,* ii.17.

6. The most detailed description of the workings of a black chamber, that of Austria, is by Harald Hubatschke in his 1973 dissertation for the University of Vienna, 'Ferdinand Prantner (Pseudonym Leo Wolfram), 1817–1871: Die Anfänge des Politischen Romans sowie die Geschichte der Briefspionage und des Geheimen Chiffredienstes in Österreich', at pp. 1269–1328, 1445–60.

7. *Livy,* Vol. XXVII.xliii, pp. 1–8; *Cambridge Ancient History,* rev. ed., Vol. 8 (Cambridge: Cambridge University Press, 1961–71), pp. 91–6.

8. It is important to understand that it is the source that matters, not the method of acquisition or the method of transmission. The presence of tanks can be ascertained by a spy and reported by telephone, but this information remains physical intelligence. Enemy plans can likewise be discovered by a spy and relayed by a photograph, but the information is verbal intelligence. The difference rests solely on the objects of intelligence themselves. Verbal objects mean verbal intelligence; nonverbal, physical intelligence.

9. The Allies beat the Germans in World War II primarily because of their overwhelming material superiority. See John Ellis, *Brute Force: Allied Tactics and Strategy in the Second World War* (London, U.K.: André Deutsch, 1990).

10. Of course physical intelligence can also reveal enemy capabilities, but doing so requires an inference – an extra step. Verbal intelligence reveals intentions without that mediation. To simplify, I have reduced this to the preceding formulation.

11. Germany, Reichsarchiv, *Der Weltkrieg: 1914 bis 1918,* Vol. 2 (Berlin, Germany: Mittler & Sohn, 1925), pp. 136–7, 351; Max Hoffman, *War Diaries and Other Papers,* trans. Eric Sutton, Vol. 2 (London, U.K.: Martin Seeker, 1929), pp. 265–7, 332.

12. David Kahn, 'Edward Bell and His Zimmermann Telegram Memoranda', *Intelligence and National Security,* Vol. 14/3 (Autumn 1999), pp. 143–59, has been superceded by Thomas Boghardt, *The Zimmermann Telegram* (Annapolis, MD: Naval Institute Press, 2012).

13. R. E. Priestly, *The Signal Service in the European War of 1914 to 1918 (France)* (London, U.K., 1921), p. 106.

14. David Kahn, *Hitler's Spies: German Military Intelligence in World War II* (New York: Macmillan, 1978), p. 418.

15. United States, Congress, Joint Committee on the Investigation of the Pearl Harbor Attack. *Pearl Harbor Attack,* Hearings, 79th Congress, Vol. 3 (Washington, DC: Government Printing Office, 1946), p. 1133.

16. *Ibid.*

17. *Ibid.*

18. Eisenhower to Menzies, 12 July 1945, Folder MELO-MEN (Misc.), Box 77, Principal File, Pre-Presidential Papers 1916–52, Dwight D. Eisenhower Library, Abilene, KS.

19. This means successful intelligence, not perfect intelligence. Failed intelligence is not considered here as intelligence.

20. Carl von Clausewitz, *On War*, trans. Michael Howard and Peter Paret (Princeton, NJ: Princeton University Press, 1976), p. 210.

21. *Ibid.*, pp. 117, 102–3.

22. I have discussed this more fully in 'Clausewitz and Intelligence', *The Journal of Strategic Studies*, Vols. 9/2 and 3 (June/Sept. 1985), pp. 117–26, later republished as *Clausewitz and Modern Strategy*, ed. Michael I. Handel (London, U.K. and Portland, OR: Frank Cass, 1986).

23. David Henderson, *The Art of Reconnaissance* (New York: Dutton, 1907), p. 2.

24. David Kahn, 'The Defense of Osuga, 1942', *Aerospace Historian*, Vol. 28 (Winter 1981), pp. 242–50.

25. Germany, Bundesarchiv-Militärarchiv, 24. Infanterie Divison, 22006/11, 19 Januar 1942; 22006/1, 21 Januar 1942; 50. Infanterie Division, 22985/4, 20 and 21 Januar 1942; Hans von Tettau und Kurt Versock, *Geschichte der 24. Infanterie-Division 1933–1945* (Stolberg: Kameradschaftsring der ehemalige 24. Infanterie-Divison, 1956), p. 24.

26. Clausewitz (note 20), p. 357.

27. *Ibid.* p. 198.

28. *Ibid.*, p. 524.

29. Barry R. Posen, *The Sources of Military Doctrine: France, Britain, and Germany Between the World Wars* (Ithaca, NY: Cornell University Press, 1984), pp. 47–8.

30. As Hamlet says, in a line generals would love, 'We defy augury' (*Hamlet*, V.ii.23). For intelligence does not always resolve problems, does not always eliminate uncertainty. In footnote 19, I excluded failed intelligence from any definition of intelligence. But partial or erroneous information certainly exists in the world, and is sometimes included in the term 'intelligence'. It is in this sense that one German officer explained that what went through generals' minds when the intelligence officer approached was 'Here comes the intelligence officer with his same old stuff. But I'm going to do it like this anyway'. See Kahn, *Hitlers Spies* (note 14), p. 415. Hamlet also maintained that uncertainty weakens determination. Referring to man's incomplete knowledge (in this case of death), he soliloquized, using 'conscience' to mean thinking, 'Thus conscience does make cowards of us all,/And thus the native hue of resolution/Is sicklied o'er with the pale cast of thought,/And enterprises of great pith and moment/With this regard their currents turn awry,/And lose the name of action.' (*Hamlet*, III.i.83–8).

31. George J. A. O'Toole, 'Kahn's Law: A Universal Principle of Intelligence', *International Journal of Intelligence and Counterintelligence*, Vol. 4 (Spring 1990), pp. 39–46.

32. This is developed at greater length in my *Hitler's Spies* (note 14), pp. 528–31.
33. John Wilson Croker, *The Croker Papers*, ed. Louis J. Jennings, Vol. 3 (London, U.K.: John Murray, 1884), p. 275.
34. Clausewitz (note 20), p. 586.
35. Generalfeldmarschall Graf Alfred von Schlieffen, *Gesammelte Schriften*, Vol. 1 (Berlin, Germany: Mittler, 1913), p. 188.
36. William Shakespeare, 'Troilus and Cressida', V.ii., pp. 120–122.
37. Edna St. Vincent Millay, 'Pity Me Not', a sonnet.
38. Herbert O. Yardley, *The American Black Chamber* (Indianapolis, IN: Bobbs-Merrill, 1931), p. 365.
39. 2 Corinthians 13:8.
40. David Hume, *An Enquiry Concerning Human Understanding* (1777) § 1:4.
41. Luke 8:17.
42. Fritz Gempp, 'Geheimer Nachrichtendienst und Spionageabwehr des Heeres.' Im Auftrag der Abwehrabteilung des Reichswehrministeriums (US National Archives microfilm T-77, Rolls 1438–1440, 1442, 1507–1509), II:7:162.
43. George K. Zipf, *Human Behavior and the Principle of Least Effort* (Cambridge, MA: Addison-Wesley, 1949).

18

CLAUSEWITZ ON
INTELLIGENCE*

Carl von Clausewitz scorned intelligence. His remarks about it are mostly pejorative. He classed it negatively among the major factors of military activity. He relegated it to a secondary role in all aspects of war.

Yet, today, commanders and military theoreticians value intelligence. They use it in their plans and battles. They emphasize it in their histories. They cite it as essential to military operations.

Of course, technology has effected this change. But technology has not outdated all Clausewitz' remarks: in the age of the ICBM, he is still cited as an authority.[1] Has he become obsolete only in intelligence? Has he become entirely obsolete in intelligence? Or have some of his views retained their validity?

Part I

In *On War*, Clausewitz rests his three-paragraph chapter on intelligence on a statement that illustrates his disdain for the activity: 'Many intelligence reports in war are contradictory; even more are false, and most are uncertain' (p. 117).[2] He summarizes his main paragraph with the lapidary 'In short, most intelligence is false' (p. 117). He expresses this view throughout the text. The third of his three major characteristics of military activity is the 'Uncertainty of All Information' (p. 140). In listing the factors that affect engagements – the psychological, physical, geographical, mathematical (lines of advance, for instance), and logistical – he excludes information about the enemy (p. 183). He says that 'The only situation a commander

---

* From David Kahn, Clausewitz and Intelligence, *Journal of Strategic Studies*, 9:2–3, 117–126, 1986. DOI: 10.1080/01402398608437261.

can know fully is his own; his opponent's he can know only from unreliable intelligence' (p. 140). In discussing the engagement, he states that 'At the moment of battle, information about the strength of the enemy is usually uncertain' (p. 233). Likewise, in strategy, decisions are based in part 'on uncertain reports' (p. 210). Indeed, *On War* contains not a single example of good intelligence ferreting out an enemy's plans, let alone an instance where such intelligence led to a victory.

Nevertheless, Clausewitz does not close his eyes to the need for information, nor does he dogmatically maintain that it can never serve. He admits, usually by implication, that it is sought and that sometimes it can help. Feints and fighting patrols have as a purpose 'making the enemy show himself' (p. 236). Advance guards and outposts are needed 'to detect and reconnoiter the enemy's approach before he comes into view' (p. 302). An army 'must use its vanguard as its strategic eyes, sending out individual detachments, spies, and so forth' (p. 259). An advanced corps 'is never intended to stop the enemy's movements, but rather, like the weight of a pendulum, to moderate and regulate them so as to make them calculable' (p. 352). An advantage of high ground is 'a wider view' (p. 352). In the politico-strategic area,

> to discover how much of our resources must be mobilized for war, we must first examine our own political aim and that of the enemy. We must gauge the strength and situation of the opposing state. We must gauge the character and abilities of its government and people and do the same in regard to our own. Finally, we must evaluate the political sympathies of other states, and the effect the war may have on them. (pp. 585–6)

In a more general sense of intelligence, he remarks 'Everyone gauges his opponent in the light of his reputed talents, his age, and his experience, and acts accordingly' (p. 137). One who did so was Frederick the Great, who, in his successful campaign of 1760, 'chose these positions and made these marches, confident in the knowledge that [Austrian Field Marshal Leopold Count von] Daun's methods, his dispositions, his sense of responsibility and his character would make such maneuvers risky but not reckless' (pp. 179–80). Clausewitz specifically lists among 'the true reasons' for victories not only of Frederick but of

Napoleon 'the correct appraisal of the opposing generals (Daun, [German Field Marshal Prince Karl Philipp zu] Schwarzenberg)' (p. 196).

Nevertheless, these occasional acknowledgments of the usefulness of intelligence bow before his more fundamental disparagement of it. Examination of what he believes are the causes of the uselessness of information helps explain why he holds this negative view.

The most important ground for his suspicion of intelligence lies in the role of chance. This concept permeates his philosophy of war. Chance reduces the accuracy and predictive value of information.

> War is the realm of chance. No other human activity gives it greater scope (p. 101)... In war more than anywhere else things do not turn out as we expect... Since all information and assumptions are open to doubt, and with chance at work everywhere, the commander constantly finds that things are not as he expected.... The very nature of interaction is bound to make it unpredictable. (p. 139)

Clausewitz makes many other comments in the same vein. And, although he nowhere says so, poor intelligence probably contributes to friction in war, which increases the effects of chance.

Another ground consists of the growth of imponderables in war. For governments in the eighteenth century, 'Their means of waging war came to consist of the money in their coffers and of such idle vagabonds as they could lay their hands on either at home or abroad. In consequence the means they had available were fairly well defined, and each could gauge the other side's potential in terms both of numbers and of time' (p. 589). But in the new wars of the French Revolution, in which not just a small professional army but the whole nation took part, 'there seemed no end to the resources mobilized; all limits disappeared in the vigor and enthusiasm shown by governments and their subjects' (pp. 592–3). Although Clausewitz does not say so explicitly, mass conscription had to lead to greater complexity in warmaking and so to greater difficulty in determining enemy potential. Support for such a view appears in his discussion of the tactical level. While Frederick did not maintain strong outposts, Napoleon 'almost always used a strong advance guard' (p. 303). One reason for this was 'the increased size of modern armies' (p. 303). Another was 'the change that had occurred in tactics... with the old system of tactics and encampment it was far easier to find out the position of the enemy than it is today' (p. 273).

A third reason for Clausewitz' suspicion of intelligence is the limitation inherent in observation. 'After all, a troop's range of vision does not usually extend much beyond its range of fire' (p. 302). Enemy forces 'may be hidden by every wood and every fold of undulating terrain' (p. 210). Night, too, 'is a great source of protection' (p. 241). Lack of strength may constrain investigation of the enemy. A small detachment cannot satisfactorily observe the enemy, 'partly because it would be more easily driven back than a large one, and partly because its means, its tools of observation, would not be sufficiently powerful' (p. 308). To these restrictions must be added a temporal one.

> Unless the enemy is so close as to be in full view (as Frederick the Great was to the Austrians before the battle of Hochkirch), knowledge of his position will be incomplete. It will be acquired from reconnaissance, patrols, prisoners' statements and spies, and it can never really be reliable for the simple reason that all such reports are always a little out of date, and the enemy may in the meantime have changed his position. (p. 273)

Finally, not even the most energetic intelligence operation can penetrate an enemy's brain; he will succeed in keeping at least some of his secrets: 'He will not just shoot his guns off blindly' (p. 273). Some things will thus remain unknown until 'the final third of battle, when the defender has revealed his whole plan' (p. 391). Battle, Clausewitz is saying, is the ultimate reconnaissance – but then it is too late.

To the limitations of collection are added those of analysis. So numerous and so nebulous are the factors involved in determining what an enemy will do that they prohibit a scientific approach. So 'colossal' a task it is for a state to assess its own and an enemy's political aims, strength, character and abilities 'in all their ramifications and diversity' that "Bonaparte was quite right when he said that Newton himself would quail before the algebraic problems it could pose" (p. 586; see also p. 112). During consideration of how much effort should be expended for a military objective,

> intellectual activity leaves the field of the exact sciences of logic and mathematics. It then becomes an art in the broadest meaning of the term – the faculty of using judgment to detect the most important and

decisive elements in the vast array of facts and situations. Undoubtedly this power of judgment consists to a greater or lesser degree of the intuitive comparison of all the factors and attendant circumstances; what is remote and secondary is at once dismissed while the most pressing and important points are identified with greater speed than could be done by strictly logical deduction (p. 585).

For Clausewitz, analysis is little more than intuition, and even that sometimes sinks to guesswork.

> In reviewing the whole array of factors a general must weigh before making his decision [on whether to press an attack], we must remember that he can gauge the direction and value of the most important ones only by considering numerous other possibilities – some immediate, some remote. He must *guess*, so to speak: guess whether the first shock of battle will steel the enemy's resolve and stiffen his resistance, or whether, like a Bologna flask, it will shatter as soon as its surface is scratched; guess the extent of debilitation and paralysis that the drying up of particular sources of supply and the severing of certain lines of communication will cause in the enemy… guess whether the other powers will be frightened or indignant. (p. 572)

The fifth and final reason for Clausewitz' distrust of intelligence is the dominance – at least at times – of preconception over fact. He recognized the importance of a person's theories or emotions. In another context, he called courage, or the sense of one's own strength, 'the lens, so to speak, through which impressions pass through the brain' (p. 137). That and other lenses can also distort information about the enemy. 'One may have been aware of it [that the enemy is stronger] all along, but for the lack of more solid alternatives this awareness was countered by one's trust in chance, good luck, Providence, and in one's own audacity and courage. All this has now turned out to be insufficient, and one is harshly and inexorably confronted by the terrible truth' (p. 255) – that the enemy is more powerful and that one has been defeated.

For all these reasons, Clausewitz looked askance upon intelligence.

Part II

Fundamental to Clausewitz' thought is the existence of both a physical and a psychological component in war. The physical consists of men, guns, horses, works. It finds an expression in Clausewitz's dictum that 'In tactics, as in strategy, superiority of numbers is the most common element in victory' (p. 194). The psychological factors – which Clausewitz calls 'moral elements' – include the skill of the commander, the experience and courage of the troops, their patriotic spirit and will.

Intelligence affects both the physical and the psychological components of war. In the physical realm, intelligence (that is, good intelligence) magnifies strength. Knowing where an enemy will attack enables a commander to put more men there, taking them from where they are less needed. In the psychological domain, intelligence improves command. Knowing that a town ahead is empty of the enemy eases a commander's mind, freeing him to resolve other problems.

The contrary of these theses is that failures of intelligence reduce strength in the physical realm and impair command in the psychological.

In the physical domain, Clausewitz expresses this effect through the concept of surprise, which by definition constitutes a failure of (the victim's) intelligence. Superiority of numbers is 'hardly conceivable' without the desire 'to take the enemy by surprise.... Surprise therefore becomes the means to gain superiority' (p. 198). Among the main factors in strategic success is

> surprise – either by actual [unexpected] assault or by deploying unexpected strength at certain points. (p. 198)... Surprising the enemy by concentrating superior strength at certain points is again comparable to the analogous case in tactics. If the defender were compelled to spread his forces over several points of access, the attacker would obviously reap the advantage of being able to throw his full strength against any one of them. (p. 364)

Clausewitz concedes that 'Even the higher, and highest, realms of strategy provide some examples of momentous surprises', as does tactics. But he emphasizes that 'history has few such events to report' (p. 200) – because in practice it [surprise] is often held up by the friction of the whole machine.... It would be a mistake, therefore, to regard surprise as a key element of success in war' (p. 198).

In the psychological domain, poor intelligence harms command most commonly by leading a general to exaggerate the enemy's strength and consequently to lose confidence. 'Most intelligence is false, and the effect of fear is to multiply lies and inaccuracies (p. 117).... Men are always more inclined to pitch their estimate of the enemy's strength too high than too low' (p. 85).[3] A general 'is exposed to countless impressions, most of them disturbing, few of them encouraging. With its mass of vivid impressions and the doubts which characterize all information and opinion, there is no activity like war to rob men of confidence in themselves and in others, and to divert them from their original course of action' (p. 108). In a strategic situation, lack of information will lead to 'most generals' being 'paralyzed by unnecessary doubts' (p. 179). The frequency of such references to psychological difficulties, and his couching them in general terms, suggests that Clausewitz believes that the impairment of command owing to poor intelligence is more common than the problems resulting from poor intelligence in the physical domain.

Part III

However, he would not have won a reputation as outstanding in his field had he not prescribed – though only by implication – what to do in the face of this inadequacy of intelligence.

In the physical field, Clausewitz made up for the reduction in strength occasioned by bad intelligence by adding men and guns. They usually take the form of a reserve. Clausewitz specifies that one of the purposes of a reserve is 'to counter unforeseen threats' (p. 210; see also p. 391). A reserve is necessary both in strategy and in tactics.

> In a tactical situation, where we frequently do not know the enemy's measures until we see them... we must always be more or less prepared for unforeseen developments, so that positions that turn out to be weak can be reinforced, and so that we can in general adjust our dispositions to the enemy actions. Such cases also occur in strategy.... In strategy too decisions must often be based on direct observation, on uncertain reports arriving hour by hour and day by day, and finally on the actual outcome of battle. It is thus an essential condition of strategic leadership that forces should be held in reserve according to the degree of strategic uncertainty. (p. 210)

In discussing defense, Clausewitz gives another example of force replacing lack of knowledge: a defender's reserve of one fourth to one third of his strength acts in part 'to protect him against the unexpected' (p. 310).

Psychologically, what substitutes for the confusion caused by poor intelligence is will power. After iterating that 'most intelligence is false', Clausewitz declares that 'the commander must trust his judgment and stand like a rock on which the waves break in vain' (p. 117). He uses this image elsewhere as well, and also makes the same point in other words. 'The role of determination is to limit the agonies of doubt (pp. 102-3).... With uncertainty in one scale, courage and self-confidence must be thrown into the other to correct the balance' (p. 86). Uncertainty is one of the four elements that make up the climate of war, the others being danger, exertion, and chance.

> If we consider them together, it becomes evident how much fortitude of mind and character are needed to make progress in these impending elements with safety and success. According to circumstance, reporters and historians of war use such terms as energy, firmness, staunchness, emotional balance, and strength of character. (p. 104)

Strength of will defends not only against external inadequacies but also against internal ones – incorrect presumptions. Thus Frederick's recognition during the daring maneuvers of his successful campaign of 1760 that Daun would not attack him called for 'boldness, resolution and strength of will to see things in this way, and not to be confused and intimidated by the danger that was still being talked and written about thirty years later' (p. 180)

Part IV

Clausewitz seems objective and sensible in his non-intelligence comments; we may presume he is the same in those dealing with intelligence. Contemporaries who wrote on war paid little attention, like him, to the subject. And up to his time history reports hardly any battles won as a consequence of good intelligence: of Edward S. Creasy's *Fifteen Decisive Battles of the World: From Marathon to Waterloo*,[4] only one – the battle of the Metaurus, in which the Romans defeated the Carthaginians – depended upon intelligence. So Clausewitz appears justified in viewing intelligence with skepticism.

In the century and a half since his death, however, whole new technologies have been created that can gather far more intelligence than was possible in his time.[5] Chief among them are the camera in an airplane or a satellite and the radio. Moreover, the establishment of intelligence agencies has given the field a permanent institutional existence. As a consequence, it has produced success after success. Satellite photography enables the United States and the Soviet Union to count with astonishing precision each other's missiles for delivering nuclear weapons.[6] Most dramatically in the First and Second World Wars, case after case attests to the power of intelligence – a power it did not have in the time of Clausewitz.

The defeat of czarist Russia, one of the most consequential events of modern times, owes not a little to intelligence. Intercepts of enemy radio messages all but enabled Generals Paul von Hindenburg and Erich Ludendorff to crush the Russians at Tannenberg.[7] Later intercepts paved the way to Brest-Litovsk. 'We were always warned by the wireless messages of the Russian staff of the position where troops were being concentrated for any new undertaking…. Only once during the whole war were we taken by surprise', wrote the chief of staff of the German armies on the eastern front.[8] Such methods, which sprouted during the first of the total wars, matured in the second. On the eastern front, the repeated tactical warnings of Russian moves, largely obtained through radio intercepts, gradually persuaded the conservative elite of the German general staff of the value of intelligence.[9] Allied intelligence was even more successful. Aerial photographs confirmed the existence and provided details of the German V-weapons.[10] Codebreaking led to the victories of Midway and the Battle of the Atlantic, to the cutting of Japan's lifelines by US submarines and the midair assassination of Admiral Isoroku Yamamoto,[11] to tactical victories on the battlefields of Europe.[12] Moreover, by engendering an atmosphere of knowing what the enemy was doing, the codebreaking facilitated command decisions.[13]

Far from being the negative, harmful element that it was in Clausewitz' time, intelligence sped victory. It shortened the war by several months, according to one authority,[14] by three years according to others.[15] Allied commanders of the Second World War extolled intelligence as neither Clausewitz nor any general of his time ever did.

Midway was 'a victory of intelligence', declared Admiral Chester Nimitz.[16] General Dwight Eisenhower said that the codebreaking intelligence was 'of priceless value to me'.[17] General George Marshall acknowledged that the solutions 'contribute greatly to the victory'.[18]

But intelligence is not perfect. Sometimes it is wrong; sometimes it is inconclusive; sometimes it is lacking.

In Vietnam, despite the use of all sorts of information-gathering devices, including sensors to count the vehicles passing them, intelligence analysts disagreed over how many troops North Vietnam had in South Vietnam.[19] In Iran, despite a strong US intelligence presence, despite the near-certainty that the telephone calls of the Ayatollah Ruhollah Khomeini from France were being monitored, US intelligence was surprised by the overthrow of the Shah. And military tactical surprises still take place: Pearl Harbor, the invasion of South Korea, the Yom Kippur War, the Falklands takeover. The causes of these intelligence failures are the same as Clausewitz' reasons for distrusting intelligence: chance, imponderables, limitations of observation and of analysis, preconceptions. Limitations of observations enabled the Japanese to pounce undetected on Pearl Harbor, for example,[20] and Israel's preconceptions played a major role in the failure of its intelligence at the start of the Yom Kippur War.[21]

Thus, although technology has invalidated Clausewitz' derision of intelligence, and although generals accept it where he rejected it, in the larger picture his views prevail. Intelligence can indeed magnify strength and improve command, but leaders do not always have it. Clausewitz, concerned less with the technological changes in war, such as intelligence's increased capabilities, than with the permanent aspects, such as the inevitability of uncertainty, found the solution to this perpetual problem. It consists of military strength and firmness of purpose.

Notes

1. I have found only scattered items on intelligence in skimming two other published Clausewitz works. Werner Hahlweg (ed.), *Schriften–Aufsätze–Studien–Briefe*, Deutsche Geschichtsquellen des 19. and 20. Jahrhunderts, 45 (Göttingen, Germany: Vandenhoek & Ruprecht, 1966), gives advice, in the lecture notes on irregular warfare, on how to use outposts and

advanced guards. But, unlike the passages on the same topics in *On War,* this shorter, earlier work does not connect the activities of these units with any larger considerations of intelligence. Werner Hahlweg (ed.), *Verstreute kleine Schriften,* Bibliotheca Rerum Militarium, XLV (Osnabrück, Germany: Biblio Verlag, 1979), offers occasional comments on intelligence. But these items add nothing significant to the material in *On War,* which, in fact, often repeats them in more refined form. For example, one of the selections in *Verstreute kleine Schriften* says, at p. 80, 'It is certainly a basis of the art [of war]: that one may count upon an enemy's erroneous conduct only insofar as it can be presumed probable.' *On War* says, at p. 117, that, in assessing information about the enemy, a commander 'should be guided by the laws of probability'.

Two recent studies of Clausewitz do not touch on intelligence: Raymond Aron's *Penser la guerre, Clausewitz* (Paris: Editions Gallimard, 1976) and Michael Howard's *Clausewitz* (New York: Oxford University Press, 1983). Ulrich Marwedel excludes intelligence in his discussion of the military philosopher's main statements on pp. 78–90 of his *Carl von Clausewitz: Personlichkeit und Wirkungsgeschichte seines Werkes bis 1918,* Militärgeschichtliches Studien, 25 (Boppard am Rhein, Germany: Harald Boldt Verlag, 1978). An index to Clausewitz' main ideas, *Clausewitz Casyndekan,* A Staff Project of Casyndekan, Inc. (Colorado Springs, CO: Casyndekan, 1969), likewise omits intelligence.

In seeking the application of Clausewitz' ideas on intelligence to the use of intelligence in the Vietnam War, I received responses from four Vietnam veterans. I thank them for their time: Lt. Eric Kronen, formerly in charge of enemy infiltration assessment, Joint Intelligence Command, US Military Assistance Command, Vietnam; Col. Jean K. Joyce, chief of the current intelligence and indications branch, Joint Intelligence Command; Col. Edward H. Caton, former chief, Joint Intelligence Command; and Air Force Maj.-Gen. Grover C. Brown, former assistant director for intelligence production, Defense Intelligence Agency.

2. All page references to *On War* are included in the text. The edition used is the English translation by Michael Howard and Peter Paret (Princeton, NJ: Princeton University Press, 1976).
3. Shakespeare said it more graphically: 'In the night, imagining some fear, How easy is a bush supposed a bear!' (*Midsummer Night's Dream,* V:i:22).
4. (London, U.K., 1851).
5. On p. 102, Clausewitz says, 'We now know more, but this makes us more, not less, uncertain'. But the intelligence experience of the Allies in the Second World War disproves this view.
6. John Prados, *The Soviet Estimate* (New York: Dial Press, 1982), pp. 203, 205, 284.
7. Max Hoffmann, *War Diaries and Other Papers,* Vol. 1, trans. Eric Sutton (London, U.K.: Martin Seeker, 1929), pp. 41, 18.
8. Max Hoffmann, *The War of Lost Opportunities* (London, U.K.: Kegan Paul, Trench, Trubner & Co., 1924), p. 132.

9. Gen. Adolf Heusinger (head of the operations branch, German general staff), interview, 8 Oct. 1973.

10. F. H. Hinsley et al., *British Intelligence in the Second World War*, Vol. 3 (London, U.K.: Her Majesty's Stationery Office, 1984), pp. 1, 368, 372, 403–4.

11. David Kahn, *The Codebreakers: The Story of Secret Writing* (New York: Macmillan, 1967), pp. 561–613 passim.

12. Ronald Lewin, *Ultra Goes to War* (New York: McGraw Hill, 1978), passim.

13. Peter Calvocoressi, *Top Secret Ultra* (New York: Pantheon, 1980), pp. 110–11.

14. Jürgen Rohwer, 'Der Einfluss der Alliierten Funkaufklärung auf den Verlauf des Zweiten Weltkrieges', *Vierteljahrshefte für Zeitgeschichte*, Vol. 27 (1979), pp. 335–69, especially 361.

15. F. H. Hinsley, quoted in Christopher Andrew and David Dilks (eds.), *The Missing Dimension: Governments and Intelligence Communities in the Twentieth Century* (Urbana, IL: University of Illinois Press, 1984), pp. 1–2. Major General Stephen A. Chamberlain, operations officer of the Southwest Pacific Area, quoted in Harold C. Deutsch, "Clients of Ultra: American Captains," *Parameters: Journal of the U.S. Army War College,* Vol. 15 (Summer, 1985), 55–62, especially 61.

16. Chester W. Nimitz and E. B. Potter (eds.), *The Great Sea War: The Story of Naval Action in World War II* (Englewood Cliffs, NJ: Prentice Hall, 1960), p. 245.

17. Eisenhower to Menzies, 12 July 1945, Eisenhower Library, Abilene, Kansas.

18. In a letter printed in United States, Congress, Joint Committee on the Investigation of the Pearl Harbor Attack, *Pearl Harbor Attack*, Vol. 3, Hearings, 79th Congress, 1st and 2nd Sessions (Washington, DC: Government Printing Office, 1946), p. 1133.

19. United States District Court for the Southern District of New York, *General William C. Westmoreland, plaintiff, vs. CBS Inc. et al. defendants,* 82 Civ. 7913 (PNL), Memorandum in Support of Defendant CBS's Motion to Dismiss and for Summary Judgment (23 May 1984), especially pp. 42–3, 60–72; Plaintiff General William C. Westmoreland's Memorandum of Law in Opposition to Defendant CBS's Motion to Dismiss and for Summary Judgment (20 July 1984), especially pp. 31–3 and Plates 11–A, -B, -C, and -D.

20. David Kahn, 'The United States Views Germany and Japan in 1941.' In *Knowing One's Enemies: Intelligence Assessment before the Two World Wars,* ed. Ernest R. May (Princeton, NJ: Princeton University Press, 1984), pp. 476–501, especially at pp. 500–1.

21. Michael Handel, *Perception, Deception and Surprise: The Case of The Yom Kippur War,* Jerusalem Papers on Peace Problems, 19 (The Hebrew University of Jerusalem: The Leonard Davis Institute for International Relations, 1976).

19

SURPRISE AND SECRECY*

Two Thoughts

May I offer two thoughts that I hope other scholars of intelligence will expand into theories that may explain aspects of intelligence? I presented them at the RAND Corporation conference on 'Toward a Theory of Intelligence' in June 2005 and immodestly think they may be worthy of further dissemination and, hopefully, discussion and elaboration.

(1) Surprise is a matter not of insufficient information but of insufficient time. Often, in looking back at the data available at the time of surprise, the indications of the event appear to have been present. But the analysts did not have enough time to understand them, to see a pattern in the mass of facts. Time explains why hindsight has 20/20 vision. Surprise is not a question of breadth but of depth; its dimension is not spatial but temporal.

(2) Secrecy can be quantified. The German sociologist Georg Simmel opened his section on secrecy in his *Soziologie* by saying: 'All relationships of men between themselves rest obviously on the fact that they know something about one another.'[1] This way of looking at things breaks the great amorphous mass of secrecy – what men don't know, especially about one another – into separate items. It becomes quantifiable. It resembles what the mathematician and engineer Claude Shannon did for information in his path-breaking 'A Mathematical Theory of Communication'.[2] He divided information into bits, or binary digits, each of which answered *yes* or *no* – a 1 or a 0 – to a question. He thus made information

* From *Intelligence and National Security*, 21(6) (December 2006), 1060.

amenable to mathematical manipulation. Though Simmel himself did not do this for secrecy, his insight opens the way to making it likewise amenable to testable prediction.

Of course, these are only suggestions. Whether they are worth anything or not will depend on the work of future scholars.

Notes

1. Georg Simmel, *Soziologie: Untersuchungen über die Formen der Vergesellschaftung*. In *Gesamtausgabe*, Band 11, ed. Otthein Rammstedt (Frankfurt am Main, Germany: Suhrkamp Verlag, 1992), p. 383ff ('Das Geheimnis und die geheime Gesellschaft'). An English translation appeared as 'The Sociology of Secrecy and of Secret Societies', *American Journal of Sociology*, Vol. 11 (1906), pp. 441–98. It's not easy even in English.
2. *Bell System Technical Journal*, Vol. 27 (July 1948), pp. 479–523; (October 1948), pp. 623–56.

20

INTELLIGENCE LESSONS IN *MACBETH**

More than any other of Shakespeare's plays, *Macbeth* involves intelligence. Other plays of course mention it. King John famously asks, 'O, where hath our intelligence been drunk? Where hath it slept?' In *Richard II*, Bolingbroke, the usurping future Henry IV, uses the term in its military sense when he says 'So that by this intelligence we learn/The Welshmen are dispersed...' A courtier in *Henry V* refers to another kind of information when he says that 'The king hath note of all that they intend/By interception which they dream not of.'

But central only to *Macbeth* is prediction, probably the most desired element of intelligence. Of course, the play's language is more beautiful than even the best-written President's Daily Brief. Most usefully, the play can instruct students of the field. It expresses, poetically, the frustration of those who receive equivocal intelligence. And it shows what at least one leader – and not the only one – does when he does not like the intelligence given to him.

Forecasting appears at the beginning of the tragedy. The three witches hail Macbeth with a title he does not yet have and as a person 'that shalt be king hereafter!' Banquo complains that 'to me you speak not' and conjures them, in one of the most poetic requests to reveal the future, that 'If you can look into the seeds of time,/And say which grain will grow and which will not,/Speak then to me...' They promise Banquo that 'Thou shalt get kings, though thou be none.'

Later in the play, to satisfy Macbeth's eagerness to know what will come, the 'secret, black, and midnight hags' summon apparitions. The first warns him to beware Macduff. The second promises him that 'none of woman born/Shall harm Macbeth.' And the third

* From *Intelligence and National Security*, 24(2), (April 2009) 275–276.

assures him that 'Macbeth shall never vanquish'd be until/Great Birnam wood to high Dunsinane hill/Shall come against him.'

So Macbeth thinks that he can never be killed in a fight or defeated in battle. Then the enemy British cut down branches of the trees in the forest of Birnam to conceal their advancing forces, making it appear as if the whole wood were moving toward his castle of Dunsinane. He begins to realize 'th' equivocation of the fiend/That lies like truth.' Later, when he warns Macduff that 'I lead a charmed life, which must not yield/To one of woman born,' Macduff replies, 'Despair thy charm;… Macduff was from his mother's womb untimely ripp'd.' Then, in the fury that must torment many a leader whose intelligence advisors have equivocated, offering predictions so vague or generalized that they can never be found false, Macbeth cries out:

And be these juggling fiends no more believ'd
That palter with us in a double sense,
That keep the word of promise to our ear,
And break it to our hope.

Bravely willing to 'die with harness on our back', he orders his aides to 'Bring me no more reports.' He was neither the first nor the last leader to reject information that contradicted his wants.

21

HOW GARBLES TICKLED HISTORY*

Usually the garbles that plague telegrams do not much matter. Simple telegraphic or orthographic errors, they are easily corrected. But sometimes they cause more serious trouble. They cannot be said to have altered history; the errors were not that great. But they can be said to have riffled it.

In 1887, the addition of a dot in a Morse code telegram changed the commercial codeword BAY,[1] —··· ·— ·· ·· meaning *I have bought*, into the assumed plaintext word *buy*, or —··· ··— ·· ··. More graphically:

$$—··· ·—\quad ··\quad ··$$

$$—··· ··—\quad ··\quad ··$$

The recipient of the telegram then bought, costing a Philadelphia wool dealer $20,000. The suit reached the U.S. Supreme Court. It held that, because the dealer had not requested that the message be repeated back to him, the terms printed on the back of the telegram form controlled. The dealer recovered only the cost of the telegram: $1.15.

At the turn of the year 1895-96, Leander Starr Jameson, a British colonial administrator in South Africa, staged a raid on Mafeking. It was intended to touch off a revolution that would bring the Boers and so all of south Africa under the control of Cecil Rhodes, the British colonizer of Africa and prime minister of the Cape Colony. Jameson was captured; the raid failed; the revolution never took place.[2] But Kaiser Wilhelm II's telegram of congratulations to the Boer leader Paul Krüger led to an international crisis with Britain. Years later, historians found a number of telegrams that the 1896 Parliamentary select committee, formed to investigate the raid, had not seen. They depicted an amazing sloppiness on the part of the code clerk. For example,

---

* From *Cryptologia*, 24(4) (October 2005), 329–336.

he was to give 7 November as a date, but instead of encoding it as the correct codeword STECHEICHE – commercial codes in those days used natural or artificial words as codewords instead of the five-letter codewords later customary – he encoded it as STECHHEBER, which meant 14 November. And there were others. Thanks partly to this carelessness and partly to guesses, Rhodes produced a seemingly meaningful but incorrect telegram instead of a correct but almost incomprehensible version. As a consequence the select committee never saw what Rhodes or other participants saw. The historians concluded that the garbles added one small item "to the impossibility of the task that the select committee imperfectly attempted to perform."

The assassination in Sarajevo of the heir to the Austro-Hungarian throne in 1914 set off a series of events that, like a string of firecrackers, exploded in World War I. It was an era when declarations of war were still made before hostilities began, and the German ambassador in Paris, Wilhelm Eduard Freiherr von Schoen, received a telegram on 3 August 1914 that he was to present to the French government.[3] "There was no doubt in my mind that its contents would be decisive," Schoen wrote in his memoirs. "Unfortunately, the telegram was so mutilated that, in spite of every effort, only fragments of it could be deciphered." It included such senseless language as *Schon gestern herab mp* ("already yesterday downward mp") and other nonwords such as *kel, elena,* and *erol.* Phrases intended to declare war were not legible, even obscurely. But a portion that could be read told him that the French had violated German borders, which was true in only a few cases, and that he was to ask for his passport and leave. He therefore composed a missive that emphasized some of the erroneous statements. This gave the French, he wrote, "abundant ground for asserting that we had trumped up excuses to justify our attack." He was still angry after the war, when he wrote his memoirs, that "such false reports could have been given the weight of facts in our responsible quarters." The garbles could not have helped him to check out any facts.

At the end of that war, the fear that a garble might cost Italy territory that it had gained led its government to send its armistice terms to Austria-Hungary by courier instead of by telegram.[4] It delayed the end of the hostilities by two days.

In 1941, the Canadian government dutifully informed the mother country of Great Britain that it was hiring Herbert O. Yardley to head its new codebreaking agency. But the ministry of external affairs was using an old code.[5] Its code elements were not constructed to exclude accidentally transposed numbers. So when Canada encoded 6792, meaning *yard*, it was received in London as 6972, meaning *eme*. What should have been *Yardley* came in as *Emeley*. The British did not question this at first, but a month later asked whether Emeley was in fact Yardley. Canada acknowledged it. Neither the British nor the Americans wanted Yardley working in cryptology, and forced him out. The only effect of the garble was to give Yardley a few extra weeks of employment. But two ironies color the tale. Yardley's former associates, Charles J. Mendelsohn and William F. Friedman, had published an article in 1932 showing how this garble could be avoided, and a man instrumental in telling Canada about Yardley, Friedman's later subordinate Abraham Sinkov, had discussed the same problem in a chapter in a 1939 book. It was a lesson the Canadians had not learned.

Not only telegrams but manuscript documents could fall victim to mistakes. Handwriting could be illegible – a problem intensified in encrypted texts because they lack the redundancy that allows plain languages messages to be corrected. Such a case has come down in the history of cryptology as having led to the elevation of the hunchbacked Frederick III, duke of Prussia and margrave of Brandenburg, an elector of the Holy Roman Empire, to the royal title of king. The story appeared in Johann Ludwig Klüber's excellent *Kryptographik* (Tübingen, 1809), 24-26, and has been repeated many times. Klüber writes that in the nomenclator used by the young Prussian minister to the court of the Holy Roman Emperor in Vienna, 110 stood for the emperor and 116 for Father Wolf, a politically astute German Jesuit preacher in Vienna.[6] In the negotiations to get the emperor to elevate the elector from duke to king, the Prussian minister wrote to Berlin that the elector should handwrite a supplicating letter to 110. But, says Klüber, in the encrypted dispatch the zero of the intended 110 was overextended and the deciphering clerk read it as 116. The elector, a Protestant, consequently asked Father Wolf for his help. Flattered, Wolf urged his fellow Catholic, the emperor, to recognize the elector's kingship – which he did, enabling the elector on 18 January 1701 to crown himself as Prussia's King Frederick I.

The story is cute and might be used as an instructive example for code clerks.[7] It has just one drawback: it is not true. That greatest of German historians, Leopold von Ranke, who taught the world to write history *wie es eigentlich gewesen* – as it really was – by basing its account on contemporary archives, checked the documents. He found that "In the dispatches at least the right numbers appear clearly." Wolf's involvement in the negotiations was thus independent of any electoral letter, and several other factors – among them Frederick's promise of 8,000 men for the emperor in case he needed them – further influenced the emperor's decision. It was not a garble that contributed to Frederick's achieving what he believed was "the sweet fruition of an earthly crown." It was power politics as usual.

The garble that most significantly affected history took place in 1870.

Prussia had just defeated Austria and its allies to dominate the German-speaking lands. It perhaps now hoped to beat France and become the greatest power in all Europe. Chancellor Otto von Bismarck foresaw a possible *casus belli* in Spain. Conservatives there had driven into exile the vacillating, promiscuous queen, Isabella II, who seems to have had almost as many lovers as she had had governments (sixty). The throne was vacant. Who would ascend it? Many leading Spaniards wanted Prince Leopold of Hohenzollern-Sigmaringen, a Catholic branch of the Prussian royal house. Prussia liked this possibility, just as France did not.[8]

On 19 June 1870, Leopold agreed to accept the throne if the Spanish parliament, the Cortes, offered it to him. Spanish officials agreed to hold the Cortes in session in Madrid if it appeared likely to choose Leopold; if such an election seemed unlikely, it would adjourn. Two days later, on the 21st, Karl Hermann von Thile, a North German Foreign Office official, telegraphed an encoded message to Baron Julius von Canitz und Dallwitz, the Prussian minister at Madrid. It directed Canitz to tell the president of the Cortes that he would see him again about the 26th, presumably to conclude details of the election of the German princeling. The president then would be expected to hold the Cortes in session. But the decoded dispatch as handed to Canitz gave the day not as the 26th but as the 9th—two weeks hence. He reported that date to the Spanish officials. The Cortes did not need to cool its heels for at least two and a half weeks while awaiting word from Germany. It adjourned. Its members quit Madrid and returned to their homes.

Bismarck was not pleased and ordered an investigation. An investigation in the Foreign Office showed that the encoded message had

been decoded as a check before being telegraphed to Berlin. The
Foreign Office thus held that it was exonerated and that the fault
"lies apparently entirely, or in the most favorable hypothesis *mainly*, at
the door of the Madrid Legation." This did not satisfy Bismarck. He
had the original telegram recalled from the Berlin Central Telegraph
Office and redecoded. It tallied exactly with the telegram as drafted.
Bismarck then had Canitz see what had happened in Madrid.

Canitz reported that the telegram arrived at the legation at 7 p.m.
on 21 June "and was immediately deciphered by the chancery clerk
Kleefeld, part of it in my presence." He could not "furnish a copy
of the telegram as it reached me in cipher, authenticated by my sig-
nature, since under Point 2 of the Instructions for the use of cipher
codes, which the Prussian legation had the honor to receive by
Your Excellency's communication of 21 July 1867 'the rough sheets
of the decipherment are to be destroyed immediately after the fair
copy has been made when the decipher for purposes of checking
has been entered either before or above the relevant groups' (as is
always the practice here), and consequently I am no longer in possession of the original of the telegram. In order to make up for this
loss I have requested and received a copy of the telegram in question from the Telegraph Office here, attested by the Director, which
I have the honor respectfully to enclose. In it at the relevant place
there stands, it is true, the cipher group 5714, expressing the number
twenty six...."

In the German diplomatic code as printed, the plaintext numbers
stood in a column in which the word "twenty" was represented by a
dash in the words that stood underneath "twenty two":

5710 twenty two
5711 —— three
5712 —— four
5713 —— five
5714 —— six
5715 —— seven
5716 —— eight
5717 —— nine

Clerk Kleefeld had made two mistakes. He had read the correct
5714 incorrectly as 5717 and then had ignored the dash that meant

"twenty" and read 5717 as simply "nine." Canitz said that Kleefelt, "in looking up the groups in the code book had the misfortune to make a slip, which might happen all the more easily since 'about the ninth' made as good sense as 'about the twenty sixth.'" Bismarck's reaction is not recorded.

Though that error had cost Bismarck his chance to surround France with Hohenzollerns, he did not abandon his intention to beat that country. This greatest Realpolitiker found other ways of inflaming Napoleon III, getting France to declare war on Prussia – and then mobilizing his armies, defeating France's, and making Germany the greatest power in Europe. In a glittering ceremony in 1871 in the Hall of Mirrors at Versailles, he established a new German empire – the second Reich, following the Holy Roman Empire.

And the crown of Spain? It went to an Italian duke as King Amadeo I. He lasted two years.

Notes

1. David Kahn, *The Codebreakers*, 2nd edn. (New York: Macmillan, 1995).
2. C. M. Woodhouse, 'The Missing Telegrams and the Jameson Raid', *History Today* (June 1962), pp. 395–404, (July 1962), pp. 506–514, 445.
3. Germany, Auswärtiges Amt, *Outbreak of the World War: German Documents Collected by Karl Kautsky*, Carnegie Endowment for International Peace (Oxford: Oxford University Press), pp. 531–532; Wilhelm Eduard Freiherr von Shoen, *The Memoirs of an Ambassador*, trans. Constance Vesey (London: Allen & Unwin, 1922), pp. 200–202; William Jannen, Jr., *The Lions of July* (Presidio, CA: Novato), p. 348.
4. David Paull Nickles, *Under the Wire: How the Telegraph Changed History* (Cambridge, MA: Harvard University Press, 2003), p. 188.
5. David Kahn, *The Reader of Gentlemen's Mail* (New Haven, CT: Yale University Press, 2004), p. 209.
6. Repeated in Fletcher Pratt, *Secret and Urgent* (Indianapolis, IN: Bobbs-Merrill, 1939), and in S. Fischer-Fabian, 1. *Friedrich I: Koenig von Preussen*, 3rd edn. (Berlin: de Gruyter, 1981), pp. 195, 322; and perhaps in other works.
7. Leopold von Ranke, *Neun Buecher Preussischer Geschichte*, 1, Band (2e Auflage) (Berlin: Veit, 1848), pp. 106–07. Trans. Sir Alexander and Lady Duff Gordon as *Memoirs of the House of Brandenburg and History of Prussia during the Seventeenth and Eighteenth Centuries*, I (1849; reprinted New York, 1968), p. 105; "the sweet fruition of an earthly crown": Christopher Marlowe, "Tamburlaine the Great, Part I," II: vii: 29.

8. Lawrence Steefel, *Bismarck, the Hohenzollern Candidature, and the Origins of the Franco-German War of 1870* (Cambridge, MA: Harvard University Press, 1962); *Bismarck and the Hohenzollern Candidature for the Spanish Throne: The Documents in the German Diplomatic Archives*, ed. George Bonnin, trans. Isabella M. Massey (London, 1957).

22

THE CRYPTOLOGIC ORIGIN OF BRAILLE*†

Louis Braille, inventor of raised-dot writing for the blind, got his idea from a secret communications system devised for military purposes by a French army officer, Nicholas-Marie-Charles Barbier de La Serre.

Barbier was born 18 May 1767 at Valenciennes, in the north of France. At 15, he was admitted to a military school under a provision allowing impoverished young noblemen to attend. The school was perhaps that at Brienne, where he would have been for a year a fellow student of Napoleon Bonaparte. He graduated as an artillery officer (as did Napoleon). When the French Revolution broke out, he emigrated to the United States, working as a surveyor and living with Indians until his return to France under Napoleon's empire.

He became interested in fast, secret writing and, in 1808, published a brochure entitled *Tableau d'expédiographie* ("Table of speed-writing") and, in 1809, his *Principes d'expéditive française pour écrire aussi vite que la parole* ("Principles of French Speediness for Writing as Fast as Speech"). The latter described a process that he called "impressed writing to replace the pen or pencil and to execute several copies at a time without tracing characters." Barbier was describing a writing that could be felt, perhaps recalling times when such a capability would have been useful for officers in the field to draft outgoing messages in the dark and perhaps to "read" incoming ones with their fingers.

* *Cryptologia*, 30 (April 1995) 151–152.
† This material is adapted from Pierrie Henri, "La Genèse du système Braille." In *La Vie et l'Oeuvre de Lovis Braille, Inventeur de l'Alphabet des Aveugles (1809–1852)*. Paris: Presses Universitaires de France, 1952.

Barbier refined his idea when he proposed setting out the 25 letters of the French alphabet in a 5 × 5 Polybius square and later what he considered as the 36 sounds of French (e.g., a, i, ch, e, ieu) in a 6 × 6 square. Each letter or sound could thus be replaced by a pair of numbers. He recognized that by changing the pattern of letters or sounds in the square, he would have a system of secret writing useful for soldiers or diplomats. As a mere monoalphabetic substitution, it was not very secure; perhaps he recognized this, for he did not insist on it further. Instead, he combined his ideas of cryptography and impressed writing in a machine that indented the numbers onto paper.

In 1819, he displayed this device at an exposition in a Museum of Products of Industry temporarily installed in the court of the Louvre. A report by three scientists to the Academy of Sciences the following year discussed two systems used apparently by two models of the machine to die-stamp the numbers representing the lines and columns of the square. In one of them, three raised dots formed right or obtuse angles. In the other, raised dots were ranged on an axis to facilitate determining them. All of this was for the military; none was for the blind. But, at the same exhibition, students of the Royal Institution for Blind Children showed how they could read from books – huge bound volumes – printed with ordinary letters in high relief by running their fingers over the words. Barbier perhaps witnessed the difficulty they had in figuring out the letters. By 1821, an article in the *Mercure technologique* that discussed the military and diplomatic advantages of Barbier's system also mentioned that the Royal Institution for Blind Children had adopted it for instruction, and in 1822 an entire article dealt with the use of the system for the blind.

This system utilized two parallel columns of six raised points each. The number of points in the left-hand column indicated the line of the square table of sounds, the number in the right-hand column the position within that line of the designated sound. Methods were given to punch the points into the paper.

Braille, a compatriot of Barbier's but 42 years younger, modified this system into an alphabet utilizing an array of 2 × 3 locations, in one or more of which dots are raised to indicate letters. Thus to represent a, the dot in the left column at the top is punched out, the other seven positions being left unpunched, or level; for o, the first and third dots in the left column and the second dot in the right column are raised. The 26 letters are supplemented by a sign for capital letters and a sign for numerals, which are then represented by the letters from a to j.

Braille, himself blind, was thus both honest and generous when he said of Barbier in 1829 that "it is to his method that we owe the first idea of our own."

23

THE ONLY FALSE
MESSAGE I KNOW*

In my talks about cryptology, I often say that codebreaking comprises one of the most trustworthy forms of intelligence, since it consists of the actual words of the persons targeted. In response, I'm sometimes asked whether it is not possible that some of the messages intercepted are fakes, intended to trick the eavesdroppers. My answer is two-fold. First, I say that in all my reading in the literature and in original documents I have never seen any actual phony messages that have in fact been transmitted.[1] Second, I say that this void makes sense, since fake messages would probably cause more trouble than they are worth. Ordinary, nondeceptive transmissions are not infrequently misunderstood through obscurity or incompleteness: husbands and others being assigned tasks are sometimes not clear as to what wanted, which causes difficulties. So to deliberately risk a misunderstanding for a slight possible gain seems not worthwhile. Another problem, mentioned by an experienced British deception officer in World War I in opposing "the sending of dummy messages containing information, false or real, with the intention of the enemy picking it up," is that "There is always the danger that information that is false today may be correct a week hence, i.e. just when the enemy has succeeded in deciphering the message."[2]

Recently, however, I came across some German documents from World War I that will make me change my answer somewhat. They disclose a diplomat proposing the sending of fake messages and stating that one has been sent. It is the only such proposal and realization that I have ever seen, though of course other fake messages in this series may exist elsewhere in the political records. However, given

---

* From "From the Archives a Real Fake Message," *Cryptologia*, 18(2) (April 1994), 150–152.

the perils of false transmission and the mediocrity of the ambassador, Prince Maximilian von Ratibor und Corvey,[3] I think it more likely that Berlin quashed the plan after the one message was sent. Real fake messages therefore remain all but nonexistent. As a cryptologic curiosity, however, these documents merit publication.

They come from the records of the German Foreign Office, Department (Abteilung) A, file Deutschland No. 179, Chiffre-Angelegenheiten zwischen Deutschland und fremden Staaten (Cipher Matters Between Germany and Foreign States). They are reproduced on National Archives microfilm T-149, Roll 416, Frames 771ff. The first message, while not dealing specifically with fake messages, shows the interest of the German embassy in Madrid in tricking the French by selling them an obsolete code, presumably to feed them false information. All the messages are on Foreign Office "Telegram Decipherment" forms except that of 2 May, which is on a form of the Cipher Bureau of the Admiralty Staff of the Navy, probably indicating that it was sent by naval code, since Ratibor regarded the Foreign Office code he was using as compromised, which it was, the French having solved it.[4]

/Frame 771/No. 740. 30 March 1916. 6:30. Military Attaché in Madrid to Foreign Office.

Request permission of Foreign Office to sell to the French General Consulate for 250,000 pesetas, through an agent provocateur, a photograph of an old kind of code available here, probably Number 312, which naval communications has replaced with another.

/Frame 774/No. 1850. 2 May 1916. 11:20. Ambassador in Madrid to Foreign Office.

It is now determined beyond a doubt that code including key is known in Paris. All secret telegrams go from now on enciphered in the naval code. There exist the danger that France will politically exploit the knowledge of our telegraph traffic—especially in view of the statements of the king of Spain—as soon as France has recognized that the betrayal of the cipher is known to us. I would therefore, in addition to nonsecret reports, also give false information about Morocco and political matters, which I request permission to answer in the same way. The transmission of such false information would be confirmed each time by a telegram in the naval code.

The military attaché requests that the General Staff of the Army be informed.

/Frame 775/No. 11. 12 May 1916. Ambassador in Madrid to Foreign Office.

Answer to telegram No. 196. 6.[5] ... Since telegram exchange about selling the cipher is undoubtedly known in Paris, which is also inferred from the behavior of the enemy in Barcelona, I have broken off the negotiation.

/Frame 776/No. 15. 12 May 1916. 10:35. Ambassador in Madrid to Foreign Office.

Telegram No. 1060[6] is fake telegram.

Notes

1. Claims that such messages have been sent are sometimes seen. For example, John Ferris, ed., *The British Army and Signals Intelligence During the First World War* (London: Alan Sutton for the Army Records Society, 1992), says that the British transmitted such messages intermittently in 1916 though "with little success." But even this careful historian of cryptology has not documented his claim with examples.
2. *Ibid.*, p. 180.
3. Lamar Cecil, *The German Diplomatic Service, 1871–1914* (Princeton, NJ: Princeton University Press, 1976), pp. 22, 66, 71, 73–74.
4. The French were solving German diplomatic message as early as 1905. They lost this ability in 1911, when the Germans got wind of these successes and changed their codes (Christopher Andrew, "Déchiffrement et diplomatie: Le cabinet noir du Quai d'Orsay sous la Troisième République," *Relations Internationales*, No. 5 (1976), pp. 37–64 at 50, 54–55, 58). During World War I, however, the French once again solved German diplomatic codes (Marcel Givierge, "Etude historique sur la Section du chiffre" (Paris: Bibliothèque nationale, Département des manuscripts), passim.)
5. Paragraphs 1 to 5 are not given in this telegram.
6. This telegram is not in this file.

24

THE PREHISTORY OF
THE GENERAL STAFF*

All armies have general staffs today. They became accepted after 1871 when the smaller, poorer state of Prussia defeated larger, richer France. Widely viewed as the most significant factor in this unexpected result was the general staff. The Prussian army had one. The French army did not. The world saw the Prussian staff as "a dark force, something more than human, weaving the threads of national destiny according to a terrible pattern of its own"[1]—an image of mystery and power that still shades it and explains its attraction. Nations all over the world wanted such triumphs. They emulated the Prussian system—creating staffs if they had none, elaborating their embryonic ones if they did, establishing colleges to train officers for staffs, intensifying acceptance of staff work. The general staff became universal.

Yet though useful histories of various general staffs have been written by Irvine, Hittle, Stoerkel, Goerlitz, Nelson, Hewes,[2] none has delved into their roots. None has looked into the preconditions needed before a general staff could come into being to improve the efficiency and effectiveness of an army or a navy. Perhaps some thoughts—indicative, not definitive—about that background may deepen understanding of this institution.

The job of a general staff is to prepare an army for what it will have to do. So it must look ahead.[3] "The primary function of mental activity is to face the future and anticipate the event which is to happen," wrote mathematician Gerald J. Whitrow.[4] And indeed men have always sought to "look into the seeds of time/And see which grain will grow and which will not."[5] The ancients interpreted dreams, omens, entrails, the mutterings of the Delphic oracle.[6] Sometimes they were right—Joseph correctly explained the meaning of pharaoh's dream

---

* From *The Journal of Military History*, 71(2) (April 2007), 499–504.

about seven fat and seven lean kine.[7] But often they were wrong. People today examine tarot cards and read astrology columns in the newspaper, with no better results. Ultimately the only basis for predicting events lies in the uniformity of nature: what has happened before will, under the same conditions, happen again. But since conditions may change, or not be recognized, no one can be certain of what will happen in the future. The philosopher Bertrand Russell summarized the situation neatly when he pointed out that "The man who has fed the chicken every day through its life at last wrings its neck instead, showing that more refined views about the uniformity of nature would have been useful to the chicken."[8] This should infuse a useful skepticism into a study of the general staff and its functions.

Looked at in the broadest terms, growth in three areas of life permitted a general staff[9] to evolve: in secularization, in bureaucracy, and in management.

The conquest of rational modes of thought over magical and religious modes began in the Renaissance—Copernicus is the exemplar—and intensified in the Enlightenment. Sociologist Max Weber called this profound movement the "disenchantment of the world"; Auguste Comte, "positivism."[10] It carried science, philosophy, politics with it. The world moved towards confirmable statements and thus towards facts and knowledge. Secularization succeeded because it took humankind from a passive to an active world view and gave it more control over events than religious modes did. One of the most important, most sweeping movements in history, secularization laid the philosophical foundation for the general staff, enabling it to build on a logical, verifiable basis.

As the population of Europe grew and moved from the country to the cities, rulers sought to generate income by increasing trade and markets. Around the second half of the sixteenth century, bureaucracies evolved to facilitate this by regulating currency, weights and measures, foreign affairs, armed forces.[11] Bureaucracy, which permits more rational control than the two other forms of authority, traditional and charismatic,[12] needs information. The most basic is who lives where. Governments had long conducted censuses—Joseph and Mary went to Bethlehem for one—but in the nineteenth century they intensified and rationalized these procedures. Prussia established a statistical office in 1805. The German customs union needed to know how many people lived in its constituent states so it could distribute its revenues according to population.[13] The enumeration in Britain by individuals of events led to the founding in 1835 of a Statistical Department in the Board of Trade.[14] Eventually, many if not most Western governments collected information, not just on population, but also on agriculture, trade, banking, occupation, mining, railways.[15] Tables of numbers, which improved government efficiency and control, became common. When necessary, governments established agencies to run or watch over those activities. Bureaucracy rationalized government.[16]

It evolved in the military at the same time. Since the military was already hierarchical, bureaucracy affected its form less than it did that of the civilian sector. Still, the growth of the nation-state and its permanent professional armies called for men to plan march routes, encampments, and the supply of food, fodder, and ammunition. Emerging to handle these were the quartermasters. They formed separate corps, each with its own uniform.[17] Since the quartermasters needed to know the terrain over which they would march, they prepared in peacetime by mapping their own lands and then obtaining maps of foreign countries.[18] In this early bureaucracy, with its strong aspect of foresight, lay the germ of the general staff.

The evolution of technology that defined the industrial revolution intensified specialization, demanded education, and established management. As steam replaced muscle and wind, as rails replaced roads, and the telegraph, the semaphore, the persons operating them had to know more than those whom they displaced. In armies and navies, cannonballs turned into shells and shrapnel; muskets, into breechloaders and machine guns. Soldiers and sailors specialized in their various weapons. All these people had to be able to read job instructions, safety warnings, organization directives; they had to compute fuel and raw material needs and manpower expectations. Education accomplished this. In Britain, correspondence societies, Sunday schools, Adult Schools, the Hampden Clubs, and other organizations responded to the demands of businessmen and workers by teaching literacy.[19] On the Continent, countries began requiring children to go to school.[20] As technology evolved, professional organizations emerged. In Britain, the civil engineers were the first to organize, in 1771.

The growth of knowledge and business led as well to scientific management. As managers had increasingly to spend time away from their factories, and as second and third generations took charge, owners wrote down how to run the firms. Gradually a science of management grew up.[21] In 1832, Charles Babbage published *On the Economy of Machinery and Engineering.* Conscription after the French Revolutionary Wars replaced the small professional armies of absolute monarchies with large armies of civilians. They needed instruction in handling the new weapons and leaders to direct them in combat. In 1800 no professional officer corps existed. By 1900 every armed force had one.[22] Within them, the quartermaster corps, whose job was to plan, evolved into what became the general staff.

As knowledge grew, it specialized. Since specialization splinters knowledge, businessmen assembled subordinates into a committee or board to get an overview. Through its greater range and mutual criticism, the committee collects more and better information than any single person. It prepares for the future better than the occasional genius.[23] Likewise, in the military the new specialists—railroad engineers, signal officers, supply officers, intelligence officers, fortress designers—had to focus their various expertises onto a single problem. Armies brought these specialists together under the chairmanship of the chief of the general staff to plan for the future. It is a form of committee. And, because that structure works, in the military as in business, it survives.

Notes

1. Walter Goerlitz, *History of the German General Staff, 1657–1945*, trans. Brian Battershaw (New York: Praeger, 1957), p. 95.
2. Dallas D. Irvine, "The French and Prussian General Staff Systems before 1870," *Journal of the American Military History Foundation*, Vol. 2 (Winter 1938), 192–203, and "The Origin of Capital Staffs," *Journal of Modern History*, Vol. 10 (June 1938), 161–79; J. D. Hittle, *The Military Staff: Its Function and Development* (Harrisburg, PA.: Military Service, 1944); Major Stoerkel, "Die Organisation des Großen Generalstabes," *Bundesarchiv-Militärarchiv*, Vol. H 35/2, and "Erste Einführung in die Organisation und in die Tätigkeit des Stellvertretenden Generalstabes der Armee und des Großen Generalstabes (1919) bis zur Auflösung am 30.9.1919," *Bundesarchiv-Militärarchiv*, Vol. H 35/3; Otto L. Nelson, Jr., *National Security and the General Staff* (Washington, DC: Infantry Journal Press, 1946); James E. Hewes, Jr., *From Root to McNamara: Army Organization and Administration, 1900–1963*, United States Army, Center of Military

History, Special Studies (Washington, DC: GPO, 1975); Huber Zeiner, *Geschichte des Österreichischen Generalstabes* (Vienna, Austria: Böhlau Verlag, 2006); Jean Delmas, ed., *Histoire militaire de la France*, Vol. 2, *De 1715 à 1871* (Paris: Presses Universitaires de France, 1992) does not mention either any quartermaster staff or the pre-Napoleonic general staff or the *Dépôt de guerre*, regarded as a predecessor of the intelligence section of the general staff. France, Ministère de la Défense, État-major de l'armée de terre, Service historique, *Inventaires des archives de la guerre: Soussérie Y a*, ed. Jean-Claude Devos (Château de Vincennes, 2000); *Côte Y a 93*, is headed état-major, 1720–1791. V. Derrécagair, *Etude sur les états-majors des armées etrangères* (Paris: J. Dumaine, 1871), 9, says the French general staff dates from 1818 but gives no details. I know of no studies of the history and organization of the British general staff.

3. The desire to know the unknowable and to control it tinges that desire with mysticism, because the black arts promise to reveal the future. That gives the general staff the image of what Goerlitz rightly called a "dark force"; it explains why Eckart Kehr has called the Prussian general staff "the mystical monster" (*Der Primat der Innenpolitik* [Berlin: de Gruyter, 1965], p. 150). Of course, as knowledge objectifies and mathematizes, it bleaches out the occult. But the desire to predict the future makes it unlikely that humans will ever extirpate mysticism from their activities (see chapter 11, on the economic basis of the belief in luck, in Thorstein Veblen, *The Theory of the Leisure Class* (1899; reprint, New York: Penguin Books, 1994). So studies of the general staff may benefit from examining the hermeticism and magic that Frances A. Yates and others have seen as a wellspring of modern science (Frances A. Yates, *The Art of Memory* [Chicago, IL: University of Chicago Press, 1966], and later books). The occult taints intelligence more strongly than it does the other activities of the staff, perhaps because while one's activities lie within one's power those of the foe do not, loosening the imagination. This may help explain the public's fascination for intelligence. And once I wondered whether Werner Heisenberg's uncertainty principle or Kurt Gödel's proof of the incompleteness of mathematics or Alan Turing's demonstration of the noncomputability of certain functions showed in part why it was hard to foresee the future. But these theories do not affect ordinary calculations or the gross events of every day.

4. *The Natural Philosophy of Time* (London: Thomas Nelson & Sons, 1961), p. 33.

5. *Macbeth* 1:3:58–59

6. Cicero, *De Divinatione*; Joseph Fontenrose, *The Delphic Oracle: Its Reponses and Operations with a Catalogue of Responses* (Berkeley, CA: University of California Press, 1978). Rose Mary Sheldon, *Intelligence Activities in Ancient Rome: Trust in the Gods, but Verify* (London: Frank Cass, 2005), vi, says that the Romans learned that such sources were not reliable. Nevertheless they used them. See also Francis Bacon, "Of Prophecies."

7. *Genesis* 41:17–42

8. Bertrand Russell, *The Problems of Philosophy* (1912; reprint, London, U.K.: Oxford University Press, 1973), chapter "On Induction."

9. This excludes early war councils. *Luke* 14:31–32 certainly expresses a truth in saying "Or what king, going to make war against another king, sitteth not down first, and consulteth whether he is able with ten thousand to meet him who comes against him with twenty thousand." But such an ad hoc council does not imply a general staff. And I believe that Bernard S. Bachrach is premature in referring to "Charlemagne and the Carolingian General Staff," *Journal of Military History*, Vol. 66 (April 2002), pp. 313–57.

10. Max Weber, *The Protestant Ethic and the Spirit of Capitalism*, trans. Talcott Parsons (1905, 1958 [English]; reprint, Mineola, NY: Dover, 2003), pp. 105, 117, 221–22. Auguste Comte, *The Positive Philosophy of Auguste Comte*, trans. Harriet Martineau (1855; reprint, New York: AMS Press, 1974), pp. 25–26. Owen Chadwick, *The Secularization of the European Mind in the Nineteenth Century* (Cambridge, U.K.: Cambridge University Press, 1975). Keith Thomas, *Religion and the Decline of Magic* (London: Weidenfeld & Nicholson, 1971). The scientific revolution may be seen as a part of this.

11. Henry Jacoby, *The Bureaucratization of the World*, trans. Evelin L. Kanes (Berkeley, CA: University of California Press, 1973), pp. 14–18, 29; "The Genesis of the Prussian Bureaucracy and the *Rechsstaat*," chapter viii in Eckart Kehr, *Economic Interest, Militarism, and Foreign Policy*, trans. Grete Heinz, ed. Gordon A. Craig (Berkeley, CA: University of California Press, 1977), pp. 141–65; Gerald Aylmer, "From Office Holding to Civil Service: The Genesis of Modern Bureaucracy," *Transactions of the Royal Historical Society*, 5th series, Vol. 30 (1980), p. 105ff.

12. Max Weber, *The Theory of Social and Economic Organization*, trans. Taloott Parsons (New York: Free Press, 1947), pp. 328–29.

13. Eugene Würzburger, "The History and Development of Official Statistics in the German Empire." In *The History of Statistics*, ed. John Koren (New York: Macmillan, 1918), pp. 333–62. Walter Heimer, *Die Geschichte der deutschen Wirtschaftsstatisik* (Inaugural-Dissertation, Universität Frankfurt am Main, Frankfurt am Main, Germany, 1928), pp. 6–7.

14. Donald A. Mackenzie, *Statistics in Britain, 1865–1930* (Edinburgh: Edinburgh University Press, 1981), pp. 7–9; Athelstane Baines, "The History and Development of Statistics in Great Britain and Ireland," pp. 365–89, in Koren, ed.; Theodore M. Porter, *The Rise of Statistical Thinking, 1820–1900* (Princeton, NJ: Princeton University Press, 1986), pp. 11, 17.

15. For example, Jean-Claude Perrot and Stuart J. Woolf, *State and Statistics in France, 1789–1815* (New York: Harwood Academic Publishers, 1984), pp. 5, 40, 81–82.

16. Lorenz Gerd Gigerenzer Krüger and Mary S. Morgan, *The Probabilistic Revolution*, 2 vols. (Cambridge, MA: MIT Press, 1987), p. 2, chapter 5; Anthony Oberschall, "The Two Empirical Roots of Social Theory and the Probability Revolution," *ibid.*, pp. 103–31.

17. Stoerkel, "Die Organisation des Großen Generalstabes," pp. 1–4; Ottomar Freiherr von der Osten-Sacken und vom Rhein, *Preussens Heer von seiner Anfängen*, Vol. 1 (Berlin: Mittler, 1911–14), p. 293; Ernst Rudolf Huber, *Deutsche Verfassungsgeschichte seit 1789* (Stuttgart, Germany: Kohlhammer, 1957), p. 230; Zeiner, *Geschichte des österreichischen Generalstabes*, pp. 164, 176.

18. W. Stavenhagen, "Die geschichtliche Entwicklung des preussischen Militär-Kartenwesens," *Geographische Zeitschrift*, Vol. 6 (1900), pp. 435–49, 504–12, 549–65 at 441; Josef W. Konvitz, *Cartography in France, 1660–1848* (Chicago, IL: University of Chicago Press, 1987), p. 167.

19. Sidney Pollard, *The Genesis of Modern Management: A Study of the Industrial Revolution in Great Britain* (Harmondsworth, U.K.: Penguin Books, 1965), pp. 209–11, 292–98, 302–14.

20. Rolf Engelsing, *Analphabetentum und Lektüre: Zur Sozialgeschichte des Lesens in Deutschland zwischen feudaler und industrieller Gesellschaft* (Stuttgart, Germany: J. G. Metzlersche Buchhandlung, 1973), pp. 69, 72–76, 101–5; P. Chevallier et al., *L'Enseignement français de la Révolution à nos jours* (Paris, La Haye: Editions Mouton, 1968), pp. 63–67. See also Alfred North Whitehead, *Science and the Modern World* (New York: Macmillan, 1926), pp. 141–42.

21. Pollard, *Genesis of Modern Management*.

22. Samuel P. Huntington, *The Soldier and the State* (Cambridge, MA: Belknap Press, 1957), p. 19. Irvine, "The French and Prussian General Staff Systems before 1870," p. 173, says mass armies require more intellectual preparation and skill than control of a visible mass of men.

23. John Kenneth Galbraith, *The New Industrial State*, 4th ed. (Boston, MA: Houghton Mifflin, 1985), pp. 14–21. "The inevitable counterpart of specialization is organization. This is what brings the work of specialists to a coherent result." Also Huntington, *The Soldier and the State*, p. 51.

PART V
PERSONALITIES

Mendelsohn, an American army codebreaker in World War I, built up the probably the world's greatest collection of antiquarian books on cryptology, which he willed to his alma mater, the University of Pennsylvania, where it continues to serve scholars. "The Man in the Iron Mask" reports a confirmation of the debunking of Étienne Bazeries' solution to the puzzle of his identity. "Students Know Better" reports that cryptologic students in 1918 solved a cipher system proposed by Bazeries that Rosario Candela independently solved in the 1930s and then wrote a charming book vaunting the solution. "The Old Master of Austrian Cryptology" reviews a solid, detailed, two-volume biography of Andreas Figl, a World War I and II cryptanalyst.

25

CHARLES J. MENDELSOHN
AND WHY I ENVY HIM*

This is expanded from a talk 15 April 2003 at the opening of an exhibition for the Mendelsohn collection of books on cryptology at the Rare Books and Manuscript Department of the Van Pelt-Dietrich Library of the University of Pennsylvania. The collection has been newly catalogued by Regan Kladstrup, who selected the books for the exhibition and wrote the descriptions and accompanying texts. The exhibit was designed and mounted by Andrea Gottschalk. The collection's catalogue may be retrieved on line at http://www.franklin.library.upenn.edu/and by then doing an "author" search.

Charles Jastrow Mendelsohn built the largest collection of antiquarian books on cryptology in the world. He became one of the greatest scholars of the history of cryptology. Those are two of the reasons I envy him. But there are many others.

His father, Samuel Mendelsohn, was the rabbi of the Temple of Israel in Wilmington, North Carolina. His mother, Esther Jastrow of Philadelphia, was the cousin of two distinguished graduates of the University of Pennsylvania. Joseph Jastrow, class of 1884, was awarded what is thought to be the first Ph.D. in psychology in the United States — in 1886 from Johns Hopkins. His older brother, Morris (Penn, class of 1881), was appointed professor of Semitic studies at Penn in 1892 and university librarian in 1898. He held the librarianship until 1919, the professorship until his death in 1921. So one of the other reasons I envy Charles Mendelsohn is his distinguished academic lineage.

When Rabbi Mendelsohn's congregation heard of his impending marriage, they showed their affection for him by carpeting and furnishing his house, on Chestnut Street between Fourth and Fifth

* From *Cryptologia*, 28(1) (January 2004) 1–17.

391

Streets. Charles was born 8 December 1880 in Wilmington. By age 7, he was captaining a baseball team, the Blue Lights, which on Monday, 8 August 1887, defeated the White Stars, 30-20. But he also grew up in a scholarly atmosphere. His father published *The Criminal Jurisprudence of the Ancient Hebrews* in 1891 and in 1893 the state university conferred an honorary doctorate of laws upon him.

Charles attended the Episcopal Academy in Philadelphia, starting at 15 and graduating the following year, winning the prizes in Latin and Greek in 1896. Of course he went to Penn, entering at age 16. In his freshman year he won the Class of 1880 prize in entrance mathematics, the B. B. Comegys prizes in entrance Greek and Latin and the faculty prize in sight reading of Greek and, in his sophomore year, honorable mention in sight reading of Latin. He was a member of the Pennsylvania Debating Union and managing editor of the *Pennsylvanian* in his junior year and assistant editor-in-chief in his senior year. In 1900, he graduated Phi Beta Kappa and twice in a row won the university's fellowship in classical languages. In 1904, Mendelsohn was awarded the Ph.D. in classics from Penn. His dissertation was on word-play in Plautus, the Roman writer of comedies one of whose plots was used by Shakespeare in "The Comedy of Errors" and another by Molière in "L'Avare." It was published in 1907.

After graduation, Mendelsohn was appointed to the faculty of the College of the City of New York as a tutor in Greek. When the United States entered World War I, he joined the censorship division of the Post Office Department. He may have been interested in codes and ciphers from childhood – perhaps his motivation for moving to the army's codebreaking agency, section 8 of military intelligence, or MI-8. This was headed by a 28-year-old former telegrapher and State Department code clerk, the capable, energetic, charismatic Herbert O. Yardley. This is another reason I envy Mendelsohn. He knew and worked with Yardley, whom I would have loved to meet.

Mendelsohn was commissioned a captain, and Yardley placed him in charge of solving German codes. (Figure 25.1) The messages Mendelsohn worked on were not from the Western Front; those were handled by codebreakers in France. Rather they were diplomatic messages that MI-8 obtained from a government radio station in Houlton, Maine. Most passed between Berlin and Madrid, Spain being neutral in favor of Germany. The messages were in four- and

Figure 25.1   Charles J. Mendelsohn as a captain in Yardley's MI-8 in World War I.

five-digit groups. Mendelsohn and his team, which included Victor Weiskopf, a former Department of Justice agent, and Edith Rickert, a University of Chicago English department professor, were greatly helped by Britain's having given MI-8 a partial reconstruction of German diplomatic code 13040 and others. When a large number of typists was unexpectedly and temporarily assigned to MI-8, Mendelsohn energetically took advantage of this windfall to have them to prepare statistics about the messages. MI-8 eventually solved six German diplomatic codes, which Mendelsohn and his co-workers determined derived from an unknown original that they called XX. His technique resembled the generation of stemmata — family trees of manuscripts tracing them back to what appears to be their source. It is a scholarly piece of work.

Two of the solved messages exposed German intrigues in Mexico. The first was sent from Nauen, the German transmitter in an exurb of Berlin, to Mexico at least 64 times between 23 January and 2 February 1918. It discussed a plan for providing Mexico with arms and machinery and with technicians for manufacturing weapons and airplanes.

Nothing came of the idea. The second, likewise from Nauen and intercepted in February, authorized the German minister in Mexico to offer the Mexican government 10 million pesetas as a "preliminary amount" "on supposition that Mexico will remain neutral during war." But the minister, who had been urging that Germany loan Mexico 20 times that amount to resist American pressures, never even mentioned the proposal to the Mexican government, perhaps as too insulting, and no significant German capital ever passed to Mexico. Though the United States merely watched these developments, the intercepts deepened its knowledge of Germany's machinations in a neighbor.

A radiogram from Germany's Madrid embassy to Berlin in Code 9700 revealed a plot to infect horses that the Allies were to buy. MI-8's reading of a 1,500-word prewar message validated its cryptanalyses, for the solution proved identical to a memorandum by the German ambassador to the secretary of state that was in the files. And MI-8 felt good about that, for while it found German diplomatic codes better than those of any other government it studied during the war, it broke them.

After the war, Mendelsohn returned to CCNY, now to teach history, and to its associated high school, Townsend Harris. But World War I had shown the United States the importance of codebreaking, and Yardley's executive ability had dazzled his government. He was placed in charge of America's first permanent peacetime codebreaking agency. This was set up in New York, at first in a brownstone on 38th Street, then in one on 37th Street, and finally in a tall office building at 52 Vanderbilt Avenue, on the corner of 47th Street. The agency came under military intelligence but was funded jointly by the War Department and the State Department. It was formally known as the Cipher Bureau but later became known as the Black Chamber, from the title of Yardley's best-selling book of 1931. Mendelsohn worked there part time apparently in the afternoons. He also joined with Yardley in a commercial codebook endeavor, in which Yardley got 49 shares, Mendelsohn, also 49, and the lawyer two. The Commercial Code Company compiled and sold a commercial code, the *Universal Trade Code*. Commercial codes were not secret but condensed a phrase or a whole sentence into a single codeword, thereby saving on cable tolls. For example, in the Yardley-Mendelsohn code, *accounts subject to discount (of)* was represented by ACKWO, which was cheaper to transmit than five words.

What cryptanalytic work Mendelsohn may have done does not appear in the records of the Cipher Bureau. It may not have been much, since no German codes seem to have been solved. Indeed, after the solution of Japanese diplomatic codes, which helped the United States win a diplomatic victory at the Washington naval disarmament conference of 1921-22, the Cipher Bureau languished, solving few foreign intercepts and having no influence on America's foreign policy, which was, in any event, isolationist. Yardley spent most of his time during the real estate boom of the mid- and late '20s buying and selling property in the New York City borough of Queens, where he lived. He and his wife transacted two property matters with Mendelsohn on 4 December 1928. Yardley's Cipher Bureau was closed down in 1929 by Secretary of State Henry L. Stimson on the ground, as he said later, that "Gentlemen do not read each other's mail." Yardley wrote a best-selling book, *The American Black Chamber*, about the work of MI-8 and the Cipher Bureau in which he cited only one collaborator, Dr. John M. Manly of the University of Chicago. Mendelsohn was not mentioned. Yardley was always broke, and at one point he sold his share of the code-making company to Mendelsohn. Sales of the one code that it had produced, with an addendum for the Tanner's Council, were handled by another code company, C. Bensinger Co. at 15 Whitehall Street, New York.

The end of Yardley's bureau did not end Mendelsohn's interest in cryptology. He was on good terms with William F. Friedman, a brilliant cryptologist who, with the demise of the Black Chamber, headed all Army codemaking and codebreaking. Friedman had served as technical consultant to the American delegation to the International Telegraph Conference at Brussels in 1928, one of whose major rulings dealt with the cable rates to be charged for the various kinds of codewords used in commercial codes. He joined with Mendelsohn in a paper that utilized Mendelsohn's mathematical ability. It sought to determine the maximum number of codewords permitted under the rules of the International Telegraph Union in force starting 1 October 1929. Codewords could be ten letters long but had to contain at least three vowels to make them "pronounceable" for the telegraph operators, who used not teletypewriters but Morse keys. To keep codebooks to a manageable size, codemakers used codewords five letters long, which they combined in pairs. But each five-letter codeword had to have at least two vowels to ensure that, when any two were joined, they would have at least three vowels. This reduced the number of usable five-letter codewords from the theoretical maximum of $26 \times 26 \times 26 \times 26 \times 26$, or 11,881,376.

In addition, Mendelsohn and Friedman, who had experience with the practical problems of transmitting the gibberish of code, imposed two further safety restrictions on codewords. One was to have them differ from one other not by just one letter but by at least two. In other words, if AAAAA were a codeword, AAAAB would not be allowed, but AAABB would be. So if a garble mangled one letter, the resultant five letters would not appear in the code word list. This would signal an error and the cipher clerk could search the five letters to find the one that would produce a coherent plaintext. The second restriction was to prohibit codewords that differed from one another by the transposition of adjacent letters. Such switching is a common psychological error — FEIND for FIEND, for example. Mendelsohn and Friedman sought to determine how many five letter codewords they could produce with these restrictions. Their calculations showed that an alphabet with an odd number of letters would make it possible to avoid transposition of alternate letters. But an alphabet of 25 letters would, by eliminating one letter, reduce the number of possible words. So they cleverly added a dummy letter, λ, lambda, to create a 27-letter alphabet. This would produce more combinations than a 25-letter alphabet. They then deleted all words with the λ, leaving codewords made up of only the letters A to Z. With a 25-letter alphabet, they would have had 390,625 words. With the 27-letter alphabet without the λ, they had 440,051. They published this article in the August-September 1932 issue of the *American Mathematical Monthly*, alongside articles on "Quasi-Cyclotronic Polynomials" and "Real Roots of a Class of Reciprocal Equations." It had little effect, because the advent of teletypewriters impelled what was now called the International Telecommunications Union in 1932 to drop the pronounceability requirement and permit five-letter codewords without any restriction. Still, the article showed Mendelsohn's breadth of knowledge. He was truly a polymath. I envy him that ability.

He and Friedman were good friends. They passed personal information back and forth in their letters, and lots of chit-chat. Mendelsohn, telling him about a bookplate by Yardley, said, "If you don't laugh at the following you're really sick." They lent material to each other. They visited. When Mendelsohn planned to pass through Washington, Friedman asked him to make sure to let him know at what time he would arrive as he wanted to meet him at the station. Mendelsohn told Friedman about cryptology books that were available. After he bought a 1726 work by Solbrig for $10.50, he wrote Friedman that "I ... am now offered another copy. If you want it for the files let me know at once, as it may be gone. It will cost $9." On 29 September 1936, he wrote Friedman, "I have been offered H. O. Yardley, 'Le Cabinet Noire' [sic] at 20 francs. Do you want it?" Friedman asked him to buy it. This is another reason I envy Mendelsohn. He got to know well and to work with Friedman, another of the giants of American cryptology. I would have loved to do that.

After the closure of Yardley's Cipher Bureau, Friedman, who had worked alone in the 1920s, hired and trained cryptanalysts. Mendelsohn's World War I report on the German codes would help teach them. Friedman asked Mendelsohn to prepare the report for confidential Army publication. Mendelsohn accepted, arranging to pick up the documents in Washington on his way to vacationing with his mother in Wilmington (his father had died in 1922) and to work on them during the summer. Friedman planned to meet him at the rail station, saying, "It will be a great pleasure to go over the stuff with you." It gave me a very nice feeling to see that indication of their personal and intellectual friendship.

Mendelsohn edited and expanded the report and returned the papers to the Army on 10 August 1931, saying, "It has been a source of real pleasure to renew acquaintance with this code material. Besides some miscellaneous odds and ends, I have written a study of some of the matter, which I am sending direct to Major Friedman." (Friedman, a civilian employee of the War Department, held a reserve commission.) But publication was delayed for one reason or another and the Army did not print it as a technical paper until December 1936. *Studies in German Diplomatic Codes Employed During the World War* had three sections: I, "Code 18470 and its Derivatives," which traced the relationships of the codes back to the unknown XX code; II, "The 'Fuenfbuchstabenheft," dealing with a five-letter code; and III, "German Methods of Code Encipherment." He later supplemented that third part with *An Encipherment of the German Diplomatic Code 7500*, another Army technical paper.

He and Friedman then tackled the cryptanalytic problems involved in the greatest intelligence coup of all time. This was the Zimmermann Telegram — a cablegram sent in 1917 by the Kaiser's foreign minister, Arthur Zimmermann, to the president of Mexico. Zimmermann, believing that Germany's unrestricted submarine warfare would bring America into the war against Germany, proposed that Mexico join Germany in the war. When they won, Mexico would get back the territories it had lost in 1848 — Texas, Arizona, and New Mexico. Britain intercepted and solved this message. Realizing that this was the propaganda weapon that would finally bring America into the war on her side, Britain gave it to President Wilson. He made it public. America exploded in outrage. Six weeks later, Congress declared war on Germany. Two German codes were involved in this — the modern 7500 in the message from Berlin to Washington, and the older 13040 for the relay from Washington to Mexico City, whose German legation did not hold 7500. Mendelsohn and Friedman examined and partially reconstructed the German codes involved and clarified the cryptology of this most important cryptogram in history.

The pair planned to write a scholarly history of cryptology. The professor of Latin would deal with the works written in that international lingua franca in the cradle years of the science. The active modern cryptologist would discuss the later evolution. The book was never written, but Mendelsohn translated two fundamental items as a warm-up. One was the 1466 manuscript of the father of Western cryptology, Leon Battista Alberti, an architect and a model of what came to be called a Renaissance man. His manuscript, of about 26 pages, included the first Western exposition of cryptanalysis, the first polyalphabetic substitution, and the first enciphered code. The other item was the world's first tract devoted entirely to cryptanalysis. By Cicco Simonetta, a secretary of the dukes of Milan, on two narrow strips of paper dated 4 July 1474, it comprised 13 rules for solving monoalphabetic substitutions. Friedman published it in the *Signal Corps Bulletin*.

These two translations served as forerunners to Mendelsohn's four scholarly articles on early cryptology, primarily of the Renaissance. Scholarly articles present fresh information, they're interesting, they deal with a single topic, and they're short. I like to read them and to write them. This is another reason I envy Mendelsohn. He did what I like to do, and he did it well. The first of his articles appeared in 1939 in a journal called *Scripta Mathematica*. It dealt with the brief sections on cryptography in two works in Latin by Girolamo Cardano, an Italian physician, mathematician and polymath of the 1500s. Mendelsohn, who claims Cardano's style is not the easiest, says that he gives what he calls a lazy man's example of the autokey. It was in fact a defective form of the cryptosystem, carelessly printed, and it is not surprising that only a few of the many post-Cardano writers on it whom Mendelsohn cites understood it.

Mendelsohn elucidates it and sets it into its place in the evolution of cryptology. He quotes Cardano's observation about the number of alphabets that a monoalphabetic cipher would make possible and remarks that "Trust in large numbers has been an *ignis fatuus* of cryptographers throughout the centuries." He describes Cardano's mask cipher, or grille. This developed into the turning grille, a transposition, which later had a vogue and which mathematicians analyzed to determine how many different grilles can be made with a fixed number of squares.

His next article, an important one, was published in 1939 in the *Signal Corps Bulletin* — almost certainly through Friedman's influence. Mendelsohn showed how another Renaissance cryptologist, Giovanni Battista Porta, had, in the 1602 edition of his *De Furtivis Literarum Notis*, come within a hair's breadth of finding the general solution for a repeating-key polyalphabetic, which had just completed its development (Figure 25.2). This would have anticipated the Prussian Major F. W. Kasiski's discovery of its solution by 250 years and would have destroyed the polyalphabetic's reputation as "the indecipherable cipher" almost before it had gained it. Mendelsohn says elsewhere of Porta, "He was, in my opinion, the outstanding cryptographer of the Renaissance. Some unknown who worked in a hidden room behind closed doors may possibly have surpassed him in general knowledge of the subject, but among those whose work can be studied he towers like a giant." Only someone who had read widely and deeply in the literature of the time could offer so confident an opinion.

Mendelsohn's most impressive article was published in 1939 in the prestigious *Proceedings of the American Philosophical Society*, submitted

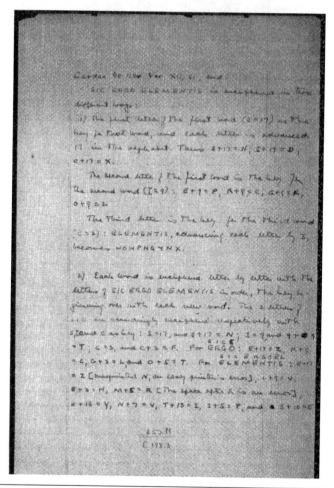

Figure 25.2 Notes by Charles J. Mendelsohn for his article on Porta and his solution of a poly-alphabetic substitution.

apparently at Manly's suggestion. In it he showed how the most famous form of the polyalphabetic – the Vigenère, named for the 16th-century French diplomat Blaise de Vigenère – had been misunderstood for hundreds of years since its publication in Vigenère's 1586 volume. Mendelsohn says that this book may properly be called "a part of the cryptographer's Bible," adding acidly that "Like the Bible, it is often spoken of but generally unread." Vigenère had devised a far better cipher than the one ascribed to him by the 23 authors from 1624 to 1935 whom Mendelsohn cites. Mendelsohn ascertained this by reading Vigenère's original text — a feat that, astonishingly (or perhaps not so astonishingly) — almost nobody else had done for the previous 350 years. He traces polyalphabetic substitution from its source in the Alberti manuscript, through other cryptologists' additions and refinements in obscure publications of the 1500s, up to Vigenère's book. He then sets out what Vigenère really devised, which was the perfected form of the autokey.

Mendelsohn's last article, "Bibliographical Note on the 'De Cifris' of Leone Battista Alberti," was published in *Isis*, the journal of the history of science, in 1947, after the hiatus of World War II.

I found all three of his articles of value and used them extensively to improve the accuracy of *The Codebreakers*. His reference in the Vigenère article to the cabalistic work "Sefer Yezirah" helped me later while I was tracing the origin of polyalphabeticity back past Alberti to the philosophical disks of the Catalan mystic Ramon Lull.

Mendelsohn was the first real scholar of the history of cryptology. Other authors — such as Johann Ludwig Klüber in his excellent *Kryptographik* – included historical material. But none approached Mendelsohn in the range, precision, and soundness of his scholarship. I envy him that as well.

Still, the activity with which Mendelsohn's name will be forever associated is less his scholarship, less his monographs and articles, than his collection of antiquarian books on cryptology. He was a bachelor and thus perhaps had more time and money to devote to this pursuit than married men, who have to support a wife and children. During the 1930s, Mendelsohn was collecting the antiquarian books on cryptology that form the basis of his fabulous collection. I have not checked a list of his books against the collections of the British Library in London or of the Bibliothèque Nationale in Paris or of the remarkable one of David Shulman in the New York Public Library. But I have no doubt that Mendelsohn's compares well with those of the two centuries-old libraries and may even exceed them, even though those institutions were buying books decades before Mendelsohn was born. The reason is that he worked at collecting on that subject. For example, he may have many more works in German than they have, because British and French libraries may not have paid as much attention to works in a foreign language on a curious but unimportant subject as he did. Moreover, Mendelsohn had the means, the knowledge, and the energy to pursue these works. Of course, he collected before the explosion of interest in cryptology, occasioned by the rise of computer security, the revelation of the World War II Ultra secret, and the invention of public-key cryptography. So his collection on cryptology does not include any works on those subjects — though the library containing his collection must surely include some. But in earlier "classical" periods, it is, if not the greatest in the world, certainly one of the greatest.

The prices, compared with those of today, make one green with envy. He refers to a book by Bazeries (he does not say which one) as costing 38 cents! He "lost out on the Thicknesse [a nice English book of 1772] at $3.75." Even at those prices, Mendelsohn did not throw his money around. When Colonel Parker Hitt's very little, very elementary *The ABC of Secret Writing* came out in 1938, Mendelsohn asks Friedman, "Is Hitt's new book worth the dollar it costs?" Friedman replies that "Hitt's new book is worth at most 25 cents.... I bought one, but that is only because I am collecting." Mendelsohn comments interestingly about the books in his correspondence with Friedman. "'Allgemeine Schrift' by David Solbrig, Saltzwedel, 1726, is one of the earliest codes I know, and elaborate and interesting. I do not aim to have a complete set of codes, but this book, with its introduction and method I am very glad to own. I should call it almost a 'must have' book. I paid $10.50 for mine." On 21 January 1938, he wrote, "Today I received what I regard as a prize — DuCarlet, 'La Cryptographie,' 1644. In its contents the book is not great, but it seems to be a rarity. I know of no copy in America; do you? It was offered me a year ago by Maggs (morocco bound, for which I don't give a damn) at $78.00 (*sic!*), and I just forgot about it. Through a friend I came on the track of the present copy (calf bound) for $15.50 (*sic!*)." He has been unable to find the Kasiski that he has been looking for — a fundamental work of 1866, explaining for the first time how to solve polyalphabetic substitution with a repeating key, regarded for centuries as unbreakable (though it is now in the collection, perhaps from another source). He and Friedman agreed that the 566-page *Étude sur la cryptographie, son emploi à la guerre et dans la diplomatic*, by the Belgian army officer, A. Collon, which appeared first as articles in the *Revue de l'Armee Belge* in 1899, is one of the best works on the subject.

In November 1938, six weeks or so after the war scare before France and Britain capitulated in Munich to Hitler's demands on

Czechoslovakia, the U. S. Army's Signal Intelligence Service, whose technical head was Friedman, sought to bring Mendelsohn back into active cryptanalytic service. The World War I cryptanalyst was "looking forward to this work with pleasure," but warned on 23 November that "A certain amount of red tape must be unwound in connection with any application for leave from an academic institution." In Washington, he would "require nothing more than a room and my own bath, preferably about fifteen minutes' walk from the Munitions Building, with street car or bus facilities available in bad weather. Quiet, especially within the place where I live, is balm to my general well-being." The army told him it wanted him because "We have a 4-letter code in the language with which you are familiar [German, not Latin], and on which we are making fair progress. The final filling-in of the code is the work for which we are going to depend upon you. In any case, this job will have progressed pretty well by the time you come. We also expect to have done quite a little preliminary work upon a more difficult code in the same language, and shall hope for your help in that. Also, if time permits, we hope you can go through our files of World War material and assist in classifying it." He began work on 24 January 1939 for six months at $400 a month, being paid by confidential voucher because "disclosure of Dr. Mendelsohn's name in connection with this work would indicate the exact nature of the work."

On 6 September, a few days after Nazi Germany had invaded Poland and Britain and France had declared war, Friedman told Mendelsohn that "We are most anxious to continue with where you left off here." Could he "obtain another extended leave of absence?" The red tape began again to be unwound, with a letter to the acting president of the City College. Then, on Saturday, 23 September, George and Alice Bernheim, friends whom he was visiting in Port Chester, a suburb of New York, found him, as Alice, a doctor, wrote to Friedman, "limp, cold, sitting on the edge of his bed. He had had a cold and a cough, had gone to bed the night before feeling chilly. I first thought he had had a stroke. I got him warm as fast as possible then sent him in an ambulance to the Mt. Sinai Hospital. He seemed to recover somewhat that evening — but on Sunday morning he showed signs of a full-blown meningitis" and he died Wednesday, 27 September, aged 58.

This meant, bitterly, that the articles of the greatest historian of early modern cryptology were – with the possible exception of the one in *Scripta Mathematica* – all published posthumously. Friedman edited the ones on Porta and Vigenère for their publication. Mendelsohn's mother was his sole survivor, and the Chief Signal Officer, General Joseph O. Mauborgne, who had known him since World War I, expressed his condolences. The Army, worried that its cryptologic expert had been poisoned on the eve of his coming to work, asked the Justice Department to investigate. Evidently, it soon discovered the unsuspicious truth. But what was to be done with his things, particularly the books. He had left everything to his mother.

What would happen, above all, to his books? In a letter to Alice Bernheim, Friedman wrote: "I cannot imagine anything more disquieting than to contemplate the dispersal of this collection by individual sale. So much time and labor of love has gone into the making thereof that it would be extremely unfortunate to have this happen. Furthermore, I doubt very much whether the sale of the books would bring in enough money to make a real difference in the well-being of Mrs. Mendelsohn, unless it is the case that she is much worse off financially than I have reason to suspect. It should be brought out that in my opinion nobody, in this country certainly, and perhaps nobody in the world, had made as serious a study of the history of cryptography as Charley did, and in making this study his collection was of course invaluable. For this reason it should be kept intact if for no other reason." (An Austrian historian, F. Stix, who had written some scholarly articles on the Austrian black cabinet of the 1700s and on other aspects of absolutist cryptology, was Mendelsohn's only rival in this field. But his papers were lost in World War II and, discouraged, he did not resume his studies.)

Friedman said he was astonished that "so meticulous a person as Charley ... had made no provision in writing with respect to the collection of books in his library." He went on: "I must tell you how vividly I recall the circumstances of his telling me of his wishes. At least two years ago, after he had spent a considerable sum of money and much time in gathering together his collection, I asked him what his intentions were with respect to the disposal of the collection after he passed on. He replied that he intended to will them to his alma mater. I pointed out to him that it would be in a way too bad to have the collection deposited there because they would not be easily accessible to the people most likely to want to consult them, namely, persons in the cryptographic services of the Government. This argument left him cold, however. About a year afterwards I repeated my question, simulating a poor memory on my part, but I received exactly the same answers and I did notice a small degree of irritation which was aroused by my query. Finally last winter I had the temerity, in a more or less jocular mood, to repeat my query, and this time Charley burst out with an oath, saying that if I asked him that question again he would brain me. Little did I suspect how near the day was that the question would be of immediate importance."

George Bernheim, a lawyer, was Mendelsohn's executor. Friedman wrote him as well "how unfortunate it would be to have Charley's collection of books on cryptography dispersed by sale and I hope that this will not be necessary." He also pointed out that Mendelsohn had purchased Yardley's share of their code publishing firm and thus became sole owner. "Just how much business the Code Compiling Company was able to do in recent years I do not know, but possibly there is enough to make a material difference in the financial affairs of Charley's mother." (Its code had gone into a second edition in 1928.) Bernheim replied that he knew that Mendelsohn was sole owner and "in due course I will have to wind up that company and see what I can get for it." As for the books, "I feel quite sure that there will be enough money available for Mrs. Mendelsohn so that the books on cryptography will not have to be sold." A month later, on 8 November, he wrote Friedman that he had written Herbert Bluethenthal, whose wife was a first cousin of Alice Bernheim and a friend to the Mendelsohn family, to send him, Bernheim, the books and papers. Bluenthenthal apparently had custody of them, for Mendelsohn had lived for many years at the University of Pennsylvania Club, which probably did not allow him room for his collection and which moved four times just during the 1930s. The books may have been kept in Bensinger's office or in Wilmington. Presumably they went via Bernheim to Penn, giving it custody, as their owner had wished, of one of the greatest collections on cryptology in the world, in the hope and expectation that it would serve future scholars. As it has! And as it commemorates their collector!

Of course, we are all only custodians of the things of this world. We cannot take them with us. Still, it would have been nice to have enjoyed that collection for a while. And that is the final reason I envy Charles Jastrow Mendelsohn. He had all those books!

Acknowledgment

The sources for this chapter lie in a study "The Mendelsohn Family — Misc. History" marked "From the files of Bill Reaves, Wilmington, N.C. 1996" and generously made available to me, in Mendelsohn's correspondence with Friedman, now in the Friedman collection at the George C. Marshall Library in Lexington, Virginia, and in the work of curator Regan Kladstrup. Photographs are courtesy of the University of Pennsylvania.

THE MAN IN THE IRON MASK

Encore et Enfin, Cryptologically*

The Man in the Iron Mask has intrigued people ever since Voltaire first told the story in *The Age of Louis XIV* and Alexandre Dumas père popularized it in his novel *Vicomte de Bragelonne*. Voltaire relates that several months after the death 9 March 1661 of Louis XIV's great minister, Cardinal Mazarin,

> An unknown prisoner, of height above the ordinary, young, and of an extremely handsome and noble figure, was conveyed under the greatest secrecy to the castle of the island of Sainte-Marguerite, lying in the Mediterranean, off Provence. On the journey the prisoner wore a mask, the chin-piece of which had steel springs to enable him to eat while still wearing it, and his guards had orders to kill him if he uncovered his face. He remained on the island until an officer of the secret service by name Saint-Mars, warden of Pignerol [a fortress at the foot of the Alps, now in Italy and called Pinerolo], who was made warden of the Bastille in 1690, went in that year to Sainte-Marguerite, and brought him to the Bastille still wearing his mask. The Marquis de Louvois [Louis' minister of war] visited him on the island before his removal, and remained standing while speaking to him, evidently regarding him with respect. The unknown prisoner was conducted to the Bastille, where he was accommodated as well as was possible in that citadel, being refused nothing that he asked for.... The unknown man died in 1703 and was buried by night in the parish church of Saint Paul. What is doubly astonishing is that when he was sent to the Island of Sainte-Marguerite no man of any consequence in Europe disappeared. Yet such the prisoner was without doubt, for during the first few days that he was on the

* From David Kahn, The man in the iron mask—encore et enfin, cryptologically, *Cryptologia*, 29:1, 43–49, 2005. DOI: 10.1080/0161-110591893753

island, the governor himself put the dishes on the table and then withdrew, locking the door after him....

   M. de Chamillart was the last minister to be acquainted with the
strange secret. His son-in-law, the second Marshal La Feuillade, told
me that when his father-in-law lay dying, he implored him on his knees
to tell him the name of this man, who had been known simply as *the
man in the iron mask*, Chamillart replied that it was a state secret and
that he had sworn never to reveal it.

The mystery grew. Historians have asserted variously that the masked
prisoner was the illegitimate son of Anne of Austria, queen to Louis
XIII, and hence a bastard elder half brother of Louis XIV, the Sun King,
or the second-born identical twin of the future Louis XIV, or the count
of Vermandois, or the duke of Monmouth, or Francois de Beaufort, or
Nicolas Fouquet, or Count Mattioli, or, finally, Eustache Dauger, a
valet. And less scholarly writers have spawned a vast literature.

   In the early 1890s, the great French cryptologist Commandant
Etienne Bazeries joined the crowd of sleuths with a new theory. His
was based on cryptology, which had never before been invoked to solve
the mystery. It began when a fellow officer who was studying the campaigns of one of Louis XIV's greatest marshals, Nicolas de Catinat,
found a number of Catinat's coded messages in the French military
archives. He asked Bazeries to solve them. In doing so, Bazeries read
a message of Louis to Catinat dated 24 August 1691. It stated that
the king was displeased at the raising of the siege of the Italian town
of Coni by one of his generals, Vivian Labbé, seigneur de Bulonde
(sometimes Bullonde), and directed Catinat that "His Majesty desires
that you immediately arrest General Bulonde and cause him to be
conducted to the fortress of Pignerol, where he will be locked in a cell
under guard at night and permitted to walk on the battlements during the day with a 330 309." Those two codegroups occurred only that
one time in the Catinat correspondence, which totaled 11,125 groups.
Their solution could therefore not be confirmed by other appearances.
But Bazeries verified that Bulonde's conduct in raising the siege had
been cowardly and that he never again held a command in the royal
army. He therefore concluded that 330 stood for *masque* and 309 for
a full stop. In 1893, he published *Le Masque de fer*, declaring that
General Bulonde was the man in the Iron Mask.

Other writers criticized it. As Fletcher Pratt put it in his 1939 *Secret and Urgent*, another historian, wishing to disprove other theories before offering his own, demonstrated that Bulonde had been alive and at liberty two years after the death of the mysterious prisoner. And indeed the *Dictionnaire de Biographie Française* states that, while Louis had ordered Bulonde arrested, jailed at Pignerol and then at the Bastille, he was still alive in 1708. (Louis died in 1715.) But the bibliography of cryptology records no reference to any cryptologist's going back to the original nomenclator to see whether Bazeries's hypothesis stood up.

In 1925, Emile-Arthur Soudart, a wartime chief of the French army's Cipher Section, and his assistant, André Lange, accepted in the first edition of their elegant and handsome *Traité de cryptographie* the Bulonde thesis of Bazeries, whom both very likely knew from his cryptologic work for the army and the Foreign Office during World War I. But they changed their minds in the second edition, of 1935. Its Errata [*sic*] No. II, states:

> A lucky circumstance having led us, a little after the printing of our work, to ourselves study the dispatch of Louvois solved by Mr. Bazeries, the examination of the ciphers of Louis XIV in the Historical Section of the Ministry of War enabled us to determine that none of the variants of the cipher of 1691 included the word *mask*, which is moreover not a word usually liable to figure in a repertory consisting of only 587 groups. Consequently, the intrinsic cryptographic motives invoked by Mr. Bazeries in favor of his solution appearing rather to weaken it, we have been led to think that the solution was doubtful if not erroneous.

They go on to say that "Marius Topin has demonstrated, moreover, that the Man in the Iron Mask was the Count Ercole Mattioli, prime minister of the duke of Mantua, and the works of Messrs. Funck-Brentano and Henri Robert confirm this hypothesis, unless further information comes along." Apparently, they did not find the nomenclator used in this cryptogram, which would be easily identifiable from the plain-to-cipher equivalents that Bazeries gave in his work. Nor do they give the plaintext or plaintexts of the codegroups 330 and 309 in any of the variants that they did see.

Bazeries dubbed the nomenclator he solved the Great Cipher of Louis XIV. He does not say why. Was it bigger than the others? Scores of other nomenclators of that reign exist. No one, to my knowledge, has compared them with the one Bazeries reconstructed. Lange and Soudart say that the ciphers they studied were in the Historical Section of the War Ministry but they do not specify which ones they examined. Spurred by their work, I went on a recent visit to Paris to the successor to the Historical Section, the Service historique de l'Armée de terre, now housed at the château de Vincennes, at the eastern edge of Paris. In its archives I looked for any Catinat nomenclators or, indeed, any of that period. The Service historique's catalogue for the relevant dates includes nomenclators of Louis XIV's reign, but none for Catinat and none for 1691 or a little earlier except for one in Carton LXXXVII for 1690 (Figure 26.1). But this gives no indication of who was to use it. It included no term *masque* and no marks of punctuation. The term *virgule* ("comma") does not appear, and *point*, which would stand for "period," is needed for many other senses. The other nomenclators listed either postdate the 1691 dispatch to Catinat or serve other correspondents: in other words, I found no candidates for nomenclators for the Iron Mask period. My work therefore substantiates that of Lange and Soudart. All of which further clouds Bazeries's solution, which few have accepted anyway.

Here is the catalogue listing: *Service Historique de l'Armée de Terre. Index à Série A de Correspondance général de la [Ministère de] Guerre, page 84. Chiffres de correspondance. Items nos. 6, 529, 1129, 1183, 2308, 2335, 2642, 351, 3000, 3728, Carton LXXXVII, Recueil des chiffres de correspondants diverses, 1709-1760* [though it includes one for 1690, as stated above].

Detail of this: #6, from 1577-1581. #529, from nov 1677. #1129, sept 1692. #1183, clef du chiffre entre Asfeld et Heiss 1688. #2308 includes jargon code, *pour Marlborough*. #2335, *renouvellement du chiffre de correspondance pour les gouverneurs et commandants de place*. #2642, *1707-1728, pièces 30 et 31, clefs pour chiffrer et déchiffrer la correspondance*. #351, no cipher listed. #3000, includes *chiffre et correspondance du maréchal de Belle-Isle pris par les ennemis*. #378, includes *chiffre de correspondance diplomantique, avec traduction* (undated) but others dated 1776-1783. Carton LXXXIII, *Recueil des chiffres de correspondances diverses, 1709-1760; 62 pièces et liasses.*

Before I visited Vincennes, I checked the enormous *Catalogue général des manuscrits français* of the Bibliothèque Nationale in the hope that that vast and ancient library, once the possession of Their

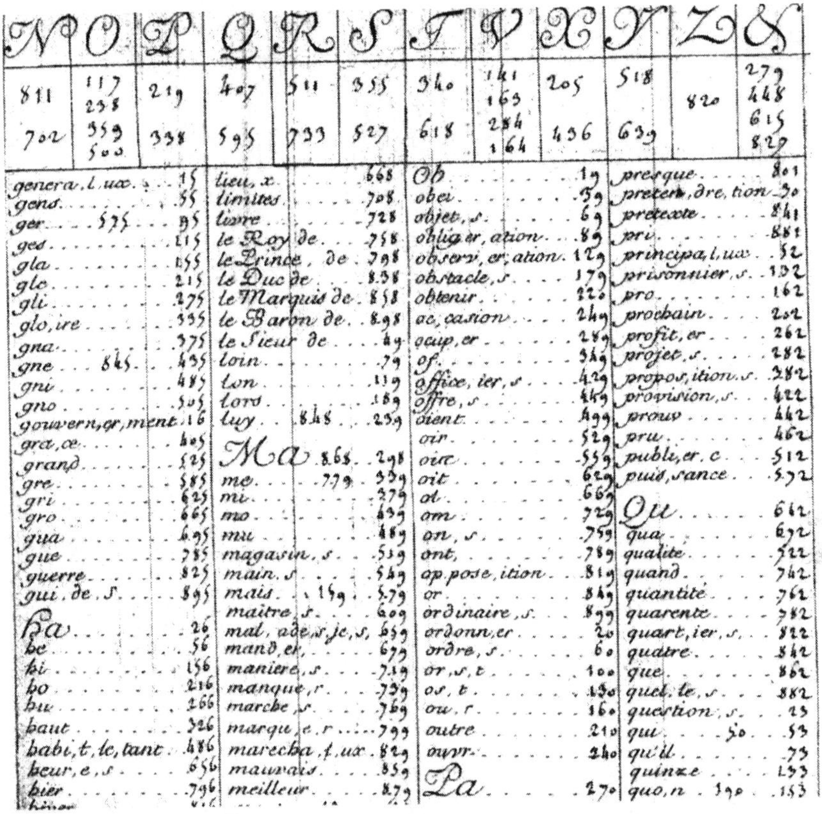

N	O	P	Q	R	S	T	V	X	Y	Z	&
811 702	117 238 359 500	219 338	407 595	511 733	355 527	340 618	141 163 284 164	205 456	518 639	820	279 448 615 829

genera,l,ux	15	lieu,x	668	Ob	19	presque	801
gens	55	limites	708	obei	59	preten,dre,tion	30
ger 575	95	livre	728	objet,s	69	pretexte	841
ges	115	le Roy de	758	obliger,ation	89	pri	881
gla	155	le Prince, de	798	observ,er,ation	129	principa,l,ux	52
gle	215	le Duc de	838	obstacle,s	179	prisonnier,s	132
gli	275	le Marquis de	858	obtenir	220	pro	162
glo,ire	335	le Baron de	898	oc,casion	249	prochain	202
gna	375	le Sieur de	49	ocup,er	289	profit,er	262
gne 845	435	loin	79	of	349	projet,s	282
gni	485	lon	119	office,ier,s	429	propos,ition,s	382
gno	505	lors	159	offre,s	459	provision,s	422
gouvern,er,ment	16	luy 848	259	oient	499	prouv	442
gra,ce	405			oir	529	pru	462
grand	525	Ma 865	298	oie	559	puble,er,c	512
gre	585	me 779	339	oit	629	puis,sance	572
gri	625	mi	379	ot	669		
gro	665	mo	439	om	729	Qu	612
gua	695	mu	489	on,s	759	qua	692
gue	785	magasin,s	519	ont	789	qualite	722
guerre	825	main,s	549	op,pose,ition	819	quand	742
gui,de,s	895	mais 159	579	or	849	quantité	762
		maitre,s	609	ordinaire,s	899	quarente	782
ha	26	mal,ade,s,je,s	659	ordonn,er	20	quart,ier,s	822
he	56	mand,er	679	ordre,s	60	quatre	842
hi	156	maniere,s	719	or,s,t	100	que	862
ho	216	manque,r	739	os,t	130	quel,le,s	882
hu	266	marche,s	769	ou,r	160	question,s	23
haut	326	marque,e,r	799	outre	210	qui 50	53
habi,t,te,tant	486	marecha,l,ux	829	ouvr	240	qu'il	73
heur,e,s	656	mauvais	859			quinze	133
hier	796	meilleur	879	Pa	270	quo,n 390	153

Figure 26.1 A part of the upper portion of a nomenclator of 1690, during the reign of Louis XIV, while the Man in the Iron Mask was still alive. This is not the nomenclator recovered by Bazeries. It depicts the type of cryptosystem generally used at that time and it shows as well that it does not include the questionable term *masque,* which Bazeries guessed at to resolve the mystery of who the masked man was. The nomenclator does not name the correspondent who used it. From Paris, *Service Historique de l'Armée de Terre,* Archives Série A, Carton LXXXVII (Recueil des chiffres de correspondents diverses), 1690.

Most Christian Majesties, the kings of France, might contain the wanted nomenclator. It catalogues its nomenclators on page 140 of volume II under *Chiffres diplomatiques* with item numbers. But these were diplomatic nomenclators, not military, and so probably did not include the Catinat one I was looking for. I therefore did not investigate them further. Still, I present them here in case some intrepid researcher wishes to look at them. He will need more energy than knowledge in this probably futile hope of discovering the final answer to the cryptologic mystery of the Man in the Iron Mask. Still, he may find a nugget or two in the items listed near the end.

Chiffres Diplomatiques

The numbers in parentheses are presumably item numbers in the volume whose number precedes; *na* stands for "nouvelle acquisition." The difference between *chiffres* ("ciphers') and *clefs* ("keys") is not set out; perhaps *chiffres* are nomenclators and *clefs* are cipher alphabets. 2988, 3022, 3029, 3034, 3053, 3081, 3251, 322, 3315, 3323, 3344 – 3400, 3409, 3413, 3414, 3422, 3462, 3564, 3618, 3619 (73), 3621, 3629, 3805, 3808, 3820, 3837, 3944, 3976, 3984, 399, 4053, 4471, 6204, 6556, 15913, 15915, 1600, 16093, 16156, 16913, 18009, 20746, 20991, 22882, 23026, *na* 5371, *na* 1045, *na* 4206 (in Italian), 3234, 3243, 3254, 3255, 3281, etc. [The B.N. does not explain why it has not placed these with the others in numerical order, whether it dropped the *na* for 3234 to 3281, and why it put in "etc." instead of listing the remaining nomenclators. The listing goes on:] To communicate by night, 3212 (150). *Clefs*: 1045, 3022 (48), 3234 (1), 3323 (1), 3329 (1), 3349 (1) 3364 (2), 3388 (15), 3395 (19), 3462 (91), 3618 (3 – 4), 3629 (42), 3657 (8), 3662 (24 bis), 3761, 3808 (1), 3820 (122), 3837 (5), 20974. Under ambassades, Louvois, chiffre diplomatique, 6204.

The library has a supplementary *Catalogue générale des manuscrits français. Ancien supplément français* whose Tome I: *Nos. 6171 – 9520 du fonds français*, lists the following cryptologic items: No. 6204. *Recueil de chiffres diplomatiques (1688 to 1713), chiphres [sic] de Louvois avec Maumort, et Avaux, Tirconel, Usson, Tallard, Martin, Bouchu, Lauzun et M. le Premier, Villeroy, Boufflers 2 anonymes, Tirconel, St. Aurice, anonyme, Vendosme, anonyme.* See also *Supplément français, 3283. Nos. 6493 – 6501. Papiers de l'abbé Capmartin de Xaupt. 6493, fol 76, Traité de l'art d'écrire en chiffres. 20975, Stéganographie, chiffres et déchiffremens. XVIIe Siècle. Papier, 79 feuillets. 17538, Mélanges politiques et diplomatiques de M. [Brûlart] de Léon. Un traicté des chiffres* and, at *folio 48*, a *Traicté des chiffres sous Louis XIII du XVII siècle.*

27

STUDENTS BETTER THAN A PRO (BAZERIES) AND AN AUTHOR (CANDELA)*

Rosario Candela was a successful New York City architect and an excellent amateur cryptologist. For several years after World War II he served as president of the New York Cipher Society, lecturing to the half-dozen members in his excitable, Italian-accented manner at evening meetings in his offices at 654 Madison Avenue. He owed his reputation in part to his 1938 book *The Military Cipher of Commandant Bazeries: An Essay in Decrypting*. An attractively designed and printed work (the result, no doubt, of Candela's publishing it himself) of 137 pages, it charms its readers with idiosyncratic opinions and entertaining digressions.

The military cipher of which he wrote was that of the successful and famous French cryptologist Major Etienne Bazeries. After the French general staff had turned down in 1891 what has come to be called the Bazeries cylinder (the inspiration for the U. S. Army's M-94 cipher device), Bazeries devised a new cipher. It was to meet the general staff's requirements of a system that would require only pencil and paper and that could be retained in memory without notes. He did not claim to have found an unbreakable system but did say that if three sample cryptograms that he submitted as tests could not be solved, he may have found the solution to the army's needs. The army requested an explanation of the system. He supplied it, together with another test cryptogram of 43 five-letter groups. It was a monoalphabetic substitution whose key changed each message with a transposition superimposed upon it and interspersed with some nulls.

On 19 April 1899, the army declined the system, saying only that it "does not present sufficient guarantees of security to be

---

* From *Cryptologia*, 23 (January 1999), 63–64.

adopted." Bazeries published this story in his lively 1902 book, *Les Chiffres secrets dévoilés* ("Secret Ciphers Unveiled"), ending with a bitter query of how this reply could be reconciled with the failure to solve the 43-group cryptogram.

Candela wrote that "The bibliography of cryptography shows that no attempt has yet been made to decrypt this pencil and paper cipher since its publication." He "succumbed to the temptation" of trying to gain through its solution "that measure of gratification which is the reward of any accomplishment." *The Military Cipher of Commandant Bazeries* describes his work, focusing on the solution of the 43-group message and giving the results as well of his solving the three earlier test messages. But, however charming the book is as an addition to the literature of cryptology, the system does not merit so exhaustive a study. William F. Friedman has said as much.

He may have based his opinion on something more than a general feeling that no monoalphabetic system can withstand cryptanalysis. In 1914, the Army Signal School at Fort Leavenworth, Kansas, was apparently instructing young signal officers in cryptology. Problem No. 5 described the Bazeries system on a mimeographed page and then gave the student cryptologists a sample cryptogram to solve. One worksheet is dated 11 December 1914 (a copy is in the folder Cipher Problems, Box 15, Bacon Cipher Collection, Manuscript and Rare Books Division, New York Public Library). Several of these problems were sent to the Riverbank Laboratories, a research institution in Geneva, Illinois, where Friedman was undertaking serious cryptographic work and where he quite likely saw them. Knowing that Bazeries' system was serving as an exercise may have given him his perspective on it. But one can only wonder what Candela would have thought had he known that his great effort had been matched a quarter of a century earlier by mere students!

28
THE OLD MASTER OF
AUSTRIAN CRYPTOLOGY*

Book Review

Otto J. Horak. *Andreas Figl: Leben und Werk, 1873–1967.* Vol. I: *Altmeister der österreichischen Enträtselungskunst und kryptographischen Wissenchaft, Hofrat i.R. und Oberst a.D.* Vol. II: *Was Übrig Blieb: Kommentare und Dokumente.* Schriftenreihe Geschicht der Naturwissenchaft und der Technik, Band 3 und Band 6. Johannes Kepler Universität Linz. Linz: Universitäts Verlag Rudolf Trauner, 2005. 303 and 292 pp. ISBNs 3–85487–770-X and 2–85487–790–0.

The name Andreas Figl resounds in the history of cryptology. He founded Austrian cryptanalysis in the years before World War I and led it to great successes during that conflict. He wrote a standard work on cryptography that was published in 1926, a study of cryptanalysis that the Austrian government kept from being published, and a memoir of his World War I work. During World War II, he was drafted into doing cryptanalysis for Nazi Germany but served only 18 months in Berlin before being released. He died in Salzburg in 1967 at 95.

For decades, the only information about him was the sketches in the history of Austrian intelligence in World War I by Colonel Max Ronge and an unpublished memoir by General August Urbanski von Ostrymiec. He deserved more. Now Otto Horak, a retired general of the Austrian army and an electronics specialist, has written the definitive biography. (The titles in English: "Andreas Figl: Life and Work, 1873–1967," I, "Old Master of the Austrian Solving Art and

* From *Cryptologia*, 31(2) (April 2007), 188–191.

Cryptographic Science, Retired Official and Retired Colonel," II, "What Else Remains: Commentary and Documents").

I cannot imagine any detail that Horak has missed. He includes a photograph of the Schubert School that Figl attended as a child, a map of the neighborhood in which he grew up, the heraldic arms, the date of his parents' wedding—two years after his birth on 22 June 1873. Horak provides the details of Figl's military career, starting with cadet school, and his successive postings, all in office work, none, apparently as a troop commander. In the multinational Austro-Hungarian empire, in which several languages were spoken, his record said that he had mastered German (his native tongue) and Serbocroatian, Italian well enough for military service, and French "well." His annual reports gave him the praise that all officers got unless they were utterly useless: in 1908 he was said to be "calm, serious, honorable,... militarily very able,... knows how to judge his subordinates and inspires trust in them." The one original comment is that he "gives the impression of a clear head." But then as of 23 May 1909, he was discharged because of an accident that blinded an eye.

Two differing stories claim to tell how Austria started in modern cryptanalysis. One is by Colonel Max Ronge, in World War I a head of Austrian intelligence, dealing with codebreaking in particular. In his memoirs, he writes that, in 1908, with Austria-Hungary and Russia opposing one another over pan-Slavism in the Balkans, the Austrian navy began intercepting Russian messages to and from the radio station at Antivari (or Bar, in Montenegro). They went to Ronge, then a captain and head of the Kundschaftsgruppe, the collection unit within the Evidenzbüro, the general staff's intelligence-evaluating agency. Buried in his unit's papers, Ronge found a Russian consulate cipher that enabled him to begin reading Russian intercepts. Then, helped by espionage, he extended his readings to the cryptograms of neighboring Serbia, Russia's client. When, in 1911, two of Austria-Hungary's neighbors, the Ottoman Empire and Italy, went to war over Libya, "it rained intercepted dispatches," Ronge said. The cryptanalytic work soon exceeded his capabilities and he was able to obtain an officer to help him: Figl.

The other story comes from Ronge's later boss, Urbanski, who was head of the Evidenzbüro at the time. Urbanski claims to have recognized long before World War I how important codebreaking would become. He sought help from the cryptanalysts of the Foreign Office. They refused it. Realizing that his unit would have to teach itself cryptanalysis, he asked his subordinates for help. Captain Hubka recommended one of his former regimental comrades: Figl. Urbanski brought in the retired officer, who in 1911 attacked Italian intercepts. Then Urbanski expanded this unit by bringing in a Russian-speaking officer.

Figl's own manuscript, "War Memories of the World War" does not credit one or the other with starting modern Austrian military cryptanalysis—nor does Horak. Still, a successful start did not assure the future of Austria's military cryptanalysis. Many officers remained skeptical of the value of codebreaking. In mid-June 1914, Figl relates, the head of the Evidenzbüro, Colonel Oskar von Hranilovic, summoned Figl to his office. He gave him a sheaf of some 40 intercepts from various countries, saying, "If these can't be solved by the 20th of September, I will end your service that day." On 28 June the Austrian crown prince was assassinated in Sarajevo, touching off World War I.

The Austro-Hungarian cryptanalysts, supplemented by those of its ally, Germany, helped the Central Powers armies stop the Russian "steamroller." And on the southern front, the Austro-Hungarians beat the Italians in the decisive 12th battle of the Isonzo, generally known as Caporetto. Figl regarded as one of his greatest rewards an unintended compliment by a postwar Italian inquiry into the loss: "the enemy knew all our ciphers, even the most secret and most important."

The outlines of the major successes have long been known, but Horak adds many new details about many new episodes—on the organization, the personnel, the results. He gives few cryptologic details, though he discusses an early cryptanalytic mechanism, the Scheuble apparatus (more details in *Cryptologia*, April 2007, p. 164–178) and provides the hierarchy of Italian field ciphers: the *cifrario tascabile* for front-line messages, the *cifrario servizio* for communications between field commanders, the *cifrario rosso* for the high command. The book is exceptionally well illustrated, with some unpublished photographs of Figl (Figure 28.1) and reproductions of important documents. Horak names many of the cryptanalysts. Sometimes he goes a little overboard, as when, because the Austrians used as the name for their intercept posts "Penkala," a pencil whose advertisements showed a

Figure 28.1   Andreas Figl.

giant ear with a pencil behind it, he gives a potted biography of the pencil manufacturer, Eduard S. Penkala.

After the defeat of Austro-Hungary, Figl got a job with the national police working in or with the Criminalistic Institute, perhaps because its scientific director, Dr Siegfried Türkel, was interested in cryptology: he later authored a solid, well-illustrated book on cipher machines. In 1924, Figl wrote "Kryptographische Erinnerungen aus dem Weltkrieg" ("Cryptographic Memories from the World War"). It relates the major Austro-Hungarian solutions—though not the cryptanalytic details—and their effects. It was never published. But a photocopy is going to the library of the National Cryptologic Museum at Fort Meade, Maryland.

In 1926, however, Figl did publish the first of two or three planned books on cryptology under the auspices of the Criminalistic Institute. *Systeme des Chiffrierens* described cryptosystems and their use in 243 pages. Its 46 technical appendices, printed separately and tucked into an envelope glued to the back cover, provided more information, in giving details of ciphers used during the war, than the rather diffuse text itself. The book hinted at Austro-Hungarian cryptanalytic successes, but did not detail what these were or how they were achieved. This seems planned for a future volume, "Systeme des Dechiffrierens." The publisher had set it into type when, in 1927, the Austrian defense ministry blocked publication on the ground of national security. It paid Figl nothing and indemnified the publisher merely for his typesetting costs. A few proofs were seen in the German Foreign Office code-breaking agency during World War II but did not survive. However, a copy of the manuscript exists, and a photocopy of it, bound in three volumes, is also going to the cryptologic museum. It is not worth much: it discusses mainly classical cipher systems, whose solutions are explained more clearly elsewhere, and hardly any of World War I; as a textbook it lacks rigor. Still, the suppression of the book understandably pained Figl for the rest of his life.

Afterward, he retired, writing nothing more of any significance in cryptology. He returned to cryptanalysis in 1941, when an Austrian cryptanalyst, Albert Langer, suggested his name to the Nazi Party's Foreign Intelligence Branch, Amt VI of the Reichssicherheitshauptamt. Figl went to Berlin on 2 January 1940 to work at Amt VI's Radio Observation Post. When other cryptanalysts were stumped, the story goes, Figl took his pot of black coffee into a rear room and emerged with the solution. But the post solved only the systems of minor nations, and it was dissolved in 1943. Figl returned to Austria on 28 July 1941. He solved no more and wrote no more but lived on, later in Salzburg, honored by comrades of the Austrian army, until, on 11 November 1967, he died, aged 95. He is buried in Salzburg's Maxglaner Cemetery.

These two volumes constitute more than just a biography. The supplemental volume II includes a 10-page bibliography, a listing of letters to and from Figl, a bibliography of his unpublished writings on cryptology, on the establishment of a cipher bureau and memoranda on the solution of historical and challenge cryptograms, clippings from magazines and newspapers, the table of contents of his unpublished book, his obituaries, organizational charts of Austrian intelligence in World War I (which show that Figl never headed any of the cryptanalytical branches), and more. One curious omission is any mention of the Ronge papers. Surviving in Vienna's Kriegsarchiv, they consist of Ronge's handwritten memoirs supported by many documents; a three-volume photocopy has been given to the National Cryptologic Museum.

Otto Horak has performed an outstanding service to historians of cryptology. It is extremely unlikely that any more facts about Andreas Figl will ever be discovered than those that Horak has found in his comprehensive, extraordinary work. Horak's book is definitive. It could be tighter, better organized, and set better into the contexts of the war and of Austria's long history of codebreaking—its black chamber in the 1700s was reputed to be the best in Europe, and several valuable scholarly studies exist on it. But, these are petty complaints. Otto Horak has given us a permanently useful work, and cryptologists will forever be grateful to him for it.

PART VI

A COUNTER-
FACTUAL AND
THE FUTURE

"Enigma Unsolved" speculates that Rommel, supplied with fuel by tankers that the British had been unable to locate and sink, would have advanced to the Caucasus, but would have been unable to link up with Army Group South, 600 miles to the north, ending the dream. "The Future of the Past" lists some questions in the history of cryptology that await resolution.

29

ENIGMA UNCRACKED*

The Allies Fail to Break the
German Cipher Machine

The Allied domination of enemy secret communications is universally regarded as an important contribution to their victory in World War II. In the Pacific, American solution of the Japanese naval code JN-25b enabled the U.S. Navy to spring with surprise upon the Imperial Combined Fleet at Midway and all but destroy it, turning the tide of the war in the Pacific: Japan never again advanced, but only retreated. In Europe, the Allies' reading of German cryptosystems—code-named ULTRA—helped them win victory after victory. In the battle of the Atlantic, the most fundamental struggle of the war, their knowledge of the location of U-boat wolfpacks let convoys steer around them, avoiding crippling losses and helping bring men and material to Britain. Later, in the great invasion of Europe that conquered Hitler's Reich, solution of German messages helped the Allies to foresee and ward off counterattacks and drive more successfully through German weak points toward the Ruhr and Berlin. Soviet codebreakers, too, exploited German communications intelligence to help win the war in the East.

But what if the Allies had not been able to crack enemy communications? The question cannot be answered with a single response. The Axis utilized many different communications systems. The Japanese, for instance, depended not only on its chief naval code, but also an administrative code, a flag officers' code, an army transport code, air codes, and many low-level military tactical codes, to mention only some. The Germans likewise used not only their famed Enigma cipher machine but also the tactical double-square cipher, whose key

---

* In Robert Cowley (ed.), what If? 2: Eminent Historians Imagine What Might Have Been, New York: G. P. Putnam's Sons, 2001, pp. 305–316.

changed every twelve hours, two different on-line teletypewriter cipher machines, the naval dockyard cipher, a plenitude of constantly changing ground-to-air systems, and some local cryptosystems. Even the Enigma was used in a variety of ways. Each service gave each of its communications nets its own key for the Enigma. Every corps in the army, for example, had one. The Kriegsmarine in particular divided its Enigma settings keys between U-boats and surface vessels and between various coastal commands. Solution of messages in one key did not automatically give the Allies access to messages in other keys. And some Enigma messages, like those used by the Luftwaffe, were relatively easily and almost constantly solved, while others, like those used by the U-boats, sometimes were solved and sometimes were not.

As a consequence, even a question that can be put simply—What if the Allies had not cracked Axis codes?—is complex. It hides many parts. The answer depends upon the cryptosystem under consideration. The matter may be simplified somewhat by eliminating the Japanese. This is fair because Japan's military and naval codes were not modern mechanical marvels but old-fashioned book codes. Such codes and their ancestors had been solved since the Renaissance. Thus, though Japan changed its codes at intervals, the new ones were constantly being solved on the basis of widely known principles of cryptanalysis. There was little chance that the Allies would entirely lose that source of information. This situation differs from that of the Enigma. Though the Enigma was employed with different keys and in slightly different ways in the several services and their various communication nets, it remained a single machine cloaking a great many medium- and high-level operations in all theaters of war. And its solution rested in the end upon a few ingenious ideas that applied to all its uses. If Marian Rejewski in Poland in 1931 and Alan Turing and Gordon Welchman in England in 1939 had not had those ideas, the Enigma might well not have been solved. So the suggestion that the Allies may not have cracked Enigma is not a blue-yonder possibility but one that enjoys substantial probability.

Again, the question—What if the Allies had not cracked the Enigma?—hides many parts. Which Enigma is being talked about? When and where was it used? Managing the question means reducing it to a single case. And that case must be relatively simple. To ask what would have happened if the Allies had not cracked the U-boat Enigma engages so many other factors as to make it all but unanswerable. Were there so many U-boats in the North Atlantic that convoys could not divert around all of them? Conversely, was air cover so complete that even if the Allies steered right through wolf packs the U-boats would not attack? And it must not be forgotten that the enormous successes of the U-boats off the eastern coast of the United States in the first half of 1942 owed nothing to the temporary inability of the Allies then to read Enigma. Rather that so-called "killing time," just after the United States had entered the war, came before convoys had been introduced and while the seaboard cities still blazed with lights, silhouetting tankers and making them easy targets for submarines, who often sank their targets in sight of watchers on the beach.

Still, though numbers cannot easily be attached to the question of what effect the Allies' reading of the U-boat Enigma had, a vague answer can be: It helped. It reduced the number of U-boat sinkings of Allied cargo vessels and so raised the quantity of supplies that crossed the Atlantic from America to Britain. This meant that the buildup of ammunition, guns, fuel, food and the other necessities of war proceeded more rapidly than it otherwise might have. As a consequence, the invasions of North Africa, Sicily and Italy, and Europe itself were not delayed and had a greater chance of success than if ULTRA had not worked its wonders on the Enigma messages.

One case, however, permits a relatively straightforward response. What if the Enigma messages that told the Allies where and when ships would carry fuel to Rommel's forces in Africa had not been solved? For those solutions enabled the Allies to sink many of those vessels and choke off the fuel that was critical to his motorized campaign.

Rommel's panzer army used 300 tons of gasoline on quiet days for supply deliveries and other routine activities. In battle, it needed 600. This came to him by tanker across the Mediterranean from Italy. It had fueled his race hundreds of miles across the desert by the end of October 1942, ending near a railroad stop called El Alamein. A glorious prize glittered ahead: Cairo, the Suez Canal, and the gates to the Middle East. He wanted to leap forward. But the advance had exhausted his gasoline stock. As the enemy fortified the ridge of Alam el Halfa, Rommel felt that he had enough fuel only to advance thirty miles. On October 24, he was informed that he had only enough for three days' battle. One reason was the sinking of the tanker *Panuco*, which had been carrying 1,650 tons of gasoline. One of his staff officers demanded another tanker immediately and insisted on being told when it would arrive. Headquarters in Italy enciphered a reply in Enigma and radioed it to Africa: "Tanker *Proserpina* sailing evening 21st with 2,500 tons army gasoline, arriving Tobruk early 26th. Tanker *Luisiana* ready to sail with 1,500 tons army gasoline on 25th; if tanker *Proserpina* arrives tanker *Luisiana* will sail with tanker *Portofino* from Taranto evening of 27th, put into Tobruk approximately 31st. *Portofino* has 2,200 tons army gasoline."

But the British code-breaking establishment at Bletchley Park, sixty miles northwest of London, had solved a message of Rommel's reporting that his fuel consumption had exceeded his resupply and that he had enough fuel to last only until August 26. Based on this information, the British chiefs of staff instructed the forces in the Mediterranean to do all they could to interrupt Rommel's fuel supply. And they did. Ship after ship was sunk—either by Royal Air Force bombers or by submarines based in Malta. Rommel's fuel situation grew tighter and tighter, limiting his ability to maneuver and to fight. Thus, when General Bernard Law Montgomery fell upon him at El Alamein, Rommel could do little more than put up an ineffectual defense—and retreat. It was, as Churchill said, "the end of the beginning."

But imagine that Britain cannot learn of Rommel's precarious supply situation and that Enigma solutions do not let her partially choke off his fuel supply? Of course, some of the tankers are sunk even without that information, but the panzer army is now not thirsting for gasoline. Rommel, no longer restrained by fuel problems, has the freedom to continue the advance that had taken him so many miles along the coastline of North Africa.

He is aided in this advance by a useful bit of German codebreaking. They had obtained the U.S. military attaché code, named the black code for the color of its binding, and were reading the messages of the American observer in Cairo, Colonel Bonner Fellers.

Fellers was an intelligent, energetic officer. He sought to send home information that would enable his army to learn the lessons of desert warfare. And the British, who desperately wanted American help, gave him access to almost everything. Visiting the British front, he discussed the capabilities of their forces, analyzed tactics, revealed their strengths, weaknesses, and expected reinforcements, even foretold plans. He dutifully encoded his messages in the black code and sent them through the Egyptian Telegraph Company by radio to the War Department.

So rich, so full of information were these messages that the Germans assigned two radio intercept posts, one at Treuenbrietzen and one at Lauf-an-der-Pegnitz, to pick them up to make sure that they missed not a precious word. The solutions were then radioed to Rommel, encrypted in Enigma. He called them his "good source," for, coming from an observer who had unparalleled access in the enemy camp, they gave him fabulous insight into his foe's intentions. Hitler himself commented that he hoped "that the American minister [attaché] in Cairo continues to inform us so well over the English military planning through his badly enciphered cables." Rommel probably had the broadest and clearest picture of enemy forces and intentions of any Axis commander during the war.

Early in 1942, for example, he was getting information like this from the Fellers intercepts:

Jan. 23: 270 aircraft being withdrawn to reinforce Far East
Jan. 29: List of all British armor, including number in working order, number damaged, number available and their locations
Feb. 6: Iteration of British plans to dig in along the Acroma-Bir Hacheim line

This helped him rebound in the seesaw desert warfare starting January 21, 1942, with such vigor that in seventeen days he threw the British back 300 miles.

Momentum hurls him along. His new adversary, General Bernard Law Montgomery, does not have time to build up his defenses at El Alamein, much less prepare an offensive. Rommel sweeps the few score miles into Cairo. Fellers flees but his intercepts are no longer needed. The British destruction of bridges across the Nile does not slow Rommel; he throws pontoons across and sends his tanks rumbling across their shaky spans. The populace cheers its relief from the hated British colonizers, who run south to Ethiopia, which they had liberated in 1941 from its Italian conquerers. Rommel, with greater visions in mind, ignores the remnants of Montgomery's army.

Wearing his goggles atop the visor of his cap as he rides a scout car, he waves back at the Arabs. Mussolini sits atop the white charger he has had flown in for his entry into the capital of a country that was bounded south (until recently) and east by Italian territory and that, he believes, naturally belongs to the ruler of the Mediterranean. He thinks himself a successor of the emperors who 2,000 years ago rode in golden chariots through the triumphal arches of ancient Rome, captive kings and lions crouching before them.

He and Rommel then drive the eighty miles to the Suez Canal. They watch amazed as vessels, behind the levees that hold the water higher than the desert, seem to sail through the sand. No Royal Navy warships, no freighters flying the red ensign of the British merchant marine will henceforth take that shortcut from India and the dominions beyond the seas. They will have to steam around the Cape of Good Hope, adding weeks to their voyage and subtracting effective men and supplies from the Allies' armory. The Mediterranean is again for Italy, as it was in Roman times, a *mare nostrum*.

The world is as shaken by the fall of Cairo as it had been by that of Paris two years earlier, and armchair strategists and pundits foretell dire results. But they do not know of all plans. Some things happen that they never foresaw; some that they predicted do not happen at all, and some not when they said. Gabriel Heatter, a newscaster with a lugubrious voice on New York's radio station WOR, forecasts that Spain will soon join the Axis. It doesn't happen. Franco sees no loot to grab, any more than he did when France fell in 1940. He was cooperating with Hitler anyhow, and while Britain was still standing, as was the United States, he sees no reason to stop hedging that bet. Like Switzerland, Spain remains neutral.

Everyone realizes that Malta, though it had bravely withstood Luftwaffe air attacks, is now utterly isolated, with support possible only from Gibraltar through a hostile sea. Emotionally, Britain would have liked to sustain its faithful colony, and militarily it would have liked to retain its powerful naval base there. But to what end? What could its ships do from there? Harass the Italian fleet, perhaps, only to be sunk by overwhelming Axis naval and aerial forces. Could help be sent? Churchill would dispatch neither ships nor men on a suicide mission that could bring no hope of positive results. He abandons the island. Hitler, who had promised Mussolini to invade Malta and then postponed doing it, recognizes that he can redeem that promise the easy way. He will let the isolated island wither. Il Duce is happy to get a coveted new possession so easily.

Momentous as is the fall of Cairo, it cannot stop other events that have been set in motion. The United States and Britain have been planning for months finally to shift to the offensive. Convoys had sailed even as Rommel and Mussolini were marching through Cairo. And on the night of November 7 and 8, American and British troops come ashore at Oran and Algiers and western Morocco. The areas are poorly or not defended at all and the Allies are soon lodged on the continent of Africa—their first holding beyond the island of Great Britain.

It worries the Axis not at all. To them, it is a mere pinprick, and in their rear at that. It cannot stop their march of conquest. Rommel dispatches a corps—infantry, not panzer—to stop the silly, inexperienced Americans. And for a few months, at Kasserine Pass in Tunisia and elsewhere, he does so. Meanwhile, true to the German tradition of aggressive action, he focuses on his next advance. Where will it be?

The decision, of course, is not his alone. It will be made in Berlin. And Hitler must choose between two axes of advance. One is east. It would strike through Arabia and its oil toward Iran; it would sever the Allied supply lines across Iran to Russia and across India to China. The Germans would shake hands with the Japanese advancing from Burma and outdo Alexander the Great. The other axis drives north. Rommel would roll through Palestine and Iraq to bite the underbelly of the Soviet Union and shake neutral Turkey into the Axis camp. Oil does not figure into this scenario because Hitler is confident that Army Group B, driving southeast through the Ukraine, though temporarily slowed at Stalingrad, will soon capture the fields around Baku on the Caspian Sea. Moreover, the Axis control of Egypt means that Allied bombers will no longer fly from there to strike the oil fields of Ploesti in Romania. In the end, Hitler decides on the northern advance. It will speed the defeat of the Soviet Union, both through the German invasion from the south and Turkey's attack on its old enemy Russia. The Mideast oil is far away and not immediately available. Moreover, with the Soviet Union gone, Iran, which cannot defend itself, even with British help via the Persian Gulf, will submit to Hitler's demands.

With the British neutralized in the Mediterranean, Hitler can send major reinforcements to Egypt.

After a short rest and refitting, Rommel's panzers mount up, and, gas tanks full, thunder into the desert east of Cairo in December. They cross the canal and traverse the top of the Sinai Peninsula, then turn north through Palestine and northern Transjordan, across Iraq to Kirkuk, and then north again through the outliers of the Caucasus to enter the Soviet Union through Armenia. As the armored columns pass threateningly close to Turkey, that country, bordered by Axis partners or conquests, seeing no option other than cooperation, and hoping for the destruction of Russia, jumps onto the Axis bandwagon. It doesn't gain the advantages it hoped. Armenian troops, remembering the massacres of their fathers by the Turks during World War I and resisting the invasion by Turkey's new allies, fight hard for their homeland. They cannot turn back Rommel's armor and battle-hardened troops. But they delay them. And while they do so, Army Group B gets stopped at a city of rubble and doom and glory named Stalingrad. Rommel indeed reaches Baku at the end of the winter of 1943. The German troops that reached the western Caucasus the previous summer have already been forced to retire. Soviet troops keep Rommel from driving the 600 miles to link up with Army Group B. And then what? He is stuck. He can't get the oil out. Hitler's grand plan has failed. To save himself, Rommel turns tail and returns home to Africa—a wornout corps, with no mission, no heroes, and no future.

In western North Africa, meanwhile, the Americans have learned to fight better, and their greater material strength—more men, more airplanes, more tanks, more ammunition—is gradually telling. They are advancing more and more against the battle-tested but now battle-weary Germans. In the months that Rommel has been away, the Allies have pressed eastward. The British forces in Ethiopia are reinforced from India, Australia, and New Zealand and move northward to squeeze the Germans out of Africa. This takes time, of course, and Rommel and his troops escape to Greece and Italy. By 1944, the Allies hold all of North Africa. They consolidate and consider invading Italy.

The Russians slog forward in the bitter, ideological, racist war that Hitler forced upon them. They are helped by their code breakers, who frequently resolve German tactical cryptosystems. It is often noted that Russians are good in music, mathematics, and chess—three characteristics that seem to predict ability in cryptanalysis. But no more than the Western Allies can they achieve a general solution of the

Enigma. At best, they occasionally capture a machine with its associated key lists and read messages during the key's validity. Throughout 1943 and 1944 and into 1945 they bleed as they advance against the Wehrmacht. And they scream for a second front.

They are not alone. The American and British publics call for the same thing. Why haven't we invaded northern Europe, they cry? That is the only way to drive a stake through Hitler's Reich. But the buildup for that operation lags, as the U-boats take their toll on the growing number of Liberty ships and sometimes troopships that lumber into packs of submarines. Direction-finding is not precise enough to locate these underwater fleets. The Allies indeed intercept the reports from the U-boats and the directions for their attacks from Germany. The code breakers count the letters in the messages, seek repetitions, analyze them, hypothesize, but hammer futilely upon the impregnable walls of the Enigma. Occasionally they read a cryptogram or two, when a code clerk errs and resends one plaintext twice, each at a different machine setting, giving them an isomorphism that they use to pry open the pair. But most messages remain unreadable. The U-boats roam at will. The Allies seem unable to get enough men and supplies to Britain to mount a successful invasion.

Then suddenly it is all over. A new weapon, in which something too small to see makes the biggest explosion men have ever seen, obliterates Berlin. That nuclear flash makes codebreaking unnecessary. World War II in Europe ends.

30

THE FUTURE OF THE PAST*

Questions in Cryptologic History

When I think of Hank Schorreck, whom I knew all too briefly, I remember what Isaac Newton said: "If I have seen further [than others], it is by standing on the shoulders of giants." That's how I feel about Hank. He began the work that I followed. He broke much of the new ground. The rest of us are standing on his shoulders.

When I was asked to do this talk, I asked myself what would be a good way to talk about the problems that face the history of cryptology. And I thought back to a talk that David Hilbert, the great German mathematician, gave to the International Congress of Mathematicians in Paris in 1900. In it he set out twenty-three problems that mathematicians should be attempting to solve during the forthcoming century. For example, one of them was to prove that every even integer is a sum of two prime numbers, as 8 is the sum of 3 and 5. It seems to be true, but a proof of this was needed. Hilbert's problems served as a program for people working on mathematics in the 20th century and continue to do so still in the 21st century. Some have been solved; some are still being worked on.

I am going to try to do the same thing for a number of problems that interest me in the history of cryptology. Some may be solvable, some not. Some are purely historical; some are more philosophical and spread out from the purely cryptologic into the larger area in which we are all involved, namely intelligence. Perhaps the answers to some of these might serve as an article or, for the larger ones, as the subject of a dissertation.

---

* This chapter is the text of the Henry F. Schorreck Memorial Lecture given by Dr. Kahn at the Center for Cryptologic History: National Security Agency on 24 May 2007.

433

One of the first problems that interested me was the origin of the square tables, like the one now generally called the Vigenère table, but which appeared before Vigenère in the first printed book on cryptology, that by Trithemius in 1518. I first thought about the connection with cryptology when I was at the Cloisters, a museum in New York City, in which I saw a table for the construction of the dates of Easter. Easter is a movable feast on the first Sunday after the first full moon after the vernal equinox. The church, I learned later, constructed tables to determine the date of Easter for years to come. It occurred to me that perhaps this might have been the inspiration for Trithemius to set up his table for polyalphabetic substitution, which is one of the first uses of those square tables. The first form of polyalphabetic substitution, invented by Alberti in 1466, used discs. Tables were first published by Trithemius, who was a Benedictine monk. So when I saw the Easter table at the Cloisters, it occurred to me that that might have been the source for the polyalphabetic table. So this might be a matter for someone to look into.

Another problem arose in my mind after I discovered, while writing *The Codebreakers*, that the Arabs had been the ones to invent cryptanalysis.

They were very early in advancing new forms of cipher and in combining transposition and substitution. This was done in the 600s, 700s and 800s of the Christian era, in a time when Arab civilization was flowering in many fields – not only in codes, but in many areas of science and mathematics.

Their civilization was burgeoning and expanding at a great rate. The question that I asked myself was, "Did the Arabs have black chambers?" These arose of course in Europe much later. But did the Arabs have enough commerce between the various cities? Was there enough communication of ambassadors and regional governments to be intercepted? If there was, and if it was read, what effects did this have? To the best of my knowledge, nobody has ever looked into this question. So some student of medieval Arab history might want to see if the Arabs began to do cryptanalysis as did the West many years later.

A smaller but similar problem would ask whether the small principalities of Germany during the absolutist period had black chambers.

The major powers did. Austria's black chamber has been well studied. So have France's, Britain's, even the Netherlands'. Spain, I have just learned, had its equivalent of France's Antoine Rossignol and England's

John Wallis: Luis Valle de la Cerda, many of whose solutions may be found in the Biblioteca Nacional in Madrid in mss. 994. But did such principalities as Prussia, Saxony, Bavaria, and the Hanseatic cities open letters? In all my reading of cryptologic history, I have come across only two case histories of the black chamber of a small German state. One, by K. L. Ellis, deals with the Hanoverian "secret bureau" at Nienburg. The other, by S. P. Oakley, details the interception of posts in Celle, a small town north of Hanover once the residence of the dukes of Brunswick-Lüneberg-Celle. If such small states had such a unit, perhaps others did as well. But to the best of my knowledge nobody has looked into their archives to investigate this aspect of cryptologic history.

Another question is that of China. China had an old and great civilization. But because reading and writing required memorizing hundreds or thousands of the logograms that represented words, instead of an alphabet of a few letters that stood for the sounds of the words, literacy was not widespread. A letter was itself almost a cryptogram. So there does not seem to have been a great deal of interest in cryptology. Moreover, the Chinese writing system does not tend to lend itself well to encryption by transformations in the ideographs. I once asked a Chinese historian, "Could you move some of those strokes of the ideograms to different places as a form of encryption?" He said that it wasn't doable. On the other hand, a codebook seems feasible (and served after the introduction of telegraphy to transmit the ideograms). So it seems to me that China, which had a great empire, an extensive mandarinate, and an old, proud, and advanced civilization, might have developed some kind of cryptology. Nevertheless, to the best of my knowledge, nobody has investigated whether any Chinese ever worked on codemaking or codebreaking. This seems like a ripe field for research.

A much more secondary issue is the evolution of nomemclators. "Nomenclator" is a term I adapted and redefined for *The Codebreakers* to designate the half code, half cipher in widespread use in European cryptography from the Renaissance to the telegraph. Nomenclators list proper names and common words of maybe 2,000 at maximum. The cipher secretaries of the Italian city-states, who were charged with creating cryptographic systems for use with their ambassadors, began with simple monoalphabetic cipher systems and added proper names, as "the pope," "the king," and the like. Thus nomenclators evolved.

At first the substitution symbols were neither letters nor numbers but fanciful signs like + or ♥. But nobody has looked into when, in the later evolution, as nomenclators ran out of easily distinguishable symbols and began using numbers, the cipher secretaries began forming two-part nomenclators. This research requires merely examining the many nomenclators in the archives of Italy and France and timing and quantifying the change. I suppose it will be tough, living in Europe for a year and having an aperitif after a day examining antique manuscripts. But somebody should do it!

A question that has interested me is the evolution of German army cryptology in the years between the war with France, 1870-71, and the start of World War I, when Prussia-Germany was the most powerful country in Europe. One would think that it would have wanted a good cryptosystem or cryptosystems to protect its field communications. To the best of my knowledge, nobody has looked into what that army had during those years.

Of course there is a problem. The Prussian military archives were bombed in October 1944 and April 1945, destroying all the records of the Prussian Army – including, of course, its signal and cryptographic files. But hope glimmers yet. The imperial German army in those years had several components under the emperor of Germany, who was also the king of Prussia. Though the Prussian army was the largest, units also came from Baden, from Württemberg, and from Saxony. They had to communicate, so they must have had cryptographic systems in common. The archives of these states survived both wars. So it is possible to look into those records to see how German military cryptology evolved from the creation of the Second Reich in 1871 to its end in 1918. And there may also be some indications of cryptanalytic work. A few shards of this work exist in the naval files, which likewise survive. Present knowledge has it that neither the German army nor its navy did cryptanalysis until World War I was at least a few months old. Perhaps some archival research will yield a fuller and more precise picture.

In connection with that, two important battles in WWI were helped to victory to a considerable degree by codebreaking. One was the battle of Tannenberg. Barbara Tuchman devotes a chapter to it in her Pulitzer Prize-winning book *The Guns of August*. In that opening month of World War I in 1914, the Russians invaded East Prussia with two armies. The Germans intercepted many of the Russian messages and, using that information, encircled one of the armies and destroyed it, winning that battle and defending the sacred soil of the Reich from the horrid footprint of the Slav.

Later interceptions helped the Germans defeat the tsar's armies, driving Russia to revolution. The head of the German eastern front operations department acknowledged the significance of cryptanalysis in those events: "We had an ally that I can only talk about after it is all over. We knew all the enemy's plans. The Russians sent out their wireless in clear." So I think that it can be said that the establishment of communist power, probably one of the supreme facts of the 20th century, was made possible to a significant degree by radio intelligence.

The other important battle whose victory was greatly helped by radio intelligence took place on the southern front, in which the Austrians were fighting the Italians. In the 12th battle of the Isonzo River, better known as the battle of Caporetto, the Austrians, who had excellent codebreaking, defeated the Italians. At the end of war, the Italians inquired into the defeat. The commission found that one of the reasons for it was that the Austrians "knew all our ciphers, even the most secret and most important."

I would like to have greater detail on the role of codebreaking in those two victories of the Central Powers. Though the German documents were destroyed, periodical literature, memoirs, and diaries dealing with the battle do exist. A historian will have to go to the Italian and Austrian archives and find what he or she can. Of course, the historian will face the usual problem in dealing with a part of a whole: not to overstate the role of that part, in this case, intelligence, when other factors also mattered.

In World War II, I would like to know more about Alan Turing's contributions to cryptology. We all know that he had the great idea for the bombe. This enabled the British to compare a proposed plaintext with an intercepted message and see if any arrangement of the Enigma rotors would permit such an encipherment. If it did, it provided the cipher key for that network for that day and so enabled the British to read all the other messages for that day. That was his great contribution. But he also helped solve the German on-line teletypewriter encryption systems collectively called FISH, and he came to the United States to help out with SIGSALY, the one-time system for telephony. It was used by the United States in a great many operations, including the telephone conversations between Roosevelt and Churchill. What did Turing do in this? Incidentally, though I have looked fruitlessly for transcripts of those conversations, perhaps a better – or luckier – researcher than me might find them and thus add to our knowledge of the relationship between these two leaders. I'm not very sanguine, though.

Another question that has always intrigued me is, what was the first electrical cipher machine? Though Alberti's disk can be considered a device, as can Jefferson's cylinder, probably the first truly mechanically driven cryptograph – using gears, for example – was Sir Charles Wheatstone's. Others followed. But when did electricity begin to play a role? I don't know, and to the best of my knowledge nobody has ever looked into that. This should not be difficult methodologically: one need only look through the patents in the several national patent offices.

Whitfield Diffie, who had the idea in America of public-key cryptography, said it would be interesting to find out why the Japanese decided to use telephone stepping switches in their PURPLE diplomatic encryption machines. He thinks this is one of the great cryptographic ideas of the first half of the 20th century. His reason is that because stepping switches are sold on the open market – they don't need to be manufactured specially, as rotors are – they are more reliable than rotors. I don't know that I agree with him about the significance, but Whit has a good mind and so that may be worth pursuing.

Another issue, though to me of secondary importance, is when did people begin encrypting telemetry? Knowledge of a missile's flight path, and perhaps commands to it could have nation-saving importance. I have never seen anything about the origins of encrypted telemetry.

Another question that has interested me is whether there are any precursors to asymmetric cryptology. One form of asymmetric cryptography is public-key cryptography, which has made electronic commerce possible – you can send your credit card number to Amazon. com without having to give it to a trusted courier. Asymmetric cryptography is a truly original concept. When I was a kid doing codes and ciphers, the thought that there might be two separate keys, one for encoding and one for decoding, never occurred to me, never entered my mind. And yet perhaps it should have. I will tell you why.

Imagine a columnar transposition. Enciphering is straightforward. You inscribe your plaintext from left to right under your key number until you have written it all in. Then you transcribe by columns. It doesn't matter how long the plaintext is. But deciphering is different. You have to count the number of letters in the cryptogram so that you know how deep each column will have to be when inscribing the letters. This is not public-key cryptography; it is not asymmetric, but a germ of asymmetry lives in it. None of this ever occurred to me at the time. But perhaps someone before Diffie and the British independent inventors of public-key, Clifford Cox and Malcolm Williamson and James Ellis, who in 1969 asserted the possibility of cryptologic asymmetry, may have devised a cryptosystem whose encryption and decryption methods differed. He or she evidently never carried it to the length of public key, but it would be interesting to know whether there were any precursors to asymmetric cryptography.

I'd love to know more about what successes the Soviet Union had in codebreaking. The USSR was a great power. It excelled in three areas associated with success in cryptanalysis: chess, mathematics, and music. It almost certainly accomplished a lot. I once interviewed the former head of the Soviet Union's 16th Directorate, which solved codes, and interviewed at greater length a lower-level employee. But these few hours naturally gave me only an overview, with not enough of the specifics that I, and others, want. Tatiana Sobolyeva's history of Russian cryptology stops before World War II. I have been told that the 16th Directorate, which solved codes, published a book – "privatized" may be a better word, since it is secret – dealing with its successes. I asked Tatiana for a copy, but never got one. This work could give us the detailed study the world needs.

I would love to see an article on business interception of business messages – if any. I've been looking for one for decades. Looking for stories about AT&T wiretapping IBM messages – something like that. I have never found one. People say, "Well, they're not going to talk about it because it's secret." But people change jobs; the events lose their force as time goes by; people want to tell their stories. Now it may be that it never happened. Perhaps businesses felt the risk was not worth the gain. Or perhaps the interception took place, but nothing worthwhile resulted. I don't know.

But I should think that what interception has done for business would be a worthwhile subject for somebody to look into. Did it take place? If so, what effect did it have?

These are the main technical matters that I would like to see investigated in cryptologic history. A much larger issue underlies all of cryptology. It is the question of honor. Honor plays a very significant role in the world of espionage and of codebreaking. Codebreakers shatter honor by breaking into other people's communications, just as spies do by stealing secrets. I would like to know what the origin or origins of honor is or are.

Perhaps it comes from altruism, which some biologists see as having a biological origin. Perhaps it has an economic basis, as Thorstein Veblen implies in the very first chapter of *The Theory of the Leisure Class*. My thoughts on this are very unformed. I would like others to think about this.

Indeed, I would like newer, younger scholars to think about all these questions, and so join in the great human endeavor that is history, to understand our past and ourselves and so perhaps guide us better into the future. It is the endeavor in which the man we honor today participated.

Just as I began with a quote from one great 17th-century thinker, I would like to conclude with a quote from another: Sir Thomas Browne, a physician, who lived in Norfolk, England. The last chapter of his book, *Hydriotaphia: Urne Buriall; or, a Discourse of the Sepulchrall Urnes lately found in Norfolk,* a meditation on life and death, has been called the most extended piece of sublime English prose ever written. He asks, in a phrase that rings for historians, "Who knows whether the best of men be known? Or whether there not be more remarkable persons forgot, than any that stand remembered in the known account of time?" Henry Schorreck inscribed names in that account. It is an honorable endeavor, and Henry was inspired to do so. Browne also wrote, "Life is a pure flame, and we live by an invisible sun within us." Henry Schorreck lived by that sun, which lights and warms us all. That is why we thank him, and that is why we honor him.

[The CCH thanks Ms. Barbara Wade for transcribing Dr. Kahn's talk.]

Index

Hitler's Spies (Kahn), 9
Hitt, Parker, 402
Hittle, J. D., 381
Hoffmann, Max, 176
Holtwick, Jack S., 33, 47n29
Holy Roman Empire, 210, 367
honor, cryptology and, 440
Hood, Edwin M., 117, 132n19
Hooper, Joe, 8
Hopkins, Harry, 71, 91, 140, 149, 262
Horak, Otto J., 415–420
HORNET (German code), 243
Hottelet, Richard C., 59
House (no first name), 125
Hranilovic, Oskar von, 417
Hubka, Captain, 417
Hull, Cordell
  diplomatic reports and, 61
  Finnish relations and, 281, 287n34
  Grew report to, 70
  MAGIC intercepts and, 81
  MAGIC Summary to, 89
  on radio intercepts, 59
Hume, David, 344
Hungary. *See also* Austria or Austria-Hungary
  Brazilian codes given to Finland by, 278
Hurley, William L., 119–123, 124–25, 132n25, 133n34
Hurt, John B., 107n10

I

IKA machine, Japanese, 47n28
Illustrious, aerial reconnaissance for, 190
India
  concerns about Pakistan by, 7
  Russia's advance toward (1869), 172

individuals, private, intelligence data in reports by, 53, 60
"Indoctrination into Special Intelligence" (British file), 322–23
Indonesia, Soviet comint on, 297
industrial revolution, modern intelligence and, 334–35
information age, 180
Inman, Bobby, 179
An Inquiry Concerning Human Understanding (Hume), 344
intelligence
  as academic discipline, 333
  from aerial reconnaissance, 187–190
  from captured documents and weapons, 186–87
  codebreaking and, 190–96
  defeats and military staff development, 170–74
  empowerment of men in charge of, 178–79
  failed, partial, or erroneous, 347n30
  from the frontlines, 184–85
  future theory of, 341–45
  of Germans vs. Allies, 201–2
  historical theory of, 333–38
  history of, 167–68
  limitations of, 179–180
  offense and, 174–75
  photo reconnaissance, 190–91
  from prisoners or deserters, 185–86
  rise of, 167–180
  as secondary component of war, 339
  spies and, 196–201
  staff for military commanders and, 168–170
  20th century theory for, 338–341
  World War I and, 175–78
  in World War II, 183–205